Resistance on the National Stage

This series of publications on Africa, Latin America, Southeast Asia, and Global and Comparative Studies is designed to present significant research, translation, and opinion to area specialists and to a wide community of persons interested in world affairs. The editor seeks manuscripts of quality on any subject and can usually make a decision regarding publication within three months of receipt of the original work. Production methods generally permit a work to appear within one year of acceptance. The editor works closely with authors to produce a high-quality book. The series appears in a paperback format and is distributed worldwide. For more information, contact the executive editor at Ohio University Press, 19 Circle Drive, The Ridges, Athens, Ohio 45701.

Executive editor: Gillian Berchowitz
AREA CONSULTANTS
Africa: Diane M. Ciekawy
Latin America: Brad Jokisch, Patrick Barr-Melej, and Rafael Obregon
Southeast Asia: William H. Frederick

The Ohio University Research in International Studies series is published for the Center for International Studies by Ohio University Press. The views expressed in individual volumes are those of the authors and should not be considered to represent the policies or beliefs of the Center for International Studies, Ohio University Press, or Ohio University.

Resistance on the National Stage

MODERN THEATER AND POLITICS IN
LATE NEW ORDER INDONESIA

Michael Bodden

OHIO UNIVERSITY RESEARCH IN INTERNATIONAL STUDIES
SOUTHEAST ASIA SERIES NO. 123
OHIO UNIVERSITY PRESS
ATHENS

© 2010 by the
Center for International Studies
Ohio University
www.ohioswallow.com

To obtain permission to quote, reprint, or otherwise reproduce or distribute material from Ohio University Press publications, please contact our rights and permissions department at (740) 593-1154 or (740) 593-4536 (fax).

Printed in the United States of America
All rights reserved

18 17 16 15 14 13 12 11 10   5 4 3 2 1

The books in the Ohio University Research in International Studies Series are printed on acid-free paper. ♾ ™

Library of Congress Cataloging-in-Publication Data

Bodden, Michael.
Resistance on the national stage : theater and politics in late new order Indonesia / Michael H. Bodden.
  p. cm. — (Ohio University research in international studies, Southeast Asia series ; no. 123)
Includes bibliographical references and index.
ISBN 978-0-89680-275-9 (pb : alk. paper) — ISBN 978-0-89680-469-2 (electronic)
1. Theater—Political aspects—Indonesia. 2. Theater—Indonesia—History—20th century. I. Title.
PN2904.B74 2010
306.4'84809598—dc22
2010033643

Contents

Acknowledgments	vii
Introduction	1

ONE The Modern National Theater and the Indonesian New Order State   22

TWO Indonesian Grassroots Theater: Arena Teater, Rural Development, and the Travails of Creating a Media For the People   56

THREE *Asas Tunggal* and Laughter in the Mosque: Indonesian Islamic Theater on the National Stage   96

FOUR Teater Sae, Teater Kubur, and Avant-Garde Performances of Urban Alienation   131

FIVE The Limits of *Bahasa Indonesia* and Teater Payung Hitam's "Theater of Pain": Crisis of Representation of the Nation and Political Allegory   188

SIX Workers' Theater and Theater About Workers in 1990s Indonesia   221

SEVEN Staged Openness: Theater and Censorship in Indonesia's 1990s Era of *Keterbukaan*   273

Conclusion	310
Glossary	317
Appendix	327
Notes	333
Bibliography	361
Index	381

Acknowledgments

Though I may have authored this volume, collating much information I gathered and formulating analyses, my efforts would not have even begun had it not been for the help and companionship offered so enthusiastically and openly by many colleagues, friends, and institutions over the years. This is especially true for the many Indonesians with whom I came into contact and who assisted me in more ways than I can enumerate. Often, these Indonesian friends provided invaluable insights into the meaning of particular performances, allowed me to photocopy stacks of newspaper reviews and play scripts from their own or institutional archives, and eagerly discussed the workings of the theater world and its many actors, often patiently helping me to understand much of what went on behind the scenes.

I owe a special debt of gratitude to Saraswati Sunindyo, who first introduced me to Indonesia and the world of Indonesian theater and whose companionship over the years included many, many hours of conversation and shared reflection on Indonesian cultures old and new. Her encouragement and advice through the writing of the earlier versions of several of these chapters helped me greatly to persist and take my analysis ever deeper. Her family has also opened their home to me whenever I am in Jakarta. In particular, the late Pak Sunindyo, Bu Fatimah, and Mas Mek helped me navigate the sometimes daunting and exhausting course of daily life in Indonesia's sprawling capital city.

Halim Hd has been a crucial friend and colleague over many years, sharing his time and insights into modern Indonesian theater and society, and frequently steering me towards exciting new developments about which I otherwise might not have been aware. Putu Wijaya was my first teacher of Indonesian theater history, giving me copious amounts of time, advice, and camaraderie; also he introduced me to several members of his Teater Mandiri. Those members, Budi Setiawan, the late Alimin Lasasi, and Egy Massadiah, graciously and tirelessly helped me in my early travels around Java, Jakarta, and South Sulawesi, and introduced me to many well-known figures of modern Indonesian theater. Among those figures, I was especially grateful to the late Arifin C Noer and N. Riantiarno for always welcoming me into their homes and for generously setting aside their time to talk at length about their writing and theater work.

I have also been fortunate enough to have spent one year in Yogyakarta, where, while studying Indonesian literature and theater at Gajah Mada University, I benefited greatly from the knowledge of Umar Kayam and Faruk. At the same time I also was taken in as a member of Teater Dinasti. To Emha Ainun Nadjib, Agung Waskito, Godor, Narto, Roni and the others whose companionship and creative activities sustained, aggravated, and inspired me all at the same time, as well as to Mbak Wiwit whose cooking helped me greatly to enjoy eating rice morning, noon, and night, and whose housekeeping allowed me to function effectively, I owe more than I can express.

In investigating the case studies presented in this book, I owe special thanks to Fred Wibowo, Indra Gunawan, Simon Hate, Joko Kamto, Emha Ainun Nadjib, Agung Waskito, Boedi S. Otong, Margesti Ningsih, Afrizal Malna, Dindon, Rachman Sabur and Yanti, Tony Broer, Nandi Riffandi, Arist Merdeka Sirait, Linda Gemeulis, Wowok Hesti Prabowo, various members of Sanggar Pabrik, TBI, and Teater ABU, John Roosa, Ayu Ratih, Ratna Sarumpaet, and N. Riantiarno. They offered me various forms of support and assistance in the course of my studies and, by sharing their work and lives with me, enabled this study. In particular, I am especially grateful for many spirited and fascinating discussions with Boedi S. Otong, Margesti, Afrizal Malna, Dindon, and Rahman Sabur.

Other colleagues have offered invaluable help and feedback as well. At the University of Victoria, Joe Moore, James Keefer, Greg Blue,

Radhika Desai, Khoo Gaik-Cheng, Kevin Dixon, Micaela Campbell, Sikata Banerjee, Yvonne Hsieh, Joanne Lee, Hiroko Noro, Peter Vandergeest, and Astri Wright have offered warm friendship and much intellectual nourishment. Barbara Hatley has been my most consistent critic and source of conversation about all aspects of modern Indonesian theater over the past 20 years, and more recently, Matthew Cohen has offered much appreciated encouragement.

During my years in graduate school, Ellen Rafferty introduced me to Bahasa Indonesia and continually encouraged my research into modern Indonesian culture. The support of Keith Cohen, Marc Silberman, Reinhold Grimm, and Mary Layoun was invaluable as I finished my Ph.D. and began the journey towards this book. Mary Layoun, in particular, has been a source of guidance, friendship, and inspiration over many years.

Faculty Fellowships from the University of Victoria's Centre for Studies in Religion and Society and the Centre for Asia-Pacific Initiatives released me from teaching duties for two terms and thereby enabled me to substantially complete the research and rough drafts for chapters 3 and 7. Earlier versions of two of the chapters appeared in the following publications: the core of chapter 2 first saw print in *The Brecht Yearbook* No. 20 (Summer 1995) and a much shorter version of chapter 6 was originally published in *Review of Indonesian and Malaysian Affairs* 31.1 (June 1997). In addition, sections of chapter 1 and chapter 4 first appeared in "Satuan-satuan kecil and uncomfortable improvisations in the late night of the New Order: Democratization, postmodernism and postcoloniality" in Keith Foulcher and Tony Day, eds., *Clearing a Space: Postcolonial Readings of Modern Indonesian Literature* (Leiden: KITLV Press, 2002); and several short fragments of chapter 7 were part of an article, "Teater Koma's *Suksesi* and Indonesia's New Order," published in *Asian Theatre Journal* 14.2 (Fall 1997). In each case, I have added much new material and changed some of the analyses contained in the earlier works.

Helen Hok-sze Leung deserves special thanks for her warm and loving companionship, astute advice, and encouragement during the time when some of those earlier versions were initially composed. In recent years,

Tracy Lowe has tolerated my long work hours and regular impatience with seeing this work through to completion, and has helped me to find better ways of coping with the stress. Her love and trust have now led to a new and different kind of project: raising our young son, Kiran, safely in this troubled world. To Tracy and Kiran, then, this book is dedicated with the deepest love and sincere, amazed humility.

Resistance on the National Stage

INTRODUCTION

The final decade of President Suharto's New Order in Indonesia witnessed a highly publicized series of confrontations between the Indonesian state and a number of theater groups over performances banned by the government. These clashes began with the banning of N. Riantiarno and Teater Koma's *Suksesi* and *Opera Kecoa* in late 1990, at the same time that President Suharto and key state officials were calling for increased openness in public discourse. The government's attempts to muzzle modern theater continued with prohibitions against performances of other plays by groups from the Yogyakarta-based Komunitas Pak Kanjeng (1994), workers theater groups from the greater Jakarta Region (1995–97), and Ratna Sarumpaet's Satu Merah Panggung company (1997). This series of incidents brought theater into the center of national politics at a time of increasing public dissatisfaction with the Suharto regime. The bannings received extensive media coverage and became the occasion for wide-ranging public debate of a variety of related issues such as the law, good governance, democracy, and economics. They also demonstrated the resolve of the modern national theater's practitioners to resist the state's efforts to limit their freedom of expression. In the process of resisting the state's censorship apparatus, cultural workers gained new solidarity, found common cause with journalists, industrial workers, and other social groups, and grew increasingly bold in the subject matter that their plays broached. Through ever sharper criticism of the government's actions and rationales for banning performances, the theater workers and their allies from other sectors of society managed to put government spokespeople on the defensive well before the Suharto regime was brought to an end in May of 1998.

This series of incidents highlight the important role that the Indonesian modern national theater was able to play, albeit briefly, on the national political stage. Yet the resistance to government censorship must be seen as emerging together with and, to some extent, building upon the ways in which elite theater workers, from the mid-1980s on, were exploring new modes of theater making: from difficult avant-garde performances to performances undertaken by and for Central Javanese peasants, Jakartan industrial workers, and other groups not normally involved in this form of modern national culture. These modes of theater making raised new critical perspectives on New Order Indonesian society and politics, and presented them to wider and more diverse audiences at a time when typical modern theater patrons were also becoming increasingly interested in such perspectives and issues. Thus, modern national theater in the late New Order era was becoming a site both for fostering germinal alliances between different social classes and groups, and for broaching new and daring themes in the process. These new alliances facilitated an expansion of public discussions about the significance of theater and theater bannings. Such discussions of censorship and of the themes taken up in the banned plays and other theater works helped mobilize public opposition to Suharto's New Order regime.

One of the central aims of this book is to illustrate how and why this happened. I will show how modern theater became a key arena for expressing political dissent under the authoritarian New Order regime, the ways in which modern national theater workers forged new theater practices in concert with a variety of social groups, how these practices were embedded in the social and political contexts of the time, and how they contributed to a sharpening of theatrical resistance to the New Order regime, including the intensifying struggle of theater workers against censorship.

Censorship struggles are an obvious instance of the relations of power between theater and the state, and Indonesia is no exception. In this case, the Indonesian state, claiming to uphold the laws and social norms of society, assumed the power to represent the nation by policing what could and could not be said and done on stage. On the other hand, theater workers insisted that their right to speak to, and often for, the nation and various groups within it by representing the nation in performance was abrogated by seemingly arrogant state officials using specious arguments or, even worse, state officials who were unable or unwilling to conform to laws which the government itself had promulgated.

Loren Kruger has argued that the attempt to "stage the nation" to represent and reflect the people in the theater arose in the European Enlightenment, but "manifests itself fully only in the course of the 19th century with the rise of mass national politics, 'universal' (male) suffrage, and the demand of the people for legitimate representation as protagonist on the political stage" (Kruger 1992, 3). Although there are good reasons for caution when comparing Indonesia to 19th-century Europe, nonetheless, the rise of nationalism in Indonesia during the early 20th century also produced mass movements, mass national politics, universal suffrage, and demands of the people for legitimate representation on the political stage. It also foregrounded the notion of cultivating feelings of "deep horizontal comradeship," to use Anderson's term (Anderson 1992 [1983], 7), among those imagined as citizens of the nation. In Indonesia, these feelings were often subsumed into the elite's sense of *noblesse oblige*, strengthening the idea of its duty to protect the "little people" from the vicissitudes of life and unjust treatment. Under the New Order, this *noblesse oblige* became transformed into a kind of corporatist paternalism in which leaders felt empowered to make decisions and speak on behalf of the "people" under their protection (and most importantly, guidance). Arguments for legitimacy thus have often circled around perceptions of who can speak for and advance the cause and prosperity of the *rakyat* (people). In the modern theater, such attitudes became intertwined with aesthetics and notions of national culture's responsibility to speak of relevant and pressing social issues, especially when they impinged on the lives of the ordinary people. But splits within the elite created differing visions of who should lead and with what ideological and cultural orientation. One result of this was that modern Indonesian national culture often took an antagonistic stance towards the state and its political leadership.

In such circumstances, we see the nation as a setting in which contests of legitimation are staged in various venues, among them theaters. To assert their legitimacy in the face of an authoritarian and sometimes arbitrary state, Indonesian theater workers continually claimed to want to speak the truth about social conditions and, occasionally, to speak on behalf of the masses, although this was implied more often than actually stated. Eventually, at a time when the New Order government of President Suharto appeared to command its greatest power over the state and society, some theater workers even began to work with peasants, workers, and other mass constituencies, aspiring to speak for, and with, the people and in so doing, to use theater more effectively for social purposes (see especially chapters 2, 3, and 6). At the same time, avant-garde groups within the realm of the national art theater pursued, in their performances and theoretical articulations, a radical critique of both pre-existing theatrical form and dominant social relations, including politics. Seemingly alienated from larger popular audiences, some of these groups nonetheless drew part of their material from the daily lives of Indonesia's lower classes and shared ideas with members of the non-government organization (NGO/LSM) community. Their texts and ideas for staging were not simple by any means, coming, as they did, not only from society's marginalized but from diverse sources, sometimes rooted in the nation's political history, popular traditional theater forms, or local intellectual traditions of experiment and dissent, thereby still staking a claim on national identity and legitimacy within the nation (see chapters 4 and 5).

Thus, one of the things I will demonstrate in this book (specifically in chapter 1) is how national culture, and specifically, theater, often came to be in an antagonistic position towards the state. In so doing, I will demarcate the background assumptions and ideologies—the operative *doxa*—for some of the theater work to be described in subsequent chapters. Yet this antagonism was not total. It was more a dominant theme and mode of operations that became more acute at some times, less pressing, seemingly unnecessary, or of necessity more submerged at others. Accordingly, I will illustrate some of the ways the national art theater resisted, negotiated with, and at times accommodated itself to the state in independent Indonesia.

However, from the mid-1980s on, theatrical relations with the Indonesian state began gradually to shift towards a more consistently critical or even antagonistic mode. This forms the key narrative thread of this study. This theme of growing and more assertive resistance to the state is first taken up in each of the various chapters, but culminates in chapter 7 with a detailed account of the ways in which these varied efforts and practices created linkages among different social groups and ultimately contributed to building momentum towards the struggle against censorship, as well as to helping undermine the legitimacy of the Suharto government. Indonesian national culture has long been the preserve of a small cultural elite whose members generally know one another. In this way, social networks are a constant feature of national cultural life. However, in the late Suharto period, these networks or *jaringan* expanded in the realm of theater work in interesting and strategic ways to include ties with peasants, industrial workers, Muslim students and organizations, and lower- and lower-middle-class urban slum dwellers. This was facilitated both by new kinds of practices (*teater rakyat*/people's theater techniques) that helped elite and middle-class cultural workers reach out to other social groups, but also by the entrance of new constituencies into the world of modern national culture. Lower- and lower-middle-class urban residents, for example, then proceeded to create new kinds of avant-garde performances that spoke powerfully to the cultural elite of the lives of fellow citizens from different social strata. This expansion of jaringan enabled theater to speak in different ways and to different social groups about material normally not within the range of modern national theater productions. It thereby joined the modern national theater more closely to the pro-democracy movement of the late New Order.

Thus, the new theatrical jaringan acted in at least two ways to offer resistance to President Suharto's New Order regime. On the one hand, they brought together new constituencies in creating theater and protesting censorship, building a more complex social movement around issues of socio-economic justice and freedom of artistic expression. On the other, they brought new themes and material to public attention. Victor Turner argues that theater can create symbols, which in turn can instigate action and channel its direction by saturating goals and means with affect and desire. Turner asserts that these symbols help us order meaning or question the established order through creative disorder (Turner 1982, 21–23). To illustrate this point, the ways in which reviewers and other observers made sense of avant-garde productions show how form and content helped social critics to formulate new insights about and expressions of social problems confronting New Order society. Similarly, grassroots and workers' theater productions broadened and deepened public awareness of the ways in which the prevailing system put these social groups at a disadvantage. In discussing the examples of Indonesian theater in the following pages, therefore, I would argue that the Islamic theater of Emha Ainun Nadjib and his collaborators, grass roots theater, workers' theater, the satirical plays of N. Riantiarno and Teater Koma, the angry productions of Ratna Sarumpaet's Satu Merah Panggung company, and the critical avant-garde productions of Teater Kubur, Teater Sae, and Teater Payung Hitam all assisted their primary and occasionally overlapping constituencies to solidify particular kinds of critiques of the regime and to imagine a better form of social life. At the same time, the performative and discursive alliances constructed by embattled theater workers, journalists, and workers' theater groups, among others, contributed to wider social articulations of those criticisms of the New Order and increased discursive, social, and legal pressure on the government to change policies and governing assumptions in the lead-up to Suharto's fall from power.

In the chapters that follow, I will present several cases from the late New Order (1985–98), the time during which these processes of expanding *jaringan* and growing critical interventions became more evident. I will examine several crucial performances and texts created in the course of these collaborations, analyzing their form and content so as to bring out a number of the key meanings they suggested, as well as to indicate tensions in their visions. In particular, I want to show how some of those thematic and formal tensions reflected dilemmas or tensions within the groups, tensions tied to the nature of the relationship between mostly middle-class cultural workers and their modern national arts ideologies on the one hand and the goals, aims, and visions of those groups with whom they worked to construct these performances.

Given that much of the theater I will present here was involved in a project of taking theater to, and making theater with, diverse groups, a second important thrust of this study will be to place the works in their complex social contexts and thereby describe theater's wider connections with society. By looking at the examples of modern theater that I have assembled, we will begin to see how theater was used to respond to problems confronting peasants, Muslims, lower-middle-class and lower-class slum dwellers, industrial workers, and middle-class university instructors and students. We will also see how the theater forms used by these groups to express their views of Indonesian society arose from rich, productive, and, at times, problematic combinations of social perspectives and cultural practices and materials.

One of the ways to illustrate this best is by highlighting the idea of theatrical works—scripts, performances, the ideologies and aesthetics that underpin them, and the institutions that support or hamper them—as always under construction, drawing on a variety of social discourses and cultural forms in the attempt to articulate their creators' often conflicted visions of society and nation and, in so doing, to connect more deeply, more satisfyingly with specific or even more vaguely imagined audiences. This requires at least two lines of investigation. The first is the construction of a genealogy of the theater practices and forms concerned, from which it will be easier to see the many ways theater is connected to and interacts with social and political communities, aesthetic ideologies, and cultural forms. It will also necessitate providing evidence of how the productions, or the groups staging the productions, changed to respond to social circumstances, that were themselves continually undergoing transformation. As Kershaw has noted, it is necessary in judging the efficacy of theater to understand the context in which audiences "read" the meaning of performances. Therefore, critical analysis must move beyond formalism and treat theater in relation to the aesthetic movements of which they are a part, the institutional structures of art, and the cultural formations they inhabit (1992, 5–6).

In all the cases that I will take up (grassroots theater, Islamic theater, avant-garde theater, workers' theater, banning struggles), we will be able to see how the practitioners involved drew upon diverse constituencies, experiences, theories, and aesthetic backgrounds to construct the particular practices and ideas they produced. We will also be able to discern clearly how specific productions can be seen as snapshots of a process. This is especially true for those instances (grassroots theater, Islamic theater, workers' theater, and banning struggle) in which the collaborations and conflicts between socially differing participants in these projects, involving the search for aesthetic forms that could engage particular audiences and satisfy their expressive desires, and desires for action of creators and audience alike, lead to a more layered understanding of theatrical performances (and scripts, aesthetic ideologies, institutions, etc.) as moments in a complex set of aesthetic and social contestations. That is, such performances are always constructed from ongoing processes of collaboration, conflict, exclusion, and incorporation worked out to satisfy both the relations of power among the creators, audiences, and official institutions, and the aesthetic demands and expressive desires circulating among such groups that are connected to relations of power but never fully explained by them. These processes continue after each performance of a specific work and in the intervals between performances of succeeding works or between those of one group and another. By approaching the work of the groups to be considered in such a frame, we will also be able to grasp something of the dynamics of New Order society and politics from which modern theater arose, to which it responded, and upon which it had an impact.

Methodology and Theory

With the overarching focus of this book on theater's resistance to the New Order, it is necessary to be clear about what "resistance" means. Susan Seymour offers the following useful definition: "In a context of differential power relationships, resistance refers to intentional, and hence conscious, acts of defiance or opposition by a subordinate individual or group of individuals against a superior individual or set of individuals" (2006, 305). The Indonesian theater that I will discuss in the following chapters clearly fits within Seymour's definition. Yet the kind of resistance the book will present are hardly simple instances of resistors versus a superior power. As Seymour and Sherry Ortner have pointed out, there has been a burgeoning literature on resistance, especially in anthropological and historical studies over the past few decades (Ortner 1995; Seymour 2006). Ortner cautions that many such studies are ethnographically thin for a variety of reasons: they do not look at the internal politics of subordinate or sub-altern groups, they do not give due consideration to the importance of culture, and post-structuralist scholars have often sought to dissolve the subject and have ended with incoherent subjects seemingly incapable of mounting resistance.

I find Ortner's arguments persuasive, and though I have no pretensions to writing a work of ethnography, nonetheless I hope to address some of Ortner's concerns about studying resistance. As should be clear by now, my primary view of the theatrical resistance offered by the groups I will discuss is that it was a resistance formed from diverse and often conflicting constituencies, ideologies, and forms. As theater workers from the mid-1980s on began to explore new kinds of theater practices and engage with new social constituencies, their resistance to the state became more complicated. No longer was it simply a matter of a relatively homogenous cultural elite voicing its criticisms, sometimes uneasily, of society, but theater workers from that elite were constructing socially critical works together with peasants, industrial workers, slum-dwellers, and others. Such collaborations were never simple, and conflicts about themes and aesthetics often showed not only common goals, but also the tensions and differences that separated those offering resistance to the state. Thus, this study offers compelling evidence that resistance cannot be assumed to be homogenous, nor can resistors be essentialized as a "single, unitary subordinate."

Similarly, in a study of theater, it would be absurd to discount the impact of previous cultural patterns and forms on the modes of resistance of the various groups. Accordingly, in chapter 1, I have tried to summarize the complex aesthetics and the social ideologies with which modern Indonesian theater is intertwined in order to present a cultural baseline on which many modern theater workers in Indonesia have operated. This baseline is not a stagnant cultural tradition but is itself a site of contestation in which relations between dominant and subordinate elements are complex and continually being tested and shifted. I have also tried to highlight important aspects of the cultural backgrounds of particular groups, for example, the mosaic of Islamic traditions which formed the context for Emha Ainun Nadjib and the Yogyakarta Islamic theater groups' work, the lower-middle-class and high arts backgrounds for Teater Sae and Teater Kubur, or the rich high art theater background of Bandung's Payung Hitam. Additionally, I have tried to pay special attention to particular elements of a number of the performances and practices discussed herein that stem from the cultural life and forms of specific communities. In the process, I have indicated how elements drawn from different communities and traditions came into productive tension or dissonance within the newer performances and practices.

Finally, I have sought to place individual groups and participants within these complex backgrounds in order to display the ways in which they grapple creatively with the cultural patterns, ideologies, and aesthetics that condition them and provide templates for their cultural work. One of the clearest examples of this, which will be evident in chapter 1, is the ambivalence many theater workers feel about being too "political" in their productions, while at the same time facing personal and social pressures to contribute to the advancement of the nation by voicing issues of concern to fellow citizens. The chapters that follow will show how different groups attempted to resolve or dispense with that ambivalence.

The body of theory that underpins my work is drawn from a variety of sources, but one of the most prominent is a combination of structuralist Marxism and neo-Marxism. My primary background is in comparative literature and drama/theater studies, and, as a result, I will devote considerable attention to scripts or performance texts. The work of Pierre Macherey, Frederic Jameson, and Terry Eagleton has been particularly helpful in seeing such texts as incomplete, full of tensions and conflicts generated within the texts themselves by the complexity of the issues they raise and the forms they deploy. Yet, in discussing theater, looking at written texts, though highly useful and necessary, is also inadequate in itself. Obviously, written texts are only one point of entry into the world of the Indonesian modern national art theater and some of its related cultural projects like grassroots or workers' theater. I have, whenever possible, tried to watch the performances that I discuss in this book, either in person or through recordings. I will, accordingly, have more to say about the actual staged performance of some of the case studies than others, although I have tried to supplement my personal knowledge of all the performances discussed with local news media reviews, observations about and descriptions of performances by some of the participants, and occasionally remarks from audience members. Applying the same method for reading performances—seeing them as full of tensions and contradictions—is as productive as in the case of written texts, and at times even more suggestive when the performance versions depart significantly from the text contained in a written script.

At another level, theater work, like other cultural work, is enmeshed in a web of social relations. These relations have an impact on many details of theater production, from the aesthetics deemed proper to producing and staging a script or performance, to the reception of a particular piece of work. In considering such socio-cultural processes, I have been guided by the work of such theorists as Pierre Bourdieu, Raymond Williams, and Stuart Hall. What my analysis draws from this body of work is a set of tools for seeing cultural tastes, genres, and forms as tied to, though not completely defined by, specific social groups, and representing arenas in which differing groups within society struggle as they attempt to attain dominance over the process of meaning making. As I will detail in chapter 1, their work has allowed me to understand the process of cultural production as one which is never complete and which, though it involves dominant groups as well as subordinates, is nonetheless a continual dance of accommodation and opposition, hegemony, and resistance. It has also allowed me to think of cultural practices and institutions as sites with considerable autonomy within a social system in which, nonetheless, hegemonic forces work to reconcile challenges and incorporate differing ideologies and practices into an acceptable framework of rules and guidelines.

The pursuit of understanding modern national theater in Indonesia at the level of its system as well as understanding individual productions as both conforming to and reacting against that system has also necessitated that I gain an idea of how popular particular plays were and how they were viewed critically in the media and among other theater workers. In some cases this was made easier because media reviewers are often themselves well-known theater workers or other arts figures. Similarly, I have tried to gauge audience responses by scattered comments in the media and other indicators such as invitations to perform in other locales and the reactions of critics. By comparing audiences' and critics' responses with the dominant aesthetic ideology, through whose lens national art theater is most often viewed and evaluated, I have been able, to a limited extent, to pursue the kind of analysis described by Susan Bennett in her book *Theater Audiences: A Theory of Production and Reception*. Bennett is concerned with viewing theater audiences as cultural phenomena subject not only to the world created on the stage, but to the institutions of theater and the expectations of theatrical events generated outside the actual performance time and space as well. Yet for Bennett, the public incorporates a diversity of critics and audiences with different horizons of expectations. She argues that the assumptions of middle-class, mainstream audiences should not be seen as an uncontested norm (Bennett 1990, 100–101). In Indonesia this would seem to hold particularly true. Though productions of modern national theater may have been dominated, especially since 1965, by intellectuals who embraced a particular set of artistic values resembling those of middle-class artistic ideologies and values in most developed countries, their productions were not always popular with the bulk of the Indonesian middle-classes. In turn, the assumptions of those middle-classes or intellectuals and art theater practitioners did not always dominate other forms of theatrical activity, most notably the large variety of folk theater productions. In such circumstances, national art theater productions occasionally came under attack for being alienated from popular audiences or from traditional Indonesian values and aesthetics. The situation became even more charged during the 1990s as segments of the middle-class attempted to gain more political power within the New Order state, despite the fact that they still constituted a small percentage of the overall population. This meant these middle-class groups began searching for allies, including peasants, workers, and the broader Muslim constituency. In the sphere of theater, this necessitated undertaking experiments with using theater for *conscientizing* those sectors of the population as well as reaching out to form ongoing links with social activists in the NGO/LSM (non-government organization/*Lembaga Swadaya Masyarakat* or Self-Reliant Community Institutions) community. In all cases, this involved to greater or lesser degrees theater workers from the modern national theater sphere, and their involvement posed anew and more deeply the problem of bridging and combining the horizons of expectations and aesthetic ideologies of differing groups. I unravel some of the negotiations and tensions involved in these attempts in chapters 2, 3, and 6.

An additional significant set of ideas vital to my analysis resides in postcolonial theory. Helen Gilbert and Joanne Tompkins begin by defining postcolonialism as an engagement with and contestation of colonialism's power structures, discourses, and social hierarchies (Gilbert and Tompkins 1996, 2–3). However, as we shall see in the Indonesian case, engagement with colonial systems does not necessarily mean a clean binary opposition between the cultural values and forms of the colonizer versus those of the colonized. Furthermore, fetishization of the colonizer-colonized binary as the only axis of struggle can lead analysts to overlook the real divisions and struggles that occur within and among the formerly colonized peoples of a newly independent nation. For example, different groups within the Indonesian nationalist movement continually vied with one another for leadership. Each brought varied systems of values and meanings into the debates and struggles. In the process of give and take, the cultural values and forms of colonizer and colonized were often combined in interesting and unusual ways. And in fact, Gilbert and Tompkins argue that hybridity can be seen as the positive recombination of forms by formerly colonized subjects who are attempting to define themselves (Gilbert and Tompkins 1996, 11). We see this hybridization process in the formation of modern theater practices and aesthetic ideologies briefly touched upon in chapter 1, but also in the very diverse ways nearly every group discussed combines elements of local tradition with conventions of performance or aesthetics borrowed in part from the West. Similarly, some of the groups discussed, especially those involved in grassroots theater and Islamic theater, consciously sought to set themselves in at least partial opposition to what they perceived to be Western mass culture, while at the same time adapting specific ideas or practices from such mass cultural phenomenon in an effort to compete. The resultant tensions suggest the extreme difficulty, if not impossibility, of cultural purity in the creation of cultural works in a postcolonial and globalized world. They also remind us once again of the complexity of the theatrical resistance I will be examining.

* * *

Chapter 1 will summarize the history through which the process of theatrical contestation with the state actually unfolded in Indonesia. Looking at the development of both the modern national theater in Indonesia and the aesthetic ideologies that govern much of its production, I will show the ways in which a struggle between different segments of the indigenous colonial elite led to a discursive and political divide, with those favoring a more conservative cultural vision of the nation eventually gaining more power within the state and government, and those with a relatively more egalitarian and modernizing perspective holding principle sway in several spheres of national culture. This led to a situation in which state and modern theater were often counter-posed in an antagonistic relationship. I will show how this situation was nonetheless always fluid and under contestation, with the state at times asserting more influence in the realm of modern theater, at other times less. I also demonstrate the ways in which leading cultural institutions such as the print media and the Jakarta Arts Center engaged with and exercised some influence on the development of modern national theater. Subsequent chapters will show the continued development of avant-garde and other groups within this matrix of ideology, aesthetics, and theatrical practice. In addition, subsequent chapter will discuss the ways in which some modern national theater workers attempted to expand the reach of the modern art theater and its ideas of social change and critique by creating specific types of theater practices in conjunction with peasants, workers, and Muslim youth.

In chapter 2, I use the example of the Arena Teater based in Yogyakarta (Central Java) to demonstrate the complexities of producing grassroots theater that aims to speak on behalf of peasants and other disenfranchised groups, often in their own voices. Arena's grassroots theater practice, developed over the 1980s through the incorporation of a variety of sources and direct experiences, shows the way in which one group of modern theater practitioners attempted to transcend the limits of conventional modern stage productions for promoting social change. It illustrates the successes that Arena achieved in *conscientizing* peasants and mobilizing NGO workers to use theater tools in their own work, thus contributing to a growing movement of peasants over land rights and rural development. Yet the chapter also concentrates on the tensions and conflicts that arise when mainly middle-class theater workers attempt to speak for, or even in conjunction with, the Indonesian disenfranchised. I examine the ways in which Arena's practices changed over the years to fit its evolving understanding of grassroots theater as a tool for grassroots empowerment, and point out the difficulties and dilemmas that Arena and a number of other grassroots theater groups encountered in obtaining funding and working with state institutions, factors that limited the reach and continuity of their efforts.

Chapter 3 investigates the work of Emha Ainun Nadjib and a group of collaborators based in Yogyakarta, to create a popular form of Islamic theater between 1989 and 1991. Like Arena Teater, though in a more limited sense, this theater showed its own connections to grassroots concepts. It thereby hints at the appeal expanding modern theater's constituency and its socio-political functions had for diverse cultural workers in Indonesia during the 1980s. Aside from a detailed portrait of the social context and cultural roots of this florescence of Muslim theater, I show how the group surrounding Nadjib continually shaped and transformed its works in order to tailor them to particular audiences and occasions. Evolving to create a Muslim form of stage spectacle that could contend with secular national mass culture associated with the West, this form of theater presents a typical postcolonial dilemma: adapting elements of a foreign (neo-colonial) culture in order to compete with it on something close to its own terms. Nonetheless, Nadjib's and his colleagues' efforts enhanced the image of a cultural Islam as part of the general movement of social protest and reform then underway.

In chapter 4, I discuss the rise to prominence in modern national theater circles of two avant-garde theater groups from Jakarta, Teater Sae and Teater Kubur. These groups exemplify the rise of modern theater ensembles that combined the lower-middle-class sensibilities of many of their members with high art conventions and aesthetics to shape startling and distinctive new styles of avant-garde theater that questioned both the formerly prevailing practices of modern theater and the social conditions of late New Order Indonesia. I show how these groups forged practices that emphasized disjuncture and fragmentation at the level of form, and that thematized urban alienation, the confusion of rapidly changing contexts and identities, and the crushing weight of national histories and ideologies upon ordinary people. I will also show how Teater Kubur challenged conventional practices of modern national theater by taking its theater to a variety of previously neglected locations and constituencies. Finally, by analyzing the contexts and the performances of these two groups, I will reveal some of the contradictions and tensions in the postmodern visions of society present in Teater Sae's later plays, and show how Teater Kubur's particular rebellion against artifice in theater, related to the work of Teater Sae, was nonetheless characterized by key differences that in large part stemmed from the different bases of support and membership prevailing in each group.

The Bandung-based performing arts academy (STSI) group, Teater Payung Hitam, forms the focus of chapter 5. Though showing distinct similarities with Teater Sae and Teater Kubur, Payung Hitam's origin in an academic milieu and its series of seminal performances between 1994 and 1997 mark it as both hailing from yet another different social constituency and signalling a new, more aggressive phase in modern theater's critique of New Order society. My argument examines the rise to prominence of Payung Hitam, investigating its 1994 national theater festival performance of Peter Handke's *Kaspar*, and its interrogation of the role of the national language in shaping the consciousness of Indonesian citizens. I look at the progressive disappearance of the national language, Bahasa Indonesia, from Payung Hitam's original productions in succeeding years as a symptom of a crisis of national identity. Furthermore, I show the way in which the group's three original and highly acclaimed performance pieces of this period foregrounded a growing militant tendency of the modern national theater to tackle current political issues head on, a tendency that was in part also indicative of the influence of the student protest movement of the 1990s.

Chapter 6 narrates the rise and development of several workers' theater groups (TBI, Teater ABU, Sanggar Pabrik, and TABUR) in the Jakarta area from 1989 to 1998. I pay particular attention to the difficulties encountered in the interactions between worker participants, NGO activists, and modern theater trainers and supporters, including some from the avant-garde groups mentioned in the previous chapter, which point to different understandings of the goals of these theater practices held by the respective social groups involved. I go on to compare the productions of TBI, ABU, and TABUR to the more artistically oriented modern national theater performances of Ratna Sarumpaet, who took up worker themes through her interest in the Marsinah murder case. This comparison demonstrates the differences in treatment and theme between worker groups and modern theater practitioners, but also shows how the two constituencies were slowly drawing closer to an alliance of interests and themes around the struggle for democratization. I also show how the New Order state tried to control and limit this type of theater, a theme that leads into the final chapter.

In the chapter 7, I focus on the series of bans of theatrical performance that began with Teater Koma's *Suksesi* in 1990 and reached a climax in the at times covert, and finally, open attempts to ban performances during Ratna Sarumpaet's 1997 tour of her *Marsinah Menggugat* (Marsinah Accuses). By concentrating on several key characteristics of the evolving debates over government bans, I show how the New Order government's legitimacy was eroding long before Suharto's sudden fall from power in 1998. Further, I demonstrate the way in which the media discourse that facilitated the public debates allowed a variety of voices to emerge and find common interests in deploring and protesting such government censorship. Finally, I highlight the fact that modern national theater workers found new solidarity and courage during the course of these struggles, mounting productions that challenged more aggressively than ever before the New Order's unwritten codes for theatrical expression.

These case studies of theater in the last thirteen years of Suharto's New Order present vivid illustrations of the complex political relations, social conditions, and artistic processes involved in the production of various kinds of modern theater. They show diverse constituencies working together, though not always in agreement, to shape new forms and practices for creating theater that its participants hoped would speak to particular publics about specific issues. They provide glimpses of the manner in which theater workers continually shape and reshape their work in response to audiences, critics, and their own members. And they offer evidence of the diverse and changing paths by which theater contributed to a rising tide of resistance to a regime riddled with corruption and bent on authoritarian control. As a whole, they suggest why theater was able, for a time, to play a modest though significant role on the Indonesian national political stage.

Obviously, in a study of this size, I could not possibly hope to cover all the groups that resisted the New Order and its social, political, and aesthetic ideologies on the stage. There have been many important modern theater groups in a variety of cities and other locations, who contributed to an ongoing theatrical critique of the Suharto regime, using a number of styles and occasionally drawing on the experiences and support of mixed social constituencies. These groups include, but are not limited to, Studiklub Teater Bandung, Bengkel Teater Rendra, Teater Dinasti, and Teater Gandrik in Yogyakarta, Teater Gedag-Gedig and Teater Jagat in Surakarta (Solo), Teater Kecil, Teater Mandiri, Teater Saja and others in Jakarta, Teater Bumi in Padang, West Sumatra, and Sanggar Merah Putih in Makassar (then Ujung Pandang), South Sulawesi. A number of scholars have already written about some of these groups and the figures who led them. Barbara Hatley has been particularly dedicated in following the development of modern theater mainly in the Central Javanese cities of Solo and Yogyakarta, often analyzing the ways in which local modern theater groups attempted to turn local codes of meaning making against the state's oppressive power. Combining theater studies and anthropological-style field work over several decades, Hatley's work has found one important culmination in her recently published *Javanese Performances on an Indonesian Stage*, which documents and analyzes the ways modern national theater and traditional *ketoprak* theater celebrate "the shared identity of particular social groupings" (Hatley 2008, 155), resist or acquiesce in state power, and adopt to changing conditions. My work owes much to Hatley's earlier studies of the 1980s and early 1990s. Younger scholars like Cobina Gillitt and Evan Winet have also contributed more recently to the study of some of the key groups in the early New Order. Gillitt (2001) has examined the rise of the "New Tradition" of theater in New Order Indonesia, looking at the significance of their pioneering efforts to blend Western dramaturgy with elements of traditional theater, noting in particular the fact that figures such as Rendra, Arifin C Noer, and Putu Wijaya paralleled the ideas of "indonesianness" propagated by the state in combining elements of various ethnic traditions, but arguing that they did so in a manner that refused the state's more static concepts and often criticised the state as well. Winet (2001), whose work I will discuss in the next chapter, has used a performance studies lens to examine the conflict between the theater and the state, using three examples from different historical eras, including Rendra and his Bengkel Teater. Yet many of the groups examined by these scholars achieved their greatest popularity and impact in the first two decades of the New Order (1965–85). I note some of their particular achievements in passing, while laying out the historical background for what happened in modern theater during the last thirteen years of Suharto's long rule.

My examples were chosen based on my own fieldwork in Indonesia beginning in 1986, and indicate a number of the trends in modern theater that I personally found most exciting, but which also seemed to be attracting significant attention in the media or in wide social circles within Indonesia. They were also selected because they drew upon key sectors of society for support and thematic material, and thus, when taken all together, present a complex overview of how Indonesian society was able to contribute to theatrical efforts of the artistic modern stage to analyze, criticize, and resist the regime that for so many years had governed its life. It was precisely this combination of public attention and excitement, the participation of or connections to diverse social constituencies, and the limiting factor of my own arrival in and history of visits to Indonesia that determined the framework for much of my research and eventually this study. Yet there are also clear patterns and connections that emerge from the groups and movements selected for examination here. In all cases of grassroots, Islamic, or workers' theater included in this study, avant-garde or high art theater participants played roles, while the struggles of peasants, workers, and women often provided themes and inspiration for high art and avant-garde theater performances. Furthermore, not only do the individual chapters show this dynamic and conflicted relationship between the modern national theater and efforts to create more popular types of theater practices, but they also bring into focus connections and developments between the different groups and movements. For instance, the grassroots theater described in chapter 2 had ties, through individuals, common goals or shared history, with the Islamic theater of Yogyakarta in the late 1980s and the worker's theater movement in the greater Jakarta area in the 1990s. Similarly, key members of Jakarta avant-garde companies like Teater Sae and Teater Kubur also participated in the workers' theater movement. Teater Payung Hitam, though not involved in such grassroots or workers' theater efforts, nonetheless also shows connections to the student movement of the 1990s as well as taking up themes that resonated with many of the issues raised by grassroots, workers', and other avant-garde theater groups alike. Finally, there is a certain historical momentum in moving from one chapter to the next; the early chapters lay the groundwork and indicate ways in which some modern national art theater practitioners were engaging with broad social constituencies other than the relatively small middle-class base long supportive of such high art theater. These chapters show the ways theater paralleled and at times assisted the broader movement of young middle-class activists attempting to build greater social equality and democratic relations through work with peasant, worker, and other socially less advantaged groups. These chapters also demonstrate the manner in which theater was articulating various criticisms of the New Order regime and Indonesian society, which contributed to the rise of a sharper kind of resistance to the Suharto government from the mid-1990s on. All of this momentum and work led, both in society and in theater, to the increasingly daring articulations of dissatisfaction and regime criticism illustrated in the realm of theater by the cases presented in chapters 5, 6, and 7.

When taken altogether, the studies gathered in this volume offer a varied and detailed portrait of the ways in which modern national theater resisted the power of Suharto's New Order regime and helped contribute to its eventual downfall. However, the role of theater as an important and visible forum for and form of public social criticism in the late New Order did not spring into being overnight or without a lengthy process. It is to the analysis of that longer process that enabled theater to play an important critical role in Indonesian society from 1985 to 1998 that I now turn.

Chapter 1

THE MODERN NATIONAL THEATER AND THE INDONESIAN NEW ORDER STATE

During the 1990s, modern national theater practitioners in Indonesia frequently displayed a critical attitude toward society and even clashed with the Indonesian New Order state over several theater banning incidents in a dramatic series of confrontations from 1990 to 1997. Such attitudes on the part of theater workers, and the resulting battles with the state over censorship of the theater, can best be understood in the context of the development of an often antagonistic relationship between the two institutions in the preceding decades, as well as in the confluence of larger political circumstances with this basic antagonism. For if the modern theater was often at odds with the New Order state, this friction was amplified and heightened during the last fifteen years of President Suharto's rule by the increasing restiveness of large numbers of the Indonesian middle-classes, professionals, peasantry, and industrial working classes, as well as by a protracted fissure in the ranks of regime supporters. These developments created an atmosphere in which theater workers felt encouraged to mount bolder critiques of conditions under the New Order, and in turn pro-democracy movements may well have drawn strength, images of desire, and sources of rhetoric from the various critiques, experiments with new actors and audiences, protests, and acts of defiance carried out by modern theater workers at roughly the same time.

To better understand the rift between the New Order state and the modern national theater that formed the basis for much of the theatrical social criticism and protest that this book presents, I will first summarize in this chapter the rise of the modern theater in Indonesia in relation to the parallel rise of the Indonesian state. As a part of this background, I will demonstrate that the antagonism between the modern theater and the state in Indonesia was part of a process of social contestation that had been developing for some decades, reaching back even to the pre-independence period. Furthermore, I will show how ideologically, and in form and practice, the modern theater's practitioners were, as is common in postcolonial circumstances, already culturally hybrid from the very beginning of the process of constructing national culture. Yet the process of hybridization continued and led modern theater practitioners to deepen their engagement with local and traditional cultural and performance traditions. In the end, this led theater workers to contest the New Order state's own version of what constituted a properly Indonesian culture. I will then describe some of the mechanisms of control that the New Order state established in order to better police what was presented on national theatrical stages as well as suggesting several reasons why these controls ultimately failed. Finally, I will also situate the productions discussed in succeeding chapters within a wider socio-political context by providing a brief overview of New Order political developments during the 1980s and early 1990s.

Theoretical Approach

I view Indonesian national culture as consisting of cultural products in the national language, Bahasa Indonesia, but also including contemporary painting, sculpture, and graphic arts, which are considered as contributions to the new national culture that is itself related to the broad currents of international culture. This culture and the various subfields that constitute it (literature, theater, film, television, dance, music, visual arts) can be imagined as complex institutions or spheres of activity formed and constantly being reformed by the interplay of a variety of interests. These cultural fields then appear as institutions-in-process that incorporate several ideologies and sets of artistic conventions and techniques.

For purposes of my argument, modern theater has been shaped as a sphere of activity by nationalism, forms of modern Western theater, knowledge of traditional performance genres, modern and traditional aesthetic ideologies, desires to connect intimately with various audiences from the local level to the international, ideas that art should refrain from politics and, conversely, that it should take up important social issues and defend the socially marginalized. This form of theater has also been constructed by government desires to mute or restrain open criticism of its policies and actions, relations between theater and arts institutions, relations between modern theater and the mass media, and relations between the many actors, directors, playwrights, composers, set designers, and stage crew involved in theatrical productions. This list is far from exhaustive, but it suggests the complex actors, interests, discourses, and conventions that have been at play to varying degrees in the constitution of modern national theater in Indonesia. It also suggests that in order to function modern theater must in some way reconcile, or at least bring into a productive working arrangement, a large number of elements. As Stuart Hall remarks, the function of a state is to condense a diverse set of practices into a system of regulation, rules, and norms (Hall 1985). Spheres of cultural activity, including theater, must operate in similar ways to achieve a minimum amount of coherency. But this situation does not remain static. The prevailing system of conventions, techniques, styles, and themes is always under pressure to change, from both the various groups and social interests participating in theater as well as the changing social conditions and moods.

We can see the various groups competing to have their interests dominate in a sphere of cultural activity as linked to particular social or class positions. By upbringing and education, these groups possess particular sensibilities and aesthetic ideologies, certain tastes that they see as most pleasing and appropriate to legitimate art. Bourdieu sees these sets of tastes as tied to *habitus* (a set of cultural predispositions) and *doxa* (classificatory systems and principles of social order which operate below the conscious level as "common sense"). For Bourdieu, in struggles over art the imposition of a certain set of tastes is always at stake (Bourdieu 1984, 1–6, 57, 471–82). Raymond Williams relates this assertion of a set of values and tastes as the dominant cultural values in society to the concept of establishing hegemony, a process that he argues is never complete, never total, and never singular. According to Williams, hegemony, the dominance of a particular set of values, must be continually renewed, recreated, and defended against other groups wishing to assert their views (tastes, aesthetics, etc.). These other groups challenge hegemonic power, helping to shape and limit it through their opposition. Thus, hegemony is dominant, but never exclusive (Williams 1977, 112–13).

In what follows, I will look at the construction of modern Indonesian theater as a sphere of artistic activity in the light of this conceptual framework. I will look at how modern Indonesian theater formed through a historical process of negotiation, competition, conflict, and accommodation at the very least within and between groups involved in creating modern theater, between theater and media, theater and arts institutions, theater and the Indonesian nationalist movement, and later theater and the Indonesian state. I begin by summarizing some of the history of relations between the Indonesian nationalist movement and later the Indonesian state and Indonesia's modern national theater. As I do so, I will show how this theater has been the site of a constant process of negotiation among competing ideologies, aesthetics, techniques, and styles. I will also delineate the main factors and processes that have contributed to the antagonism between the state and theater, though that antagonism was never total. My thesis in this first chapter is that the dominant aesthetic ideologies of the modern national theater sphere were autonomous from and in some ways inimical to the hegemonic political ideologies of the Indonesian state. Nonetheless, the power of the Indonesian state allowed it to propose an aesthetic counter-ideology during the rule of Suharto's New Order government (1966–98) that it claimed was rooted in Indonesian tradition and that exercised a powerful influence on theater.

A number of scholars have attempted to explain the development of Indonesian national culture as a conflict between traditional social elements, practices, and ideologies, and more modernizing, internationally oriented segments of the population (Geertz 1960; Anderson 1990 [1983]; Foulcher 1990; Winet 2001). In the analysis of the development of modern national theater which I propose here, I want to make a more fine-grained analysis of the development of one sphere of cultural activity than most of these scholars have been able to do, one which shows the give and take between multiple elements and groups, including those claiming to represent traditional cultural models and those claiming to champion modernity and modernization. Winet (2001) stands as a partial exception to the general trend, for he specifically examines a growing rift between modern theater and the Indonesian state that, he argues, results from the theater's interest in developing more psychologically complex characters, while the state remained interested in categorizing citizens according to stereotypical "roles." However, he does not explain the social bases of this antagonism, the interest of modern theater in international models, or the kinds of internal tensions within the sphere of the national theater that led to its formulation as a richly hybrid practice with its own ideological underpinnings partially separate from those of the state. Elucidating these issues will occupy the early sections of this chapter.

Key reasons for the State-Modern Theater Antagonism
1. Elite divisions

As I have argued elsewhere (Bodden 2007a), a split in the indigenous elite between those of aristocratic or bureaucratic-aristocratic backgrounds who were inducted into the higher echelons of the Dutch colonial native civil service, and those from lower levels of the aristocracy and bureaucracy who were excluded from such higher level positions or who chose not to pursue them, was a key factor in the growth of a national culture that did not always see eye-to-eye with the state.[1] The latter group generally followed educational trajectories into professions such as medicine, law, and journalism. To be sure, these two groups still had much in common. Whether through class background or Dutch colonial educational training, both had a sense of *noblese oblige* toward ordinary Indonesians. Similarly, Dutch education and life in the increasingly commercialized and bureaucratized Dutch East Indies colonial society had made them both culturally hybrid. Yet though the boundaries separating these two groups were far from rigid, their existence as two distinctive life-paths did generate tension and rivalry. Those of higher rank who obtained position in the native civil service often defended their place in Dutch colonial society by claiming that their mastery of local custom and inherited tradition of leadership made them indispensable to the government. Those eschewing or ineligible for higher civil service positions often viewed the high-ranking civil servants as "feudal" in their extreme observation of status differences and in their perceived lack of interest in helping the common people. These critics of the higher ranking bureaucratic aristocrats often championed modernizing social relations (Sutherland 1979; Frederick 1989).

These different positions led to similar tensions in the realm of culture. The 1930s *"Polemik Kebudayaan"* (Cultural Polemic) saw "traditionalists" such as Sutomo advocating "knightly" values such as disinterested service, disdain for commercial gain, and traditional Islamic boarding school education as foundational, while others asserted the need to completely adopt "Western" values and methods in order to modernize Indonesia (Mihardja 1986). Playwrights of the era experimented with grafting local historical and legendary story materials as well as elements of traditional theater genres onto modern dramas (Winet 2001; Bodden 1997b). However, by the end of the 1930s and the early 1940s, modern nationalist culture was turning decisively towards the modernizers, possibly because conservative elites seemed unwilling to change, while the tradition they supposedly supported was perceived as hampering a future Indonesia in its desire to stand equal to other nations on the global stage (Bodden 2007a).

This is clearly visible in the theater world in the plays of Sanusi Pané. Unlike some of his contemporaries, Sanusi Pané was hardly in favor of discarding tradition and simply emulating the "West," as his stance in the *Polemik Kebudayaan* (Cultural Poemic) indicates. In his contributions to the *Polemik*, he advocated as the basis for national culture a synthesis of "Faust and Arjuna," of the materialism and physical accomplishments of the "West" with the spiritual achievements of the "East" (Mihardja 1986, 22–26). Similarly in his 1932 drama, *Sandhyakala Ning Majapahit* (Twilight Over Majapahit), a number of elements drawn from the *wayang kulit* shadow puppet theater are evident. For instance, the play opens with a very brief allusion to the setting for the action as the perfect kingdom, much as in a shadow play. The fact that Damar Wulan is living in an isolated forest hermitage far from society and is seeking deeper wisdom before acting, the presence of his two clown servants, and the description of the enemy who rebels against Majapahit, the "villain" Menak Jinggo, as demonic or ogre-like, all suggest traditional theatrical themes and motifs.

Yet for all Sanusi's sympathy for and willingness to incorporate traditional culture into his modernist visions and works, the play is extremely pessimistic about the role of the elites, who claim to represent and staunchly defend "tradition." *Sandhyakala Ning Majapahit* features a hero, Damar Wulan, who wishes to serve the state disinterestedly. To rescue the state from collapse, he determines that the traditional aristocratic leadership must change its ways, for such leaders are unsympathetic to the impoverished plight of the masses, and are in fact oppressing them. Damar Wulan proposes several changes to the laws of the kingdom that threaten to diminish the power of the elite and the religious orders. The latter resist, plotting Damar Wulan's downfall by presenting half-truths and slanderous accusations about him, painting him as someone contemptuous of all religion and scheming to overthrow the Queen. In the end, Damar Wulan is executed, and the kingdom of Majapahit faces destruction at the hands of its enemies. Sanusi's pessimism thereby suggests how many nationalists and in particular nationalist-minded cultural workers may have viewed the more highly placed traditional elites employed in the colonial civil service. In so doing, it demonstrates why the appeal of modernization became stronger among such cultural workers in the late 1930s, leading to the modernizers' domination of much of national culture.

2. Communities of Artistic Ideology and Technique

A second reason for the divergence of interests between the state and modern national culture lay precisely in the desire of the modernizers to achieve an equal footing in the international cultural spotlight. The choice to align with modern cultural practices meant orienting one's life, if not moving to the cities where like-minded individuals mainly congregated. Since most people in the countryside still spoke their regional, ethnic language, the cities would also have been the place where the most concentrated audience for the new national language culture and theater could be found. These factors both argued for a national culture tied to the urban and ideas of modernity. Furthermore, through education, career trajectories, and place of residence, the new makers of the national culture were partially alienated from their more rural compatriots. Imbued with ideas of modern culture, literature, and art, they would have been bound to one another by this new set of artistic practices, techniques, and ideologies. Armin Pané, Sanusi's younger brother, was one of the central figures in this newly emerging nationalist avant-garde. While Armin hardly ignored tradition, and in fact believed that modern Indonesian culture was certain to be hybrid, his ideas of the artist and artistic creation sound quite similar to liberal humanist ideas being propagated in Europe at about the same time. Armin's notions included the ideas of the writer as an independent individual whose creations came from a restless soul (although the writer was also a product of the times), the universality of great art, and the importance of continual change and innovation (A. Pané 1933a; 1933b; Bodden 2007a). In this way, Indonesia's national culture of the time looked to new techniques that were seen as international and universal, at the same time as its proponents were also staunchly nationalist. This trend was intensified to almost mythic proportions by the life and work of Chairil Anwar, the modernist poet par excellence of the 1940s and the era of the independence struggle, and by a number of writers and artists, some of whom had been closely connected to Anwar, who produced the *Gelanggang* document of 1950 stating that they were "Heirs to World Culture" (Kratz 2000, 182–86). With the dominance of such modernizing and internationalist ideas and techniques in the realm of national culture, most tradition-minded bureaucratic elites would have found its products little to their liking.

Still, traditional ideas continued to exercise some influence as well. Even as modernist and politically progressive a figure as the politician and future Prime Minister of Indonesia, Sutan Sjahrir, seemed to blend conservative Dutch bourgeois ideology with the attitudes of local aristocrats in promoting the use of "refined" (*halus*) literature in educating ordinary Indonesians, who he felt were still primitive intellectually, spiritually, and emotionally (Sjahrir 1938, 24–25). Sjahrir privileges refined works as an antidote to the "low and vulgar sentimental feelings" of the people, and in so doing suggests a doxa or assumption operating almost subconsciously at the level of common sense about what art was best for society. Similar assumptions marked Usmar Ismail's play of the mid-1940s, *Liburan Seniman* (Artists' Holiday) in which popular urban theater is dismissed as a melodramatic commercial product pandering to the vulgar desires of the audience. The nationalist-minded creations of the play's heroes, in contrast, are seen as spiritual contributions to national culture, works of profound ideas. And in fact, anti-commercialism such as in Usmar's play, continued to be strongly represented in the world of modern national theater right up to the 1980s and beyond (Bodden 2007a).

3. The Legacy of the Revolution/War of Independence

The war of independence waged against the Dutch from 1945 to 1949 also left a strong imprint on modern national culture and theater. This independence struggle was also marked by a number of attempts in different parts of the archipelago to stage simultaneous social revolutions to overthrow the traditional structures of power. Both of these struggles translated into persistent impulses to create works that would criticize injustice and engage with contemporary social issues in the spheres of modern national culture. Thus, while Anderson notes that conservative elites increasingly filled the ranks of the newly independent Indonesian state's bureaucracy throughout the 1950s (Anderson 1990, 104), in the various spheres of national culture, modernizers with a more radical imperative took deep root. In fact, the different ways in which groups of cultural workers saw this imperative eventually produced a painful rift within the ranks of modernizing cultural workers that came to a head between 1963 and 1965. On the one hand were those who followed most closely the *Gelanggang* idea of creating a "universal humanist" culture. Though they were not completely opposed to cultural workers constructing works that clearly showed nationalist and political commitments, they emphasized the sovereignty of the individual cultural worker in determining the manner and extent of that commitment's expression. Opposed to this group, though they held many ideas about art and culture in common, were those cultural workers who gathered in the left-wing cultural movement, Lekra (Lembaga Kebudayaan Rakyat or Institute of People's Culture), which was aligned, though not without tensions, with the Indonesian Communist Party. This movement saw art and culture as springing from and, of necessity, serving the "people." Its members eventually strove to develop an Indonesian relative of "Socialist Realism," which they termed "Revolutionary Realism," and they felt that in art "Politics are the Commander."[2]

For much of the 1950s, the predominant theatrical style had been a type of psychological realism, heavily colored in many works by the thematic presence of social issues as well. By the second half of the 1950s and the early 1960s, both groups had begun to experiment, for different reasons, with combining Western-style realism with elements of traditional theater. Among the members of Lekra, whose anti-imperialist sentiments worked to create a more suspicious feeling about Western culture, playwrights such as Joebaar Ajoeb, Utuy Tatang Sontani, and Emha (Ibrahim Ismail Hamid) sought to use traditional tales or forms to create works that would display Indonesian national cultural characteristics as well as appeal to wider audiences still familiar with traditional culture. Among the "universal humanists," the work of Jim Lim and Suyatna Anirun with the Studiklub Teater Bandung stand out as examples of the desire to explore how traditional elements might be adapted to create new, avant-garde performances (Sumardjo 1992, 162–65).

Interestingly, even the work of those Lekra playwrights most involved in the creation of modern "Revolutionary Realist" dramas that relied on realistic dialogue, sets, and some aspects of psychologically developed characterization were not completely devoid of traditional theatrical elements. In some of the plays of Bachtiar Siagian or P. H. Muid, for example, the coding for good and bad characters is often based on earlier local models such as the *wayang kulit* or the Malay court adventure romances, the *hikayat*. Thus, psychological realism combines, sometimes uncomfortably, with calm, polite, refined heroes who are always in the right and emotionally uncontrolled, rude villains who are inevitably defeated.

By the early 1960s, as the political atmosphere in Indonesia became increasingly tense, Lekra and the "Universal Humanists" too began to clash, where before there had often been friendships and recognition, if also pointed polemics. In this newly polarized atmosphere, just as Lekra was aligned with the PKI, other groups of arts workers sought protection and support from other political parties such as the PNI (Indonesian Nationalist Party) or the NU (Nahdlatul Ulama or traditionalist Islamic Party), and even from the military. Following the *Manifes Kebudayaan* (Cultural Manifesto) affair of late 1963–64, in which a group of cultural workers supportive of "Universal Humanism" attempted to distance their art from state and political party direction, tensions began to peak. Leftist groups, including Lekra, strongly condemned the Manifesto's "Universal Humanist" signatories as "counter-revolutionary," supportive of cultural imperialism, and attempting to subvert the state ideology, *Pancasila*. The ousting of a number of supporters of the Cultural Manifesto from their positions in state institutions and newspapers, and the eventual ban on the Manifesto by President Sukarno, demonstrated the powerful ways in which the state and social organizations could intervene in the cultural sphere (Moeljanto and Ismail 1995, 355; Foulcher 1986, 124–28) and soured more deeply non-leftist cultural workers' feelings about the idea of political art. Yet the imperative to make drama and theater socially relevant did not disappear, however much modern theater felt the need to moderate or integrate in more subtle ways its social critique. This was a particularly strong factor in assuring continued, and even increasing tension, between theater workers and the state.

The New Order period and the excavation of "tradition"

Following the coups of September 30 and October 1, 1965, and the slaughter and imprisonment of Indonesian Communist party members and other leftists, the "Universal Humanists" became the dominant group in the further construction of Indonesian national culture. Though relatively liberal towards the arts in its first few years, the New Order government of President Suharto did eventually seek to bring modern culture under closer control and into general harmony with its development plans and ideology. Hints of this could be seen in Suharto's speech during his visit to the Taman Ismail Marzuki, Jakarta's main cultural center, in June 1976. In this speech, Suharto spoke of the "guided construction of culture" as included in the outlines of state policy, and reminded listeners that the development of national culture must be in accordance with the norms of Pancasila (Suharto 1976). Ensuing years were witness to efforts to curb social, political, and cultural dissent and to exert more influence over a variety of spheres of modern national culture, including attempting to insert preferred candidates into the Taman Ismail Marzuki's governing body and ordering public bans on particular performers. It was also in this era when government spokespeople endeavored to assert that social criticism in the arts should conform to what it defined as acceptable "traditional" patterns (Bodden 2007a, 74–75, 82–86).

Running parallel to the government's assertion of a certain idea of "tradition" as a tool to legitimate its particular kind of socio-political control, modern national theater began a long exploration of traditional performance genres, including theater, dance, and music. Modern national theater workers sought to imbue their creations with aspects of the spirit, structures, and content of traditional cultural forms. In the process they fashioned avant-garde theatrical works that they believed would retain ties to Indonesia's various regional cultural traditions and thereby stake claims to national cultural legitimacy at home, and a uniquely Indonesian modern theatrical signature abroad. This experimentation was significantly aided by the fact that the Taman Ismail Marzuki, first under the enlightened direction of Trisno Sumardjo and later under others carrying out many of Sumardjo's ideas, scheduled performances by both modern and traditional groups, allowing for a kind of cross-pollination of the two during the late 1960s and early 1970s (Gillitt 2001; Bodden 2007a). This led to what Putu Wijaya has called the "New Tradition" in modern Indonesian theater (Wijaya 1997, 343–49), something that could just as aptly be described as "neo-traditionalism."

The "neo-traditionalist" trend was also shaped and assisted by the mass media in the 1970s, most notably by the theater critics writing for *Tempo* magazine, a number of whom were directly involved in the construction of this new style. These critics reinforced notions associated with "Universal Humanism," maintaining that plays should be original, individual expressions of the director (and in some cases, writer), that they should contain profound truths about human nature and psychology, and, reflecting the conservative Dutch and Indonesian aristocratic ideas discussed above, that they should avoid being "pop." Goenawan Mohamad, the editor of *Tempo* and a frequent theater reviewer in those years, defended the new trend in theater against older, more dismissive critics by pointing out the ways in which the new trend performances had appropriated traditional elements to speak more intimately to their audiences (Mohamad 1980, 91–142; Kartakusuma 1974).

Yet the vision of these neo-traditionalists in the modern national theater was nonetheless distinct from the vision of tradition possessed by the state. In line with "universal humanism," many of the theatrical "neo-traditionalists" felt that tradition was not static but rather, something that was continually changing and evolving, and that individual cultural workers needed to adapt tradition, according to their own visions, so that it could still speak in contemporary times (Rendra 1983). Furthermore, despite their suspicion of direct political statement or linkages to specific parties or movements, they nonetheless often felt that art should take up social issues, defend the poor, and oppose feudal or unjust behavior (Bodden 2007a, 75–80).

Protest and criticism of New Order society was quite prevalent in much of the innovative theater created in the 1970s by "neo-traditonalist" pioneers such as W. S. Rendra, Arifin C Noer, Putu Wijaya, Teguh Karya, Ikranegara, and Riantiarno. Yet, given the memory of the recent trauma of political polarization in the arts in the early 1960s, much of this criticism tended to shy away from direct political commentary or sensitive contemporary social issues, preferring instead to raise issues of social alienation, irrational patterns of social behavior, the difficult lives and shattered dreams of the urban poor, and allegories of state power (often clothed in adaptations of Western plays from the Greeks to Schiller to Brecht). As the New Order grew more authoritarian and began to ban performances of particular groups, playwrights, and plays, this "universal humanist" preference for less direct political content became a protective necessity. The fate of W. S. Rendra demonstrates the dangers of presenting too pointed a critique of the New Order political reality.

Rendra and New Order Control

As frustration with the New Order's development policies and corruption grew among students and critical intellectuals in 1973, Rendra became more deeply engaged in a project of regime-criticism—a stance already foreshadowed in his *tirakatan* arrest (for participating in a protest vigil or *tirakatan*) during student protests in 1970 (Aveling 1981, vi; McDonald 1980, 125–26). In the final months of 1973, Rendra attempted to stage one of his own original plays, *Mastodon dan Burung Kondor* (The Mastodon and the Condors). The play itself still retains some thematic and cognitive distance from the reality of New Order Indonesia by being set in an unnamed Latin American country, but the problems encountered—an authoritarian regime bent on a particular kind of economic development, the rhetoric of state control, the disparaging of dissidence and opposition, and the displacement and economic dispossession of large numbers of ordinary people—clearly mirror much of the situation in Indonesia circa 1973. In brief, the play narrates the rise of a movement of student opposition to autocratic ruler Max Carlos. Max Carlos leads a regime that has staked its claim to legitimacy on its ability to pursue economic development. However, the development pursued by his regime has not benefited most ordinary citizens. Eventually, the student revolutionaries launch a "planned" revolution and succeed in driving Max Carlos from the country. Yet in the process, they have become more like him, and in the end they exile a critic, the poet José Karosta, who had formerly been sympathetic to their goals.

As can be seen from this synopsis, the play is a cautionary tale both about the blindness of dictatorship and the likelihood that violent revolution will in the end lead to a discouraging reproduction of some of the oppressive patterns of governing against which the revolution arose. But there are other issues involved as well, for Rendra's play foregrounds the perceived opposition between poetry and practical political work. This binary grows to encompass a variety of associations as the play progresses. On the side of poetry Rendra posits spiritual development, pleasure, emotional strength, and charisma. On the side of practical politics, we find material development, machismo, a tendency to control (to the point of oppression), and bureaucracy. Karosta, the protagonist of the piece, is a poet who voices criticism of the government but refrains from joining any political party in order to guard his individual independence. Karosta also views violent revolution as wrongheaded, preferring peaceful, "evolutionary" change through public debate and changing individual consciousness. He is the champion of poetry, which he feels balances material life. Opposed to him are both the dictator, Max Carlos, and the man who will eventually perhaps replace him, Juan Frederico, (though there are hints that one of his comrades is conspiring to oust Juan Frederico from power in the near future). Frederico is consumed with seizing power and is willing to use any means to accomplish his goals. In order to convince Karosta to work with the revolution, Frederico has a female member of the revolutionary leadership attempt to seduce the poet, manipulates the government to martyr Karosta by imprisoning him, and takes Karosta into "protective custody" when he refuses to subordinate his actions to the goals of the revolution, as outlined by its political leaders (Rendra 1981).

Clearly, *Mastodon dan Burung Kondor* in no way advocates violent overthrow of the government. If Karosta's explicit statements opposing such action were not enough, the play's portrayal of the obsessed, manipulative, and coldly calculating revolutionaries proves this quite emphatically. Yet the play may have made the authorities uncomfortable for a number of reasons. Given the New Order regime's attempt to tie its legitimacy to successful economic development, the play's criticisms of "development" and the repeated portrayals of the ways in which the poor were not benefiting from economic development, but rather were suffering dispossession and impoverishment (Rendra 1981, 1, 3–4, 14–16, 20, 22, 27–29) were no doubt troubling. Other elements of the play, such as Max Carlos' speeches about development and his arrogant dismissals of his regime's critics, may have resonated too closely with the Indonesian reality felt by audiences of the time as well. Writing in the 24 November 1973 edition of *Tempo*, the magazine's editor and well-known poet, intellectual, and theater critic Goenawan Mohamad, basing his article on a reading of the script, praised Rendra's play for "speaking effectively about Indonesia" and for "formulating our actual problems." Further, Mohamad argued that with this play Rendra had taken an important step on behalf of "Indonesian Theater" by beginning to offer members of the public representations of the world and problems with which they themselves were already intimately acquainted. This, Mohamad felt, would help theater attain a more important place within society (Mohamad 1973).

Confronted with a growing wave of student protest, apparently the Yogyakarta police also agreed with Mohamad's assessment and banned the performance of the play. The Rector of the University of Gajah Mada in Yogyakarta, the campus on which the performance was to be held, then found "procedural reasons" for siding with the police in blocking the performance. Amazingly enough, the last minute intervention of General Sumitro, then head of the Military Intelligence and Security organization, the powerful and feared *Kopkamtib*, allowed Rendra's play to be staged in early December (Mohamad 1973). Sumitro's intervention was indicative of a split in the New Order's military between a group of so-called "professional" generals of whom Sumitro was the leader, and the "business generals" headed by Suharto aide Ali Murtopo. Sumitro's subsequent ouster from power following the Malari riots of January 1974 was one sign of the end of the New Order's "honeymoon" with its own more liberal supporters. Following the performance of *Mastodon dan Burung Kondor*, Rendra's Bengkel was not allowed to perform in his home city of Yogyakarta for the next four years. Rendra's staging of plays such as Sophocles's *Oedipus at Colonus* (1974), Aristophanes' *Lysistrata* (1975), and his own celebrated work critiquing the social disparities and ecological and cultural short-sightedness of New Order development, *Kisah Perjuangan Suku Naga* (Struggle of the Naga Tribe, 1975), were prohibited by Yogyakarta police on various grounds: that they deviated from the original script, were not appropriate in the given conditions, or were too sharply critical (Rendra 1975, 50–51; YLBHI 1994, 48). Curiously, these bans only applied to the Yogyakarta area, as each of the plays mentioned above was allowed performance in the more relaxed, liberal atmosphere of Ali Sadikin's Jakarta and TIM.

Rendra received an award for his achievements in theater, poetry, and poetry reading from the Jakarta Academy in 1975, but even at this point, many members of the arts community were becoming uncomfortable with his increasing engagement in direct political critique in his work. His "Pamphlet Poetry," mainly composed in 1977 and 1978 at a time of rising student protests against the government, was particularly sharp in its criticism. At a reading of this poetry at the Taman Ismail Marzuki in May, 1978, an ammonia bomb was thrown into the audience, providing a pretext for Rendra's arrest and detention for several months. Upon release, he was no longer allowed to perform theater or poetry for the next seven years.

The debate surrounding Rendra's arrest revealed with special clarity the divisions between the government and the arts community, as well as those within the arts community itself, over how to regard Rendra's recent work. Aside from accusing Rendra of being provocative and providing a "false" picture of the results of the government's development policies, government spokespeople, including the Minister of Education and Culture, Daud Yusuf, attacked Rendra as a publicity hound who only sought to increase his popularity for financial gain. Yusuf combined this conservative doxa about art as non-commercial with a reference to "universal humanist" ideals in declaring that Rendra's poetry contained no formal innovations, implying it was therefore doubly illegitimate as art. Though most modern theater and cultural figures polled did not agree with the government's decision to ban Rendra, several expressed criticism of his recent artistic production, characterizing it as a publicity-seeking, sloganistic, and un-artistic protest (*Tempo* 1978).

Bagong Kussudiardjo, a well-known painter and choreographer, argued that traditional theater had never been censored since it leveled its protests in humorous, refined, and subtle fashion that didn't anger those criticized (*Tempo* 1978). Though his point was debatable, many theater figures repeatedly echoed Kussudiardjo's reasoning during the ensuing years as the New Order tightened its control of the modern theater: social criticism was best raised through a subtle, humorous approach (Bodden 2007a, 84–85). At the same time, the New Order state was intent on installing a similar idea of appropriate criticism in traditional theater as well

(Weintraub 2001). All of this marks again the influence of conservative Dutch/Indonesian aristocratic notions of art in the sphere of modern national theater. Thus, during much of the New Order, the state sought, with some success, to modify the behavior and ideas of modern theater workers.

As Hatley (1990, 1993) has pointed out, theatrical protest against and resistance to the New Order's rule continued in a variety of locales, though it was most often a resistance that critiqued the state mainly in the state's own terms. Still, this resistance suggested that many theater workers were restless under the New Order's hegemonic control and that the ground was being prepared for a future resurgence of theater's autonomy and capacity for a more critical creative expressiveness.

Challenges to the New Order's Hegemony in Theater

And indeed, during the 1990s, this neo-feudal aesthetic was challenged in several ways by theater workers at a moment when the New Order was struggling to cope with the regime's own internal dissension and the rise of an increasingly vocal, critical and restive middle-class. In the chapters that follow we will see two key kinds of challenges. The first was represented by the move of some groups into a grass roots theater or *teater rakyat* (people's theater) in which middle-class and elite theater workers, together with socially marginalized groups, developed theater to produce plays about the daily lives and problems of its creator-participants. These theater forms did not abandon notions of aesthetics but laid much more emphasis on the relevance and authenticity of story material and form to the lives of its creators. They took up the idea of theater as a means of consciousness raising and confidence building, and of mobilizing peasants, workers, and others to work for social change that would benefit them directly. Such theater was produced by Arena Teater and others in Yogyakarta by workers' theater groups in the greater Jakarta region, and to a lesser extent by the Islamic theater of Emha Ainun Nadjib and Sanggar Shalahuddin.

The second challenge came in the form of postmodern aesthetics and ideas about human subjectivity. In its early years and in some of its critical and theoretical works, postmodernism as it developed in North

America could be seen as waging a cultural struggle of liberation from hegemonic and often oppressive forms of knowledge and cultural practice. It did so through its rejection of a "high," socially sanctified and institutionalized version of cultural modernism, but also by valorizing minority cultures, new technologies, and popular culture. It tended to agree with the work of Foucault (1995) that saw power as dispersed, and stressed the micro-politics of power relations as well as the coexistence, collision, and interpenetration of different realities, rather than attempting to create a sense of a complex, though unified, reality as modernism had done. Furthermore, postmodernism tended to posit the right of all groups to speak for themselves, in their own voice (Harvey 1989, 41–52). All of this suggested the rejection and deconstruction of the previously established dominant or master narratives of social and cultural meaning that postmodernists argued could no longer be taken as universal truths. In the postmodernist view, these "master narratives" emerged as the products of certain groups, constructions tied to the perpetuation and extension of those groups' own interests.

Indonesian avant-garde postmodernism shared with North American postmodernism a kind of anti-establishment cultural politics. This oppositional stance led many of its leading practitioners to become involved with, or at least, sympathetic to the Indonesian pro-democracy movement, including workers organizations, social justice NGOs, and a cautiously re-emerging women's movement. As we will see in chapter 6, in one case this led to the collaboration of postmodernist theater workers with a nascent workers' theater movement. Yet the very nature of its opposition also showed that Indonesia's postmodernists differed in a number of ways from North American postmodernism. A key difference lay in the fact that though seeing individuals as fragmented, most Indonesian postmodernists attempted to downplay or negate the dominance of local, traditional values by positing some sense of universal human values. Kwame Anthony Appiah has noted a similar pattern in second-stage African postcolonial novels that rejected potentially repressive particularistic visions of African identity in favor of ethical universals (Appiah 1996, 66).

The New Order state consolidated its political power in the early 1970s and moved to control a variety of realms of cultural production from the mid-1970s on. This included an attempt to control and limit the aesthetic ideologies of modern national culture, including theater. I have already discussed the ways in which the artistic ideologies of "universal humanism" and a kind of "traditionalism" or "nativism" contested the terrain of the modern national theater from the 1970s to the 1990s. To be sure, the traditionalism that the New Order state sought to assert in the field of theater was not the only sign of interest in elements of traditional culture in this era, nor was the state the only party interested in making use of "tradition." During the New Order, as I have shown, an interest in local cultural roots, motifs and forms was widespread in modern theater and in Indonesian literature also beginning in the late 1960s (Foulcher 1978). However, the state was a powerful force for promoting a specific kind of traditionalism. A glaring instance of this was the New Order government's own mobilization of a nativist stance in order to "protect" Indonesia from cultural and political trends it deemed inappropriate to Indonesian culture, ranging from liberal democracy, break dancing, rap music, (Dewanto 1995) and consumerism (Foulcher 1990, 301–3; Hatley 1993, 48–50), to excessive use of English on billboards. As we have seen, such cultural policing also affected the world of modern national theater.

Even more pervasive during the New Order was the state's attempt to appropriate and remold (not to mention invent) many forms of "traditional" culture and practice in order to bolster its program of nation-building and economic development (Pemberton 1994; Guinness 1994; Bowen 1986). This was complemented by a reconstructed Javanese aristocratic ideology of orderliness, hierarchy, deference to social superiors and paternalistic familial authority that came to dominate much of government and public discourse during the New Order period (Koentjaraningrat 1985, 460–62; Mahasin 1990, 91–92; Anderson 1990, 125–46; Suryakusuma 1996, 96). In the second half of the 1980s, the New Order even made a concerted effort to install a totalitarian, integralist notion of the state, presented as an expression of the "national personality," as a key part of the official state ideology.[3] In the light of all these developments, I would argue that a nativist ideology was strongly present in determining the "structure of feeling" (or "practical lived consciousness") in New

Order society,[4] and even more so in the ways in which the state impinged on cultural production.

Nonetheless, in the late 1980s and early 1990s, pressures for economic deregulation and political liberalization as well as tensions within the Indonesian ruling elite convinced the New Order government to declare a new era of political openness (*keterbukaan*). Ariel Heryanto has suggested that the Indonesian debate on postmodernism during this same period was related to the growing prosperity and social confidence of the Indonesian middle-class, and coincided with the public prominence of discussions of openness, human rights and democratization (Heryanto 1995, 33–36). Heryanto and Nirwan Dewanto were among the most influential intellectuals to discuss postmodernism as a possible counter to New Order doxa regarding culture.

Heryanto juxtaposed a list of post-modern values to those of the New Order, explaining that postmodernism, with its emphasis on slang and play with language, diversity and complexity, valuing the local, anarchy, process, openness, participation, and play represented a useful alternative to the New Order's obsessions with formal language, a sole ideological basis, the universal, stability and security, hierarchy, centralization, bureaucracy, and subservience to rules (Heryanto 1994, 80–81). Dewanto sounded a Foucauldian note in his 1991 speech to the National Cultural Congress, attacking large-scale historicizing and grand concepts. He linked Indonesian artistic and cultural modernism to the privileging of the unified nation state as the ultimate frame of reference for cultural production. Dewanto argued that culture does not conform to such grand frames of reference or "master narratives." He held that culture was in reality created in diverse locations by little units (*satuan-satuan kecil*) shaped by a variety of influences including local traditions and global trends and not just national developments. He saw this cultural production as decentered and fragmented, but he evaluated the situation as one holding positive possibilities for more open networks of communication and exchange, along with unlimited choices and plural standards of judgement for human creativity freed of uniformity, surveillance, and paranoia, freed of the master narratives and stifling cultural bureaucracy erected during the New Order (Dewanto 1996, esp. 28–46).

Cultural theorists such as Dewanto and Heryanto tried to use aspects of postmodernism to challenge and attack the prevailing ideologies and paradigms of New Order culture as part of a general movement by radical segments of the middle-class to transform New Order cultural and political life. Another aspect of the growth and rising prosperity of the middle-class generated a related but somewhat different kind of postmodernism. This was an avant-gardism that challenged New Order control and repression and as such had some affinities with the critiques offered by Heryanto and Dewanto. For instance, as we will see in chapter 4, Teater Sae's works of the early 1990s indirectly attacked ideas of a "national personality" or unified traditional ways of imagining the social human being by presenting individuals as fragmented and shaped by a variety of discourses and processes. The group also took on concepts of tradition, occasionally highlighting elements of "tradition" not usually championed by the New Order, at other times questioning the validity of officially favored "traditional" ways of imagining and organizing life. But at the same time, this avant-gardism also represented a mainly critical response to the commercialization of modernist culture in the late New Order.

By the late 1980s, the dominant ideologies of New Order high cultural production, as outlined above, were also being challenged by the commercialization of culture. This was in itself spurred by the rise of a larger, more affluent middle-class. Key features of this commercialization of culture were the growth of huge, profitable press empires throughout the 1980s (stressing, in the case of the flagship publication of one such empire, easy, pleasurable and necessary reading—"Enak dibaca dan perlu"), and the launching of several privately owned television stations, beginning in the last years of that decade (Hill 1994). Commercialization also began to affect the arts, particularly the graphic arts, an area where art collecting had become more widespread (Wright 1994, 12–13), and the modern theater. A number of leading older-generation theater practitioners began exploring ways to market their performances to a wider audience. Groups like Rendra's Bengkel Teater sought connections with particular impresarios or sponsors to help defray expenses. Ticket prices increased to cover rising production and promotional costs (Cholid et al. 1989, 105–6).

Under these circumstances, as well as the conditions of social and ideological control constructed by the New Order regime, popular new middle-class forms of art, such as Riantiarno's Teater Koma, Srimulat, the musical productions of Guruh, and innovative *wayang kulit* productions, developed and flourished throughout the 1980s (Hatley 1993, 49–50; Sears 1996, 240–44, 260–73; Zurbuchen 1989, 127–28). For the most part these new forms of cultural production and consumption were considered politically mild or safe and intellectually untaxing.[5]

Faced with the rising tide of commercialization as well as the longstanding bureaucratic restrictions on public performance, an avant-garde infrastructure began to be established in the late 1980s. It included several smaller Jakarta-area theatrical spaces,[6] intended to avoid much of the bureaucratic procedure required for larger public performance venues as well as to minimize the costs of rental and production. In such a way, the involved members of the theater community hoped to nurture more experimental works that might not be accommodated at the larger theaters for fear they could not draw enough paying customers. Ray Sahetapy of Teater Oncor suggested that these smaller stages presented an alternative to "budaya instan atau kemasan" (instant or packaged culture) (Hartojo and Fadjri 1992, 42; Chudori and Iswardhani 1993, 104). Paralleling the tendency of earlier European and North American avant-garde movements towards political engagement, such theaters often also opened their spaces to performances and discussions connected to the broadly political pro-democracy movement, including performances of Jakarta area workers' theater groups ("Kesenian di luar pabrik" 1997, 49–60). Similarly, as the market for books in Indonesia became saturated and publishers were felt to be reluctant to publish "serious" literature, smaller publishers such as the Yogyakarta-based Bentang sprang up to publish "serious" literature and cultural analysis.[7]

However, here it is possible to apprehend another difference between Indonesian postmodernism and that of North America. If North American postmodernists embraced pop culture as an antidote to what they perceived to be an institutionally sanctioned, elitist version of high modernism, Indonesian postmodernists, while certainly not rejecting pop and mass culture, were painfully aware of the way in which commercialized mass culture in the New Order was already eroding the legitimacy of, and space for, a more reflective high art. Perhaps one of the clearest indications of this development was the decline in government funding for the Jakarta Performing Arts Center (TIM), which from the late 1980s had been increasingly forced to rely on corporate support (Hatley 1994b, 244–45). Thus, Indonesian postmodernism was generated in a context where "high" art was already perceived to be in a much less secure position in regard to both the state and the market than it was in 1960s North America. Caught between a highly controlled and censored mass media on the one hand, and the difficulties of marketing "serious art" on the other, some Indonesian postmodernists such as Afrizal Malna, in particular, and avant-garde performers such as Ray Sahetapy had a tempered enthusiasm for commercialized and mass mediated culture.[8] This also partially aligned such avant-garde figures with lower-class groups such as Teater Kubur, whose works were in part a reaction against consumer culture and the alienating new reality of urban life.

Structures of New Order Cultural Control

According to Edward Aspinall, the early period of the New Order regime allowed some space for criticism, mainly for those students and intellectuals who had collaborated with the army in overthrowing Sukarno and supported the destruction of the Indonesian left. However, as the regime consolidated its hold on power, it rapidly became less tolerant of any kind of criticism or opposition (Aspinall 1996, 215–25). The greater tolerance in the early years of the New Order may be explained in part by the fact that during its first few years, the New Order government was busy promoting foreign investment-powered economic growth and securing control over the mechanisms of political power. Only in the early 1970s did the New Order move to construct broader mechanisms of control over civil society, notably by stipulating women's role in society and development (Sullivan 1990, 62–69); by banning newspapers in 1974 and 1978 and issuing rules in the early 1980s facilitating tighter, corporatist control of the print media (Hill 1987; Hill 1994, 41–51); by banning all political activity on university campuses in 1978 and mandating Pancasila ideological training in the same year for all university students, civil servants, doctors, teachers, and soldiers (Morfit 1986, 42–43; Ramage 1995, 31–32; Aspinall 1996); by promulgating a set of guidelines for censorship in the cinema between 1977 and 1981 (Sen 1994, 66–71); and by passing the *asas tunggal* law of 1985 (Morfit 1986; Ramage 1995, 35–36), stipulating that all social organizations had to embrace the national ideology as their sole foundational principle.

While its censorship of modern theater was mainly directed at quashing explicit dissent, criticism of specific policies, and direct criticism of the regime's leaders, the New Order government also exhibited more totalitarian tendencies in its regulation of culture. For example, it instituted corporatist organizations and publishing licenses with which to exercise better control over print journalists and radio and television broadcasters. Furthermore, it used the sole television station operating in Indonesia up until the late 1980s, TVRI (Indonesian National Television), to promote its programs and perspective. In addition, private radio and television stations (private television began broadcasting in the late 1980s) were required to air specific numbers of newscasts generated by government media on a daily basis. A set of guidelines for censorship over films was also promulgated in 1981 (Sen and Hill 2000, 52–56, 83–90, 109–111, 137–42).

The modern theater was not exempt from regulation and surveillance, but such regulation was less systematic for theater. As a result, the New Order's efforts to control the theater world at an institutional level from the mid-1970s on, including its censorship policies for stage performances, were piecemeal and appeared arbitrary, thus producing regular occasions for conflict. For example, the 1980s saw a regular series of bans of theater and other performances in Yogyakarta and elsewhere, usually without a clear set of arguments to support such bans. Local police generally issued some statement about the plays disturbing stability, not being "appropriate," ridiculing officialdom, or containing criticism that was too sharp (Tempo 16 February 1980; Tempo 12 December 1981; von der Borch 1988; YLBHI 1994). The less systematic nature of theater censorship thereby allowed a small opening for theater to become one element of the emerging oppositional movement of the 1990s. Though the New Order put in place an extensive apparatus for controlling modern theater through the mass activities permit application process,[9] in contrast to the way in which the government handled Indonesia's modern film industry, no set of guidelines was developed to delineate precisely which subjects could or could not be handled by theatrical performances during the first two decades of the New Order. There are several possible explanations for this lacuna.

First, vague censorship guidelines often work to the advantage of the government, for those producing cultural works must exercise extreme caution if they wish to avoid government bans or censorship. The case of the print media is instructive here. Even though a number of topics were known to be "off limits" (criticism of the first family, and the "MISS SARA" topics—anything seditious, speculative, sensationalistic, insinuating, or deemed to hurt ethnic, religious or racial or class groups) for discussion in newspapers and magazines, often there were large grey areas that forced reporters and editors to rely on official hints and their own instincts (Makarim 1978, 279; Djajamihardja 1986, 45–46; Hill 1994, 44–47). Such uncertainty caused those in charge of a publication to exercise a more cautious form of self-censorship than might otherwise prevail in order to avoid a government crackdown. Zygmunt Hübner argues that such preventative self-censorship has also been amply evident in the history of world theater (Hübner 1988, 52–62). It would appear that this line of reasoning can be partially substantiated with regard to the modern theater in Indonesia under the New Order. Playwrights often crafted their works in forms presumed to be acceptable and attempted to shape or veil their criticism so that it would pass censorial inspection.[10] Certainly, aside from aiming to prevent explicit public criticism and dissent, New Order acts of censorship against modern theater performances were also intended to serve as examples, warning and intimidating the rest of the arts community. The mere fact that censorship was a real possibility would clearly convince many cultural workers to attempt to find "more acceptable" methods of expressing themselves.

From the producers' point of view, one possible advantage of vague guidelines, or even the absence of guidelines, as opposed to clear rules for censorship is the fact that though such a situation may make cultural workers more cautious, it nevertheless does not definitively foreclose

The Modern National Theater 47

any possibilities. This leaves room for the continual testing and shifting of the limits of discussion, reporting, and criticism. This became an advantage for theater during the last decade of Suharto's rule. Nonetheless, self-censorship by producers works in the majority of cases to the advantage of the government in power. It tends to force social critics to be more careful, thus controlling the manner and tenor of dissent. And Hübner suggests that since censorship is often a "shamefaced" activity, the authorities involved might prefer to keep a low profile, allowing self-censorship to do its work rather than committing their reasons to writing, since a written record is subject to more sustained public scrutiny—both in the present and future (Hübner 1988, 50). Still, the New Order did develop more specific guidelines for cinema, which, given its predominance of fictional material, represents a cultural practice more closely parallel to theater than is the print media.

This leads to a second possible reason for the lack of guidelines for modern theater. Guidelines were developed for the cinema under the urging of film producers anxious about losing large investments if a completed film's release were to be rejected by the Board of Film Censors. The censorship guidelines for film provide an interesting contrast with theater. According to Krishna Sen, banning of cinema prior to 1980 was rather arbitrary, being subject to both a Board of Censors (BSF) and local military and government officials. The BSF was relatively liberal in the early 1970s, but as the seventies progressed the government installed an ever-larger number of government officials and security agency operatives on the Board. Partly at the urging of the film industry itself, attempts were made between the mid-seventies and 1981 to create a clear set of censorship guidelines in order to avoid financing films only to have them banned. These guidelines, issued by the government in 1977 and confirmed by industry production codes in 1981, required that films not destroy feelings of inter-religious harmony, harm national consciousness or show the individual as more important than the nation or state, exploit feelings of ethnicity, religion, or ancestry, incite social tensions, and dissent against government policies or express anything that could damage state institutions or officials of the state or associated with the state (Sen 1994, 66–71; Sen and Hill 2000,

140–42). In contrast to this specific set of guidelines, censorship in the theater appears to have been much more ad hoc.

Nevertheless, though prohibited material was not clearly delineated, the New Order government established a daunting process for bureaucratically controlling theatrical performances and mass activities: the mass activities permit system. Still, the distinction between theater and the cinema remains instructive. The difference may be explained by the fact that the modern theater, derived as it was from heavily modern, Western styles of theater, was not yet considered a sufficiently important medium to warrant more clearly formulated guidelines and cloying corporatist organizational control. In comparison to television or cinema, any given theater performance reached a much smaller audience mainly composed of youth and segments of the urban middle-classes. A second reason lies in the fact that most modern theater productions were much less expensive to mount than a feature film, and even though by 1972 several groups could attract audiences numbering between 800 and 2000 over a run of two to five nights (*Tempo* 1972c, 32–38), modern theater was nonetheless not a large-scale and consistent money-making venture prior to the late 1980s.[11] Furthermore, a number of leading groups received subsidies from the Taman Ismail Marzuki, which served to minimize a group's own private investment in the venture.[12] Financially speaking, there was less at stake and less incentive for theatrical workers to urge the government to develop clear guidelines about what could be presented. Nonetheless, since most modern theater groups attracted relatively small audiences compared to film and even some of the older theater genres, it is also possible that the New Order security apparatus may well have felt that its exhausting bureaucratic process for vetting proposed public performances was sufficient for most contingencies.

Throughout the 1980s and into the 1990s, modern theater groups wishing to perform had to obtain the necessary permit by running an entire gamut of government offices. In the Central Javanese cultural center of Yogyakarta, for instance, speakers or performers wishing to appear in the local Performing Arts Center had to get approval from the following list of government offices: the village/neighborhood office (*kelurahan*), the sub district government office (*kecamatan*), the sub district military command (*koramil*), the police sectoral office (*Polsek*), the district military command (*Kodim*), the county police office (*Polres*), the district attorney (*Kejaksaan*), and the regional government's socio-political office (*Bidang Sospol Pemda*). If a request was felt to require *special consideration* before going through the regular permit process, it would have to be screened first by the Regional Intelligence Coordinating Board or *Bakorinda* (*Badan Koordinasi Intelijen Daerah*) composed of representatives from the police, the district military command, the regional government's socio-political office and the Attorney General's District office). If a speaker came from outside the province the request needed to be made one month in advance in order for the request to be vetted by the National Headquarters of the Police Force in Jakarta (*Mabes Polri*). Purported reasons for denying permits to a particular speaker were "If the contents are intended to incite," or if the lecture was deemed to be targeted at a general audience (*Kompas* 13 May 1994)!

Reflective of the New Order's lack of systematic procedures for censoring theater, the process, though similarly laborious, seemed to vary considerably in different locales.[13] If these labyrinthine and confusingly varied sets of permit procedures were not enough, the "threat" of popularity for particular stars' or groups' productions prompted the New Order to create yet another, quasi-secret layer of permit procedures for special cases. It was long widely rumored that several figures/groups required special permits above and beyond the regular process in order to perform. This rumor was finally confirmed during 1994 and 1995 in the course of the public discussions of the banning of *Pak Kanjeng* in Surabaya in 1994 and Teater Koma's successful 1995 production, *Semar Gugat* (Semar Accuses). In both cases Pramana Padmodarmaya, the Director of the Taman Ismail Marzuki, admitted that while in the 1990s the city's key art center generally only needed to inform the police of upcoming performances (which seems to have been the case for a number of regional performing arts centers until the late 1980s as well), Rendra, Teater Koma, and Guruh Sukarno Putra (and formerly, popular *dangdut* music star, Rhoma Irama) all required a special permit (*Republika* 3 February 1994; Pracoyo and Riza [Forum Keadilan 18 December] 1995; Republika Online [24 November] 1995). This entailed applying to (1) the Cultural Office (*Dinas*

Kebudayaan); (2) the Tourism Office (*Dinas Parawisata*); (3) the Socio-Political Directorate (*Ditsospol*); (4) the National Coordinating Board for Stability, Regional Branch (*Bakorstanasda*); (5) the Jakarta Metropolitan Area Police (*Polda Metro Jaya*) (*Republika* On-Line 24 November 1995; *Forum Keadilan* 18 December 1995). Significantly, the list of those requiring special permits seemed to be focused on performers who had frequently criticized the regime in a way censors found objectionable, and who were able to command large audiences, the latter attribute in itself constituting a peculiarity among modern theater groups that certainly singled them out for the extra scrutiny that the government trained upon them. The two attributes seemed to be mutually reinforcing. In the case of Guruh, the additional vestigial charisma of being the son of Sukarno most likely was also a cause of concern for New Order censors. Even so, no set of guidelines was developed, but rather an extra layer of review and "negotiations" was added. Most likely, then, the establishment of guidelines was dependent upon the insistence of those involved in producing the performances/cultural products, as was the case with film.

For all the above reasons, modern theater, though operating under heavily constrained circumstances, was nonetheless better positioned than a number of other media to become a significant socio-political lightning rod by the late 1980s. The Indonesian middle-classes were becoming more restless under New Order harness and more assertive in voicing their opposition. Since other media were more heavily systematically regulated and involved a more substantial financial investment, theater became a more ready-made medium for expressing that opposition. In contrast to other media, its productions tended to have smaller overheads and its practitioners therefore were correspondingly less afraid of losing money. As detailed earlier in this chapter, there was also a strong tradition of insistence on the integrity of plays, as artistic creations and social commentary, among "universal humanist" cultural workers longing for relatively unmediated self-expression. This was coupled with a desire for theater to represent the ordinary people's problems and the real issues facing Indonesian society. And finally, since there was a lack of clearly defined guidelines regarding content, this form of theater had somewhat more room to maneuver in airing criticism than other cultural media—in censorship battles during the 1990s, the security apparatus displayed frequent confusion in explaining the reasons for its censorship. This implies that officials within the apparatus were often not really sure of the reasons why particular works should be banned. Yet it also points to the skill and daring with which theater workers began to find new ways of opposing the Indonesian state's restrictions as well as criticizing the social conditions the state had created. Among others, these strategies of resistance and opposition included linking their creativity to that of ordinary Indonesians in several kinds of grassroots theater, constructing new avant-garde forms that could voice radical criticisms in less obviously transparent ways, and eventually fighting to expand the space for even direct kinds of political and social commentary and criticism in the 1990s. A number of these practices, as we shall see, even challenged the formal expectations about what artistic national theater should be or do, and ideas of what constituted good or important uses of theater. Exploring some of these strategies of resistance as well as examining the communities and situations out of which they grew and the social momentum to which they contributed will be the key foci of the following chapters.

New Order Politics in the 1980s

If the New Order began as an alliance between the military, Muslim groups, segments of the tiny middle-class, students, and intellectuals, it soon became apparent that the new state, dominated by military interests, would tolerate very little opposition. Its prohibitions against the reconstitution of the Sukarno-era Islamic political party, Masyumi, were one indication of this, as were its early efforts to meddle in and weaken the traditional parties such as the PNI (the Indonesian Nationalist Party) prior to the first general election over which it presided in 1971. Thereafter, it forced all opposition parties into two variegated umbrella parties, significantly hobbling their political coherence (Crouch 1988, 246–72; McDonald 1980 87–111). At the same time, many middle-class intellectuals were becoming dissatisfied with the regime's continuing domination by the military as well as its economic policies that they felt favored foreign corporations and a coterie of generals and Chinese-Indonesian business tycoons over the masses of ordinary people. Further exacerbating the growing disaffection, the regime was proving to be highly corrupt (Aspinall 1996, 218–19). Protests against government corruption began at least as early as 1970, and large-scale student protest movements erupted in 1974 and 1978. The government's response—increasingly heavy-handed repression in the form of arrests, the banning of newspapers, and eventually policies designed to limit student activism on campus—further alienated the regime from its initial base of support (MacDonald 1980, 112–42 and 232–54; Robison and Hadiz 2004, 64–65).

Still, through opening Indonesia to foreign investment and through strategic use of international loans, government revenues, and funds channeled into government and military-controlled foundations, the New Order was able to promote fairly sustained economic growth throughout the 1970s and early 1980s (Schwarz 2000, 57–59; Vatikiotis 1993, 32–59, 96). Similarly, it made progress in the alleviation of poverty as well as setting up rudimentary universal health care and education provisions for most of its citizens (Liddle 1990, 56; Hill 1994, 105–107; Guinness 1994, 272–74).

As the economy grew and Indonesia became more economically prosperous, however, new problems emerged. Foreign investment led to growing industrialization in the 1980s, which in turn generated a burgeoning industrial working class and eventually a rising number of strike actions and demands for more independent labor unions (Hadiz 1993 and 1994; Bourchier 1994b; LaBotz 2001). The increasing power and wealth of Suharto cronies and other members of the emerging oligarchic economic elite led to a rise in what David Harvey has called "accumulation by dispossession" or "primitive accumulation" (Harvey 2005, 159–75), with numerous cases of peasants and others being forced off their lands for minimal or no compensation, and on some occasions with little or no prior consultation (YLBHI 1996, 1994, and 1990: Human Rights Watch 1994, 109–21; Lucas 1997). A large share of the New Order's development occurred in and around cities, and landless peasants and others flooded into the urban areas seeking long-term or seasonal work (Guinness 1994, 284–95) often as a result of lack of profitable work and a growing imbalance in wealth and ownership of land in rural areas (Hart 1986; *Inside*

Indonesia 1983). The expansion of the urban areas and the increasing commodification of life, coupled with a rising awareness of gaps in wealth and ability to buy consumer goods, also created new kinds of social tension and alienation, such as a growing distance between *gedongan* (people living in large houses close to main streets) and *kampung* (urban slum dwellers and lower middle-class families living off the main streets) residents (Sullivan 1991; Guiness 1990; Price 1997).

In the realm of power politics, one of the key events that unfolded from the late 1970s on and intensified in the 1980s was Suharto's move to edge the military out of the center of state power through a reduction in the number of military and ex-military men holding cabinet positions as well as by the transfer of military companies and assets into the hands of Suharto family members, cronies, and other members of the new economic elite, undertaken mainly by Sudharmono and Ginandjar Kartasasmita and their Team 10 within the State Secretariat (Vatikiotis 1993, 52; Schwarz 1994, 117–18). This caused a widening rift between Suharto and the military. The latter found its strongest champion in former Suharto confidant and intelligence chief Benny Moerdani, who was Commander in Chief of the Armed Forces and Minister of Defense from 1983 to 1988, and who continued on as Minister of Defense from 1988 to 1993. Moerdani helped coordinate military initiatives to curb Suharto's personal power and regain some of the ground ABRI had lost in the preceding decade (Vatikiotis 1993, 81–91; Schwarz 1994, 283–86; Honna 1999, 84–86).

Given the rebelliousness of his former base of support in the army, Suharto began to court an Islamic constituency more assiduously as a counter balance. This became most evident in his making the pilgrimage to Mecca as well as in his sanctioning the formation of the Indonesian Islamic Intellectuals Organization, ICMI, in 1990 under the leadership of his protégé, then Minister of Research and Technology B. J. Habibie (Vatikiotis 1993, 123–38 and 158–60; Hefner 2000, 128–166; Schwarz 1994, 176–91; Robison and Hadiz 2004, 66 and 110–15). In itself, this constituted a highly strategic move since Islamic culture had penetrated much more deeply into the fabric of Indonesian (and especially Javanese) society during the 1970s for a number of reasons, including lack of other venues for social protest, social anomie inherent in the dislocation of many from rural backgrounds into urban areas, and the spread of new forms of Islamic thinking (such as the "neo-modernism" promoted by Nurcholish Majid, Djohan Effendi, Dawam Rahardjo, Abdurrahman Wahid and others) which made Islam seem more inclusive and less threatening to many (Hefner 1993, 8; Barton 1994; Schwarz 2000, 162–94 ; Vatikiotis 1993, 120–38).

All of this created a situation in which growing social protest and criticism from the middle-classes and others mixed with elite fractures and power struggles. As Indonesia moved towards the 1990s, discussions of a new "openness" (*keterbukaan*) began to resonate publicly, with both Suharto and his supporters and military and other vocal opponents of the ruling clique vying to outdo one another in promoting openness and a new accountability in the parliament and in public discourse (Vatikiotis 1993, 88–91; Schwarz 2000, 283–86, Aspinall 2005, 30–44). This was the juncture to which the modern Indonesian theater of the 1985–98 period responded and that it helped produce and intensify.

Chapter 2

INDONESIAN GRASSROOTS THEATER

Arena Teater, Rural Development, and the Travails of Creating a Media for the People

One response to the growing dissatisfaction of Indonesia's middle-classes with the Suharto government came from art theater workers in the city of Yogyakarta (also known as Jogja). This response took the form of a search for ways to make theater more relevant to larger numbers of people. In the case of the Arena Teater and other grassroots theater groups, the search led to the pioneering of a kind of theater constructed jointly by middle-class theater workers and marginalized constituencies—especially peasants—who were not perceived as having benefited equally from the New Order's development strategies. The practice of this kind of theater, so different in aims and constituencies from most art theater productions, also encouraged, eventually, a nearly complete rejection of the liberal humanist aesthetic that dominated the national art theater. The resulting grassroots or "people's" theater (*teater rakyat*) practice was widely influential among non-government development activists and organizations (NGOs) in Central Java and throughout Indonesia from about 1987 to the mid 1990s, and helped give birth to the workers' theater experiments of the 1990s in the greater Jakarta area. Additionally, it may well have helped foster a much more assertive, critical attitude among both NGO workers and peasants and other socially disadvantaged groups. Yet it also raised complex and persistent questions about the nature of inter-class cultural collaboration, questions that would also haunt the development of workers theater throughout the 1990s (see chapter 5).

This chapter investigates the work of Arena Teater and other groups involved in developing and spreading grassroots theater practices in Indonesia beginning in the 1980s and reaching a climax in the early 1990s. In so doing I will show the diverse sources and practices from which this kind of theater was constructed as well as demonstrate how these practices—and the audiences for whom they were developed—changed over time. I will also show how they contributed to a broad process of social change in Indonesia, eventually even being incorporated into at least one major government program. Because Arena Teater was the most successful of all the grassroots theater groups, a major portion of this chapter will be devoted to its development and some of its most important projects. Yet I will also draw on the experiences of several other groups and participants in order to flesh out the scope, ideas, practices, and problems of this type of theater.[1] The sort of theater practices these groups developed were heavily marked by several legacies including local and national theatrical performance traditions, Freirian ideas of popular pedagogy, notions of the need for empowerment of local communities then burgeoning among non-government organizations, as well as indirectly by Bertolt Brecht's ideas of theater. Practitioners from Teater Arena/PUSKAT and other Indonesian grassroots groups selectively combined all of these elements in order to create a distinctive theater practice that addressed significant local needs for social change. Their engagement with the Brechtian, local, and national theater traditions was thus as much concerned with grassroots development strategies and initiatives and social and cultural democracy as it was with the mechanics of staging a performance.

Arena Teater and Grassroots Theater Practices

Yogyakarta has long been a center for modern theater activity. As mentioned in the previous chapter, a talented group of "psychological realist" playwrights made Yogyakarta their home base in the 1950s. The premier Islamic theater of the early 1960s, Teater Muslim, also gave additional luster to Yogya's modern theater scene. At no time, however, was Yogyakarta's important role in modern national theater more evident than the early New Order when W. S. Rendra's Bengkel Teater made one of the city's *kampung* (lower-class neighborhood) its home. Not only did Rendra's plays take up vital social issues, but they also presented those issues in new and formally innovative ways, combining Western classic scripts with elements of traditional Indonesian theater genres such as *wayang*, *ketoprak*, and *ludruk*. For many younger theater workers and observers, the fact that Bengkel's alternative lifestyle also seemed to combine elements of traditional Javanese culture with aspects of Western youth counter-culture (Hatley 2008, 120–25) also added additional interest. As recounted in the previous chapter, Rendra's original socially critical plays eventually brought him into conflict with the New Order state, at the same time that they increased his stature as a spokesperson for Indonesia's dissidents and ordinary people.

In 1977, even before Rendra's arrest and prohibition from further public performances in mid-1978, a group of former Bengkel members founded Teater Dinasti, a group that went on to continue and extend Bengkel's tradition of social criticism. By the mid-1980s, a young poet, Emha Ainun Nadjib had joined Dinasti and became the writer for several of the company's most outspoken plays. Similarly, several student activists had joined the group, contributing to its vibrant intellectual development and critical stance. From 1983 on, Dinasti, too, began to run afoul of government censors as its works became more openly critical (Hatley 2008, 127–34; von der Borch 1988).

Arena Teater developed in parallel with, sometimes drawing inspiration from these groups. Arena was formed in the mid-sixties, initially staging European and American plays as well as Indonesian plays corresponding roughly to notions of theatrical psychological realism. Much as other Indonesian theater groups of the times, Arena, too, experimented with folk forms in the late 1960s and early seventies. In 1971 Arena affiliated itself with a Yogyakarta-based catholic media production center, PUSKAT. This move gave Arena an institutional base, helped the group to crystallize its commitment to social activism, and gave the group access to equipment and funds that would eventually aid them in many of their projects.

At about this same time, the thinking of Arena's young leader, Fred Wibowo, and of other group members was being stimulated by the rise of activist-oriented, non-government development organizations (NGOs) (Field Notes 15 August 1991). Many of these organizations, involved in community development projects, criticized the Indonesian New Order government's development strategy, arguing that it was designed chiefly to satisfy the resource needs of Japan and the Western countries, as well as the desire of the local Indonesian elite for luxury consumer items. Such policies, they felt, benefited foreign corporations and a local alliance of military bureaucrats and their Chinese-Indonesian business partners. At the same time, the economic position of small-scale entrepreneurs eroded, as did that of the great majority of Indonesian peasants, who derived few benefits as extra state revenues were used to modernize the major urban areas (Eldridge 1990, 506–7; Lev 1990, 33; Robison 1986, 156–68). National events caused Wibowo and his Arena/PUSKAT colleagues to agree with the analysis put forward by the NGOs and to sympathize with those left out of New Order development plans:

> After the Malari incident (1974 riots protesting perceived Japanese encroachment on the Indonesian economy) and the events of 1978 (student protests about government corruption which were met with severe repression), people within Arena began to feel that development wasn't really reaching a large part of the people. Arena works with PUSKAT, and they wanted to use their media for the people, as a voice for the people. The main impediment is that there is no means for horizontal communication. We are trying to become a means for creating solidarity in a certain sector, a media for the lower classes. (Fred Wibowo, Personal Communication 14 November 1987)

Members of Arena and PUSKAT's Audiovisual Studio, which was headed by Father Rüdi Hofmann, a Swiss Jesuit, spent much of the late 1970s studying liberation theology and the works of radical educator Paulo Freire, who advocated creating a more egalitarian, co-educational relationship between teacher and student. Freire's method was to begin the educational process with the students' own day-to-day experiences and codes for understanding the world. Such codes were then to be posed as a problem for the students. The method was aimed at helping peasants and others become more critically aware of the conditions of their own oppression as well as giving them the self-confidence and analytical abilities that would enable them to become active participants in the struggle for their own "liberation" (Freire, 1989, chapters 1 and 3).

In 1979, Wibowo and several members of Arena Theater, along with fellow Yogyakarta cultural workers Emha Ainun Nadjib (for more about Nadjib, see chapter 3) and Simon Haté were invited to attend one of the Philippines Educational Theater Association's (PETA) summer workshops in the Philippines. During the period 1979–81, PETA was engaged, through its Asia Theater Forum Partnership program, in training cultural workers from South and Southeast Asia in the techniques of the grassroots theater that PETA and other Philippine groups had been developing for almost a decade (Labad 1988, 4; Dasmarinas 1988, 19). Mounting grassroots theater workshops, these Philippine groups helped peasants, workers, and students to develop and produce plays based on their own life experiences. Grounded in Freirian pedagogy, children's and improvisational theater techniques, and a Brechtian notion of the role of theater in educating people for social change (Bodden 1993, 70–157), this approach used theater as a tool for creating community solidarity, for breaking the "culture of silence" so common to marginalized groups by drawing out people's stories of personal and social oppression, and for helping communities to analyze and organize against the conditions that allow those oppressions to exist. During the process, the participants' confidence and creativity would hopefully be built and strengthened. In this kind of theater, the focus was not on an actor or director, but what PETA calls ATORS (artist-trainer-organizer-researcher), whose main role is to facilitate the process of others' cultural production as well as their *concientization* or awakening of one's critical consciousness (Van Erven 1989, 26–43). The Indonesian participants of 1979 spent one month undergoing workshop training and then were sent to separate Philippine villages to immerse themselves in the daily lives of ordinary Filipinos, gather data, and create theater-related projects (Field Notes 15 August 1991).

At about the same time that Wibowo, his Arena colleagues, and the other Indonesian members returned from the Philippines, Father Hofmann was also returning from a year in Latin America. While there, Hofmann had participated in the founding of a Basic Christian Community in Columbia, and he had brought back books by Freire and the Brazilian theater activist and playwright, Augusto Boal, who had attempted to apply Freire's pedagogy to theater work (Van Erven 1992, 187; Field Notes 15 August 1991; Boal 1985, 120–56).

In his book, *Theater of the Oppressed*, Boal attempts to outline the ways in which theater can be used to "conscientize" the poor and the oppressed by offering them a new "language" with which to express themselves that will, at the same time, help them discover new concepts (Boal 1985, 121). Like Freire, Boal felt that the oppressed must take control of their own lives, becoming the agents of their own history. While drawing on the theatrical concepts of Brecht, Boal also attempts to go beyond what he sees as the limitations of Brecht's ideas and practice. In essence, Boal feels that Brecht distinguishes his theater from Aristotelian concepts of theater by creating a situation in which the spectator does not completely yield his power to act and think to the character. In Brechtian theater, according to Boal, the spectator reserves the right to "think for himself, often in opposition to the character." This promotes the awakening of critical consciousness. Boal wants to create a kind of theater in which the spectator does not even delegate the power to act to the dramatic character but instead becomes an active subject capable of transforming the dramatic action. Assuming the protagonist's role, the spectator changes the dramatic action, discusses plans for change, and tries out solutions. Boal sees this as training for real action, as "a rehearsal for revolution" (Boal 1985 121–22).

Furthermore, Boal stresses that the grassroots theater he proposes, the "Theater of the Oppressed," should not show the "correct path" but rather offer "the means by which all possible paths may be examined" (Boal 1985, 141–42). Similarly, Boal suggests that grassroots "Theater of the Oppressed" practices should "create an uneasy sense of incompleteness that seeks fulfillment through real action" (Boal 1985, 142). These formulations certainly bring to mind Brecht's idea of a theater attuned to the "scientific age" in which all of a society's actions would be treated as "experiments" using the "great productive method," the critical approach. As outlined in "A Short Organum for the Theater" of 1948, Brecht hoped that he would eventually be able to construct this type of theater so that the new thoughts and feelings that it produced among the spectators might encourage them to transform the existing "historical field of human relations" (Brecht 1986, 185–95).[2] However, despite Brecht's pedagogical experiments with turning the audience into active learner/participants in his *Lehrstücke* of the 1928–33 period, his arguments in "A Short Organum for the Theater" do indeed posit an audience that is separated from, though responding critically to the events on the stage. Boal is much more intent on using theater to prepare the performer/spectators for real action, while Brecht is primarily concerned with creating a radically new consciousness.

Building on the experiences and techniques brought back from the Philippines and beginning to slowly incorporate lessons from Freire and Boal, the Arena group constructed their own grassroots theater methodology over the course of the ensuing years, though it remained rather similar to that developed by PETA. As has been documented by Van Erven, one of Arena's first grassroots projects was the use of theater in integrating lepers of the Lewoleba colony in Lembata, Flores, into the surrounding community that had previously shunned them (Van Erven 1992, 188–89). The success of the Lewoleba workshops of 1980 and 1983 gave Arena's facilitators the necessary experience and confidence to conceive of even more ambitious uses for their newly learned techniques.

In 1981, the year following the first Lewoleba workshop, Arena staged a weekend people's theater workshop for 150 participants, most of whom were students. By setting the workshop in the rural, coastal area of Parangtritis, which was rapidly being developed as a national tourist site, Arena confronted the workshop participants with the impact of "development from above" on the people of an isolated rural area. Participants were required to undertake research into local conditions as a part of their training. At the end of the weekend, the attendees broke down into three groups and performed for the residents of the surrounding villages who grasped their own plight in the plays presented. Based on the enthusiasm and dialogue that the workshop generated between participants and villagers, Wibowo termed the event an "incredible success." Yet, as he remarked, there remained a problem of follow-up: "The students returned to the city—what was needed was the participation of someone directly involved in the situation who could help make a movement" (Wibowo, Personal Communication, 14 November 1987).

In 1983, Arena conducted another project using Freirian pedagogical methods in combination with theater to help the residents of an impoverished Central Javanese village, Tanen Pakem, overcome a number of debilitating economic and political problems. Tanen Pakem's village co-operative was dysfunctional, its irrigation systems inadequate, its residents too poor to afford basic necessary tools, while local children were having great difficulties in school. Arena surveyed village residents concerning the fundamental aspects of their life and problems, carefully drawing out the villagers' own codes of understanding. In the next phase of the project, Arena members proposed that they should work together with the villagers to solve their problems. A referendum was held to determine the key issues to be dealt with. With Arena members facilitating the process, the villagers gradually came to a decision about how to tackle each problem. A contributing factor to the overall situation of the village was the neglect of the local village chief, the local government liaison official who was influential in determining where government development money was channeled. With workshop training from Arena facilitators, village residents put on two plays addressing the situation. Both plays were based on traditional theater forms.

The play that the village adults produced in the style of Javanese *ketoprak* theater told the story of a village suffering because of the inattention of an irresponsible *demang* or district administrator. The *demang* is primarily concerned with his own family's affairs, and he demands the villagers provide help in preparing for his daughter's wedding. The villagers refuse, insisting that they must first solve the problem of obtaining sufficient water supplies for their rice fields. The village youth then plan to form a cooperative to begin tackling their problems. In anger, the *demang* refuses to allow his daughter to marry the village youth with whom she is in love. She runs to him with the news, and the *demang's* men pursue her, initiating a fight with the villagers. Finally, the village elder brings the two sides together to talk things out and settle their problems peacefully, stressing that the *demang* has to be willing to listen to those living under his jurisdiction (Studio Audiovisual PUSKAT 1984).

The play was obviously intended to criticize the current village chief, and Wibowo and the Arena facilitators had worried that he might try to stop the entire project (Van Erven 1992, 190). But after the show, the chief, who had been present, admitted that he had been made more aware of existing problems, and he requested that similar workshops be held in the other villages under his jurisdiction. He seemed to realize, now, that dealing with the current problems successfully required the mobilization of—and a willingness to listen to—the ordinary people rather than a "top down" bureaucratic centralist approach. Inspired by their success with the performance, the villagers went on to solve the other problems in a variety of ways, using available resources and services. Throughout the process the villagers continued to make all the decisions themselves (Wibowo, Interview 14 November 1987).[3]

Arena's Tumbal: Staging the Lessons of Grassroots Theater

A little over two years later Arena performed *Tumbal* (The Sacrificial Victim), an original play written by Fred Wibowo. If judged simply by the venue of the performance (the performing arts center of Gajah Mada University in the city of Yogyakarta) and the fact that the play was performed by a theater group for an urban middle-class audience whose members were not necessarily directly involved in the creation or the staging of the piece, *Tumbal* would seem to be more closely related to the kind of urban, elite-focused theater with which Arena had begun in the early sixties, and which it had continued to perform even while pursuing the development of a grassroots theater practice. Yet a brief synopsis of the play indicates that *Tumbal* was closely linked to Arena's grassroots theater work both thematically and conceptually.

As the play opens, a number of angry peasants, carrying the dead body of a village youth, waylay a student and request that he preside as judge in a trial that they plan to hold to determine who is responsible for the youth's death. The student doubts that he is qualified, but the peasants respond by declaring:

JALI: This is the people's court, sir. The highest authority in the country chooses its judges.
BOYING: Good God! Are all of you government officials charged with appointing judges?
OLA: What d'ya mean! In a democratic country, the highest authority is the people. And we here are the people. (Wibowo 1986, 3–4)[4]

Thus *Tumbal* begins with a two-fold gesture. On the one hand, through the peasants' assertions the play attempts to give Indonesia's poor and disempowered their voice, their claim to a share of social power, based on the government's own careful efforts to cultivate Indonesia's image as a "democratic country." On the other hand, the opening scene lays the groundwork for the play's courtroom frame, through which the "people's" justice will be sought. The trial that follows will invite the audience to become judges: hearing the testimony of witnesses, weighing the evidence, listening to summary arguments.

Performed for an urban audience consisting mainly of intellectuals, students, and members of Indonesia's small but increasingly important middle-classes, *Tumbal* indeed suggested that such an audience must also become judges, must educate themselves about conditions of the rural peasants. To make the point doubly clear the ex-student is given a number of co-judges to help him reach a verdict: an academic, a businessman, a promoter, and a model. All profess a lack of time for such affairs but are eventually shamed into participating by a village doctor who has become the peasants' spokesperson and advocate. They agree to hear the case after the doctor suggests that they are selfishly overconcerned with their own affairs while a large group of fellow citizens are in dire need of assistance.

The courtroom testimony relates the story of Wasa, a youth from an average Indonesian village who has to leave his home for lack of economic opportunity. On his way to the big city, a dilapidated bridge he is crossing collapses, and he is thrown into the ravine below. The villagers attempt to save him, but at every turn their efforts are thwarted by a lack of necessary facilities: the only automobile in the village has no headlights, so their departure is delayed until the following morning;

Fig. 2.1 Arena Teater, *Tumbal*: The Judge. Photo courtesy of Fred Wibowo/Arena Teater.

the bridge is impassable and the detour they must make as a result leads them over muddy and rutted roads; the phones in the nearest small town do not work, so an ambulance can not be summoned to meet them. By the time they finally arrive at a hospital in the capital, the village youth can no longer be saved.

Following this account, the heads of several government departments are called to give testimony. One after another they all deny responsibility for the lack of facilities in the village that has led to Wasa's death. Finally, two social researchers appear to help clarify the situation. Using statistical data, the two throw into sharp relief the "urban bias" of current national development programs. The villagers are forced to realize that it is not through the individual neglect of any one functionary that the village is desperately lacking in facilities, infrastructure and opportunities—the reason for Wasa's decision to leave and his death. It is the structure and logic of the entire social system that is to blame. The play ends with a call for all Indonesians to recognize their responsibility to solve these pressing problems.

It should be clear by now that *Tumbal* was also the result of the fundamental transformation that the group was undergoing as it increasingly turned from the urban stage to grassroots theater. As such, it was intimately connected to Arena's other projects, particularly to the Parangtritis workshop and the Tanen Pakem project. It is, after all, a play whose material is drawn predominantly from the conditions with which Wibowo and his co-workers became exceedingly familiar in the course of their 1980's grassroots theater work. For example, just as in the Tanen Pakem project, issues such as the existence of bad or incompetent village chiefs, a lack of job opportunities forcing the out-migration of local youth to the cities, poor rural education facilities, corrupt cooperatives, broken machinery without means of repair, and a lack of financial resources in general, all figure prominently in the action and arguments of *Tumbal*. Problems of tourism and the ideological hegemony of urban, capitalist, consumer culture, such as those encountered by workshop participants at Parangtritis, are also treated.

Even more crucial here is the fact that Wibowo and Arena attempted to duplicate some of the techniques of their grassroots theater and development projects in the play. Their strategy for accomplishing this was to implicate psychologically the members of their mostly middle-class urban audience in the plot, thereby involving the audience in an emotionally direct way in a problem-posing, educational situation roughly similar to Freirian pedagogical methods. The problems posed—Why is the village in such a dire situation? Who is responsible?—are presented within a framework in which several symbolic representatives of the majority of audience members are shamed, partly through an appeal to nationalism, into taking time to consider the problems of their fellow citizens—to sit as judges and thus to weigh the evidence. And, as in Boal's notions of theater, *Tumbal* offers no specific solution to the problems it represents. It attempts to put forward evidence that defines the problems and leaves the construction of a solution to the audience.

The purpose of the performance was to engage the audience both viscerally, and critically, in the issues it presented with the hope that audience members would be moved to discuss these issues as well as to work to resolve them in the world outside the performance space. Such an orientation marks clearly the "Brechtian tradition" in theater as Arena found it in the works and writings of PETA, Boal, and the Canadian theater activist, Ross Kidd, with whom Wibowo began a correspondence in the early 1980s.[5] Thus, though Wibowo stated in 1991 that he was only then beginning to read Brecht's plays and theories, well after the writing and staging of *Tumbal*, the play nonetheless contains several features that bear a striking similarity to those found in Brecht's dramas and indeed seem aimed at engaging the audience's critical consciousness and prompting action.

First and foremost among these is the courtroom frame, a device that appears repeatedly in Brecht's plays.[6] The importance of the courtroom frame for both Brecht and Arena as well as for other appropriators of Brechtian notions lies, of course, in placing the performers and/or the audience in a position in which members of the audience may hear a number of different arguments and witness the presentation of various bits of evidence. The audience is urged to deliberate; it must weigh the evidence critically and ultimately decide the case.

Another technique that parallels Brechtian theater is the very specific way in which the chorus of peasants defines the socially constructed personae of its members during the scene in which Wasa decides to leave the village.

> MAYA: Why are conditions in our village so very different than those in the city?
> WASA: I can't say. Perhaps some of our friends know?
> THE WHOLE GROUP: (CHORUS)
>   No, we don't know
>   We're just ordinary farmers after all
>   Loyal and obedient
>   To the authorities
>   We continue striving
>   To cope with our fate
>   Though our suffering hasn't ended (Wibowo 1986, 11)[7]

The exchange then continues through two more sets of question and response.[8] In both Brecht and *Tumbal*, these devices function to present characters and basic social situations in a spare, condensed,

Fig. 2.2. Arena Teater, *Tumbal*: The Peasant's Chorus. Photo courtesy of Fred Wiboow Arena Teater.

non-melodramatic form and to facilitate a critical approach to the issues by modeling concise modes of argumentation.

Music is also used at least once in *Tumbal* in order to offer ironic commentary on the relations of different characters. This is most evident in the scenes in which the government officials appear to testify. Each official's entrance is accompanied by a Javanese song, "Dayohe Teko" (A Guest Comes), which relates with bitter humor the embarrassment of a poor family that has nothing to offer worthy, visiting guests. Every time an official enters, the existing power relations and the humiliation of the impoverished peasants are thus underscored by a verse of the song, which narrates the peasants' feelings of social inferiority.

One final similarity with Brechtian theater is the use of a screen and projected slides during both the recounting of Wasa's death and the final summation of Indonesia's rural development problems by the "experts." The use of such technology underscores the gap between theater and "reality," distancing the audience from too close an emotional identification with the characters in the play and inviting reflection regarding the relationship between the play and the world it attempts to problematize.

Yet for all this, Arena's play is also quite different from those of Brecht. It draws on local theater forms such as *ketoprak* for some of its sets and adapts the comic, clown-figure conventions of a number of Javanese stage genres from the classical shadow theater to the 1980s populist *sampakan* theater style and popular comedy routines commonly called *banyolan*. Such clowns usually represent the "common people" and have often been used to voice commentary and criticism relating to current conditions. Yet, ironically, they also often present the ordinary peasants and villagers as bumbling, humorously flawed, ignorant and insulated from modern changes. The criticism of such clowns is usually quite good-natured (Hatley 1990, 339–40; Hatley 1971, 89–91). Arena's clowns, however, are much more bitter than usual, their criticism sharper and more aimed at the need to change the system than at the foibles of individual excess and the need for simple reform—the typical themes of traditional critical clown characters,

In addition, the Government Functionaries' Chorus of the closing scenes of the trial is highly reminiscent of Rendra's uses of the chorus in his most famous satirical play, *Kisah Perjuangan Suku Naga* (The Struggle of the Naga Tribe). Typically, and in marked contrast to Brecht's work, such a chorus baldly parodies the parties it claims to represent on stage, allowing popular audiences to laugh at their oppressors. The chorus in *Tumbal* also involves moments of parody but has been altered slightly, allowing the functionaries to present a defense of their own position that is not completely specious or motivated solely by self-interest. As such, this chorus calls for a serious response from the village doctor and the experts testifying about government development priorities. Yet the chorus is not allowed to respond in turn to this rebuttal of its arguments, thus awarding the "last word" in the debate to the critics of government policy.

These elements point to the importance of evolving local conventions of signification and social criticism. Such conventions are used to engage the audience's critical faculties, yet at the same time to channel its sympathies to certain characters and drive home some of the arguments presented. As such, they run counter to Brechtian practice that stresses distanciation. Along these same lines, the very setting for *Tumbal*'s action—contemporary Indonesia—and the final plea to the audience—to help solve the concrete problems that the play has represented—also help to distinguish the play from the dominant tendencies in Brecht's own work.

An instructive comparison can be made here. The ending of *Tumbal* is designed to prompt the audience to undertake a specific strategic task—solving the inequities of New Order development policy. Only one of Brecht's plays, *Die Mutter*, approximates this kind of orientation through its combination of experimental techniques, designed to engage and develop the audience's critical consciousness, with an attempt to channel the audience's emotions into general action on a particular social problem. *Tumbal*, on the other hand, is not a lonely exception in presenting issues of immediate relevance to its society. Such a choice, indeed, demonstrates the play's linkages to Arena's own grassroots strategy. It also shows its connection to broader discourses in contemporary Indonesian theater, as seen in the ways Brecht's plays are "contextualized" by other Indonesian theater groups (see, for example, Bodden 1997c, 382–83, 384, 389–91) as well as its connection to the common practice of much progressive theater throughout the postcolonial "developing" world.

In this way, *Tumbal* can be viewed as a supplement to Arena's grassroots activity. Still a difficulty exists in that the play's function was clearly also to create a bridge, a way of building an intellectual and emotional alliance between the rural poor and the small urban middle-class, composed of business people, intellectuals, students, and professionals. Despite the fact that the means of constituting that alliance in political practice as well as its specific goals are not explicitly stated, apparently leaving these "details" as issues for all concerned parties to deal with once the performance has ended, the play's structure and the perspective which that structure contains suggest an unequal relationship between the potential allies. Much of the difficulty can be attributed to the fact that the attempt to simulate some of the grassroots theater methods in the performance and text of *Tumbal* was handicapped by transposing the problems of rural Indonesian peasants from their original environment to an urban stage and performing them for a middle-class city audience.

To begin with, the play was performed on an arena stage in an auditorium where more conventional contemporary theater performances often occurred. The performance only symbolically attempted, through

Fig. 2.3 Arena Teater, *Tumbal*: Appealing to the Audience. Photo courtesy of Fred Wibowo/Arena Teater.

an implicit identification of the audience with the five "judges," to break down the audience/performer barriers existing in such conventional venues—by symbolically appointing the audience as "judge." Secondly, in contrast to the Tanen Pakem project, though the play's themes are immediately relevant to middle-class Indonesians who are concerned with "national development" policies, this play does not present the every-day problems of the urban audiences for which it was performed. These factors distort and subvert the Freirian co-intentional educational methods that characterized Arena Teater's grassroots practice. Thirdly, in the performance of *Tumbal* before urban audiences, egalitarian relationships of co-educational dialogue are replaced by a hierarchy in which the urban middle-class audience can see itself as the judge of the peasants' problems and teacher to peasant students.

Acting as a voice for the concerns of the rural populations, Arena took its case to the middle-class, the professionals, and the intellectuals, writing them into the play as judges, but also as spokespeople for the villagers and experts who clarify the common people's confusion. In so doing, *Tumbal* makes it possible for the middle-class audience members to visualize themselves as patrons and benefactors, rather than someone whose own situation is in question, as would be common in the grassroots theater projects. Indeed, the critical consciousness of the villagers, as found in characters such as Kewa, Igo, and the wisecracking Gopil, completely disappears in the final pages of the script when Engineer Banda and Professor Darma present the expert testimony. Ironically, even Dr. Juha, the professional who acts as spokesperson for the villagers, ultimately bows to the analysis of these progressive-minded experts, shifting the play even farther in the direction of promoting a "vanguard" group's analysis and solutions.

To be sure, *Tumbal* remains a remarkable and lively play precisely because of what it attempted to accomplish. Still, the problems generated by this attempt to build an emotional and critical alliance between two distinct social groups, as well as to synthesize several distinctive theatrical practices into a new stage approach, necessitated further work. Between 1986 and 1991, Arena began to search for the means to transcend those problems.

Grassroots Theater Workshop Training for Non-Government Organization Workers

The appeal to the nationalistically oriented urban middle-class contained in *Tumbal* implicitly posed once more, but on a larger scale, the issue raised by the Parangtritis workshop: how to create a sustained development effort, using theater, nation-wide? Arena's work in Tanen Pakem had shown that sustained efforts were possible and productive, but Arena did not have the resources to undertake such efforts nationally. Drawing on the arguments of Ross Kidd, a theater activist from Canada who had been involved with grassroots theater projects in Botswana and Bangladesh, Arena and Wibowo determined that theater, as a rehearsal for social change (to alter Boal's phrase), needed to be tied to organizational activity that could provide an ongoing framework for actual material improvements (Kidd 1979, 7).

Arena had already begun to alter the format of the 1984 and 1985 workshops before taking a decisive step in 1987, a year after the performance of *Tumbal*. For the 1987 workshop held in the coastal village of Pantai Baron, the invited participants consisted entirely of NGO field workers. These participants were trained in Arena's grassroots theater techniques with the hope that NGOs would gain both the necessary skills and interest in combining their sustained, grassroots development efforts throughout Indonesia with cultural and theatrical tools for *conscientization*. Since such training would eventually be given by the NGO field workers, in turn, to the groups with whom they worked, it was assumed that peasants, workers, and others would themselves increasingly gain the skills to become more critically conscious as well as the confidence to articulate that knowledge. This approach was continued in subsequent annual workshops.

Meanwhile, in the mid-1980s, another of the Yogya cultural activists trained by PETA in the Philippines in 1979, Simon Haté, had also begun working on a grassroots theater project. Unlike Arena, Simon, working together with two other fellow former members of the Yogyakarta theater group Teater Dinasti, Agus Istiyanto and Joko Kamto, did not have the resources of PUSKAT and its Audiovisual Studio to help support his efforts. Instead, Simon and his collaborators sought to work under the umbrella of area non-government organizations and later sought funding from international donors. Their experiences illustrated some of the potential pitfalls of working with NGOs and foreign funding agencies on grassroots theater projects. As Van Erven has recounted, following an ideological disagreement within Teater Dinasti, whose plays were often critical of the New Order government, Simon, Joko, and Agus decided to devote their time to practicing grassroots theater, so as to pursue more effectively cultural work as a means of promoting positive, democratic social change. According to Van Erven:

> In 1985 and 1986, Simon Haté and several associates targeted twelve communities in Central Java that they hoped would form the nucleus of an emerging grassroots theater of liberation network. They were sponsored by a non-government funding agency for rural development. Haté and his team used the same strategy and methodology as Teater Arena, but . . . they gave participants simple "instamatic" cameras loaded with slide film. After the integration period, the villagers were instructed to photograph the things they considered to be the

most important landmarks of their community. The public slide show that followed produced a flow of stories that were later used as the basis for scenarios. (Van Erven 1992, 204)

Yet soon after, Simon and his colleagues had a falling out with their NGO sponsor, whom they felt was pressuring them to move the project along too quickly (Van Erven 1992, 204). They had also felt that the leadership of their NGO sponsor was too top-down and that they hadn't been consulted enough about their views on how the project was progressing. Yet Simon regarded the fact that the sponsoring NGO decided to continue the grassroots theater work after Simon and his friends had left as a sign that grassroots theater was now more widely seen as a potentially important alternative media for development. Simon and his friends next worked with another NGO in different villages, but in this project they were not directly involved with using grassroots theater techniques. Rather, they became engaged in helping villagers design and implement basic social welfare development projects. In addition, they facilitated the process of improving village cooperation in order to construct work teams for plowing and preparing rice paddies in shorter periods of time, a strategy which would enable them more effectively to compete with expensive, mechanized farming methods (Field Notes, 21 November 1987). From 1989 to 1991, Simon obtained a grant from the Australian Freedom From Hunger Campaign to undertake a large grassroots theater project in three base areas in Central Java, but the funding was not continued after 1991 (Field Notes 17 August 1991). In 1990–91, Simon was also active in grassroots theater training with Yasanti, a Yogyakarta NGO working on empowering women factory workers in Unggaran and elsewhere in Central Java. When it became difficult for Simon, as a man, to gain access to women workers housed in barracks, Yasanti had asked Simon to train two of its own field workers. However, Yasanti's efforts to use theater for building solidarity and confidence were halted after soldiers surrounded the area where they had assembled the workers for a performance practice (Field Notes, 17 and 23 August 1991).

At about the same time (December–January 1990–91), the group formed by Simon and his colleagues, Kelompok Teater Rakyat Indonesia

(KTRI), obtained funding from the Asia Foundation for a grassroots theater workshop with local community figures from the Asmat-Agats Bishopric in West Papua (then called Irian Jaya) (*Rakit* July 1991). KTRI members Joko Kamto, Agus Istiyanto, and Eko Winardi traveled to West Papua in late 1990 to conduct the workshop, which revealed a number of problems such as disputes over rights to make use of timber and other forest products. But following the successful completion of the workshop, KTRI experienced difficulty obtaining further funding and eventually dissolved (Field Notes 14 and 24 July 1994).

Though Simon and KTRI's difficulties provide evidence of some of the problems of sustaining grassroots theater work, even with the support of non-government organizations (ideological disagreements with NGO leadership, lack of funding continuity, intimidation from authorities), the dissemination of grassroots theater techniques began to precipitate other similar projects. For example, Indro Gunawan, involved in Arena/ PUSKAT's grassroots theater work since 1979, started another informal study group along with anthropology and law students from Yogyakarta around 1990. Indro's group approached issues of local development from a number of angles. First, they undertook careful analyses of current conditions in order to understand why the government and large business groups (*konglomerat*) act in the ways they do. Members of the group then used these analyses to help in cases where ordinary Indonesians ("*rakyat kecil*" or the little people) were being displaced from their land or given unfair compensation. In such cases, the group also used theater. They would use a local person as a go-between in order to gain access to the affected area and conduct research into the local conditions and power dynamics. After gathering data, Indro and his group would produce a dramatic scenario, rehearse it (often at PUSKAT's Studio) and bring local residents to PUSKAT to watch the play. The performance would be followed by a discussion about the issues. This would open a process of critical analysis of the situation, usually facilitated by Indro (Field Notes 13 July 1994). In other cases, Indro and his colleagues held grassroots theater workshops in villages near Yogyakarta and helped form teater rakyat groups. One group in particular, located in a village some 22 kilometers East of Yogya, which Indro referred to as his group's *desa binaan*,[9] performed eight times over one and one-half years beginning in 1993 using different kinds of styles such as poetry readings with music and traditional music. The group performed on every holiday so that their activities would not simply be regarded with suspicion as critical interventions into local conditions. In their performances, questions were usually addressed to the audience. If anyone from the audience responded to the questions, they were later invited to join in a dialogue with the group. In some of the workshops and village projects that Indro and his colleagues had taken on, Indro admitted that the group had had to emphasize to local authorities that they were mounting workshops or performances for the sake of developing local traditional culture. Participants usually enjoyed comparing folk stories and histories with current conditions, and officials generally supported traditional art forms. Only if the performances were tied to some sort of social action would local officials move to stop the cultural activities (Field Notes 13 and 18 July 1994).

Buoyed by the momentum of their past projects and the general atmosphere of interest in grassroots theater projects prevailing at the end of the 1980s, Arena and other grassroots theater activists even convinced a government agency, BAPPENAS (The National Planning Board), to use grassroots theater techniques as one component of its 1990 program to promote integrated pest management, undertaken in conjunction with the FAO (Food and Agriculture Organization of the United Nations) (Wibowo, *Teater Rakyat*, n.d., 1).[10] At this time the government was looking for an alternative method to controlling crop-destroying insect outbreaks for two reasons: subsidizing pesticide use was becoming financially too burdensome and the Indonesian government was under pressure internationally to reduce its subsidies (Vatikiotis 1993, 35–36; Hüsken and White 1989, 259); and widespread application of pesticides had wiped out natural predators and thus made more devastating a resurgence of resistant pests that were inflicting severe damage on rice crops (Wibowo n.d. 1; Röling and van de Fliert 1998). The government consequently responded positively to the FAO's integrated pest management initiative. Yet farmers had become dependent on following the advice and instructions of government agriculture officials. The idea of using grassroots theater techniques was intended to wean farmers from simply following top-down instructions and to instill a greater sense of self-initiative. Fred Wibowo argued that using "horizontal communication" in a Freirian manner—having farmers draw pictures and perform plays about their problems—would help them articulate, study, and understand better the ecological issues they were facing in their fields (Field Notes 15 August 1991). Results from some early experiments prompted Wibowo to conclude that having farmers engage in theatricalizing the problems in their village actually increased their confidence in expressing their views and conveying their knowledge to government agricultural officials (Wibowo n.d. 5).

Simon Haté also became involved in this project as a field worker in the *Sekolah Lapangan Pengendalian Hama Terpadu* (Integrated Pest Management Field School) and saw both positive and negative patterns emerging. Haté felt that those who took the most initiative in such grassroots projects, including the theater components, were usually the relatively well-off small farmers who wanted to improve their situations even more. Consequently, in most cases the focus came to center solely on economic issues. He also added that use of pesticides had become so naturalized after years of government advice and promotion that it was exceedingly difficult to convince farmers to believe they were not indispensable. Further, given the government's connection to the program, some top-down government instructions were prone to slip in to the training programs. Still, like Wibowo, Haté saw a positive side to the entire project. He argued that it gave farmers a reason to gather regularly and that they didn't easily stop doing so, even after a performance or the program had ended. Group solidarity thereby increased, especially during the theater part of the program. Haté maintained that the program did succeed in freeing farmers from excessive top-down control by giving them experience making their own decisions based on training relevant to their own lives and work, and by showing them that this process could work well for them (Field Notes 17 August 1991). The experience with the Integrated Pest Management Program also convinced Fred Wibowo and members of the Arena/PUSKAT group that the grassroots theater techniques would work best if they were not simply conveyed to NGO members, who in some cases might act like outside experts on whom farmers and peasants could also come to depend, but if these techniques were also given directly to the people themselves. They began to ponder ways in which ordinary people and NGO workers could mix in workshops so that the knowledge of the NGO cadres did not become too exclusive, and so that they experienced things together with the people with whom they were intending to work (Field Notes 14 July 1994).

Pesta Rakyat and Ombak-Ombak

By the beginning of the 1990s, grassroots theater activities had become the central focus for Arena, and its original thrust, producing performances for the stage, declined in significance. This is illustrated by the group's lack of stage productions in the early 1990s, when they mounted only two plays, one of which, a March 1993 adaptation of Aristophanes entitled *Perempuan-Perempuan Pemimpi* (Dreaming Women), critically took up the theme of women who must always subordinate their interests to those of men (Field Notes 14 July 1994). Already in 1991, Wibowo had stepped down as leader of Arena in order to devote himself more exclusively to his work at PUSKAT and to community animation and grassroots theater projects. In line with this decision, Wibowo was preparing three short books covering the orientation, methodology, and performance of "people's theater." Based on pre-publication manuscripts available in August 1991, Wibowo's approach can be summarized as follows.

Wibowo asserts that people-oriented theater cannot be separate from the contexts of daily life. Secondly, he insists that the basis of such cultural activity is not some dogmatic notion of aesthetics but rather originality and honesty of expression. Borrowing from Boal's reading of "Aristotle's Coercive System of Tragedy," which holds that Aristotle's theory, when put into practice, converts the viewer into a passive observer who surrenders her/his authority to the characters on the stage, Wibowo criticizes modern theater, television, and film (Wibowo 1991b, 1:2, 6, 8–9). Not only is the viewer rendered passive by such productions, she/he is "alienated" from her/his normal surroundings, drawn into a culture that is not her/his own. This is particularly true in Indonesia where most films and television serials are about the lives of the well-to-do or upper-middle-class Indonesians. Modern plays, while often concerned about the plight of the poor, present such themes in relation to issues and clothed in styles more familiar to the urban intelligentsia. Viewers, especially the poor for whom such entertainments seem so alluringly alien, can never become "creators" in these situations. For Wibowo, becoming a creator is crucial—it means becoming critical (Wibowo 1991b, 1: 3).

According to Wibowo, people's theater should allow the broad masses of people an opportunity to express themselves; it should take the side of the people's interests and be the voice of conscience and reason; and it should not differentiate between the protagonist and the audience. In such a way, it will become a true *"pesta rakyat"* (people's festival). Theater that does not serve the interests of the people for whom it is performed will have little relation with the primary concerns of the audience. It will form one more part of the "culture of silence" in which the poor have to depend on the culture and the sympathy of the rich. In such a culture, drama will mainly convey messages from above. There is no opportunity for the people to become creators (Wibowo 1991b, 1:10). For Wibowo, this is inhuman, because the essence of life is change and development. Those who are not allowed to become creators are eventually unable to change and develop. They are denied life, are virtually dead (Wibowo 1991b, 1:15).

Wibowo goes on to list six essential characteristics of People's Theater, which I have summarized below:

1. *The story must have its origins in local social conditions.* It should be based upon research and open dialogue among the performers and the community with which they work or in which they themselves live. It should touch on awareness of history and should raise critical consciousness and a discussion of the issues presented.
2. *The script should be created and arranged by the people themselves.* The people must be involved in the performance from the very beginning. They should write the story and thereby begin to take charge of their own history.
3. *Performance should be kept simple.* It should be interesting enough to get everyone involved and should make use of resources that are easily accessible, locally available. This is a chance for the people to show and develop their creativity.

4. *Break down the barriers between audience and performers.* Create a dialogue between performers and the audience. No professional performers should be used.
5. *No catharsis.* The performance should make participants more aware of the problem and instill in them a desire to deal with the problem. This begins with discussions during and after the performance.
6. *Build a dialogue.* Dialogue occurs between two (or more) people in the same life circumstances—it is intended to change conditions, to create a better, more just, harmonious, and peaceful world (Wibowo 1991b, 1:16–18).

As with Boal and Kidd, Wibowo perceived people's theater to be but a part of a larger cultural process aiming for complete social change. One or two performances are not enough. Continuous, directed activities are needed. Borrowing a term often used by Kidd, "animateurs," people who help form, train, and motivate locally based theater groups (Kidd and Rashid 1983, 271; Kidd 1979, 7). Wibowo suggests that such figures should not tell people what to do. Rather, they are present in any given situation to help discover and utilize people's talents to analyze and solve their own problems (Wibowo 1991b, 1:18, 20–21).

Arena had already tried to realize a number of the elements of this approach in an earlier play, *Ombak-Ombak* (Waves), written in stages by Indro Gunawan and other members of Arena, and finished by Fred Wibowo (Field Notes 13 July 1994). Based on Arena's research into the conditions of Parangtritis and other coastal villages in 1981, *Ombak-Ombak* was originally performed at the 1981 workshop at Parangtritis. Subsequently, it was revived and performed several times during the late 1980s and early 1990s, becoming more integral to Arena's efforts as Arena devoted itself more to grassroots theater activities and deemphasized middle-class-oriented urban stage theater. The play's 1991 performance at the grassroots theater workshop at Pantai Sundak, Central Java, coincided with a growing awareness among the members of Arena, fostered by the experiences of the integrated pest management program, that grassroots theater training skills must not become the exclusive domain of middle-class NGO

Fig. 2.4 (above) and 2.5. Arena Teater, Studio A.V.: Two scenes from the Pesta Rakyat Workshop. Photos courtesy Studio Audio-Visual Puskat.

workers. One way in which Arena adjusted its practices accordingly was to have local villagers create and perform plays along with the NGO workshop participants at Pantai Sundak. This was done in order to begin breaking down the barriers between the young activists and ordinary villagers and to increase the confidence of the villagers in dealing with urban, educated Indonesians (Field Notes 14 July 1994). *Ombak-Ombak*, with its focus on villagers rather than on urban, university-educated intellectuals, was another component in Arena's strategy to shift the thinking of the participants and local villagers alike with regard to the existing relations of power within the development process.

The Sundak performance of *Ombak-Ombak*, staged by Arena members in an open Javanese-style *pendopo* pavilion for an audience of local villagers and NGO theater workshop participants, also shows how Arena's performance strategy had changed in response to the problems illustrated by the structure and performance venue of *Tumbal*, which in turn suggested the existing gap between middle-class NGO activists and ordinary villagers that was becoming apparent to Arena members. Using cultural images, forms, and language which the play's creators perceived to be taken from the villagers' own daily life, *Ombak-Ombak* was designed to stimulate dialogue with local villagers about their economic problems, and thereby model the techniques of the *pesta rakyat* for both the villagers and the NGO workshop participants.

The play opens with a ritualistic atmosphere—the sound of waves crashing and voices chanting, with human figures discernable on stage. The chanting lapses into silence, followed by a sung lament telling of the difficult life of the fishermen of Java's south coast but praising their courage and determination. A gong then signals a break from the ritual and poetry, as a group of villagers appears onstage to await the arrival of the village chief. However, the chief is late in arriving and the villagers engage in a *banyolan*, humorously but sharply criticizing the chief for making them wait and bemoaning the fact that they are called to so many "upgrading" sessions they no longer have time to take care of their families. Finally, the chief arrives with two student volunteers who are to give yet another upgrading session, teaching the villagers about gardening and making tarts. Hilarity ensues when the villagers, seeing the drawings of tarts, misinterpret them as hats or the minaret of a mosque. Even the lecture on gardening, dotted with many English terms unfamiliar to the villagers, who already know all about gardening, creates more confusion. The villagers protest at having to attend so many upgrading sessions, especially when they seem remote from the villagers' own daily lives. Yet the village chief insists they must undergo such training in order for the village to progress.

In the second section of the play, Pak Soma and Mbok Soma, the parents of an unemployed youth named Pardi, argue with their son about what they perceive as his lack of ambition and initiative. Pardi argues that he wants to work but finds no satisfying options in the village. They also argue about the value of the upgrading sessions, with Pardi maintaining they are not relevant to the real problems in the villages, while his father insists that Pardi shouldn't presume to contradict those with a higher education than he. Pardi's mother suggests they pray to the Queen of the South Sea, Kanjeng Ratu Kidul, in order for Pardi to find work as quickly as possible. Pardi leaves and soon the village chief and the two urban-based students arrive, lamenting the laziness of village youth, especially in comparison with the dynamism of city life.

In the final section of the play, Pardi and his sweetheart, Isah, lament their loss of hope and ideals. In contrast to the conversation of Wasa and Maya in *Tumbal*, however, Isah states that running to the city presents just as many difficulties as staying in the village. The training and ideas presented in upgrading sessions seem useless without access to money and resources. Yet Pardi and Isah also blame the villagers themselves for not telling the student trainers what kind of training and assistance they really need. After Isah leaves, Pardi falls asleep and has a fantastic dream in which his and some of his friends' wishes are granted by Kanjeng Roro Kidul, including making them rich. They imagine a fantasy project of village development that eventually leads them to embark on a trip to the city to buy necessary materials and supplies. Pantomiming riding in style, in Pardi's dream the village youth comically act out taking a plane flight to the city, then proceed on an exaggerated buying spree, while dancing to the popular Indonesian music genre of *dangdut*.[11] Yet on return to the village, Pardi and his friends are challenged by Isah to stop being selfish, to stop amusing themselves with far-fetched fantasies. She suggests, rather, that they should join with the waves now covering their village or be overwhelmed by them. She ties the idea of becoming one with the waves with the notion of working for the common good to destroy all obstacles. The village youth then converge on the village chief's house and list the obstacles confronting them: dropping out of school, lack of activities, lack of work, lack of income. The students and the village chief agree to help them, with the village chief vowing that if the villagers assert their own true needs and act creatively rather than simply carrying out orders, then programs can no longer be "dropped on us from above."

According to Wibowo's concept, people's theater should be "an expression of the identity or a realization of the culture of a particular social environment" (Wibowo 1991b, 1:16). As Wibowo wrote, "In this context the dialogue which needs to be developed for this democratic, social interaction should take the form of the symbols, codification, or language with which they are familiar. In addition to the verbal language, people's art consists of symbols which are very often more effective and which, in a very precise way, are able to articulate and express their intentions...."(Wibowo 1991b, 3:5).[12]

Ombak-Ombak was fashioned by Wibowo and his co-writers with these thoughts in mind. This can be seen in both the play's theme—the problems caused by uneven development in an isolated coastal village—as well as in the consistent use of the Kanjeng Ratu Kidul mythology. This spirit, to whom the Sultan of Yogyakarta is supposedly ritually married, is well known among the Javanese of the Yogyakarta region. The play's writers hoped to evoke local associations by tying the play to this mythology. The ritual scene at the beginning of the play seems to support the myth, since it suggests that the play itself is a "ritual," perhaps an offering to Kanjeng Ratu Kidul in order to gain her favor and thereby make the village prosper. Yet the way in which the plot presents the myth, only to reinterpret it later, gives a different twist to the "ritual" function of the play.

From out of the opening incantations, flute music, and smoke, women emerge as though summoned by magic to sing a song of the suffering, hard work, determination, and courage of the coastal villagers. The last

Fig. 2.6. Arena Teater, *Ombak-Ombak: The Village Youth's Dream Plane Ride*. Photo courtesy of Fred Wibowo/Arena Teater.

three lines of their song assert that out of such struggles the future generation will be born ready to carry on the effort. The entire play seems, in this sense, to be a ritual designed to overcome the problems that it depicts. The opening incantations summon images and sounds of the problems that the performers and audience wish to overcome so that they may be struggled with collectively, yielding fortified resolve and new strategies.

In the play's second act, the characters discuss praying to Kanjeng Ratu Kidul to grant their wishes, a practice still employed by many Javanese today. This leads to Pardi's dream, the first part of which culminates in the surreal "development" spree. Yet this section of the dream is an implausible solution to the village's problems and, thus, the figure of Ratu Kidul is temporarily displaced by the image of the sea as a threatening collectivity of waves. These waves are in fact the villagers themselves who have begun to assert themselves, to be *conscientized* about the problems facing them. Isah, who speaks for the waves, tells Pardi and his friends to become one with the waves, to break through the difficulties confronting them. This is how they can avoid the curse of Kanjeng Ratu Kidul, for the spirit queen of the south coast does not favor those who desire but do nothing to bring about the fulfillment of those desires (Wibowo 1991a, 21). The local belief is thus transformed and reintegrated by the end of the play. If previously one had to practice austerities or throw gifts into the sea to gain the blessing of Kanjeng Ratu Kidul, now the play suggests the villagers themselves can become a force of nature, like the spirit queen, if they join together, learn to articulate their desires and needs, and struggle collectively for positive change. The ritual here is not simply an offering to Kanjeng Ratu Kidul, rather it produces a strategy for overcoming problems. Pardi's dream is crucial here, for within it the impracticality of the first utopian vision is transformed into a positive program for action, just as the myth of Kanjeng Ratu Kidul is reinterpreted to become a call for critical thinking and taking initiative.

Another link to local culture is the *banyolan* style of joking discussed earlier. In contrast to most *banyolan* routines, however, the peasants' humor in *Ombak-Ombak*, as was also the case in *Tumbal*, includes sharp, radical criticisms of the existing system. Such criticisms can be found in the villagers' jokes about the fact that the village chief forces them to wait for an hour before he arrives (3, 4); their near rebellion against the upgrading sessions that deprive them of any free time (3, 9); and their humorous conversation about the lack of connection that many of the upgrading sessions have with their daily conditions (3–4). Much of this dialogue is spiced with Javanese words and phrases, bringing it closer, linguistically, to the inhabitants of the area in which the play was performed. These *banyolan* sections do not only draw upon the peasants for their humor, but by showing the interaction between the student volunteers and the peasants, these joking sequences also underscore the absurd mismatch between the information that the students impart to the villagers and the difficulties the villagers face in their day-to-day struggles for survival. How do tarts, cosmetics, and lectures full of foreign words relate to a situation in which few people know where their next meal will come from? Thus, the dialogue in these sequences not only highlights the villagers' relative lack of knowledge, but it also uses that lack, and the humor arising from it, to demonstrate that the student volunteers and the government program that they represent are frustratingly out of touch with the villagers' real conditions and needs.

Fig. 2.7. Arena Teater, *Ombak-Ombak: Dangdut dancing*. Photo courtesy of Fred Wibowo/Arena Teater.

The play makes use of popular culture in other scenes as well. Pardi's melancholy songs and the *dangdut* accompaniment to the villagers' shopping spree add elements of popular musical culture that are quite widespread throughout Central Java and much of the rest of Indonesia. These mobilizations of popular legend and cultural forms are highly appropriate in a play that centers on the problems of the peasants and attempts to present these problems from the perspective of the peasants themselves.

How then are the peasants and their perspective represented in *Ombak-Ombak*? Even though the attitudes and limited horizons of the peasants are gently made fun of in some of the *banyolan* sections, another side to the villagers is also shown, distinguishing *Ombak-Ombak* from most genres of traditional theater. We are presented with the toiling women of the opening "ritual" section who sing of the difficult lives of coastal villagers and praise the perseverance of such ordinary people, suggesting their determination and resilience. In the upgrading session the villagers are not simply the butt of jokes but are also seen to be critical, rather desperate, and weighed down by their struggle for survival and the obligations to participate in government-administered programs. The dynamics of Pardi's family further illustrate the depth of the villagers' dilemma. The father is estranged from his son, whom he perceives to be lazy. The mother, also concerned about her son's seeming aimlessness, nevertheless plays the role of mediator between father and son. Pardi himself is seriously attempting to discern a solution to the village's, and his, difficulties. Pardi's sister defends her brother with sympathy, if also caution. Taken as a whole, these characters show the audience a village family full of complexity, conflict and nuance. Similarly, Pardi's conversation with Isah reveals the village youth as intelligent analysts of their own conditions, showing them to be potential subjects of their own history. This is confirmed by Isah's reincarnation in Pardi's elaborate dream as the spokesperson of the waves/movement for self-development and initiative. Furthermore, though the village youth return to seek the approval of the village chief in the play's final scene, the concluding lines leave little doubt that the real, substantive initiatives must come from the mass of ordinary villagers and not from the chief or student volunteers. On the whole the villagers are represented as thoughtful, complex human beings who can make decisions and act to change the conditions of their lives.

Perhaps the least convincing element of the play is the sudden conversion of the village chief at the end. Previously he has been presented, at best, as concerned but hopelessly out of touch with his fellow villagers and, at worst, as a condescending authoritarian leader. Suddenly, in the last scene, however, he transforms himself into an enthusiastic supporter of the villagers' newly found assertiveness and sense of initiative. This ending is so harmonious in contrast to the sarcasm and concern (bordering on despair) in the earlier scenes, as well as the giddily chaotic atmosphere of the "development spree" of Pardi's dream sequence, that it hardly seems believable or consistent with what has preceded it. Indeed, given the fact that the dream sequence never explicitly ends, the viewer/reader might well dismiss this ultimate vision of social harmony achieved through mass *conscientization* and mobilization as just another part of a generally impractical utopian fantasy.

This incongruity points to some of the contradictions operating in grassroots theater practice. First of all, given their own life experiences and the techniques of social analysis which Arena and other cultural workers and community "animators" were providing by 1991, peasants participating in the workshops in villages such as Sundak would likely have had something to say about their disadvantaged position in the national scheme of development as well as about possible official corruption in the development plans that had been formulated for their area. The Tanen Pakem peasants' plays of 1983–84 centered thematically around the poor stewardship of the village chief and on his hierarchical attitudes toward the villagers under his supervision. Surely, Arena's play could have pushed these themes further, while trying to stay true to peasants' perspectives. Similarly, the ultimate failure of the dream sequence "development spree" seems to debunk get-rich-quick fantasies tied to ideas of urban culture with "Westernized" jackets, airplanes, telephones, and industrialization. Yet the peasant characters in the play are not allowed to offer an articulated critique of why these fantasies will not work for them or of why they cannot eventually accomplish such things through intelligence and hard work. Nor do the villagers have a chance to discuss how precisely to organize themselves to become a human "breaker." An analysis of how the system has made them poor is not offered in the course of the drama. Were it not for the persistent return to the themes of the inappropriateness of the upgrading sessions, the condescending attitude of the student volunteers and the village chief, together with the concluding statement of the village chief that "Programs can no longer be dropped on us from above, rather our actual needs will become clear and we can finally overcome our challenges together," one would be tempted to conclude that the play even blames the victims for not realizing sooner that all they had to do was speak up.

However, these nagging indicators that the system has not been functioning in the villagers' favor, that it has not been encouraging them to speak up, are indeed present in the play. How then do we account for the lack of structural analysis and sharper social critique in *Ombak-Ombak*? Why is it so important that the village chief and students be incorporated into the project for social change and positive development initiated and controlled by the common people? Is such a move merely a replay, with a more grassroots democratic twist, of traditional theater genres in which commoner clowns ultimately remain loyal to their masters?

By the early 1990s, Indonesian progressives had still not succeeded in forging a powerful oppositional coalition that could actually challenge the programmatic momentum of the forces exercising control of the state apparatuses. At best, they had been able to further their own organizational growth and agendas by taking advantage of divisions within the powerful military-bureaucratic elite that dominated the Indonesian state and economy. At the same time, their pressure had perhaps forced the elites to modify their approaches (Aspinall 2005). Yet they were still vulnerable in the face of the state's coercive apparatus. In this respect, a statement that PUSKAT AV Studio's Father Rüdi Hofmann made during an interview with Dutch scholar Eugène Van Erven in November 1987 is revealing: "The situation here is very dangerous and that is why we have to be pragmatic. The bishops are also quite conservative and have already created difficulties for us. If necessary, we are prepared to take risks. We are not scared, but we prefer to operate cautiously. What's the point if the authorities stop us?" (Van Erven 1992, 194).

Furthermore, given the still traumatic memories of the massive slaughter of communists and suspected communist sympathizers in the 1965–66 period as the New Order government was being established, many progressives like Wibowo were concerned to avoid violence. Wibowo felt that any violent attempts to create social change would most hurt those who are poor; the very people Arena had dedicated itself to helping. This belief led Wibowo to embrace non-violence as a component of his work for social change (Field notes 25 September 1987; 15 August 1991). This provides another reason to downplay a type of sharper social analysis that might lead to heated, confrontational scenes in *Ombak-Ombak*. As Wibowo wrote in the manuscript version of *Tiga Buah Buku Teater Rakyat* (Three Books on People's Theater): "People's theater is not for revolution, but for creating the structure of a new world based upon brotherhood/sisterhood, peace and justice" (Wibowo 1991b, 3:30).[13]

Viewed in this light, *Ombak-Ombak* appears to be designed simply to model a people's theater play for the participants of the Sundak workshop and to engage the villagers of Sundak in a preliminary round of thinking about their difficult economic situation, without offering a coherent and directed structural analysis. It was hoped that the play would help villagers and NGO workers rethink the relationship of urban intellectuals to peasants. As in *Tumbal*, the play concludes by suggesting the need to work together to overcome the desperate economic situation in which the village finds itself. However, there is no specific solution given, once more leaving the audience to construct its own methods of solving the problems. Yet unlike *Tumbal*, no "experts" are summoned during the course of the drama to provide a well-articulated critique of the current program of development. In a related change, it is the peasants, particularly the village youth such as Pardi and Isah, who are constituted as the critical, reasoning subjects in *Ombak-Ombak*, though their framework for understanding seems frustratingly partial. Still, with such a move the play suggests that only the villagers will be able, ultimately, to determine the best ways to address their own needs. Used in such a fashion, Arena's new approach attempted to initiate critical discussion among the direct subjects of its material, while endeavoring to minimize the amount of "vanguard" guidance that middle-class voices provided in *Tumbal*.

Similarly, the play was deployed in the workshop as a model that might inspire and encourage the workshop participants to formulate their own plays and critiques of the problems facing ordinary villagers. It was hoped that such a process might eventually produce a sharper social critique and a more powerful, cohesive grassroots movement. Yet it would have been crucial in the early stages of building such a movement to maintain the good will of local village officials, who, while officially part of the government, may nevertheless have been sympathetic to the problems of their fellow villagers. Such an analysis, while highlighting the acumen of Arena's cultural animators in analyzing the social situation, nonetheless also shows that *Ombak-Ombak* still contains a tendency for urban professionals and intellectuals, as mainstays of the NGOs and grassroots theater organizations, to determine protectively the general strategy of grassroots development efforts on behalf of those whom they seek to help.

Climax and Decline

From 1990 to 1994, then, with funding from WACC (World Association for Christian Communications) Arena devoted itself more completely to promoting and spreading grassroots theater practices. Arena/PUSKAT undertook grassroots theater workshops in Irian Jaya (West Papua), Kalimantan (Borneo), Mentawai, West Sumatra, North Sumatra, West Java, East Java Cirebon, Central Java, and East Timor. Fred Wibowo felt, in 1994, that Teater Rakyat was spreading and that the workers' theater that had appeared in the Jakarta area since 1989 (see chapter 5) was connected to the spread of grassroots theater. As an indicator of such progress, he pointed to farmer groups started during the Integrated Pest Management Program that continued to use theater to promote Family Planning and other ideas but always with a more critical attitude. He noted that they used traditional theater forms such as *ketoprak* and joking styles like *dagelan* that no longer contained "feudal" content and expressed issues important to their locales. Wibowo also noted the some NGOs had even formed their own theater groups, for example, YPKS (Yayasan Pimpinan Kesejahteraan Sosial or Leadership for Social Prosperity Foundation), which had developed its own *ketoprak* group that performed plays reflecting the needs of society, including doing a play about the well-known Kedung Ombo land dispute in Central Java. Finally, Fred considered the empowerment approach of grassroots theater to have had a wide influence in helping many people to conclude that top-down development was irrational (Field Notes 14 July 1994).

Similarly, Indro Gunawan believed Teater Rakyat had helped produce a change in rural society. Gunawan argued that people no longer accepted whatever comes their way and that they had a more critical attitude. He also noted a number of other grassroots theater groups were active by 1994, citing in particular the Kelompok Pinggiran (Marginal Group) in Solo whose membership included students and others, and the ITRJ (Institut Teater Rakyat Yogyakarta—Or the Yogyakarta People's Theater Institute) which was composed of students and informal street vendors (Field Notes 18 July 1994). It seemed then, in 1994, that theater had been appropriated, developed, and opened up to entirely new audiences and performers.

Yet in the next few years, interest among NGOs for grassroots theater practices quickly drained away. By 1997, Surowo, a member of PUSKAT's Audiovisual Studio and participant in Arena/PUSKAT's workshops, admitted that Arena/PUSKAT AV Studio no longer did many workshops for NGOs. He was uncertain as to why this had happened but suspected the NGO community may have reached a saturation point (Field Notes 26 July 1997). Others speculated that international donors had lost interest in funding grass roots empowerment through theater, or that they distrusted some of those involved in grassroots theater projects as a result of poor management of funds (Field Notes 24 and 27 July 1994). It is also possible that many activist and grassroots empowerment NGOs became more interested in using direct social and political protests as a means of empowering and conscientizing peasants, workers, and other groups as the Suharto regime began to unravel, especially after the 1996 attack by government-backed thugs on PDI headquarters in July 1996. Such protests, after all, were another kind of performance (see, for example, Heryanto 2006, 154–56; Aspinall 2005, 96–100, 139–44).

As a result, Arena/PUSKAT grassroots theater workshops now focused on secondary school students, hoping to train them to be sensitive to problems in the villages and to increase their creativity and feelings of independence. Students and their teachers would usually conduct research in the village, work up a script based on the results of their research, and put on a performance (Field Notes 26 July 1997). Clearly, helpful as this might be in creating a new generation of urban middle-classes sympathetic to the plight of their rural compatriots, it represented a step back from the more socially radical vision of earlier workshops and Wibowo's *Teater Rakyat manuscript* formulations (1991b.).

Still, if the assessments of activists like Wibowo and Gunawan are correct, the decade from 1985 to 1994 was one in which grassroots theater practices helped to build critical consciousness among activists and peasants alike and may have contributed to the growth of the thriving, more assertive movements to oppose cases of land seizure and in the end the authoritarian rule of the New Order government itself. Yet even as it did so, it raised problems of the persistent gulf between those with higher social status, access to wealth, education and media, and the lower classes of society, in this case, small farmers and landless agricultural laborers. The constant reformulation of workshop aims and participants, along with the obvious differences in the form, themes, and venues/audiences for the two Arena plays analyzed, mark most clearly the process of continual adjustment that grassroots theater activists pursued in their attempts to grapple with and overcome this problem. However, who would speak on behalf of the peasants and with what media were nagging dilemmas never completely surmounted. In engaging with Brechtian and Boalian theater and Freirian pedagogical methods as well as with forms of folk theater and culture, grassroots theater workers pursued a utopian impulse to create a better, more equitable world, and they achieved some noteworthy results. If their efforts fell short of their desires, this was not due to a lack of courage or vision on their part. Rather, the reasons were the constrained political circumstances in which they had to work, the imperatives governing international funding, and the fact that many NGOs and activists turned to more immediate kinds of social theater and performance as the New Order regime first experimented with more openness, then tried to crack down on political dissent from around 1994 on. Still, there were other kinds of theater, drawing on some of the same roots, and flourishing at about the same time as the peak of grassroots theater efforts, that built momentum in other constituencies for criticism of Indonesian politics and society, broadening critical modern theater's reach into and relationship with Indonesian society. It is to one of those efforts that the next chapter is devoted.

Chapter 3

ASAS TUNGGAL AND LAUGHTER IN THE MOSQUE

Indonesian Islamic Theater on the National Stage

For about three years, from mid-1988 until August 1991, Emha Ainun Nadjib and his collaborators from the Central Javanese city of Yogyakarta electrified Javanese and other Indonesian audiences with a new form of mass Islamic theater. Capitalizing on Nadjib's fame as an Islamic orator and poet and building a successful media marketing approach, this group of cultural workers created a series of plays that drew large audiences everywhere they were performed and caused a number of national and local arts figures to dream of Islamic aesthetics and of using art as a media for promoting the faith. These productions of Nadjib and his group also attracted a fair amount of public controversy and political attention.

For example, the performance of Nadjib's unabashedly Islamic play, *Lautan Jilbab* (Sea of Jilbabs), staged in the provincial East Javanese city of Madiun on 27 and 28 April 1991, shows in remarkable ways how Nadjib's theater was enmeshed in a complex web of social and political relations. *Lautan Jilbab*, as a performance piece, grew from the need of its creators to oppose the New Order government's policy of prohibiting young Muslim women from wearing the jilbab (the loose fitting dress with a hood-like habit that covers the hair and shoulders, leaving only the face visible) in public schools. The setting for the Madiun performances of *Lautan Jilbab* was Stadion Willis, a large sports stadium, filled with approximately 17,000 spectators each night. The enormous size of the audience was rendered even more noteworthy because ticket prices started at the top of the normal price range for such events in provincial cities, Rp.1.000, and went up to what was, by Indonesian standards of the time, a rather startling Rp.5.000 (US$2.50). As if this expense were not enough, the first night's audience braved a heavy downpour, which delayed the start of the evening's performance for over an hour. The circumstances of this event were made even more interesting by the fact that Nadjib and his collaborators received some rather special support: B. J. Habibie, then the powerful Indonesian Minister of Research and Technology and chair of the new government-sponsored Islamic intellectuals organization, ICMI (and in May 1998 to become Suharto's successor and the third president of the Republic of Indonesia), donated Rp2.5 million worth of funds to rent a more adequate sound system for the second night. Despite this support by one of President Suharto's closest political allies, the local police of Madiun demanded a number of changes in the script before they would grant a performance permit. It was reported that several criticisms were judged to be "too strong" (*Surabaya Post* 29 April 1991). To add to all of this, an anonymous letter was delivered to the play's writer, Emha Ainun Nadjib, declaring that the play, after all was said and done, was un-Islamic: it was contrary to the sense of modesty conveyed by jilbab because it included several male performers with long hair and worn-out clothes (*Harian Umum Karya Darma* 1 May 1991).

Here, we see all the elements of a real life drama that frames and threatens to overwhelm the contents of the actual plays Nadjib and his collaborators created, not only *Lautan Jilbab* (Sea of Jilbabs, 1988-91), but also *Dajjal* (Tempter at the End of Days, 1989) and *Keluarga Sakinah* (The Virtuous Family, 1990). What exactly were these plays about and what brought all the actors—those jostling to get a good view of the stage, those on it, and certainly all those behind the scenes—into action?

The plays in question were part of a resurgence of Indonesian Muslim pride and identification. This key phenomena shaping Indonesia today is by no means a simple one led by a unitary movement with a clearly outlined program. Within contemporary Indonesia, a whole spectrum of groups is in dialogue and is competing to form new visions of and roles for

Islam. This Islamic resurgence is itself embedded in a process of social and economic change that is rapidly eroding or transforming old structures of family life, traditional livelihoods, social norms and ideologies, and cultural practices. In the late 1980s and early 1990s, although in a very uneven fashion, Indonesia was industrializing and urbanizing at an astonishing pace. A predominantly rural, agrarian society was then racing toward a different and, in some ways, very disturbing new mode of existence. As related in chapter 1, the system seeking to shape, guide, and control these processes during the time of the major performances of the Yogyakarta Islamic theater groups was presided over by an aging but extremely powerful president, who attempted to maintain his personal grip on power by wooing Muslim support to counterbalance sections of the resentful military chafing under his continued rule.

Of course, other processes and discourses were also involved. The rise of an urban industrial and finance-based society engendered new social classes, including the very wealthy and middle-classes who were able to use their excess income to purchase and consume goods and services. Up until 1997, a mass-media market, dominated by a menu of national and international cultural products, had been growing steadily over several decades. Its expansion had accelerated in the late 1980s with the liberalization of television, a move that allowed several new private channels to begin operating, often with extensive foreign programming. This entire trend alarmed sections of the Indonesian public concerned about losing local cultural traditions and economic control to the onslaught of a consumer culture propagated first and foremost by the advanced industrial nations and secondly by wealthy urban Indonesians often in tune with Western culture. Against this, Indonesian Muslims were drawing on local traditions of Islam and upon social currents flowing across the wider Islamic world. Islamic theater thus was one attempt to respond to the perceived cultural inundation that is one aspect of "globalization" for many less industrially developed countries.

Finally, the plays also participated in a dialogue with the aesthetics and practices of modern theater detailed in the first chapter, including the productive tension between Western modern drama and traditional performance and cultural elements. But the plays were also created with modern mass music and dance spectacles in mind as well as with the idea that social issues should be tackled head on. They also responded to debates about what types and forms of Islamic art should be considered appropriate. Grassroots theater practices comprised a last element in the mix of ideologies, practices, and discourses shaping these plays, detailed in the previous chapter. How all these elements were articulated is the subject of this chapter.

Islamic Resurgence

Since it began to take substantial root in the Indonesian archipelago, Islam has had an extremely complex history marked by various stages and currents. Between roughly 1200 and 1800, the predominant type of Islam in the archipelago was based on a blend of Sufi mysticism and local spirit beliefs as well as adherence to the Shafi'ite School of jurisprudence.

However, beginning in the eighteenth century with the Wahabi movement in Arabia and continuing with the late ninteenth- and early twentieth-century modernist movements, which sought to purge Islam of all alien beliefs and practices, mystical Sufi Islam came under increasing attack. In the Indonesian context, the rise of Islamic modernism coincides with the beginnings of nationalism, modern education, and urbanization. Early twentieth-century modernists in Indonesia specifically rejected all "alien" elements, including syncretic "pagan" beliefs and what they deemed profane mysticism. In their view, the four *madzhab*, which comprised compilations of Islamic jurisprudence followed by many traditional *kyai (venerated scholar)*, also were not valid in determining proper conduct for Muslims. Modernists believed that the *Qur'an* and the *Hadith* were the only sources of authority and encouraged individual and group interpretation of the scriptures by contemporary Islamic scholars. The modernists held public prayer meetings, discouraged all practices deemed as not purely Islamic, founded modern-style schools that taught religious subjects in combination with secular ones, and stressed that women had rights, especially in pursuing education. Historically considerable tension has existed between Indonesian modernists and more traditional Muslims, whether the latter were oriented to a more mystical form of Islam or were simply legalist or scripturalist Muslims adhering to one of the schools of jurisprudence (once again, in Indonesia, usually Shafi'ite) not accepted as valid by modernists (Nakamura 1980; Dhofier 1980; Noer 1973, 73–96).

Since Muslim party politics were rigidly controlled and then manipulated and engineered by the New Order government beginning in the late 1960s, an argument within modernism led to the birth of a "neo-modernism." The military-dominated New Order government held a deep suspicion of Muslim political activity, as a consequence of the fundamentalist Darul Islam uprising of the 1950s and the association of prominent modernist-oriented Masyumi party leaders with the PRRI rebellion of the late 1950s. The neo-modernists therefore argued that direct Islamic political party activity was counter-productive and likely to give rise to sectarianism. They maintained that Islam's role was to offer ethical and cultural guidance to society. Strategically, they sought to deepen the Islamic roots of Indonesian society while avoiding military and government suspicion (Hefner 1993, 4–5).

Like the modernists before them, these neo-modernists argued for the right of *ijtihad* (interpretation), but they expanded it by stating that absolute truth can never be achieved because interpretation is an ongoing process. They combined classical Islamic scholarship with modern critical inquiry and rejected orthodox dogma. Similarly, they placed more emphasis on the essence of Islamic teachings than on their form or obscure points of correct ritual and behavior (Schwarz 1994, 178; Vatikiotis 1993, 124). More strongly than previous modernists, the neo-modernists supported democracy and took a pluralistic, inclusive stance toward other faiths (Barton 1994, 144–49).

The arguments and approach of the neo-modernists seemed increasingly appropriate as the New Order government forced all Islamic parties to merge into one party in 1973 and then, through constant meddling, undermined the credibility of that party as a representative of Muslim political interests in Indonesia. The final blow, generating considerable anger and resentment among Indonesian Muslims, came after 1982, when the government promulgated its *Asas Tunggal* law. It forced all mass organizations to adopt the official government ideology, the *Pancasila*, as their sole ideological foundation (Morfit 1986, 42–43). Throughout the seventies, the government had also attempted not only to buy Islam's good will but also to control it, through mosque-building programs, the establishment of state-run Islamic universities (IAIN), and funding for study abroad programs in North America and Europe (Hefner 1993, 9–11; Vatikiotis 1993, 127). By the mid-1980s, Indonesia was experiencing a full-fledged revival of interest in Islam. due to a number of factors. Many youth looked for a realistic and stable set of values and guidelines in the face of a rapidly changing, modernizing society. Additionally, if ironically, the *Asas Tunggal* law, by forcing all Islamic parties to tolerate other religions under the Pancasila's vague "Belief in One Supreme God" principle, made Islamic identification more comfortable for those Muslims who had previously feared the potential for intolerance within their own community. Finally, the suppression of most overt political activity forced many to turn to Islam as an avenue for voicing "political" concerns and aspirations (Schwarz 1994, 173–74). In such a context, Islamic neo-modernism offered a model for an attractively tolerant, intellectually broad, pro-democratic Islam that appealed to many urban and rural Muslims.

Yet the profuse growth of semi-oppositional NGOs, tied to the resurgence of Muslim pride and confidence, was becoming a worry for the government. The New Order's success in controlling Muslim party politics was thus threatening to move most active Muslims beyond the reach of its normal bureaucratic restraints (Vatikiotis 1993, 123–24). This problem was made even more critical for President Suharto and his supporters within the government by the fact that he had been feuding with the leadership of the military beginning in the late 1980s. In part to counter the loss of much of the military support he had previously enjoyed, Suharto courted the strategic Muslim middle-class by various means, including the formation in 1990 of the government-sponsored organization of Islamic intellectuals, ICMI.

Emha Ainun Nadjib, Engaged Art, and Islamic Culture: the Lautan Jilbab *Poem Cycle*

Emha Ainun Nadjib was a figure uniquely able to contribute to the complex discourses and representations of Islam embedded in the social and political history described above. Born on May 27, 1953, in Jombang, East Java, a center of intense Islamic faith, Nadjib grew up in a traditionally devout Muslim family and began his education in the renowned *pesantren* of Gontor, in the Ponorogo region of East Java[1] After completing high school in Yogyakarta, he established himself as a journalist and poet in the 1970s. In the early 1980s, as noted in the previous chapter, he became intimately involved with the Yogyakartan national theater group, Dinasti, which came increasingly under the scrutiny of the local police as a result of its angry criticisms of New Order government and society (Borch 1988, 39–55). Nadjib himself collaborated in writing some of the offending scripts.

At about the same time, Nadjib was also frequently invited to NGO forums to discuss a range of social justice and development issues, in his distinctive humorous style that often used striking metaphors to illustrate social problems. All of this work linked him to the socially critical current within Indonesian national theater and culture as well as to the Indonesian arts world in general and critical NGO circles. But while he established his reputation as an artist critical of contemporary society through his theater work, he also built a name for himself as a Muslim thinker, activist, and speaker, highly sought after by many groups. His intense religious beliefs and strong commitment to Islam featured prominently in his poetry, essays, and mass-media columns. Thus, by virtue of family background, education, and religious and cultural activism, Nadjib draws on a rich blend of both traditional and modernist Islam, modern national arts culture, and ideas about social and economic development.

In his writing, Nadjib makes use of elements from all of these traditions. One of the great literary traditions within Islam is the Sufi poetry of the middle ages—from al-Hallaj to Farid Uddin Attar, Rumi and Hafiz. Intimately connected to Sufi mysticism, this poetry took up themes and images of god as the beloved, even a lover; of a mystical path or journey of suffering which the believer took back to the source, Allah; of ecstasy and intoxication caused by love of and yearning for the beloved; of Allah as sole agent of creation and source of everything to which everything would return, as captured in the image of water returning to the ocean (Schimmel 1982).

As a mystical, ecstatic strand of Islam, Sufism was in frequent tension, even antagonism, with the religious scholars, the *ulama*, who tended to confine themselves to interpretation of the formal laws and rules. The Sufis' antagonism towards legalistic ulama served them well as defenders of the poor and dispossessed in opposition to autocratic states supported by a legal system staffed by such religious scholars (Schimmel 1982, 137–39; Rahman 1966, 150–55).

Though Nadjib would hardly identify himself as a Sufi, echoes of Sufi poetic expression nonetheless appear in his literary work. A closer examination of the themes of *Lautan Jilbab* (1989),[2] a poem cycle that became the point of departure for the best known of Nadjib and his collaborators' plays, confirms that Nadjib is conversant with the images, tropes, and themes of the Sufi poetic tradition and has harnessed them to a project closely tied to modernist or neo-modernist versions of Islam. In such a way, Nadjib's work appears to embody a rich amalgam of the most powerful Islamic traditions that have influenced Indonesia over the centuries.

Written during the mid-eighties, the poems respond to a series of incidents involving Muslim girls sent home from school for violating a national law prohibiting wearing of the jilbab at public schools (Triyanto et al. 1991, 76–77; Triyanto, Nugroho, and Fadjri 1991, 100). The poems strike back at the logic of a system that professes to ban atheism yet denies Muslims the practice of their faith according to the forms they deem proper.

Traces of the Sufi poetic tradition are present in images scattered throughout the poems. Many of them speak of separation from and longing for the beloved Allah, who is the source of all things:

And they sing:

> My beloved. Yes, my beloved!
> If our beginning and our end are one and the same
> Why must we endure this long pursuit!
>
> If our past and our future are one and the same
> Why place this illusory gulf between us
> If you are the source from which your servants come
> Why must they wait for You to the edge of madness?[3]

Others describe Allah as the one whose reality is hidden as if behind a screen or a veil (19–20). The poems also use the image of God as the source of all light (20, 24–27, 37), and those wearing jilbabs are portrayed as drops of water in a river running back to the ocean or source/Allah (8, 12). Some of the poems display a pattern of repetition and variation that could be connected to Sufi chanted prayers or *zikir* (17–18, 26–27). Another important motif from popular rural Sufism echoes idiosyncratically in the final poem of the collection. The motif glorifies the unrefined and uneducated person who, because of spiritual purity, is more holy and wise than the greatest scholar. In the poem, angels with no human attributes and no refined language or culture are nonetheless better able to sense the importance of those wearing jilbabs than many of the more educated and cultured (47). This final image connects to the populist, anti-ulama strand of Sufism, conveying an attitude that links to a distinct mistrust of the modern "state" with its bureaucracy, official culture, secular educational institutions, and consumerism. It thus yields a blistering critique of what Nadjib sees as the oppressive, secular system established under the New Order. In the last poem of the thin volume, "Maka Inilah Jilbab" (This, then, is the Jilbab), Nadjib lists some of the things that oppress the Jilbabs:

> school books consume us
> spectacles and broadcasts devour us
> advertisements and consumer goods herd us on
> stages and bureaucratic desks befuddle us
> stupid-ifying machines we take to be school benches
> livestock pens we believe to be places of worship
> our mouths are gagged, our eyes weep blood
> life consists of climbing on the backs of others. . . .[4]

In this apocalyptic passage, Nadjib positions the notion of official education as something that can actually make people stupid, as part of an all-encompassing ensemble of modern society's oppressive structures and processes that includes consumer culture and the modern bureaucracy. Just a few lines later, Nadjib also criticizes Muslim ulama who gather Qur'anic verses in support of the New Order's security state. It is a scathing reference to religious scholars who, like the old enemies of the Sufis, are too subservient to the government. Taken together, all of these images construct a vision of the modern, profane nation state as a nightmarish prison of the soul.

Elsewhere, the poems equate the modern state with power and violence; in contrast, religion is equated with love and salvation. The nation state, in other words, does not follow God's desire for the constant circulation of the earth's wealth among the *umat* (community, especially the community of faith) in a circuit of intimate love and affection, but is based upon greed and the lust to build fences, establish boundaries, accumulate possessions. In this prison of the soul, moral corruption is rampant. Like the conventional image of the pre-Islamic jahiliya era in the Arabian Peninsula, Nadjib's vision of modern Indonesia sees all values turned upside down. Advertising and pornography are conspicuous evidence of this depravity. This set of images intertwines with the idea of Muslim women wearing the jilbab.

Veiling and covering are highly contentious topics in contemporary Islamic societies. A number of Muslim scholars assert that the injunction for women to wear the veil must be understood in its historical context as Allah's revelation of a compromise solution to a complex set of issues centered on the relations of men and women within the early community of believers (Mernissi 1991, 85–188; Ahmed 1992, 50–63). Within this context and that of the Qur'an, such solutions must be seen simply as first steps toward a greater liberation of the entire community of believers (Rahman 1966, 38–39).

In order to explain present discourses about veiling and covering, Mernissi suggests that the movement of women into the realm of education and the workforce in the Arab world threatens Arab men long trained to believe they should inherit and control the public sphere. Foremost among those protesting such developments are young, rural men who for the first time have received a modern education and have relocated to regional or national urban centers. Though invited closer to the table of power in a broadly democratic process that has expanded education and the civil service, such men are faced with competition from women, whom they have been taught to believe they should control. Such problems then articulate with struggles for national autonomy in the face of predatory intrusions by multinational corporations and foreign governments—governments that used the "women's issue" to further their own domination of colonized Muslim lands (Mernissi 1987, vii–xxix; Ahmed 1992). Thus, the idea of equality for women is construed to be a foreign imposition. In Muslim communities, a frequent response to these rapidly changing conditions has been to summon notions of the present as a second jahiliya, that is, the time of "ignorance" predating the establishment of Islam. This period is said to have been dominated by a confusing plethora of sexual, religious, and political practices now deemed abhorrent and the very symbol of chaos (Mernissi 1987, 84–85). Perhaps in response to such discourses, Leila Ahmed has explained the donning of the veil or head covering as a positive way for Egyptian Muslim women to protect themselves in a potentially threatening urban environment and to assert their right to participate in the public sphere (Ahmed 1992, 221–25).

Distinct from the Middle-eastern and North African cases cited by Ahmed and Mernissi, donning the jilbab was never a widespread tradition in Indonesia. In fact, many of the women wearing such clothing in the 1980s and early 1990s faced stiff opposition from parents, even discrimination and harassment on the streets (Brenner 1996, 675, 683). Thus, wearing the veil in Indonesia cannot be said to be a return to tradition as a defense against the political, economic, and cultural intrusions of the advanced industrial world. Even so, the use of the jilbab is becoming more common. Brenner argues that such a gesture symbolizes a new historical consciousness in Java, one that wishes to dissociate itself from the local past and identify as modern. The women she interviewed saw the decision to don the jilbab as one of self-definition.[5] By accepting what they felt to be a new, modern Islamic discipline, they incorporated themselves into a global community of Muslims. Relying upon this sense of identity and the authority of the sacred scriptures, these young women often defied parents' opposition to their style of dress and challenged their own parents' understanding of Islam (Brenner 1996).

Still, while Indonesia is certainly neither the Moroccan or Egyptian Arab society that Mernissi and Ahmed write about, it is nonetheless undergoing dramatic social and economic changes that are creating some of the same pressures. Many youth involved in the current Islamic movement come from lower-middle-class backgrounds. They are the children of teachers, business people, and low-ranking civil servants. As such, they have benefited less than the upper-middle-class and the elite from the New Order's boom years and have tended to see more clearly the injustice of the elite's conspicuous displays of power and consumption in the face of wide social disparities in wealth and well-being. For many such young Muslims, Indonesian society during the New Order displayed the symptoms of moral degeneration and the disintegration of social solidarity (Brenner 1996, 276–78). Even in Indonesia, then, the donning of the jilbab was implicated in a kind of moral resistance to what was perceived as a New Order jahiliya, often characterized as slavishly imitating Western modernization.

As mentioned above, Nadjib's *Lautan Jilbab* poem cycle thrusts the idea of wearing the jilbab[6] into the midst of an apocalyptic vision of contemporary Indonesian society as a new jahiliya. The jilbab thereby acquires a certain symbolic value as a counterweight to the surrounding depravity. A number of the cycle's poems contrast those who wear jilbab with women who reveal their thighs or wear miniskirts. One poem asks whether jilbabs are more useful socially than pornography or corruption. The sense that the modern era is a new jahiliya arises from the litanies of present conditions that contradict all expectations, notions of propriety, and norms of society. Such rhetorical features do portray a world turned upside down, one of confusion and chaos. And indeed, a dominant image in the poems is that of a sea of Jilbabs struggling resolutely through a history that rejects them, embarking on a long journey of suffering, endurance, and love of God, but heading towards the day of judgment and reunion with the sweetness of Allah. The Jilbabs are seen as religious heroes under constant threat and harassment by a profane world.

Inscribed in these themes and conventions, it seems, is an already amalgamated discourse. It is rooted historically in both rural, traditionalist Islam and in the fervor of modernist reform Islam. With its Sufi undercurrents and communal solidarity, the discourse of traditionalist Islam is part of a way of life under singular stress, whose participants are being forced into a confrontation with threatening social changes. For its part, modernist reform Islam in Indonesia, which sought to combat the pernicious aspects of Western cultural influence by revitalizing Islam has, from the early decades of the twentieth century been the clearest proponent of the idea that women should veil, or at least cover their heads and hair (Nakamura 1980, 276). A part of this discourse, then, appropriates the symbol of women as a device. It reaches into the strongest, most private fantasies of a masculinist heterosexual society to mark the immorality of the other. Not surprisingly, there is also a link to nationalist notions of gender here, notions that place women as bearers of cultural tradition. Such an idea is directly equated with the Jilbabs in the fourth poem of the cycle.

Yet *Lautan Jilbab*, whether from the point of view of traditionalist or modernist Muslims, is more than a simple, conservative response of fear and rage towards a profane modernity, a modernity that, it must be admitted, certainly possesses its horrors. Like many modernists, Nadjib is not advocating that women be kept in the home. The persecution of jilbab-clad women as well as their being expelled from school, are events that spurred the composition of the cycle. Similarly, Nadjib would certainly not advocate that women be kept off the stage. I will now turn to the stage versions of *Lautan Jilbab* and their engagement with the Muslim community—and the broader Indonesian national political stage.

Art that "Mingles" with Its Audience

Nadjib's experiments with poetry readings, backed by an often startling and raucous use of a Javanese gamelan orchestra as well as his marked tendency to insert political criticism into his plays and poetry (Massardi 1980, 38), earned him rebukes from some arts critics and writers for obscuring the literary value of his poems with music, or for tarnishing his work with political slogans. Nadjib's characteristic response was to argue that the boundaries of artistic genres and categories such as "literary value" were never clear or pure. The important thing was to contribute to the creation of a better society, and for that it was necessary that literature "mingle" with its community, communicate with it and be altered, improved, and enriched by this process (Nadjib 1984a, 76–82; Nadjib 1984b, 238–44). The process of writing, staging, and rewriting the play *Lautan Jilbab* is a striking realization of Nadjib's ideas.

Lautan Jilbab was converted into theatrical form beginning in July 1988 and first performed as a play on September 10–11 of the same year. The process by which the poem cycle was transformed into a stage performance is in itself important. In early 1988, a campus Islamic student organization, Jamaah Shalahuddin from Gajah Mada University (UGM) in Yogyakarta, had invited Nadjib and several collaborators to give a *pesantren seni* (Islamic boarding school for art). In early June, several participants in this workshop asked Nadjib to write a script for the first attempt of Sanggar Shalahuddin, Jamaah Shalahuddin's new theatrical group, to perform theater. He responded by constructing his script on the *Lautan Jilbab* poetic cycle (Field Notes 10 June 1988).[7]

The play's first performances in Yogyakarta in September drew record crowds for a modern-style theatrical performance—5000 over two nights. This record attendance was certainly due in large part to the fact that it was a Sanggar Shalahuddin production involving a group of Muslim students from an active campus organization, part of a much larger activist Muslim community on campus. That theater performance was a new, and sometimes controversial, kind of venture for a Muslim group may have stimulated additional interest. The fact that the play drew such a large crowd established a kind of "buzz" of excitement, but it also confirmed the tantalizing potential of its mode of performance—that of involving local Muslim students and thus creating new participants who in turn would attract new audiences, composed of local friends, family, and networks. In these two ways, the play's Yogyakarta success laid the groundwork for the play's future triumphs as well.

The play was performed in the East Javanese city of Malang in December 1988, Ujung Pandang in South Sulawesi in August 1989, in Yogya once more in April 1991, then in Madiun later that same month. It was mounted for the final time in August of the same year in Surabaya, the great port metropolis of East Java (*Masa Kini* 9 Sept. 1988; Kertaraharja 1988; *Pedoman Rakyat* 10 Aug. 1989; *Fajar* 10 Aug. 1989; *Kedaulatan Rakyat* 20 Aug. 1989; Sofian et al. 1989; *Suara Merdeka* 27 April 1991; *Surabaya Post* 28, 29 April 1991; *Jawa Pos* 28, 29 April 1991; *Surabaya Minggu* 1st week of May 1991; *Surabaya Post* 13 Aug. 1991; *Jawa Pos* 13, 14 Aug. 1991; Hartoyo 1991). At every performance the work involved local Muslim students and drew remarkable numbers of people.[8] In response to criticism as well as to insert material about current national and local events into the text, Nadjib rewrote the play at each new staging. In this section, I will describe the first version of the play, then discuss how the script changed from the first to the last version, in order to demonstrate how the process of performing and rewriting the play displays a dialogic kind of interaction between cultural workers and their "audience."

Unlike most modern plays up to that time, the first version of *Lautan Jilbab*, as staged Yogyakarta, has very little plot. The play consists of sections of rhapsodic poetry often taken word for word from the earlier poems, arguments about the appropriateness of wearing the jilbab, and long comedic sections commenting on contemporary politics. Following Nadjib's stage plan, director Agung Waskito divided the area into a central stage (on which the action occurred) and a "surrounding" area (in which actors not currently participating could sit or stand and watch the action). This positioning some actors as "spectators" at various times sought to blend the action/actors and the audience area proper in a *teater rakyat* (people's theater) style. It also served to demarcate an "ideal" space (the central stage) from an "everyday" space (Nadjib 1988).

Waskito had already had some experience as an actor with Teater Dinasti, and he had directed school theater groups, including a rather ambitious production of Arifin C Noer's *Kapai-kapai*. This particular production of *Lautan Jilbab* gave evidence of Waskito's talent for creating innovative stage tableaux for large numbers of people. It also suggested a potential for imaginative visualization of abstract concepts through use of blocking, costumes, and other elements of the mis-en-scene. In the first performance of *Lautan Jilbab* at the Gelanggang Mahasiswa UGM in Yogyakarta, Waskito was challenged to deploy and develop his skills, given a cast of around twenty-seven actors and the plotless, segmented nature of Nadjib's script. Working with Sapto Rahardjo's orchestration, which combined a synthesizer, electric keyboard, traditional instruments like the *kecapi*, and improvised metal can percussion (*Masa Kini* 9 Sept. 1988), he choreographed a varied series of visually interesting group movements (Kertarahardja 1988; Waskito, 1988).

A key change from poems to stage perhaps indicates a concession to the modernist aversion to Sufi ideas. It can be found in one alteration to the second poem of the cycle, which was also used in the play, namely, a vision of a sea of Jilbabs meeting with Allah on judgment day. In the original poem, one line reads: "Menyeru belaian tangan Kekasih" (Greet the caress of the Beloved). In the script for the first version, the line reads "Menyeru belaian kasihNya" (Greet the caress of His/Her love). Here, the Sufi notion of Allah as lover, possibly seen as blasphemous, has been modified to suggest simply that Allah loves the faithful.[9]

The poems chosen from the collection for inclusion in the play represent the Day of Judgment, show the purity and difficulty of young Jilbabs striving in a hostile society, and touch upon the meaning of the jilbab. Throughout the play, the jilbab is again represented as a prophylactic chosen to erect a physical barrier against profane modernity. Yet more importantly, in the first stage script, it is also seen as a spiritual and symbolic barrier against all the threats and invasions of that profane world. This distinction is significant. While in the poems there is a clear sense that the actual physical donning of the jilbab is important because it conceals a woman's body, in the first version of the play the idea of the jilbab as a symbol of commitment to spiritual striving, to purifying oneself, and to struggling toward God becomes more prominent. In the course of one of the arguments between the jilbab-clad women and their male interlocutors, Emha's script explicitly states that what matters is not so much the womens' physical appearance, but the process by which they determine their identity and position toward things. One of the Jilbabs declares, "Jilbab-clad women are not a symbol of oppression! Naked women are not a symbol of freedom!" A male youth replies, "But the opposite is also true, right! Naked women are not a symbol of oppression, jilbab-clad women are not a symbol of freedom." To which the Jilbabs reply, "So why are you getting so worked up?"

The debate sections also involve an argument between a father and his daughter over the dangerous nature of wearing a jilbab because it can be construed as a political statement, which is a perilous act in contemporary Indonesia according to the father. In this particular debate, the Jilbabs assert that children have the right to question and refute the views of their parents. This view, something that one would not expect if the play were to be dismissed as purely a threatened traditionalist response to modernity, matches Brenner's analysis of current young Muslim activists' attitudes. There are also clear signs of the social commitment for which Nadjib is so famous. As they were in the poems, at one point the Jilbabs are equated with the struggles of all the marginalized and oppressed groups in Indonesian society. Furthermore, the poems' reflections on the nature of the jilbab do not claim that Muslims should simply follow the teachings of the authorities, but that they should also depend upon their faith, conscience, and, crucially, their thought. In another passage falling in the *dagelan* or joking sections of the play (which present political commentary in the form of a comic dialogue between two angels), the Jilbabs argue that Muslims need to use their creativity to reach paradise. All of these elements suggest that Nadjib is not only articulating the discourses and concerns of rural-based traditionalist Islam and twentieth-century modernism, but he is also dialoguing with young Muslim activists. As Brenner suggests, they are the generally more urban-based, more pluralistic, democracy-oriented neo-modernists who stress critical interpretation of the sacred texts, advocate democratic relations in society, and place the core of religious teachings above specific details of practice and ritual.

The dagelan joking sections featuring the two angels are fascinating in their own right. Based upon Central Javanese joking styles, these scenes rely upon the slippage of meaning from one key word to another. This technique of reading between the lines of official statements by twisting the meanings of government euphemisms is used with devastating effect to undercut official pronouncements. A special target of the angel's commentaries is the official national ideology, Pancasila. Pancasila is so powerful an ideology, one angel declares, that everyone should be *forced* to follow it. Much is made of the power of Pancasila: God has even been made subservient to it, a comment that clearly refers to the *Asas Tunggal* law. Other political comments were specifically designed to engage with the mainly university-related crowd attending the Yogya performances.

This last point suggests how the group's work was constantly changing and incorporating new material that its members assumed would appeal to particular audiences. At each new performance, the play was altered. The blocking and movements had to be adjusted by Waskito at every step of the way to accommodate increasingly large numbers of performers, and Sapto Rahardjo continuously revised the score. The alterations in Nadjib's script, however, appear to be the most context-oriented element. In Ujung Pandang (Makassar) in August 1989, for example, given the local Muslim population's concern about young couples living together out of wedlock, *Lautan Jilbab* contained a section about a pregnant young Jilbab whose child would have no legal father. This version also criticized sending girls wearing jilbabs home from school and the state-sponsored lottery, SDSB, whose revocation would become a cause celèbre for Muslim activists about two years later (*Kedaulatan Rakyat* 20 Aug. 1989; Heryanto 1996, 258–59).

The version performed at Madiun in April 1991 included a prayer of thanks for the government's recent repeal of the regulation forbidding girls to wear the jilbab to public schools (Triyanto et al. 1991, 76–77; Triyanto, Nugroho, and Fadjri 1991, 100). In addition to criticizing the continued existence of the state lottery this version also touched upon issues like the Bank Duta corruption scandal and the *Monitor* media case of the previous November, in which many felt Islam had been insulted (*Surabaya Post* 28 April 1991). Still the various versions of the plays not only commented on the sensitivities of the Indonesian Muslim community, they also became the target of criticism engendered by such sensitivities. Nadjib and *Lautan Jilbab* thus became part of a long process of debate about the propriety of Islamic art and culture.

Modern Islamic Literature and Theater In Indonesia

A long-standing tradition within Islam, based mainly on verse 227 of Sura 26 of the *Qur'an* ("Poets are followed by erring men. Behold how aimlessly they rove in every valley, preaching what they never practice."[10]), held that poetry was evil and sinful activity ill-suited for honest, industrious Muslims (Schimmel 1982, 12–13; Kratz 1986, 62). Despite the fact that the next verse of the same Sura could be interpreted to admit that there are exceptions (Kratz 1986, 62) and despite the existence of a long and remarkable tradition of Islamic poetry dating back to the companions of the Prophet himself, these notions of poetry as evil remained common among Muslims in the Dutch East Indies during the late colonial period.

In the 1930s, modernists who wished to use modern media to spread a revitalized Islam and counter what they perceived to be the pernicious effects of the onslaught of modern, Western culture on traditional society and morality were continually in the difficult position of arguing both against the colonial order and the bad aspects of modernization (which it was seemingly encouraging) and against Muslims who, relying on traditional assumptions about appropriate behavior or selective and narrowly literal readings of the scriptures, held that modernist novelists such as Hamka were "Obscene Kyai" or pornographers. Islamic novelists countered by claiming that modern literature was a new way of propagating the faith: it should not simply be seen as propaganda but should strive for aesthetic value as well (Kratz 1986, 64–66).

During the 1960s, Islamic theater was briefly cultivated in a number of cities, in part in response to the rapid politicization of the entire cultural arena under Sukarno's Guided Democracy. At this point, Islamic literature and theater were seen by many Muslims as vital to the defense of Islamic values against the onslaught of communism and secular nationalism (Federspiel 1973, 413–15; Sumardjo 1992, 169–71). However, though successful in capturing the imagination of many Muslims throughout Central and East Java, the best known of the Muslim theater groups of the time, Teater Muslim, often encountered criticism from within the Muslim community. As Teater Muslim's leader, Muhammad Diponegoro, noted in the post-play discussions, audience members inevitably would question the group on the basis that it allowed adult women to appear on stage. Diponegoro argued that this was one sign that the Muslim community needed to be educated about the values, purposes, and uses of art (Diponegoro 1983, 60–63).

According to the common pattern, then, certain segments of the Muslim community, in criticizing literature or theater, mobilized discourses based upon issues of gender and sexual morality. Muslim artists, therefore, needed to defend art's ability to convey specifically Islamic messages and ideals, while at the same time trying to address concerns about the "autonomy" of art and aesthetics, questions particular to a modern, secular idea of art. Muslim cultural workers had to look over both shoulders, as it were, toward both the realm of urban, internationalized high art and the traditional and puritanical segments (which do not necessarily coincide) within the Muslim community.

As early as 1980, Nadjib had already entered this field of discussion, agreeing with Hamka and Diponegoro that literature was a possible vessel for Islamic *dakwah* (proselytizing, raising awareness), but cautioning doctrinaire ulama that spontaneity should not be crushed by the burden of the message. Dakwah had to be skillful, shrewd, and artistic, and the psychology of the performance event needed to be taken into account (Nadjib 1980, 42). Like others before him, Nadjib seemed to be balancing between conservative Islamic desires for a clearly moral and educational art and modern notions of the importance of aesthetics. Yet he was also plainly committed to art as a political intervention and a social process.

The nature of the interaction between Nadjib and his collaborators and the audience is difficult to determine with precision. A few scattered comments in newspaper reports on the performances suggest the group's work was met with great enthusiasm. Clearly, the participation of large numbers of Muslim students in many of the performances also indicates that many Muslims were supportive and even enthusiastic about being involved in such Islamic cultural and artistic practices. In similar fashion, the large numbers of people who came to witness the performances suggest their powerful attraction. Nadjib and his collaborators, as well as some of the play's sponsors in the cities where it was performed, spoke of the play as demonstrating that theater could be a powerful new medium for dakwah, raising the Muslim community's artistic capacities.[11] Some audience members felt the play even taught them about the *duty* of Muslim women to wear the jilbab (Sofian et al. 1989). But certainly, not all of the feedback was positive. In Ujung Pandang, young Muslims in the audience criticized the play for containing what they deemed "un-Islamic" elements, such as dancing, rock music, and men and women together (Sofian et al. 1989). Upon returning to Yogya, Nadjib, as though echoing Mohammad Diponegoro, wrote a column for a newspaper stating that this paranoia about men and women mingling was one of the greatest obstacles facing the development of a truly vital Islamic culture (Nadjib 1989b). The criticisms did not stop, however. At the Madiun performance, as related previously, accusations of "un-Islamic" elements again arose (*Surabaya Post* 29 April 1991; *Karya Darma* 1 May 1991).

Clearly responding to all of this, in the last version of the play performed at Surabaya in August 1991, the theme of the jilbab became less central in the dialogue sections since the government had meanwhile relented and promulgated a law allowing girls to wear jilbab to school. The customary political humor was now trained even more pointedly on government "double-speak," bureaucratic-authoritarian hierarchical thinking, the police permit system for theater, and gentle pokes at then-Minister of Technology Habibie's plans to erect nuclear power plants in Indonesia, while the dialogue sections accordingly focused more on what Nadjib perceived to be the obstinacy, lack of imagination, and dogmatism of the Islamic community in relation to art and politics. This script included several debates about the nature of proper Islamic art, and it clearly advocated allowing all sorts of performances and other events to be staged in mosques as a way of making them cultural centers attractive to all. The basic problem is stated quite early in the play. In response to the Poet's surprise that people are dancing in the mosque courtyard, the following exchange occurs:

> FIRST DANCER: Dancing isn't prohibited either you know, Mas Poet. There once was a friend of the Prophet who, out of pure joy at hearing the beauty of the Prophet's speech, spontaneously began to sing verses of poetry and to dance. The Prophet didn't prohibit it—in fact he smiled and enjoyed it.
> THE POET: But this is Indonesia, youngster, remember? You have to be careful. At the mosque you don't laugh, you don't clap your hands, and you certainly don't dance.[12]

Nadjib's advocacy of a more open attitude comes across clearly. Earlier in the very same scene, the head of a local Tasyakuran committee (which wants to celebrate the government's decision to "liberate the Jilbabs"), remarks:

> As we've all agreed, we have to make the mosque a more cultural place. We must turn the mosque into a place that makes people happy,

that attracts their attention and stimulates the love of all Muslim youth for a healthy, quality life.

The mosque is the cutting edge for deepening the faith. The mosque has to be able to speak beautifully of Allah's teachings, which transcend all other beauty. The mosque must never be boring, don't let its atmosphere become dry. Each and every activity has to make all Muslim men and women feel completely at home, while making those friends who aren't Muslims yet feel that they really, really want to get involved in what's going on.[13]

In the play's third scene, the "poet" figure upbraids members of the Muslim community for wanting only to criticize others' cultural efforts, while never doing anything themselves, and indeed, for not having many clear goals or strategies for achieving those goals they do have. A debate in scene five also ridicules the notion that Islamic art should not criticize the Muslim community but should show only good examples.

This final version of *Lautan Jilbab*, then, contained Nadjib's most vivid expression of his frustration with the Muslim community's stance toward culture and the arts. Such debates also indicate the presence of another discourse, one that prompted the Islamic theater group's efforts in the first place and that continued to haunt them throughout the three years they worked together on specifically Islamic theater. In scene five of this final version, during the course of one of the comic debates undertaken by two *malaikat* (angels), one of the angels states: "Even about art the Muslims bicker endlessly. Others already control television, the stage, the market for cassettes, the advertisements lined up the length of the street, newspapers, magazines—and they're still making a racket about looking for the definition of Islamic art. And these people want to achieve economic 'take off'! Advancing to greet the 21st Century! The era of industrialization!"[14]

From other passages in the play, it is evident that Nadjib abhors the crass materialism encouraged by the New Order government's own programs and attitudes. He feels it to be taking control of Indonesian culture. In scene two, for example, several characters mock the poet figure for reciting poetry about such "arcane" things as the field on which the Last Judgment will be enacted. According to them, at a time when Indonesia is

Fig. 3.1. *Lautan Jilbab*, "Pak Takmir" in the Surabaya Performance. Photo courtesy of the *Surabaya Post* (13 August 1991).

about to enter the government's second long-term development phase, something more concrete is required. Though the poet agrees that he too would like to write about "development" within the context of the play, he maintains that those who have no time for his more religious poetry, who chase after material progress while belittling the spiritual dimensions of life, appear to be one symptom of the moral corruption of society. In the angel's comments about the divisive bickering about culture indulged in by Muslims, at a time when others control the media that exert such widespread influence, we can detect Nadjib's desire to use an Islamic counter-mass-media to combat the secular mass media that constitute one locus of the crass materialism he finds so destructive.[15]

Materialism, Family and Morality, the New Order State, and Islamic Aesthetics in the Group's Other Plays

This concern with crass materialism and the pernicious effect of the mass media, which spreads desire for materialistic hedonism, was also a major theme in two other productions undertaken by Nadjib's group: Agung Waskito's *Dajjal* (Tempter at the End of Days, 1989) and Nadjib's *Keluarga Sakinah* (The Virtuous Family, 1990). Yet the attack against materialism and a perceived loss of a moral/ethical/religious compass with which Indonesians might navigate the straits of modern society is first and foremost a critique of the New Order government and its version of development, which is represented as an oppressive imitator of Western development.

Agung Waskito's *Dajjal*[16] was the second play the group performed, again working with the Sanggar Shalahuddin of Gajah Mada University. It shares a number of common concerns and features with *Lautan Jilbab*. Unlike the latter, *Dajjal* does feature a rough storyline, though the story is quite simple and is often overshadowed by a cabaret-style presentation much like that of *Lautan Jilbab*. This style combines *Qori* (chorus members) chanting specific Quranic verses with a number of actors commenting *en masse* on contemporary social issues and alluding to social problems in a Central Javanese joking style known as *dagelan mataram*. In it the thing being discussed becomes a kind of elaborate comic metaphor for something else that cannot be so openly talked about. Similarly, like *Lautan Jilbab*, *Dajjal* is a play conceived in the apocalyptic mode.

The text of the play uses the figure of the *dajjal*, traditionally conceived as an evil tempter appearing before and signalling the approach of the last judgment and the end of time. In the actual performance, the dajjal was represented by a huge head in the upper background of the stage. It possessed a glowing fanged mouth and one good eye (its materialistic eye) that emitted a bright light that at times literally, as well as symbolically, blinds the audience to spiritual values with "material desire." The play's music, again composed by Sapto Rahardjo, opened with oppressive and frightening tones, complementing the first appearance of the dajjal and the blinding light of its eye. Screams and moans of suffering issued from a group of men and women wearing jilbabs (in this case meaning veil-like gunny sacks), with ropes tied about their necks. They became symbols of the way in which the material world has enslaved modern Indonesians (video performance of *Dajjal*). The language of the play also often reaches an apocalyptic crescendo in describing the present in terms of the filth and corruption of a humanity mired in materialism and rationalistic arrogance and in the belief that it can solve any problem. Later in the play, this age is also referred to as the return of the *jaman jahiliya* (jahiliya times).

Ostensibly, all of this symbolism is connected to the domination of the "East" by "Western nations," in keeping with a long-standing Orientalist discourse picked up with a vengeance by some nationalists in the early decades of the twentieth century. This discourse maintained that the natures of "East" and "West" were different and unchanging. The West was equated with rationality and technological and social progress, while the East was considered to be spiritually rich but socially and technologically backwards (Mihardja 1986 [1948]). The play richly describes what the dajjal has wrought: technological wonders such as flying to other planets and monitoring the galaxy, but also weapons of mass destruction that throw all spiritual values into confusion. This identification of materialism and spiritual barrenness/moral decay with modern Western culture becomes quite obvious, as does its dissemination through Western political and economic dominance throughout the world of nations (1–2). This linkage is confirmed later in the play. In the early scenes, the Cinde Tua character tells his pupil that mainly *faranji*, including Indonesian faranji, have embraced the dajjal of materialism as their god, but in the closing scenes, the word faranji is equated with the European colonial powers whose brilliant minds have awed many Indonesians (36). The businessman Amsyo, too, has previously said, "Aku anak negeri. Aku bukan bangsa faranji" (I'm a child of this nation. I'm not one of the faranji–(29). Thus, *Dajjal* presents a vision of Westernized modernization and thus, globalization, as a process that destroys humanity through material greed and spiritual degradation.

Yet the play's plot, along with much of the serial comments on politics and joking, are directed at conditions in contemporary Indonesia. The play situates Amsyo and his spoiled, pouting wife as paragons of New Order society. They are materialistic, greedy, and will stop at nothing, including violently evicting their fellow citizens from legally owned land in order to obtain what they want. Although Amsyo is a businessman, he is in fact represented more as a conflation of New Order businessman and bureaucrat. He not only works closely with local officials at the site of his future satellite-city development, bribing them when appropriate, but he also gives voice to the rhetoric of the security-conscious New Order state with its top-down vision and obsession with the outward, material manifestations of modernization. In the closing scenes, his speech about the world he will create is a cynical comment on the perceived ideals of New Order leaders at the time the play was written. It portrays an Indonesia in which Amsyo himself will rule arbitrarily, locking every mouth shut, creating a social stability without protests or demonstrations because everyone does what they are told and the thoughts and sensitivities of youths are tightly controlled and shaped. A later scene visually cements this dimension of Amsyo's representation. The suffering victims from the opening scene emerge, pulling Amsyo's cart by the ropes tied around their necks. Here, materialism and arbitrary power combine in one powerful image, demonstrating that "globalization" in the text and performance of *Dajjal* is primarily, though certainly not exclusively, an opportunity to critique the Indonesian state and the "Westernized" society it has created.

Waskito's *Dajjal*, then, reconfigures, expands, and foregrounds some of the feelings of anti-materialism as well as the critique of the New Order's version of a modern society tied to anti-Western sentiments and notions already introduced in the jahiliya of Nadjib's poem cycle, which also persisted in the stage versions of *Lautan Jilbab*. Ironically, this critique of corrosive, Western materialism and rationalistic modernization, as selectively imposed upon Indonesia by the New Order, takes the form of a Western-derived stage presentation. Though the "Western" origin of the form is once again heavily inflected by local traditions and needs (for example, many of the characters are still marked by stylized movements reminiscent of traditional *wayang wong*[17] performance), even these harsh critics of Western modernity felt the need to construct a more modern form of counter discourse.

Such an impetus lay behind the analyses of several critics as well. For instance, Ahmadun Y. Herfanda and Nur Sahid tried to use the play to demonstrate a set of Islamic counter-aesthetics (Herfanda, 1989; Sahid, 1989). Herfanda, for example, saw in *Dajjal* an exemplar of modern Islamic art based holistically upon three interconnected values: beauty (aesthetic value), truth (commitment to Islamic law), and goodness (social usefulness). In contrast, he pointed to Western art, in which beauty and aesthetic values could be separated from other values, as in *l'art pour l'art*. Then, tapping into the discourse on sexual morality, which I have shown to be at work in Nadjib's poem cycle and dramatic version of *Lautan Jilbab*, Herfanda privileges "Islamic aesthetics," suggesting that such "Western" style "permissiveness" sanctioned the appearance of half-naked women on stage.

These recurrent images also link the reviews of *Dajjal* to another of the group's plays, *Keluarga Sakinah*. Written by Nadjib and directed once again by Waskito, this play was performed from 16–19 December 1990, for the 42nd Congress of the Islamic modernist organization Muhammadiyah.[18] *Keluarga Sakinah*, like *Dajjal*, unfolds in cabaret-like format around a simple plot. Full of songs and mass dance scenes, performed mainly by local Muslim school girls in white jilbab, and featuring extended comic exchanges between male and female "narrators," *Keluarga Sakinah* tells the story of a teenage boy who is alienated from his modern professional parents, who are too busy to give him proper love, attention, and discipline, and a girl whom he rapes and who becomes pregnant. The play poses this dilemma: should the boy, Dodi, be dragged before the courts or should he be forgiven as long as he admits his fault and endeavors to reform himself.

Taking a thematic approach that clearly resonates with other plays the group has created and performed, *Keluarga Sakinah* attributes the misbehavior of youth to the neglect of parents who are too wrapped up in modernized life-styles, but also to pornographic and permissive "Westernized" culture, in whose movies and magazines women's "private parts are revealed and put on display."[19] Once more, the play's content was geared specifically to the audience. The play was organized to coincide with the Muhammadiyah Congress of Aisyiyah, the Muhammadiyah women's auxiliary organization. Catering to middle-class modernist Muslims, it took up family themes such as what a good family should be and what causes the current breakdown in families and the attendant youth problems.

Islamic Commercial Culture vs. Grassroots Empowerment

The work of Nadjib and his collaborators was, in fact, intended as one possible antidote to what they viewed as the prevailing profane condition of culture. Ironically, however, and as is often the case, the antidote was closely related to the poison itself. As each new staging of *Lautan Jilbab* occurred, the scale of the productions grew, ticket prices rose, and the status

Fig. 3.2. *Keluarga Sakinah*. Photo courtesy of *Bernas* (20 December 1990)

of Nadjib as a nationally known, media-star figure in his own right was played upon and elaborated. In the same vein, for the Madiun and Surabaya performances of 1991, nationally known film and rock stars Neno Warisman and Gito Rollies, whose readings of Nadjib's poetry or singing of his song lyrics were inserted into the fabric of the play, were added to enhance the events. Publicity dwelled upon these guest stars, and media reports marvelled that *Lautan Jilbab* and Islamic culture actually could draw such attention and huge audiences. The attendance statistics for the play's performances were compared to commercial rock concerts.[20]

Nadjib was aware of the problem of becoming a pop idol. Though he did not necessarily resolve the contradiction of using his own celebrity to market the play, in the final Surabaya stagings, the script presents a poet character who, much like Nadjib himself, speaks about contemporary social problems and defends the mosque youth's right to hold activities without government permits. But the poet character eventually acts like a crazy man in order to avoid being idolized by the youth and to force them to rely on themselves.

Other elements, beyond the attempt to fight profane consumer culture on its own ground, were also at work in the Yogya group's pattern of performance. Nadjib had long had links to NGOs and to the cultural movement that had pioneered grassroots theater techniques as a means of democratizing culture, building solidarity, and raising critical awareness of the oppressive effects of existing social structures. While not exactly duplicating the techniques of such grassroots efforts, from August 1989 on, it is clear from his statements to the newspapers that Nadjib and his collaborators saw their theater productions as a possible means for building self-sufficient, independent Muslim cultural groups. In each instance, groups of young local Muslims interested in culture were involved in the productions, which also increasingly took on the character of mass spectacles.[21] In part, the hope was that those involved would build a vital local group after the performances were over. Nadjib explained his group's objective as making Muslims subjects rather than objects of their own culture, to use Freirian cultural liberation terminology (*Surabaya Post* 27 April 1991). This objective prompted the final words of the last version of *Lautan Jilbab*, "Let's carry on by ourselves" (*Kita teruskan sendiri!*).

Furthermore, the Yogya group was also attempting to balance its modern "media marketing" and publicity "gimmicks" with a commitment to "traditional" and "Islamic" culture, all folded, perhaps a bit uncomfortably, into one modernized cultural package. As mentioned above, Nadjib's poetry contained traditional Sufi elements, which the vocal music of *Lautan Jilbab* seconded through its use of Islamic *zikir* (chanted prayers). Prior to the last performance of the play in Surabaya, composer Sapto Rahardjo admitted to being preoccupied with the idea of blending traditional music with sophisticated modern technologies and instruments in order to demonstrate that Muslim culture had not been left behind by modernity (*Jawa Pos* 12 Aug. 1991; *Memorandum* 12 Aug. 1991). In line with such aims, and possibly in the hope of balancing the presence of the modern rock musician Gito Rollies, the group mobilized various emblems of traditional Indonesian Muslim culture for the final performance. These emblems included the incorporation of ten *bedug* drums and a *samroh*[22] chorus into the play and its soundscape (*Surabaya Post* 13 Aug. 1991). Jujuk Prabowo and Whani Darmawan, two of a team of four co-directors who replaced Waskito for the Surabaya performances, also added combinations of traditional dance movements from Aceh and East Java in order to "enrich the movements and body rhythms" of the performers (*Surabaya Post* 11 Aug. 1991). In these ways, the experiments of the Yogya group surrounding Nadjib also found confluences with the efforts of much of Indonesian national art theater from 1968 to the late 1980s to root a Western-derived theater practice in local idiom.

All of this activity should also be seen against the background of a growing middle-class consumer market tied to the increase in identification with Islam. Dangdut (see note 11, chapter 2) star Rhoma Irama, a dedicated Muslim whose lyrics often reflected that commitment, had become Indonesian pop-music's first superstar in the 1970s and had made some inroads in creating an image of modern, mass Islamically oriented culture (Frederick 1982; Lockhard 1998, 94–105). By the early 1990s, popular Muslim preachers such as Jakarta-based Zainuddin MZ were able to sell large quantities of their lectures in cassette form (*Tempo* 2 April 1988, 43). There were signs that other business-people were interested in encouraging and getting in on this trend. Setiawan Djody, a high-flying business figure with connections to the presidential family, and himself an aspiring electric guitarist, followed up on the *Lautan Jilbab* phenomenon by joining pop stars Iwan Fals and Sawung Jabo and the poet Rendra to create a mass event billed as the *Kantata Taqwa* or Cantata of Devotion in Jakarta's Senayan Stadium in June 1990 (*Editor* 23 June 1990, 11–12). The trend was further elaborated by the participation of Djody, Rendra, Rhoma Irama, and Zainuddin MZ in a *Tablig Akbar* (Great Religious Meeting) in January 1992 in the Senayan parking area, which may well have been connected to the efforts of the ruling party, Golkar, to win the hearts and minds of the Indonesian Muslim community (*Editor* 25 January 1992, 11–15). Djody was also negotiating with Nadjib in August 1991 to bring *Lautan Jilbab* to Jakarta, a deal that eventually seems to have fallen through (*Jawa Pos* 9 Aug. 1991; *Jawa Pos* 16 August, 1991).

Lautan Jilbab *on the National Stage*

The presence of Djody in the wings of the Surabaya performances of *Lautan Jilbab* also points to a particular intersection of business and top-level political interest in the phenomenon. After all, Djody's comments following the Surabaya performances not only touched upon the play's suitability for performance in Jakarta, for which he was willing to offer financial backing, but also praised Nadjib for being clever enough to "neutralize" his play's sharp criticisms.[23] Such comments hint yet again at the persistence of the New Order government's preferred set of norms and sense of taste, especially in regard to theatrical social criticism, as detailed in chapter 1.

Indeed, the Indonesian power structure seems to have followed the Islamic theater/culture trend with unusual interest. Given the Suharto regime's strategy of courting Islam as a counterbalance to the military, coupled with Nadjib's stature as a prominent Islamic cultural figure and the huge crowds the Yogya group's productions attracted, this interest appears logical. Following the first performance of *Lautan Jilbab* in Yogyakarta, Waskito and the Sanggar Shalahuddin group were invited to work together with members of the Indonesian Military Academy in Magelang, Central Java, in order to put on a joint performance of an Islamic-oriented play titled *Abu Zar al-Ghifari* (Waskito 1989). In Ujung Pandang in August of 1989, the local military commander gave his personal permission for the play, which was performed in the military's own hall, while the cast and crew were housed in a local military complex (Nadjib 1989b).

The financial support received from B. J. Habibie for the second night's sound system in Madiun is another startling piece of evidence of top-level attention to *Lautan Jilbab* (*Jawa Pos* 29 April 1991). Minister Habibie's support may well have been another sign of government attempts to co-opt Islam. Nadjib, long critical of the New Order, was at the time campaigning (unsuccessfully, in the end) within ICMI, the organization of Muslim intellectuals that Habibie led, to have it intervene on behalf of displaced peasants in the Kedung Ombo land seizure case (a World Bank/Indonesian government joint project). Nonetheless, local police saw fit to censor the Madiun version of the play in a demonstration of a more typical kind of New Order "interest" in national art theater.

The Surabaya version of *Lautan Jilbab* included a scene in which police arrive to ban the mosque youth's celebration, a gesture that might have found at least partial consensus among Islamic critics of Nadjib's vision of a joyous, critical Islamic art. This scene, apparently, was cut during the

Figs. 3.3 and 3.4. Two programs showing the increasing commercialization of the productions of Nadjib and his collaborating groups and sponsors. The first is from late 1990, while the second is from the final Surabaya performance of *Lautan Jilbab* in August 1991.

Madiun performances, supposedly to shorten the play. Whether or not the Madiun police objected to it in particular is unclear (*Surabaya Post* 28, 29 Apr. 1991). Certainly, the scene as performed in Surabaya could also be viewed as a commentary on what had happened in Madiun.

The Surabaya performance was remarkable for another reason as well. The play received the full support not only of regional military commander, General R. Hartono (a Suharto loyalist, who later was to rise in the ranks to become Chief of Staff of the Armed Forces and eventually Minister of Information and a rival of Habibie for the Vice-Presidency in 1998) but also of other government-related figures (e.g., the head of Golkar's regional branch, the head of the regional police, and the head of the government-sponsored Council of Indonesian Ulama [*Surabaya Post* 11 Aug. 1991]). Hartono, identified as strongly Muslim, wrote a greeting for the play's performance program. In it, not only did Hartono adopt the stance of concerned protector of the faith, advising the group to make a good showing in the name of Islam, but rhetorically he also tried to suggest that the play supported national development (Pagelaran Drama Kolosal *Lautan Jilbab* 1991). Following the play, Hartono praised the depth of its Islamic content, but momentarily becoming an paternalistic art critic, so typical of New Order officialdom, he asked that the play's scenes not be organized in such a choppy fashion (*Surabaya Post* 13 Aug. 1991).

In the midst of so much government attention, it is likely that the performances of *Lautan Jilbab* provided additional impetus for the government to rescind its regulation prohibiting the jilbab from being worn in public schools, and to abolish its national sports lottery. Still, despite creating a powerful nexus for diverse Muslim dreams and desires through its work, the Yogya group walked a fine line. This balancing act became evident only days after the Surabaya performances of *Lautan Jilbab*, when Nadjib withdrew from ICMI in protest over its refusal to take serious action on the Kedung Ombo issue. Almost immediately, Nadjib was banned from speaking in Central Java.

As Hatley has noted, as a result of a number of factors, the group's activities came to an abrupt halt after the 1991 Surabaya performance. Nadjib had become discouraged by the lack of support from ulama and tolerance for theater only as long as it presented religious messages. His conflict with ICMI may well have diverted some of his energies at that juncture. He and Waskito had also experienced a period of personal tension. Waskito had gone to Sulawesi for a time, expressing a desire to work on new projects, specifically, several non-religious plays (Hatley 2008, 153). Still, for a brief three years, this group had helped foster one of the most spectacular popularly received flowerings of modern national theater to date.

Cultural Products as Social Articulations

The work of Nadjib and his collaborators on the serial performances of *Lautan Jilbab*, along with *Dajjal* and *Keluarga Sakinah*, represents something quintessential about cultural products. The way in which Nadjib, Waskito, Rahardjo, and the various actors, at the request of Sanggar Shalahuddin, created the work, then changed and adapted it to different audiences and circumstances, suggests something of the way all theater pieces and, in general, works of art are formed out of many processes. As we have seen, these include several systems of ideas, aesthetic concepts, formal devices and structures, social discourses, political debates and contexts, expectations regarding the intended audience, as well as feedback from audiences as individuals and as groups, both during and after performances. The willingness of its creators to continually change and adapt the text and performance of *Lautan Jilbab* merely facilitates our recognition of the presence of such a diversity of processes working beneath the surface of each text/performance.

The success of *Lautan Jilbab*, *Dajjal*, and *Keluarga Sakinah* can be accounted for by a combination of factors. The plays incorporated traditionalist poetic tropes of God as beloved and the ocean to which Muslims seek return. It also took up themes associated with modernist and neo-modernist strands of Indonesian Islam, such as the issue of women wearing veils and the need for Muslims to exercise all their creativity and critical thought to meet the challenges of the times. The plays thus offered wide religious resonances. But there was more to their appeal. These works caught the temper of the times for many young Muslim Indonesians in their criticism of New Order society and the version of modernity it proffered to Indonesians as well as the New Order's handling of religious and social issues. In addition, the plays presented these criticisms in a distinctively vibrant and attractive modern form, using music, comedy, group movement on stage, as well as bare-bones moralistic social parables. The strategy of involving groups of local Muslim youth in productions was equally important in attracting huge crowds and reflected a different kind of legacy of grassroots theater.

The plays in effect rode a wave of Islamic resurgence and mounting social disaffection, slaking a public thirst for vital and lively Islamic artistic expressions while at the same time offering familiar discourses and images, packaged in an exciting new way, to a variety of Indonesian Muslims. Furthermore, as cultural products produced and "consumed" by certain segments of society, either by direct "consumption" (reading the poetry, listening to it, or watching a play) or through second-hand "consumption" (through word of mouth, media reports and the like), these products themselves contributed to the articulation of other social processes and structures. The Yogyakarta group's work affected Indonesian society a number of ways: by increasing excitement about Islamic culture, contributing to ideas of Islamic aesthetics, involving large numbers of youth in artistic expressions, deepening some audience members' understanding of their faith, and adding to pressure on the government to change specific policies.

At the same time, they also projected the image of the New Order as being on the wrong track in developing Indonesian society. This image resonated with those pursuing grassroots theater as well as with two avant-garde groups operating in Jakarta, which put their distinctive stamp on modern theater for years to come.

Chapter 4

TEATER SAE, TEATER KUBUR, AND AVANT-GARDE PERFORMANCES OF URBAN ALIENATION

At the same time that Nadjib was writing scripts critical of the Suharto regime for Teater Dinasti, composing his *Lautan Jilbab* poem cycle, and developing it into a popular stage performance, a very different kind of theater was taking shape among members of a young generation of theater workers in Jakarta. This theater was in part a response to some of the same conditions that had helped stimulate the brief florescence of Islamic theater created by Nadjib and his Yogyakarta collaborators. If the Yogya group was attempting to revitalize Islamic cultural life in the face of profane, commercialized culture, the journey to prominence in the world of modern Indonesian theater of groups like Teater Sae and Teater Kubur was also in no small part spurred by feelings of alienation from a modern urban space, including the increasing inundation of the social imaginary with commercialized images from television, films, newspapers, magazines, and mass advertising. The commercialized images that buffeted urbanites in Indonesia often seemed distant from the everyday reality of those group members who hailed from lower and lower-middle-class *kampung* (neighborhoods, slums) while offering their middle-class and intellectualized participants empty or too narrow visions of identity. At the same time, the pace of life grew faster, harsher, and less comfortable for those used to the slower rhythms and tightly knit solidarity that could sometimes characterize kampung and even middle-class existence. Implicit in much of the theater developed by these groups was a critique of the New Order government and its politics, as these related to the daily struggles and search for meaningful identities of a range of Jakarta's inhabitants from the middle to lower classes, though there were also moments of more direct social criticism.

Like *Lautan Jilbab*, the defining works of avant-garde groups like Sae and Kubur were chiefly non-narrative. Yet there were crucial thematic and stylistic differences between the Jakarta avant-garde groups of the late 1980s and 1990s and the Yogyakarta Islamic theater groups of the same period. Instead of interrogating faith and religious practices in relation to state power and commercial culture, the new theater appearing in Jakarta was more focused on issues such as urban alienation and the heavy weight of national histories and ideologies upon individual identities. Formally, the performances of this avant-garde were characterized by disjuncture and fragmentation. They emphasized poetic yet spare visualizations of everyday life and extreme emotional reactions to the constraints of urban conditions. In contrast to the theater of Nadjib and company, the work of these pioneering urban avant-garde groups was formed at the intersection of high-art-inspired artistic experimentation and a relatively more secular view of development, as experienced by a mix of bewildered lower- to middle-class urban residents.

Given the economically precarious backgrounds of many members of Sae and Kubur as well as the predilection of middle-class and educated modern Indonesian theater practitioners to advocate for the nation's economically marginalized, in order to critique existing conditions, it should be no surprise that during their formative periods (Sae, 1977–83; Kubur, 1985–88) both groups found affinities with the plays of Arifin C Noer. Of all the director/playwrights rising to prominence during the New Order, Noer most consistently took up the theme of the fate of Jakarta's urban poor. Yet by the mid-late 1980s, both groups were separately feeling their way towards a much different kind of performance than Arifin's tragi-comic, poetic presentations of the unfortunate lives of Jakarta's have-nots. In so doing, they cemented their place in modern Indonesian theater history and sparked a whole new trend in modern performance whose traces can still be found in the productions of most of today's leading avant-garde groups.

The works of Sae and Kubur shared many commonalities. This was in part due to the fact that Kubur's leader and director, Dindon W. S. had served as a Sae actor in the early 1980s. Similarly, both groups had ties to Arifin C Noer's Teater Kecil. Yet they also diverged in significant ways formally and thematically. These formal and thematic differences had much to do with the differing composition of the two groups. Nevertheless, in each case, whether with regard to Sae's intense, highly philosophical, thematically labyrinthine, and text-heavy performances, or Kubur's physically demanding, thematically focused, and linguistically spare productions, the story of their transition to leading avant-garde groups is again one of diverse influences percolating through groups situated in specific social contexts.

Teater Sae

Teater Sae was first formed in 1976 by a group of mostly unemployed youth under the leadership of a West Sumatran painter, Asril Joni. He had recently moved to Jakarta and was trying to find a place for himself in the world of modern Indonesian culture. With no clear plan for mounting a performance, the group dissolved after less than a year, in part because Joni began to devote his attention to preparing for an art show that included some of his paintings. Yet about a year and a half later, in August 1978, Sae was resurrected by Boedi S. Otong, a young member of Arifin C Noer's Teater Kecil, who had briefly trained the members of Sae in its first incarnation under Joni's leadership. Otong, the son of a well-placed father of Sundanese (West Javanese) *priyayi* origins, was raised in Bandung but had intentionally distanced himself from his family for personal reasons. Thus, Otong was not from a lower- or lower-middle-class background, like Busyra Yoga, Zainal Abidin Domba, Dindon W. S., and several other members of Sae during its early years.[1] Nonetheless, he found some common ground with them since he was by choice in a socially marginalized position as a struggling artist. As such, Otong, Yoga, and other Sae members frequently lived a fairly simple, communal life in the urban kampung of

Jakarta, further familiarizing themselves with the conditions of ordinary Indonesians (Yoga 1994, 16). A second crucial factor in the group's formation was the haphazard nature of its constitution, which forced Sae to recruit members from various circumstances on an *ad hoc* basis.[2]

Sae's first few years were marked by an astonishingly high turnover in personnel, making it difficult to know with certainty if the group would have enough actors to participate in any given production. One factor was the casualness with which group members came and went according to their own life circumstances, without necessarily possessing a high level of commitment to the group or to theater. An additional factor is noted by Yoga in remarking that as the date for the group's inaugural performance approached, Otong became increasingly demanding in rehearsals, a trait for which he would later become well known. His demands also caused those not completely committed to the group's ongoing productions to quickly drop out (Yoga 1994, 8). Thus, Teater Sae slowly developed in such a way that members, places to practice, and performance opportunities were always difficult to come by and in flux. Even committed members such as Otong and Yoga might disappear for months on end as the result of personal or family crises. But those like Otong and Yoga, who endured "starving artist" vicissitudes, achieved a sense of common purpose and an enduring camaraderie.

Sae's first actual production occurred in 1978, during a time of rising student protests against the government. The group's experiences with the piece *Dilarang untuk Melarang* (Forbidding is Forbidden) illustrated both the inclination of many youth theater groups to insert social criticism into their plays (especially at charged moments such as the 1977–78 juncture) and the countervailing tendency of the New Order government's security apparatus to attempt to control and prevent such criticism. Based on a very short, schematic script written by Otong himself, *Dilarang untuk Melarang* was then built through improvised dialogue and action. The piece was first performed at the Central Jakarta Gedung Sumpah Pemuda (Youth Oath Building) in commemoration of the October 28, 1928 nationalist movement Youth Oath, which declared the nation's activist youth committed to "One Nation, One People, and One Language." But as Yoga recalled, "Our performance also had criticism of the government, because of that Boedi was summoned by the police to give an explanation. But fortunately nothing dangerous happened" (Yoga 1994, 8). However, when the group tried to perform the same piece again at the University of Indonesia campus in Rawamangun, they were told the permit had been denied. The Student Council at the adjoining IKIP (Teacher Training College) campus then invited the group to perform, but no sooner had Sae members begun to prepare the stage than the building was surrounded by military troops who asked them to cancel the performance. After negotiations with the Student Council, the soldiers allowed the performance to proceed though the army had dispersed much of the audience already (Yoga 1994, 9).

After many changes of personnel, Sae was able to stabilize its operations by basing itself in the Matraman community in East Jakarta. It went on to win the Jakarta Youth Theater Festival three years in a row (1981–83). This success earned Sae the status of "senior" group, entitling it to practice space and regular stage time for performances at the Taman Ismail Marzuki as well as a subsidy for productions from the Dewan Kesenian Jakarta. It was during the festival years that Sae began to mount productions of Arifin C Noer's plays. These included *Mega-Mega* (1979, Clouds), *Kapai-Kapai* (1980, Moths), and *Umang-Umang* (1983, Crabs).

These plays about the hopeless fantasies of the urban poor or about the ways in which these kampung denizens were twisted into criminal and anti-social ways of existing in harsh city environments seemed to have a strong attraction for the members of Sae. Many of them came from, or were well-acquainted with, relatively humble social environments (though as Dahana points out, by the early 1990s those members of Sae still remaining with the group possessed on average at least a high school level education (2001, 51–52). Most likely, this attraction was stimulated by the time Otong spent with Arifin's own Teater Kecil company. Otong's stint with Teater Kecil may well also have instilled in him a general sense of the dominant theater aesthetic (as discussed in chapter 1). Through his early associations with Joni, Yoga had also been inculcated with such ideas, along with the romanticism of the "artist's" life. Joni introduced him to the painter Nashar as well as the arts figures who frequented the Balai Budaya at Jalan Gereja Theresia No. 47 in Central Jakarta (Yoga

1994, 3). During this period, as a consequence of their general introduction to the prevailing ideas circulating in the arts and theater worlds of the time, Otong and Sae members also developed a fascination with more experimental works from absurdist plays by Harold Pinter, Eugene Ionesco, and Slawomir Mrozek to German Expressionism (Rolf Lauckner). The process was also facilitated when Otong witnessed a performance of Sardono's dance-theater piece, *Meta-Ekologi* (Meta-Ecology), which convinced him to begin investigating new directions for theater (Field Notes 15 August 1994). Many of the experimental plays Sae staged during these years explored extreme or absurd human situations, and as time went on, Sae found its metier in the performance of humanity in conditions of psychological and social torsion.

Fortuitously, one of the audience members watching Sae's final festival performance, a staging of Arifin C Noer's *Umang-Umang* (Crabs) in 1983, was the poet Afrizal Malna. He characterized the performance as "full of hatred!" This comment shook Otong and led him to ask to be introduced to Malna.[3] Sometime after witnessing Sardono's *Meta-Ekologi*, Otong asked Malna's permission to base a performance on the poet's prose piece "Konstruksi Keterasingan" (Construction of Alienation), published in February 1983 in the leading literary journal, *Horison*. As a result, in September 1983, Sae performed *Teater Hitam Konstruksi Keterasingan* (Black Theater: Construction of Alienation). Its run (September 6–10 in The Teater Tertutup in TIM) took place shortly after Sae had received "senior status" through its consecutive victories in the Jakarta Youth Theater Festival.

Indeed, the genesis of *Teater Hitam Konstruksi Keterasingan* lay in Malna's personal alienation caused by the experience of leaving for work and returning home on an 8–4 daily schedule through the bustling and often jammed-to-a-crawl streets of Jakarta. Malna sometimes found it difficult to even cross a street, given the aggressive and near continuous flow of traffic, which left him feeling as if he were confronted by animalistic machines driven by zombie-like creatures. At such moments he experienced an intense longing for *manusia* (humanity) (*Kongko* 1984, 35). Otong read Malna's story and found himself experiencing similar feelings about life in Jakarta. Thus, in the mid-late 1980s, Sae's work began to move towards a thematic focus on the alienation of the individual in urban settings. In so doing, it resembled an important strand of European Modernism from the mid-nineteetnth to the early decades of the twentieth century.[4] Sae was thus able to give more geographic and chronological specificity to its theme of human beings in extreme psychological and emotional conditions. Elaborating on this theme would preoccupy Otong and his colleagues for the next eleven years of the group's existence. During that time, Otong and Malna formed a collaboration in which Malna provided much of the literature upon which Otong and Sae built their increasingly experimental performances.

The theme of human alienation was accompanied by a transformation in the approach Sae's actors would take in embodying this alienation on stage. A poster announcing the performance contained the following statement: "In the *Black Theater: Construction of Alienation*, the performers involved don't perform roles that are given to them. Rather they appear as human beings who perform themselves, and who are always in dialogue with their bodies, spirits and thoughts which are tied to tradition as well as their own surroundings." This was the first public statement of an approach to acting that would become central to Sae's most seminal performances over the next decade and which would be elaborated in later statements by both Malna and Otong. The shift away from actors playing roles to actors using a given script as a vehicle to express their own innermost feelings had begun.

While details of the actual performance are not readily available, its style and themes stimulated some attention within the Jakarta intellectual scene. This notice is attested to by the discussion or *kongko* (chat, dialogue) that was organized by a group of Indonesian-Chinese students at the Youth Arena in Bulungan, South Jakarta, on 2 October 1983.[5] Those present for the apparently well-attended discussion included members of the literature and theater worlds (Ikranegara, Hamid Jabbar, Noorca Massardi, Sardono, H. B. Jassin), intellectuals and representatives of NGO circles (Nasir Tamara, Permadi, the kongko group themselves), and members of the younger generation of theater workers (Boedi S. Otong, Afrizal Malna, Bambang Dwi). This sense of connection not only to people in the arts world, but to activists, intellectuals, and members of the NGO community also became an important feature of Sae's development.

Though its presentation of themes may always have been abstract, the themes it raised often suggested a link between personal identity crises and larger social issues. This link was highlighted by the interest of NGOs in Sae's highly experimental work. In *Teater Hitam Konstruksi Keterasingan*, these themes apparently circled around ideas of individual alienation in industrialized Jakarta and included references to the threat of nuclear destruction. The topics ran throughout the Kongko discussion and generated extensive commentary. However, another aspect of the discussion, the persistent issue of originality in art, points to the new style that Malna and Sae were beginning to shape. This received its clearest articulation in the ways some members of the older generation of literary and theater figures reacted to the performance. Acclaimed choreographer Sardono viewed *Teater Hitam Konstruksi Keterasingan* as an interesting new development— one that broke free of previous conventions by merging poetry and theater. H. B. Jassin, a leading literary critic dubbed the "pope" of Indonesian literature, found the performance intense and captivating, while playwright, actor, and director Ikranegara panned the performance, arguing that Malna's poetry ruined the visual presentation of the piece and that the theme of alienation was clichéd. Furthermore, he held that Malna's text was "not the language of art: it was unconvincing as the product of a deep reflection, but rather represented quotations from other readings; or possibly it was from life experience, but... What emerges so far is merely formulations: like algebra. In short, it's very dry"[6] (Kongko 1984, 29).

This comment reveals the radical break Malna was pioneering with regard to previous conventions of dramatic script and poetry writing. In fact, Malna's style of poetry juxtaposed philosophical ideas with snippets of everyday life in a fragmentary, disjunctive fashion. And indeed, the texts Malna provided as "literature" for Sae's performances often incorporated, along with his own poetry, sets of quotations from diverse sources placed in puzzling juxtaposition. Thus, what Ikranegara saw as "dry" and not containing "deep reflection" was in fact part of Malna's attempt to forge a new kind of poetic expression, based on frequent use of quotation and collage.

This style was also highly evident in Sae's next performance, again with "literature" by Malna, *Teater Pengantar Ekstase Kematian Orang-Orang* (Theater Introducing the Ecstasy of Human Death). In this script, death is conceived as a normal "dance" performed by all humanity, though contemporary conditions made it difficult for humans to recognize it as such. Malna's text bemoans the everyday conditions of life such as work, boredom, and time, which he feels oppress people, but he also laments the tyranny of words, especially the ways in which they give static names to things and to human beings, thereby obscuring the fact that our real identities are always in process. One passage ends with the wish: "But those are only words. Meanwhile what I want is only my own self. My self who is free of all roles" (Malna 1984, 4).[7] Later, the actors recite a chant-like poem in which humans are consumed by all the objects and social structures surrounding them: buildings, automobiles, markets, institutes, rules, machines, ships, weapons, language, words, and other people. All of these are seen to participate in robbing human beings of their own lives. Malna's text metaphorically suggests that things and static names have become more important than the complexity of human beings and their multifaceted interactions and that these objects take over our lives by defining us in relation to themselves. The piece then presents how our lives are also hemmed in by clocks, by a sense of urgency and the need to work, and exclaims: "It's been nine months now, nine months that my spirit has been stored away in a hospital. And I just let people tinker with the hands of the clocks in the places they live out their lives in work. And the death which inhabits the hands of the clock, I just let it happen, the economic competition that chases itself in the barrel of a weapon in order to maintain the world of industry" (Malna 1984, 18).[8] In this passage, the personal unites with the political and larger processes, in order to present a sense of personal helplessness in the face of a brutal economic system, one also fuelled by the arms race. This leads to the piece's "climax" in a statement of confusion, but also a statement that affirms the possibility of a different choice, one in which humans are not defined by a religious or political affiliation, but one in which economies function for the sake of human beings and nature, not for profit :

... where does the future of modernization lead? And it's clear, it's not in my name. A name that tries to see what kind of economic structure can take more consideration of humanity and nature. And not an economic structure that only bows down to the bottom line. Nor is my name a religion or a political institution. Nor do I wear layer after layer of clothing only to cover the poverty stored within my body. A future death carried by modernization. (Malna 1984, 19).[9]

Visually, the staging of the text had also included the incorporation of elements of technology suddenly going "dead," as though being interrupted by electromagnetic interference, such as a nuclear explosion. In such a way, Sae again tried to join the personal search for definition and meaning to the power relations and political issues then confronting the world. This point was underscored by Malna, who asserted that he had originally written the text for *Teater Pengantar Ekstase Kematian Orang-Orang* in order to reshape words into a new language. He felt that Indonesian as it then existed had been flattened out and emptied of meaning by the groups holding power within the government, media, and arts world (Field Notes 1988, 20 June).

Several trends should be obvious by this point. First, Sae's performances were becoming less attached to normal scripts with plot and character, but rather took as their material Afrizal Malna's poetic reflections on individual alienation and loss of identity in modern urban life. The themes this approach raised can be seen in the examples taken from Malna's texts: words, names, and objects have become more important than humans, and they serve mainly to categorize and pigeonhole us in restricting and deadening ways. Second, these productions also express an anxiety about modernization, and, in so doing, by association they begin to critique the developmental ideology that served as the cornerstone of New Order legitimacy. But they also show Sae talking about nuclear destruction and arms races, clearly topics with global significance. Third, Sae's style emphasizes theatricality. Rather than realist-style, psychologically developed characters uttering dialogue in a causal sequence, Sae's performances featured actors declaiming Malna's poetic, fragmented, and abstract words in tones that

Fig. 4.1. Program Cover: Teater Sae, *Pengantar Ekstase Kematian Orang*, 1985. Dindon WS is on the left.

expressed their own emotional responses to the text as they moved about the stage.

During the second half of the 1980s, Sae again mounted a series of productions based on somewhat more narrative scripts, but the scripts chosen continued to reflect the group's preoccupations with experimentation and extreme human conditions: Ionesco's *Les Chaises* (Kereta Kencana, 1986), Malna's *Happening Channel 00* (1986), Georg Büchner's *Woyzeck* (Wooizeek -1987), a fragment form of Rolf Lauckner's *Schrei aus der Straße* (Teriakan-Teriakan Gelap, 1988), an Afrizal Malna adaptation of Sam Shepard's *Buried Child* (Rumah yang Dikuburkan, 1989), and Christopher Bond's *Sweeney Todd* (Sweeney Todd Help!! Seorang Tukang Cukur, 1990). At the same time, a number of these texts also pointed to the conjunction of personal crisis and social conditions. For example, *Woyzeck* shows the psychological deterioration of a lower-class soldier who is forced to take part in preposterous medical experiments in order to earn extra money. *Schrei aus der Straße* relates the murder of a poor prostitute by three blind men confined to a fenced-in hospital who fear and hate the outside world that simultaneously fascinates them. *Sweeney Todd* shows the insanity of a man driven to seek revenge by his unjust treatment at the hands of a judge who wrongfully sentenced him to fifteen years imprisonment, then raped and murdered his wife. All of these plays bear themes that resonated with social and political conditions in Indonesia at the time: how lower-class figures are driven to extreme and brutal actions by social conditions, ignorance, and fear; the corruption and arbitrary brutality of those in power; a feeling of spiritual and intellectual confinement; and the violence lurking beneath the surface of society.

However, beginning in 1991, Otong and Sae returned to their more abstract and philosophico-linguistic collaboration with Afrizal Malna for several of the group's most memorable performances. Produced in the intersection of mounting middle-class dissatisfaction with the politics of the late New Order and an increasing commercialization of Indonesian culture, these works coincided with the rise of a debate within Indonesia about postmodernism in the arts as recounted in Chapter One. As some of Sae's mid-1980s productions demonstrate, Sae had

Figs. 4.2 and 4.3. Scenes from Teater Sae's *Teriakan-Teriakan Gelap*, 1987. Photos by Michael Bodden.

already been experimenting with a disjunctive style and themes (the limits of language) that appeared to be moving in the general direction of post-modern aesthetics long before the public debates over postmodernism actually began. Yet in Sae's 1990s performances, the tendency for more fragmented scripts, collage and quotation of other texts put into apparently random juxtaposition, and disjunctive performances intensified. And in the early 1990s, Malna and Otong also articulated more detailed arguments about what they were trying to accomplish with their scripts and performances, arguments that echoed post-modern ideas while still displaying distinct differences. Finally, public debates about postmodernism coincided with an increase in the amount of attention media commentators paid to Sae's performances from around 1989 on, suggesting that the moment of growing public recognition of this new wave of avant-garde performance was a sign of the rise of a new intellectualism with a different approach to critiquing the New Order.

In this context the determinedly avant-garde, non-compromising, non-commercial theater represented by Otong and Malna's work with Teater Sae achieved increasing recognition, ironically, in the national media toward which they felt considerable ambivalence. Sae's roster had been greatly enhanced in the second half of the 1980s by the remarkable actress, Titi Margesti, who soon became Otong's wife[10] and a mainstay of the group during its rise to prominence in the following years. Bolstered by the performances of Zainal Abidin Domba, Margesti, Taslim Idrus, and a frequently changing supporting cast, Sae was attracting more attention. By the end of the 1980s, Sae's staging of Malna's adaptation of Shepard's *Buried Child* (the adaptation title was Rumah yang Dikuburkan or literally, Buried House/Home) received reviews in three major Jakarta newspapers—*Kompas, Suara Pembaruan*, and *The Jakarta Post*. Among these articles, *Suara Pembaruan* trumpeted Sae's work as the standard bearer for a New Wave Approach (*Paham New Wave*—Suara Pembaruan/Naniel K 1989). Sae's 1991 production based on literature by Malna, *Pertumbuhan Di Atas Meja Makan* (*Things Growing on the Dining Table*) garnered even more media attention with articles in *Media Indonesia*, the Bandung-based papers *Pikiran Rakyat* and *Bandung Post*, and the magazines *Prospek* and *Tempo*, as well as in the three Jakarta dailies mentioned above. In the interval between this production and Sae's next work, *Biografi Yanti Setelah 12 Menit* (Yanti's Biography after 12 Minutes, Dec. 1992), *Kompas*, Jakarta's leading daily newspaper, also published an article proclaiming the birth of a "Subjective Theater," which devoted most of its commentary to Teater Sae and the views of Boedi Otong (*Kompas* 20 July 1992). This media attention continued over the next few years.[11]

Yet a glance at a number of these reviews and reports reveals an ambivalent response. Putu Wijaya, commenting on *Pertumbuhan di Atas Meja Makan* (1991), voiced doubts, although he admired Sae's actors' discipline and meticulous performances and the uncompromising way in which Otong and Malna sought to break through the norms of most modern theater.: "SAE's presentation was heavily dominated by an atmosphere of discussion. Is it enough if theater is just ideas? Has the era of "putting on a show" passed? ... SAE's performance this time was expressive, to be sure, but difficult. It was like an essay. An exhausting essay, though that doesn't mean it wasn't important"[12] (Wijaya 1991). Nirwan Dewanto, reviewing *Biografi Yanti Setelah 12 Menit*, complained that Sae's performance was "too tumultuous," never allowing the audience time to reflect and make sense of what they were witnessing. He went on to describe the piece as too full of tense bodies, shouting, and words (1992). Yet intellectuals were not the only ones who held doubts about Sae's demanding style of theater. As Boedi Otong once remarked, Teater Sae's aim was not to "make theater with the audience," but to "confront the audience as its critical observer." To this he added that it was possible Sae never had a specific audience and that usually there were not large numbers of people attending their performances (Field Notes 9 August 1991). The limited size of the audience captures something of the social tensions, mixed with aesthetic ideologies, informing Sae's existence. The clearest emblem of this problematic situation can be found in one of Sae's key themes: a concern with alienation of human individuals—and especially, though not exclusively, lower middle-class and lower-class Indonesians—in urban settings. This theme was mixed with an avant-garde aesthetics that challenged potential audience members and attracted a relatively small audience, a fact that ironically appeared to signify Sae's own alienation from many of the Indonesians upon whose lives it frequently tried to reflect. While the group's work was highly influential among younger modern theater workers, it failed to capture the imagination of a wider, more socially diverse audience.

Nonetheless, the group's interest in social issues continued. One sign was Sae's periodic association with socially concerned NGOs, despite signs of Otong's growing frustration with demands for more explicit political criticism in Sae's work (Field Notes 1 August 1994). For example, several representatives of NGOs advocating for the rights of women and those with non-heterosexual identities participated in a forum discussion of the group's 1992 performance, *Biografi Yanti Setelah 12 Menit*. Yet as Margesti became more involved with workers' theater in the mid-1990s, including conflicts about whether workers' theater was focusing too much on artistic development and not enough on presenting issues directly linked to current labor campaigns (see chapter 5), Otong's attitude towards NGO and political activists began to change. According to Boedi, "my ears are disgusted when they hear statements that 'art must take sides' ("kesenian harus berpihak"), because usually such statements are made by people who have a very narrow view of the issues—women's issues, workers' issues, etc." Echoing an aesthetic and ideological axiom of many modern theater practitioners, Otong stated that he was more committed to defending what he saw as a larger goal—general human values (Field Notes 1 August 1994).

However, during roughly the same time (the first half of the 1990s) Otong and Malna also began to articulate their concepts of theater, which intertwined a much clearer critique of New Order society and Indonesian political discourses, while reiterating the desire for individual authenticity and a reconstruction of notions of community that modernization had seemingly dissolved. Malna asserted that theater could no longer be explained through "the self" of individual characters. For him, the individual was in crisis in an era of globalization, industrialization, the standardization of New Order culture, and the increasingly monolithic nature of its social institutions. In such a context, especially as mediated by television, newspapers, radio and film, new connections to society were opened up which worked to fragment the individual personality, both enlarging and deflating the "self" (Malna 1995, 42). Malna maintained that it was thus crucial to stop trying to portray the unified individual as the center of theatrical productions, for this would only result in playing "types." Instead, striking a chord familiar to Western postmodernists (Hutcheon 1989,

32–62), he insisted that it was more desirable to focus on how society signified people's behavior, on how people gave and received images of their own lives through various manifestations in their lifestyle and environment. For Malna, this meant presenting an "installation of ideas" (*instalasi gagasan*) rather than a play centered on plots and roles (Malna 1995, 110, 257).

Still, unlike Western postmodernists, the individual subject was not yet "dead" for the Sae group. Both Malna and Otong felt that the New Order, whether through depoliticization and the establishment of monolithic social institutions, or through the 'jargonization' of life in books, newspapers, lectures, and television (Malna 1991, 3–8; Otong 1995, 20–21), had created a society in which it was difficult for individuals to know themselves apart from the dominant institutions and definitions. This development implies that such state-encouraged attempts to impose an identity clashed and created tension with the enlarging and fragmenting of human experience and self-consciousness that other modernization processes had engendered.

Thus, both Malna and Otong wanted to get away from a theater that imposed more external paradigms on their actors through a script with a plot and characters distant from the actors' everyday lives. Sae actors would play themselves through the actuality of their bodies in contact with ideas and objects. For Malna, in this theater actors sought a "self-actualization" otherwise blocked to them in New Order society (Malna 1991, 3–8). Otong went even farther along these lines. He posits that contact with some basic reality of one's life is the greatest strength theater can possess (Otong 1995, 18–19). Otong therefore attempted to get his actors ready for performance by trying to peel away the "jargonized" identities constructed for them by society.[13] Clearly, the actualization (Malna) or "recovery" (Otong) of the individual (for Malna, precisely a complex, fragmented individual) is seen as occurring in spite of and against the New Order's socio-political organization of life.[14]

One more facet of Malna's ideas is worth noting in order to situate this theater against the background of commercialization and the rise of the middle-class. Once again, language is decisive in his theory of why Indonesian theater has developed as it has in the last decade. Related to Otong's view of "jargonized" language and consciousness, Malna sees New Order language as undergoing a process of "euphemization" or, in Benedict Anderson's term, "kromo-ization" ("highly polite, official language" Dewanto 1996, 42; Hooker 1993). Yet Malna's emphasis is rather different than Otong's, for he sees the "euphemization" of language as a result of the commercialization presided over by the New Order. One of the effects of this process is the development of the journalistic language used in the print and electronic media. Malna labelled it "bahasa-yang-enak-dibaca" (language that is fun/easy to read), following the slogan of the weekly magazine, *Tempo*. In contrast, he claimed that the new theater rejected an audience from the middle-class who only want to read or hear "bahasa-yang-enak." Groups like Teater Kubur, Sae, and even newer groups, he argued, intentionally used a language "yang-tidak-enak-dibaca" (that's not fun/easy to read) (Malna 1991, 6–7; Malna 1994b, 17). Malna added that the new theater groups often performed in less comfortable venues and handled topics that, unlike the "safe" middle-class entertainment mentioned above, created an acute sense of unease and discomfort (Malna 1991, 6–7). The theater that Sae pioneered thus stands in clear contrast to the easier, more-entertainment oriented theater of the economic boom years. This fact brings together political discontent and social alienation, including anti-bourgeoisie sentiments, into an avant-garde stance similar to those found earlier in Europe and North America.

Pertumbuhan di Atas Meja Makan
and Biografi Yanti Setelah 12 Menit *(1991–1992)*

In order to grasp more clearly Sae's groundbreaking work during these years, I will now turn to analyses of two of their best-known works. Malna's approach in the text for the first *Pertumbuhan di Atas Meja Makan* (Things Growing on the Dining Table, 1991) is predictably non-narrative. Employing a technique that can best be described as a montage of passages quoted from other sources, combined with a few bits of poetic dialogue of his own, Malna put different kinds of texts into abrupt juxtapositions that force the reader or audience member to make sense of the seeming hodgepodge of textual material. The text opens with a "domestic scene" including a Husband, Wife, and Maid. The

Husband and Wife begin by trading short speeches, she speaking the words of Sukarno about the need for press censorship, he replying with a passage taken from a letter by Mohammad Hatta describing how the Dutch colonial government censored the nationalist movement. The next scene presents the Husband and Wife acting out two altered passages from Albert Camus' *Caligula* that involve Caligula's discovery of the existential absurdity of human life and his need to kill others to feel alive. The Husband and Wife then speak dialogue from Sanusi Pané's classic 1930s nationalist play, *Sandhyakala Ning Majapahit* (Twilight Over Majapahit), in which a Maharesi and the play's hero, Damar Wulan, discuss the nature of reality and human language. A second extract from the same play presents the courtiers of Majapahit slandering Damar Wulan in order to have him executed. Once this scene ends, the husband declaims a section of a Mohammad Hatta speech on the responsibility of intellectuals. The script ends with a popular song by Franky Sahilatua, in which the singer laments being abandoned by a lover. In between these scenes, the script calls for a female maid to be moving around the married couple, cleaning and attending to their needs, while a newspaper hawker passes across the stage selling papers.

Though he was still several years away from articulating the actual concept, Malna's inclination to create something akin to an "installation of ideas," which, in post-modern fashion, would focus on the ways society and people signified their own lives, found at least a partial realization in *Pertumbuhan di Atas Meja Makan*. In *Pertumbuhan*, Malna both implanted images of mass media's influence on ordinary Indonesians and encoded discourses and images that resonated deeply with the history of Indonesian nationalism as well as that of the New Order. For the former, Malna gave the print media and popular music a central place in the text in order to suggest how the mass media and popular culture shape people's abilities to understand and articulate their lives. (Otong and his actors added to this theme by foregrounding television in their performance.) He accomplished the latter by selectively quoting from the texts of the two revered nationalist leaders who continue to serve as icons of national identity and personal identification: Sukarno and Hatta. Finally, in keeping with Malna's idea that the new theater made people uneasy, the topics included censorship, the responsibilities of intellectuals, a utopian longing for a better world that derails into madness, oppression, and murder, corrupt elite politics, and the inability of human language to describe human pain or reality. Any or all of these themes might well have made audiences uncomfortable.

From the description of the performance script above, it should be clear that there are resonances for 1990s Indonesians in the extracts taken from the words of the two nationalist leaders. These quotations deal with a leader's rationale for press censorship, its similarity to colonial government tactics for control of nationalist freedom of expression and assembly, and the responsibility of intellectuals to resist the pressures of power that seek to distort what they believe to be true or scientifically established in order to serve the politics of the moment. These materials, even without any narrative continuity, echoed the recent discursive history of independent Indonesia in ways that still reverberated in the late New Order, especially considering President Suharto's call for openness in the 1989–90 period. That call was cast into doubt by the regime's continuing bans of theater and surveillance of the mass media. The historical passages thereby constituted a significant part of the way in which many Indonesians understood national politics and made sense of their world.

In the performance devised by Otong and his actors, the mass media also exercised a haunting and at times disturbing presence on stage. For example, Busro Yusuf represented a newspaper hawker shouting out "Koran!" (Newspaper!) at the top of his lungs. Bi Sari'ah, an older kampung woman who joined Sae for this production, sat at the front of the stage, cradling a television lit with an eerie blue glow, as though the television, as object, were a beloved companion. As noted above, popular culture, in the form of the music industry, plays a role in the text/performance too. Near the conclusion of the play, in another quotation, Margesti S. Otong sang the Franky Sahilatua song mentioned above. All of these elements sought to imbue the performance with a sense of the discourses, ideologies, and technologies which, through their centrality in history or saturation of the recent social imaginary, shaped how Indonesians understood their lives and acted upon them.

Fig. 4.4. Teater Sae, *Pertumbuhan di Atas Meja Makan*, publicity shot suggesting the centrality of modern electronic media in Indonesian lives. Zainal Abidin Domba is at center top with his head on the speaker. Margesti sits holding a boom box at right. Photo courtesy of Teater Sae.

Another element in the performance's attempt to represent how Indonesians signified their own lives came in the form of a challenge to stereotypical gender roles. For instance, in an ongoing reference to the arbitrariness of normative representations of men and women, a theme that had long preoccupied the group, Margesti as the Wife spoke with a deep, masculinized voice, while Abidin as the Husband sometimes spoke in an extremely high register that might be considered a more feminine sound. Furthermore, though Husband and Wife do play Caligula and his wife, respectively, in the scenes from *Caligula*, in the scenes from Sanusi's *Sandhyakala Ning Majapahit*, the Wife plays the role of the Maharesi, the sage and teacher to the male warrior, a role usually reserved for men.

The designations given to the two lead actors, Wife (Margesti S. Otong) and Husband (Zainal Abidin Domba), aside from allowing Sae to interrogate gender roles, also served other functions. Malna's text describes them and their setting in terms of "eternal compositions," suggesting they were an ironic representation of an imagined perfect couple. Yet, by having a domestic couple speak to each other, often in angry or argumentative tones, in the words of Sukarno and Hatta, the piece cleverly and disturbingly hints that political discourse and ideology insinuate themselves into the everyday consciousness of ordinary Indonesians. For example, by letting the wife mouth Sukarno's speeches about preserving a leader's dignity and the need to censor the press (lest it prove destructive of a fledgling nation's fragile unity), Malna's script intimates that authoritarian behavior and ideas in the political realm and in families are mutually reinforcing.

Certainly, given the government's penchant for talking about Indonesia as though its citizens were simply members of an enormous extended family, the resort to presenting a play about family issues to suggest parallels with national politics was a common tactic for Indonesian playwrights. Yet unlike a number of New Order plays that used a domestic situation to allegorize or draw parallels to national politics, the fusion of personal and political in *Pertumbuhan di Atas Meja Makan* is not aimed at allegorizing the New Order. Rather, it works to assert that the *ideologies* of the two realms interpenetrate and permeate one another. In such a way, the idea of the "self of individual characters" as no longer an adequate representation of reality, another theme that resonates with postmodernism, finds its partial representation in the portrayal of historical discourses speaking through contemporary individuals. *Pertumbuhan di Atas Meja Makan*, therefore, is less about patterns of action and parallels, than it is about patterns of thought, argumentation, and the formation of individual subjectivities in a society where the political reaches deep into social life.

This idea is also embodied in the performances of the other actors, who come and go about the stage, constantly moving around the central husband and wife, virtually enfolding them within an environment that formed something like a socio-political unconscious. Physically and visually, such a staging concept connected the typical domestic sphere of husband and wife to the world of politics contained in several of the spoken passages. It also formed a subconscious "background noise," much as one always hears in kampung life in Indonesia. These connections are clear in Busro's newspaper hawker, who not only mimics (though in a rather hysterical tone) the sounds of peddlers passing along streets and through kampung, but who at one point also screams the names of a series of newspapers banned across several eras of Indonesian history. Bi Sari'ah's television-cradling woman spouted strings of rapid fire Sundanese, reminding us of marginalized regional languages within Indonesia. Another actor, Dinaldo, wearing a farmer's round bamboo hat and black garb, continually hopped around the stage like a rabbit or frog, as though representing the ignored and passive, oft-victimized small peasants of the Javanese countryside. Finally, Hare Rumemper embodied a ghostly maid figure who slowly swept the performance area, brought drinks for the husband and wife, or combed their hair, while they, as though oblivious, continued to talk. In a visually central, but verbally and thematically peripheral fashion, these characters brought onto the stage a number of troubling political issues. In so doing, they also gave physical presence to the "little people" of Indonesia, those marginalized or left out of the economic boom of the mid-late Suharto era. Their voices and presence on stage were constant, always heard and seen by audience members and, occasionally, by the husband and wife. Yet for the most part, their presence was unacknowledged, rarely gaining the conscious attention of the husband and wife. Particularly in the person of the maid, they suggest how ordinary Indonesians help free elites for intellectual, political, and business pursuits, while being subject to the often negative effects of the policies and political rhetoric of national leaders such as the play presented. This representation of the socio-political unconscious of Indonesian elites demonstrated Sae's continuing awareness of and concern for the lower rungs of Indonesian society.

Malna's text also broached ideas about the need for social change and how power is used in arbitrary and cruel ways by power-holders. To do so, it borrowed scenes from *Caligula* and *Sandhyakala Ning Majapahit*, which often seemed unconnected and in a disjunctive relationship to the text fragments taken from Indonesian political history. There were, however, ways of establishing links between these diverse fragments. In the excerpt from Camus' *Caligula* (1958 [1938]), in which the husband, now playing the role of Caligula, returns home and meets his friend

Helicon, Caligula expresses his intense longing to speak his truth to others, to change the seemingly existentially absurd world in which "men will die, and they are unhappy" and to follow the logic of his thoughts to their most extreme conclusion.[15] Caligula rebels against an absurd world, but significantly Malna has also chosen a section of Camus' play in which Caligula comments: "If everyone agrees that the treasury is the most important thing, then the human soul is of no importance whatsoever. The judgment has already been rendered. The world no longer matters."[16]

Once again, Malna and Sae's concern with modernization and capitalism re-emerges, but in the figure of Caligula who, in his awareness of the absurdity of the human condition becomes an extreme tyrant, killing his subjects in order to feel alive. And indeed, Malna has included a discussion of Caligula's need to kill in the second short passage from *Caligula* inserted in his script. Thus, in *Pertumbuhan di Atas Meja Makan*, Caligula serves as a figure to express multiple meanings: the absurdity of the human condition, the horror and anguish of Sae members at the form capitalist modernization is taking in Indonesia as well as a veiled reference to the political tyranny of the Suharto regime. Malna's script drives this last point home by embedding the tyranny passage from *Caligula* in a script in which there are also speeches about the need for press censorship and in which scenes from Sanusi Pané's *Sandhyakala Ning Majapahit* show the hero, Damar Wulan, being slandered as a result of the machinations of political rivals who desire his death, a clear representation of corrupt and violent elite politics. In an intriguing change, however, Otong and his actors decided to delete this final scene from the stage performance, replacing it instead with a stylized enactment of physical agony to which I shall return in a moment. Still, by making this change, Otong and his actors managed to forge a tighter link between the political content of the play and another of the group's and Malna's ongoing concerns, one that again ties them to post-modern ideas: the limits of words and language in expressing the truth of life, accurately representing our identities, or adequately articulating profound human feelings.

At one moment early in the play, after the wife has delivered Sukarno's speech arguing for the necessity of press censorship and the husband performs part of a Hatta letter recalling the pervasiveness of Dutch colonial control of the media and of nationalist meetings, the wife declares: "I'm not the colonial government that Hatta was accusing, nor am I the Sukarno I declaimed just now."[17] Here, in one of the few segments of dialogue written by Malna himself, the wife's statement emphasizes the gap between her reality as a complex human being and the words she utters, or positions or roles she sometimes assumes. Thus the play asserts that, while greatly shaped by ideologies inherited from the past and the present and though often measured by what we say and do, we are never completely defined by these things.

This concern appears in its most philosophical form in the segment from *Sandhyakala Ning Majapahit* containing Damar Wulan's conversation with the Maharesi, who tells him, "Whoever wants to know life must forget names and characteristics. All things are within each of us, Damar Wulan, and can't be known through thoughts dependent upon language.... And death for a human being merely means moving from one event to another, one moment to the next. Time is an illusion." Interestingly, the Maharesi ends by saying that though our understanding of life is limited and often illusory, Damar Wulan has been given a place and role in life and that he must nonetheless act responsibly to fill that role as a member of the warrior (*kesatria*) caste. In this passage, Malna attempts to come to terms with his own post-modern grasp of the arbitrarily constructed nature of language and understanding by returning to an older, traditional philosophy of knowledge, Hinduism, as conveyed through Sanusi Pané's 1932 play. Words and language are confining and their understanding of the complex world, illusory, yet we must nonetheless engage in a struggle to ensure that our duty is fulfilled. This conclusion leaves open a fundamental question: upon what basis does one construct a notion of duty? It is clear that Malna and the great majority of his Sae collaborators are not Hindus bound to follow the caste system with its notion of proper caste roles.

It is no coincidence that Malna followed this set of passages from *Sandhyakala Ning Majapahit* with the excerpt from former Vice President Mohammad Hatta's speech on the responsibility of intellectuals. Quoting from Julien Benda's *La Trahison des Clercs*, Hatta (as spoken by the husband) continues: "The intellectual who is bought by the world's power holders is a traitor to his/her function."[18] Thus, the play appears to argue that one must act in accord with what one believes to be the truth, but given Sae's radical mistrust of words and language, truth, too, seems like a slippery concept. Therefore, this dilemma remains a source of thematic tension, a fact reinforced by another facet of Sae's staging of the limits of verbal expression.

The search for individual identity and the politics of late New Order Indonesia seem thoroughly entwined with one another in *Pertumbuhan*. For instance, in a short bit of spoken dialogue that Otong and his actors added to the performance, near the piece's very beginning Zainal Abidin Domba, as the husband, states: "Hello, Good Morning. How are you? Good. Good. I hope you're well. You're a person of culture and so am I. So, can we begin now?"[19] Immediately thereafter, the newspaper hawker emits a loud, rapid-fire stream of words that included dates, the words "Watch out!" (*Awas!*), "Don't" (*Jangan*) "age/lifespan" (*usia*), and "newspaper" (*koran*). Three times in succession, the husband asks, "What is your name?" (Siapa namamu?). This sequence is then repeated again. The words the husband speaks in this short scene could well be simple words of greeting, and the question "What is your name?" the opening to a common exchange of introductions between strangers. Yet given Sae's interest in how identities are constructed and their essential instability over time, the question of the name and the invitation to begin may well have signaled the piece's intention to interrogate how Indonesian citizens' identities are formed. But there is also another possible reading of this sequence. When the newspaper hawker spouts his rapid-fire dialogue, it touches on anxieties about the all too vulnerable position of newspapers under a regime where censorship and banning are common. Thus, "Siapa namamu," and perhaps even the husband's "Good Morning" greetings, could be the beginning of an interrogation by security apparatus personal. This interpretation is supported by a scene shortly afterwards when the newspaper hawker rapidly shouts the names of a number of banned newspapers, and the husband asks: "Darimana anak itu menjual Koran-koran yang telah dibreidel?" ("Where did that kid get banned papers to sell?") The succeeding excerpts on censorship taken from Sukarno and Hatta further reinforce the theme I am suggesting. Yet the sequence of the husband's morning greeting is also repeated at the very end of the performance, just before the lights go down, suggesting that the act of beginning is never final, there is always another beginning. Thus, both the search for identity and the political struggles for controlling how Indonesians view themselves and their nation are represented as always changing, subject to revision, to starting over.

This interrogation of representation and the limits of language (or images) achieves its most intense embodiment in two scenes where language fails. The first comes at the conclusion of the Damar Wulan (husband)-Maharesi (wife) scene when the Maharesi tells Damar Wulan to go to Majapahit and fulfil his duty as a kesatria. As noted above, Otong and his actors dispensed with the next scene, in which Damar Wulan is betrayed politically. Instead, they inserted extra dialogue in which the husband figure states: "Yes, I know where I come from. Never satisfied like a flame. I burn and consume myself. I hold onto light alone. I leave behind only oil. I am fire. Just go . . . " Afterwards, as though unable to articulate any more words, the husband and wife begin to groan and writhe in place, with the wife emitting terrifying whinnies and audible shudders. She dances, strikes poses, and collapses, all the while screeching in a terrifying manner. The movement was choreographed and highly stylized, yet together, the agonized movements along with the excruciating vocal sounds conveyed a sense of a verbally inexpressible anguish and frustration. The convulsions of Abidin's and Margesti's bodies therefore became the expression of feelings that exist beyond the borders of the verbal, and, given what has come before, are a painful commentary on both the absurdity of the limits of human understanding and the agony of being trapped in duties to a questionable government and social structure.

The second instance of this representation of the limits of verbal language occurs after the Hatta (husband) speech on the responsibilities (and possibility of betrayal) of the intellectuals. As I have already mentioned, this passage seemed to be an attempt by Malna to overcome the lack of a basis for determining one's duty in an absurd world. But the tension was

Fig. 4.5. Margesti and Zainal Abidin Domba dance the verbally inexpressible. Photo by Michael Bodden.

apparently not resolved. For in the next scene, the wife proceeds to sing an *acappella* rendition of the Franky Sahilatua song "Black Sky," mentioned previously. In this song of a lost love and the ensuing emotional depression, the stars and moon have disappeared, leaving darkness. The singer feels surrounded by a strangling silence and experiences intense pain.

Fig. 4.6. Teater Sae, making the body speak in *Pertumbuhan di Atas Meja Makan*. Photo courtesy of *Kompas*.

Immediately after finishing this scene, the wife and husband break into a convulsive series of movements. Language once more has broken down into barking syllables and chattering teeth. This montage-like collision and fusion of concepts—the pain of betrayed love sharply juxtaposed to commentary about the possible betrayal of the intellectuals in the service of power again produce verbally inexpressible feelings.

The power of Sae's performance lay in its attempt to explore new languages, to endeavour to move beyond everyday language that is taken for granted as a transparent vehicle for instrumental communication, in order to understand what it meant to be a human being in late New Order Indonesia. Malna's script and Sae's performance, as directed by Otong, suggested the absurdity of human life, the constantly changing nature of our identities, the ways ideologies encroach upon our most private spheres of interaction, how our unconscious minds absorb the human environment, the emotional difficulty of remaining true to one's beliefs in New Order Indonesia, and how some emotional states can find expression only in the gestures and contortions of bodies or non-verbal vocalizations.

The group's next piece, *Biografi Yanti Setelah 12 Menit* (A Biography of Yanti after 12 Minutes, 1992), continued the group's exploration of post-modern themes and techniques of performance. This time it examined the mechanics of identity and politics through a more concentrated focus on the family. The script, once again built from diverse texts including government and UNESCO reports, Amir Hamzah's poetry, the *Asian Wall Street Journal*, and the diary of 1960s Indonesian activist Soe Hok Gie as well as Malna's own poetry, begins with a description of a mother's hope for an idealized heterosexual marriage, one in which the spouse is "a companion from a good family, successful, morally upright, protective, of the same faith, not too old, and, if necessary, with the same shirt size, too. The main thing is a love that fits with national ideals and the environment: where growth, equal distribution, and draining natural resources will not stand in opposition to one another nor go against development, success, and our future." (Malna 1992, 1)[20]

This passage, one of Malna's own invention, presents one of the play's few parodic moments in its imitation of a naive nationalist rhetoric interspersed with normative hopes for a perfect spouse. Yet, the parody dies before our laughter becomes too prolonged, as the speaker continues: "But you know, Mother, that Amir Hamzah is already dead, the one who gave his love to only one person. . . . Marriage, Mother, is now no more important than people entering and leaving their offices. People's high social mobility in urban life creates a sharply rising graph for the statistics of joinings and separations. Don't be sad." (1)[21]

These two extracts announce the play's major themes. *Biografi Yanti* is a meditation on the nature of love, marriage, and relationships between humans in the midst of a rapidly changing, modernizing urban environment. Crucially, it is an environment that, as the passage suggests, is no longer a place for the romantic love of the pre-war nationalist poet, Amir Hamzah, long viewed as the model for combining traditional Malay poetics with a modern attitude. Every bit as disjunctive as the relationships alluded to in the second passage, the play moves from highly poetic agonizing over the difficulty of finding and defining one's individual identity and knowing the meaning of love, sex, and marriage to speeches about the difficulty of third-world development, the role of cosmetics and consumption in the destruction of the ozone layer, and the drop-out rate for Indonesian students from primary school to high school. There are other levels of disjuncture as well. Even within a single sentence, phrases often seem unrelated. For example: "There are no mice in my biography, just as you can always smell aluminum on my lips." (10)[22]

Elements of the performance version of the play add suggestively to this landscape of disjuncture. The roles different actors assume, the clothes they wear, the gestures they adopt, even the ways in which they speak their lines all grate against our expectations. Zainal Abidin Domba, the lead male actor, played a role designated by a woman's name (Yanti), wore a bra, and spoke with a falsetto voice. Taslim Idrus, performing the role of narrator, spread his arms as though making a speech—or at other times monotonously strummed a ukulele at a manic pace—while reciting statistics about education and the destruction of tropical rainforests in a flat tone at high speed. Margesti, the lead actress, spoke in a deep voice full of rage—at times seemingly out of all proportion to the meaning of the words spoken—pulled her pant legs up to her hips as though challenging the audience rather than exposing herself, and violently slapped the male lead. Not only are typical gender roles confounded, but the angry shouting, shrill falsetto, and breathless but flat delivery of statistics also create a disjuncture in the emotional fabric of the play. The effect is similar to that "schizophrenic" jumping from one emotional register or "intensity" to another that Jameson claims creates postmodernism's specific brand of euphoria (Jameson 1984, 71–73).

Thus, in the juxtaposition of different sections and speeches about seemingly unrelated things, as well as in the structure of many of the play's sentences, the physical delivery of the words, and the startling roles, gestures, and costumes, *Biografi Yanti* displays a poetic rather than a narrative register, a register that juxtaposes things and acts in startling fashion in order to suggest connections rather than stating causes and effects. As in *Pertumbuhan di Atas Meja Makan*, this strategy forces the viewers/readers to become active interpreters if they are to create meaning from the play's apparent randomness.

Disjuncture is also present at the thematic level. One of the major recurring themes is the difficulty of possessing a biography, at least one that forms a coherent narrative or can be summarized in neat formulas

Fig. 4.7. Confounding gender roles and explosive anger. *Biografi Yanti Setelah 12 Menit*. From left, Taslim Idrus, Zainal Abidin Domba (with spatula) and Titi Margesti Ningsih (at the time, Margesti S. Otong). Photo courtesy of Ging Ginandjar.

such as married couples, households, or the idealized portrait of the spouse in the play's opening lines. Coherent, neatly unified identities exist only in films, television shows, and novels, one character suggests (Malna 1992, 9). In everyday life, however, identity fragments. Its world is one in which people can change their appearance with cosmetics, can change their sex, and are surrounded and affected by so many discourses and processes (politics, environmental disasters, consumerism, industrialization, the lives of many others). This fragmentation of identity is exacerbated by the fact that we can never truly know others, or even ourselves. Community, too, fragments, leaving the characters and audience for *Yanti* with no more than simple gestures of comfort, such as offering someone a pillow (13, 18).

The difficulty of possessing a biography, when identities are constructed out of formulas about family and social roles, leads to a second prominent facet of the play, namely, the explosive anger that erupts, both at unexpected junctures where words have no clear connection to the emotional charge with which the actors speak them, and when this anger does attach itself to monologues that might plausibly be connected to such emotions. These latter are most often passages expressing confusion about personal identity, about normative roles that do not fit present circumstances, alienation from others, and a number of speeches about the hardships of women's lives and roles. Thus, in an emotional score of rapidly shifting intensities, anger becomes something of a dominant tone, threading together most of the play's major themes and supplying the lion's share of the tension sustaining the performance. Sometimes this anger leaves behind words and jumps into the violent or shocking actions of the three lead performers who jerk each other's heads back by the hair and slap one another. The audience may itself be the object of aggression, for example, when the female lead defiantly challenges the audience by thrusting her pelvis toward them.[23]

The explosive nature of rage and violence in the performance, tied as it often is to themes such as ill-fitting normative identities and unsatisfying familial and personal relationships (especially for women), causes the play to project a sense of deep crisis in the New Order's ideology of *kekeluargaan*, an ideology often used to assert a "natural," "traditional" quality to paternalistic authoritarian hierarchy as well as to structure and control the actual organization of day-to-day family relations (Bourchier 1997, 164–70; Sullivan 1990; Suryakusuma 1996). This anger at a restrictive ideology, along with the confining roles it reinforces in society, carries over into equally enraged monologues about more clearly political topics, such as the domination of Third World countries by the United States, environmental destruction, the lack of a parallel intellectual development to Indonesia's physical development, and Indonesians' media-exacerbated alienation from their own country. The play's sense of crisis thus expands to envelop the entire New Order development project, indeed the affairs of the entire earth. *Biografi Yanti Setelah 12 Menit*, like *Pertumbuhan di Atas Meja Makan*, seems to cry out for a new language, for new concepts of human identity and community, and ultimately, for a new nation and international order.

Curiously, a number of elements tend to mitigate the play's devastating landscape of fragmentation. The first is far clearer in the performance version than in the script. As the three main actors go about their roles, several other performers move about the stage scrubbing the floor, pouring water, cooking, ironing, and praying. Again, as in *Pertumbuhan di Atas Meja Makan*, this constant activity creates something of a subconscious "everyday," perhaps even domestic, landscape that gives contextual coherence to the rest of the play. In *Biografi Yanti*, this activity outlines the confines of household and neighborhood, the site of marriage, relationships, community, and of the government's increasingly problematic efforts to reproduce specific identities for its citizens. It is thus the context for much of the play's anger.

The relationship of the main performers reveals another such point of connection while at the same time raising one of the play's main concerns. The three major roles are simply referred to as Yanti 1, Yanti 2, and the narrator (who also calls himself Yanti at one point early in the play). In sharp contrast to the disjunctive elements of the work enumerated above, this naming suggests a similarity or sameness, even among the major roles and is hinted at textually at more than one point. In a speech about the dropout rate of Indonesian students between primary school and high school, Yanti 1 wonders if all those lost to higher education have become Yanties, "seperti diriku" (like me) (5). Elsewhere, Yanti 2 states that Yanti is the name of the majority of Indonesian women (10). Another seemingly disjunctive element in the performance is the presence in the cast of a German citizen of Indonesian parentage who speaks no Indonesian and who thus delivers her lines in German (ironically, translated into Indonesian during the performance by a "Caucasian" German-speaker). This character is recuperated into the play's sense of commonality when the actress claims that many Germans still have difficulty living with people who are different and goes on to state "Ich nenne mich nun Yanti" (I'll call myself Yanti from now on). In the performance version, this commonality is also reinforced visually and verbally. At the end of the play, all of the major players face the audience and repeat the same speech, one after the other and then all together. This scene represents a possible moment of community: the words they speak, both in the script and the performance, confirm that they all are the same, all Yanti, all alienated and groping for an identity and connections to others in a confoundingly

Fig. 4.8. Teater Sae *Biografi Yanti Setelah 12 Menit*. The family and its "subconscious everyday landscape." Photo courtesy of *Tempo* magazine.

disjunctive world. They are all hidden in each other's and the audience's "biographies," at least for twelve minutes. While this twelve minutes is the arbitrary number chosen for the play's title, it symbolizes how all people become who they are, in small, brief, but real ways, how they are "given birth" through others they know and through objects and social processes. It represents the difficulty of composing an individual biography without also speaking of the biographies of other people, things, and processes. The horizon of fragmentation in Yanti is, after all, also an horizon of connections—perhaps too many connections to easily make sense of—and as such, it suggests that we are all part of a larger whole that is simply extraordinarily difficult to grasp given our current ways and frames of "narrating" our understanding of the world.

Biografi Yanti Setelah 12 Menit, then, exhibits many of the characteristics of Western postmodernism. It is fragmented and disjunctive on various levels, tends to create a series of emotional intensities rather than relying on building plot tension toward a clear, singular denouement, and incorporates a variety of disparate textual materials. What is interesting is how Malna and Sae changed and incorporated these elements according to their own historically specific needs as cultural workers in contemporary Indonesia. The techniques of disjuncture and fragmentation are here put together in pursuit, made more urgent by the performance's dominant tone of anger and violence, of a new conceptual language, a new way of understanding the modern world urban Indonesians inhabit, and perhaps a new way of imagining community. They are used in part to suggest connections as well as disjunctures and to prod the audience into using the new language and seeing the world at a more complex level. Furthermore, the collage of different texts is not the "blank parody" of pastiche Jameson describes. More often, these fragments of text are lifted whole from their sources, or paraphrased, in order to put them into a radically meaningful juxtaposition. What indeed does the destruction of the ozone layer have to do with cosmetics and the way they help people to change their identities? What do the drop-out rates of Indonesian students have to do with love and marriage? What do the dilemmas of developing countries have to do with the fictions of biographies? Another contrast to Western postmodernism, one that relates to a point made previously is the play's attitude toward modern mass media. As is the case with other Malna/Sae collaborations, *Biografi Yanti* does not feature modern mass media in a laudatory sense, but rather as one site, alongside normative government discourses, where traditional, inadequate and fictional biographies still exist. Rather than being a harbinger or pioneer of postmodernism, modern mass media are seen as reinforcing unified, linear modernist representations of life.

The analyses of *Pertumbuhan di Atas Meja Makan* and *Biografi Yanti Setelah 12 Menit* presented above demonstrate some of the complexity of the performance style Sae developed. It became a highly influential model for theater practice among a large number of other, younger generation groups that followed Sae onto the national stage of modern theater. This style combined avant-garde ideas about acting, theatrical performance, and theater's social role with political themes viewed from a middle-class intellectual perspective, one that is in an occasionally tense dialogue with the NGO community and is colored by sympathies with, experience of, and some roots in the urban lower-class and lower middle-class. In 1993 Sae added one more ground-breaking performance to its legacy, *Migrasi dari Ruang Tamu* (Migration from the Guest Room), but in 1994 the group collapsed under pressures that had long haunted it: the attrition of actor-members who needed to find ways to earn a living for their growing families. Eventually, Boedi S. Otong himself left Indonesia for Switzerland, and though the group banded together for one more performance without Otong in 1999,[24] it never achieved its former intensity or acclaim. The precarious, haphazard, and personalized basis for Sae's existence, along with its turn to an extreme avant-garde position, also raised questions about its ongoing links to the social groups from which many of its members had historically hailed.

Teater Kubur

However, another group with direct connections to Sae but with a very different base of support continued the legacy of avant-garde theater throughout the 1990s and into the post-Suharto Reform Era. That was the extraordinary Teater Kubur, led by former Sae member Dindon W.S. The first time I visited Dindon W. S., I had no trouble finding his home located in the maze-like alleyways of the Kober kampung of East Jakarta's Jatinegara Timur district. After arriving by taxi behind what was then the Mitra Family Hospital, I asked a pair of young men standing at the entrance to Kampung Kober if they knew where Dindon lived. They replied, "Oh, Dindon, orang teater!" (Oh, Dindon, the theater person!). It soon appeared that nearly everyone in the kampung knew Dindon, or at least knew of him. As one of the young men led me along a narrow, arm's length-wide walkway between houses, he nodded in affirmation to others who inquired about where he was taking an obvious stranger.

This first visit to Kampung Kober impressed upon me how Teater Kubur differed from Teater Sae and many other well-known modern theater groups in Jakarta. It has deeply grown and continually nurtured roots in one specific lower-lower-middle-class neighborhood.[25] Teater Kubur formed in 1983, initially in response to the desire of a group of kampung youths to stage a play for the kampung Independence Day pageant.

Dindon, who was a few years older than the others and who had been involved in Teater Sae since 1980, became the group leader and wrote at least one script for an August 17th pageant performance. Living in Kampung Kober, which was named for an adjacent cemetery and whose name is a variation of the Indonesian word for cemetery (*kuburan*), the group called itself Teater Kubur. Additionally, its main rehearsal space was on the actual cemetery grounds. During these years, Kubur consisted of around twenty-five members, including high school students, construction workers, auto mechanics, and auto painters, among others, all of whom lived in Kampung Kober. The group was accepted as a part of the community, and local kampung residents often watched their rehearsals on the cemetery grounds. After two years, Teater Kubur decided to enter the Jakarta Youth Theater Festival. For three years in succession, it finished among the winners of the Festival with highly praised productions of Arifin C Noer's *AA II UU* (1985, 1986) and *Kucak Kacik* (1987). In 1987, these victories earned them the designation of a group under "DKJ's guidance" (Field Notes 10 August 2001; Wiyanto 1987).

Newspaper reports of a number of its performances in the mid-late 1980s are one indicator of the group's intense connection to its home *kampung*. As Wiyanto noted, for its 1987 performances of *Kucak Kacik*, Kubur had brought a large group of spectators from *Kampung* Kober who appeared very absorbed in the performance and even participated at some points (Wiyanto 1987). Arwinto Syamsunu Aji, writing for *Sinar Pagi* about Kubur's 1988 production of Arifin C Noer's *Kapai-Kapai* (Moths), not only noted the large audiences, but he also argued that in choosing Noer's plays(which dealt with the problems of ordinary Indonesians from the kampung) and in creating a form that communicated effectively with its constituency, Kubur demonstrated a desire to involve the audience in its performances (Aji 1988). Dindon confirmed this by stating "I want to bridge the gap between the performers and the audience.... In my performances the spectators are also actors"[26] (Naniel K, 1988). These articles also noted the superior discipline of the group, and senior theater figures, such as Teguh Karya, Danarto, and Rendra, lavished praise and attention on Dindon and his comrades. Karya, in particular, invoked the discourse of high art in Indonesia by remarking that Teater Kubur's discipline and dedication placed the group above others. In Karya's words, Kubur's plays were more *"adiluhung"* (supreme, superb, beautiful, high art) while other groups resembled "popular arts performances" (*pentas seni rakyat*) (Aji 1988).

All this attention confirmed Dindon's and Kubur's place in the world of modern artistic theater. Yet at this point in their careers, there was also a note of rebellion toward official institutions. Though his troupe had proved itself by winning three consecutive Youth Theater Festivals, Dindon nonetheless declared that artists couldn't be "programmed" ("Seniman itu bukan diprogram" *Jayakarta* 27 December 1989)[27] and that his group wanted to distance itself from the festival as an institution. He later commented that he wanted to destroy the belief that a successful theater group had to be strengthened by the aesthetic values of the festival (Tejo 1994b). He also found it insulting that after winning the festival three years in succession, the Jakarta Arts Council, which sponsored the festival, still considered Kubur a group under its guidance (Field Notes August 2001). In the years following 1987, Kubur not only abandoned the festival, but the group also developed a new method for working and a new performance style.

Here again, the solidarity of the Kubur group gave it a distinct advantage. After winning the 1987 Festival, followed by a praised production of Noer's *Kapai-Kapai* in April 1988, Kubur took more than one and one-half years to develop its next piece, *Sirkus Anjing* (Dog Circus). Thus, its cohesiveness and commitment shone through in its ability to undergo an arduous practice process over the course of at least fourteen months, while still retaining its strongly committed core of more than twenty members.

Sirkus Anjing (1989–90) marked a departure from Kubur's previous work in several ways. Its new features highlighted the fact that Dindon had gained considerable experience with Teater Sae from 1980 to 1986 (performing in *Teater Hitam Konstruksi Keterasingan* and *Teater Pengantar Ekstase Kematian Orang-Orang* as well as a number of earlier Sae productions), but the new work also exhibited distinct differences between Sae and Kubur. First, unlike the productions of Arifin C Noer's and Danarto's works staged previously, *Sirkus Anjing*, like Sae's most experimental works, lacked a strong storyline or characters carefully differentiated according to

Figs. 4.9, 4.10, and 4.11. Teater Kubur's early productions: *Rintrik* (1987) and *Kapai-Kapai* (1988). Photos by Michael Bodden.

psychological motivations, nor did it have typical dramatic dialogue. Second, in ways similar to those practiced by Boedi Otong and Sae, the work was pieced together using a new exploratory method—improvisations by the actors with materials from their immediate environment, like nets and large metal storage drums. This method required more time for actors to explore the possibilities of interacting with common objects. Unlike Sae, which seemed compelled to mount a new production every year, Dindon was content to let the process take as much time as required to produce a striking ensemble piece. An article reviewing Kubur's 1994 production of *Tombol 13 (Topeng Monyet Bola Plastik)* (Button 13: Monkey Mask Plastic Ball), reported that Dindon didn't think productivity (in terms of number of performances) was important: "A performance is essentially an unfinished process" (Rizal 1994). A third characteristic of Kubur's new approach also differentiated it from Sae. The group, confirming Dindon's desire to distance himself from the festival as institution, chose not to perform at TIM. Instead, Kubur took *Sirkus Anjing* on tour to a variety of locations in kampung, youth centers, university campuses, and private avant-garde venues. Examples of the latter two types of locales were campuses like IKIP Jakarta and ITB in Bandung, or Rendra's Padepokan Teater Rendra at Citayam (see Syaid 1989, *Jayakarta* 27 December 1989, and Tejo 1994b). Kubur's decision to take its shows to locations other than TIM suggested a more populist inclination than could be claimed by Sae or almost any other modern Jakartan theater group of the era.

Finally, the group did not use a script developed by an avant-garde writer, as had been the case in Malna's collaboration with Sae. Kubur constructed the verbal text of its performance through the improvisational process in which Dindon and his actors selected expressions and language they felt best fit the actions and themes they were developing.

Dindon's background with Sae had certainly helped prepare him for the new direction his group took. Yet his work with Arifin C Noer's *Teater Kecil* from 1984 to 1988 had also increased his knowledge of stagecraft and the aesthetic ideologies of the world of modern national theater. In fact, Dindon's commitment to ongoing experimentation reflects this lineage. For example, he once remarked that though he didn't consciously consider himself to be an exponent of experimental theater, he found theater to be "a mystery that will never be exhausted or finished. If we feel that the map of current theater is all there is, in my opinion that is a very narrow view. In fact theater provides a much bigger space" (Sularto 1994).[28]

Yet Kubur's roots in a lower- and lower-middle-class kampung marked the group's work with a clear difference compared with most modern theater—in a more fundamental way than Sae, it was modern theater undertaken with a perspective from below. The group's "rebellion" against the festival institution was one indication of this. Similarly, newspaper reports about *Sirkus Anjing* clearly read this performance as a presentation of life from the bottom and characterized it in terms of Dindon's belief in the "honesty and divine (keilahian) quality of madness which becomes a theatrical idiom" ("... sebuah kejujuran atau keilahian dari orang sinting yang menjadi idiom teatrikal ... ")(Syaid 1989). According to a *Jayakarta* article, Dindon endeavors to express the complaints of the masses by excavating the situation that inevitably arises from the suffocating conditions, pollution, and noise of vehicles and advertisements that stir up the life of the wider society (*Jayakarta* 27 December 1989).[29] Dindon himself also commented that the group simply used the language, idiom, and images most familiar to them.

> What we performed yesterday was also our own language. Not to mention that we start from a very marginal situation. Teater Kubur doesn't have a financial supporter or a boss. We start from true poverty, which always necessitates that we must be clever in digging through whatever is around us in order to give it meaning. ... I think Teater Kubur begins with our problems and those of society. After my friends and I rub up against the values, social, economic, and political conditions, and also the system around us, I feel that this is what in the end makes us feel like something that can't be separated from society. What I mean is, whatever themes we take up, they're sure to take several social problems that are close to our lives as their point of departure (Sularto 1994).[30]

Thus, Dindon claimed that his works were based on the authentic experience of his group's members. This desire for authenticity also found expression in the fact that the group rarely, if ever, used make-up. As Dindon remarked, "The reason I don't have my actors use make up, for example, is because I believe the strength of their expressiveness already provides an original make up. If we force things, the actor's expressive talent is killed. In addition, make up contains a pretension to manipulate the value of the honesty already there" (Sularto 1994).[31]

Similarly, and indicative of the rebellious streak in Kubur's practice, in response to a reporter's suggestion that the language Kubur employed in its performance of *Tombol 13* (*Topeng Monyet Bola Plastik*) was coarse, rough, and gave too free a rein to passions, Dindon argued that such language was the daily language for those on the margins. Still, he maintained that it was more refined (*halus*) than using terms like "the authorities" or "conglomerate" (Bawantara and Sopyan 1994). Dindon thereby linked the authenticity of his group—its composition of socially marginalized people—to a kind of anti-*halus halus*-ness (anti-refined refinement). This association was as much as to say that New Order aesthetes who valorized "refinement" above all in art were in reality less refined than Kubur and the experiences of the urban poor. Ironically, though Dindon had absorbed much of the modern theater's aesthetic ideology, the social and artistic position of his group necessitated that he at times critique the limits of its assumptions.

Dindon argued that his group used the idiom of the kampung and images close to the world of its dwellers. As a result, he maintained, while Kampung Kober residents could understand and appreciate Kubur's experimental performances and idiom (Field Notes 10 August 2001), it was less clear if intellectuals could do so as easily. Although most reports stated that the meanings of symbols and language used in Kubur plays were clear enough, at least one reviewer of Kubur's *Tombol 13* (*Topeng Monyet Bola Plastik*) (1994) observed, "Not a few audience members furrowed their brows searching for the common thread of this repertoire..." (Rizal 1994).[32] Nirwan Dewanto praised the strong physicality and prop interactions (folding chairs) of *Tombol 13*'s actors, but he felt that its tendency to paint the large city in strictly negative terms was phoney and pretentious (Dewanto 1994). Still, Dindon felt that Kubur's efforts were directed towards exploring social and political themes meaningful to the group's members and to the wider Indonesian community. The introduction to a newspaper interview summarized his feelings about the role of such themes in the development of the group: "According to him [Dindon], the honesty of his friends in Teater Kubur in exploring various social problems represented the 'fuel' that united them. 'Imagine, if our orientation towards theater was merely to perform, maybe we'd have already disbanded,' remarked the director . . . " (Sularto 1994).[33]

How were the ideas of Dindon and his group manifested in actual performance? How did Kubur try to bridge avant-garde performance with the idiom of daily life in the kampung? In what follows I will attempt a descriptive analysis of two of Kubur's performances, but I first need to introduce a caveat. Though I have not managed to see either a live performance or video recording of the original performances of *Sirkus Anjing* or *Tombol 13*, my readings are based on newspaper reviews and a later production, *Trilogi Besi* (Iron Trilogy, 2001), which was a restaging of the two earlier works plus Kubur's 1998 production, *Sandiwara Dol*, and which, according to Dindon, captured much of all three original performances. This should permit us to gain at least some sense of Kubur's concerns and style.

Newspaper reports at the time described *Sirkus Anjing* as representing poverty as a disgusting situation, a place where "bums" congregated, chattering, complaining, and saying whatever came into their heads without any clear connection, jumping from one problem to another. The men wore denim shorts and were bare-chested, though at times they covered themselves in nets, while the women dressed in black with sashes made from faded banners, with their hair hung loosely-bound by assorted strings. Their utterances included mention of private television stations (RCTI), rooftop tv reception dishes, commercial advertisements, and computers as well as people engaged in corruption (corruptors), hotels, taxis, and lotteries (Syaid 1989). Another report suggested that the play offered many complaints of the "little people" as well as social criticism and that the idiom used moved audience members to trade opinions after the performance, in part representing Kubur's attempt to think through, together with the audience, solutions to the problems presented (*Jayakarta* 1989). *Tombol 13* (*Topeng Monyet Bola Plastik*) was similarly described by reporter/reviewers as representing the victims of development who suffered and were mocked, but who also tried to understand their identities in the midst of rapid urban change. One reviewer described the victims' attack on an "iron wall" that seemed to block their way, their doubts about their leadership, and their realization that *nyali* (courage) was their key weapon (Rizal 1994). Bawantara and Sopyan noted that in *Tombol 13*, Dindon didn't appear to care about a "realistic story" but rather concentrated on the expressiveness of the actors in conveying impressions to the audience through hyperbolic mimicry and movement (Bawantara and Sopyan 1994).

Yet in order to achieve a more detailed understanding of Kubur's style, we now need to examine the reconstruction of *Sirkus Anjing* and *Tombol 13* in the group's 2001 production, *Trilogi Besi*. The *Sirkus Anjing* section of *Trilogi Besi* opens with a woman carrying a baby-like doll greeting incoming audience members. She chats with and interrogates them as the other members of the troupe appear to be engaged in warm-up movements around the arena-style performance area. After approximately twenty minutes, the actors begin to become more animated, pounding rhythmically on large metal drum containers and chanting, sometimes breaking into cacophonous banging noises and moans. After a few more minutes they begin to stagger jerkily about the performance space as though suffering from some nervous disorder. While the woman continues chatting with the audience, they cover themselves in nets and hum while spinning around. Soon a man climbs atop one of the metal drums as though searching for something, while the rest put half-sized drum containers on their heads and begin to slam into one another. While the woman who has been talking now begins to move about saying "eat" and miming giving out food, the man atop the drum asks, "Where is my place?" (Mana tempat saya?) Emphatically, the woman begins to say, "Watch out!" as though silencing others, and the man on the drum worries about getting lost on the city streets. As the others sit in other drums, the man atop the drum utters phrases about the difficult environment in which they live, his desire for relations with other people, and the pervasiveness of garbage receptacles in the city. He covetously names various luxury goods, yet ends by advising "but eat first" (makan dulu). Next, he tries to get out of his drum and walk away, but is scolded each time and eventually dives head first back into the barrel and its ostensible security. The woman greeter discourses on the importance of being "smart" (orang pinter) so that one can earn money to buy goods and travel, but she also emphasizes learning to speak up for one's interests. As the performance continues, topics such as feeling pain ("Sakit!"), holding seminars, and exchanging opinions also come up. The woman greeter becomes involved in a squabble with a dancing woman (in *Trilogi Besi*, Dindon's wife, Sheila Hamzah) who interrupts her speech, and they end by violently stuffing each other into metal drums. Next, the dancing woman and a man comically enact an exaggerated love scene, in which the dialogue is very creatively built around the alliterative sounds of the words *Ku* and *Kau* (I and you), plus a few other words that similarly begin with "k." The dancing woman and her man go into convulsions until she screams in pain before shouting the piece's title, "*Sirkus Anjing*" (Dog Circus). The actors now form a circle, holding ropes over their shoulders, and as they draw the circle tighter and tighter, the ropes wrap about the man and the dancing woman who stand in the circle's center. The others don veils and step back, while the man, in a trembling voice says, "We're lost in the markets!" (Kita kesasar di pasar-pasar!). The woman adds, "With hungry stomachs we're tossed into the claws!" (Dengan perut lapar terlempar-lempar di cakar-cakar!). They retreat in fear and hide behind a drum as the others crawl around them making cooing noises. Several actors prance about the stage like chickens and the dancing woman delivers a very rapid speech. The men and women worry about people carrying weapons, talk of the water being drained from their area and of poison taking away their breath. One actor mentions arriving at a "depressing slope" and expresses a desire to leave the place, to fly with the smoke and wind. Wondering how long they have been in this place, they comment, "In the long run, we'll go mad here!" (Lama-lama kita jadi sinting di sini!).

This description of the 2001 re-creation of *Sirkus Anjing* allows us to grasp something of Kubur's themes and style and to connect them to some of the reviewers' comments about the original performance. The fact that the piece opens with a woman greeting audience members and chatting with them as they enter and wait for the show to "begin" underscores the desire of Dindon and Kubur to dialogue with the audience and break down the barriers between performers and spectators—to make the spectators part of the performance. The greeter's patter ranges from recognizing individuals and urging them to move forward for better seats to presenting gender stereotypes when speculating about whether women have become so busy with their careers that they are ignoring their children and thereby contributing to the prevalence of street brawls (*tawuran*) among different high schools. Thus, the greeter bridges the personal and the larger socio-political realm that the overall performance takes as its primary thematic material.

The piece uses other techniques to engage the audience as well, including rhythmic, dynamic drumming and the chanting of the actors. Yet its lack of narrative forces *Sirkus Anjing* to rely on producing enough interesting, discreet utterances and actions to retain the audience's attention. The metal drum containers with their visual-, aural-, and spectacle-laden properties helped accomplish this goal. Kubur's actors not only rapped on the drums to create musical rhythms and chaotic, cacophonous effects, but they dived into them, sat in them, wore them like body armour or shells, and perched atop them. The drums became shabby dwellings, metaphors for ways of protecting the self but also symbols and causes of restricted vision. In this last capacity, they recalled the common Indonesian expression for designating ignorance and lack of wider knowledge of the world outside one's own narrow, guarded sphere, a "frog beneath a coconut shell" (*katak dalam tempurung*). Yet in both the ideological and literal senses of restricting vision, the drums also blocked the eyesight of those within them, leading into jarring collisions among the drums, a richly suggestive metaphor of conflict born of ignorance and fear.

Another significant element in holding audience attention is the everyday language that alludes to a multitude of commonly acknowledged problems: the gap between rich and poor, conspicuous consumption, pollution, garbage, corruption, violence, and the generally inhospitable environment of Jakarta. *Sirkus Anjing* names these issues, provides brief verbal cues, or symbolic or exaggerated enactments of them. At no point does it build a causal, continuing story based upon them.

Structurally, therefore, *Sirkus Anjing* resembles a collage of actions and comments that evoke the feelings, dreams, and vicissitudes of the socially marginalized and/or mentally challenged kampung dwellers. This structure is reinforced by stage design. The set in the performance area is extremely spare, consisting of the metal drums, while the actors wear only cut-off denim shorts (for the men) or black pants and sleeveless blouses. The lighting is subdued and creates a soft but austere chiaroscuro effect. Both of these elements evoke a stifling and impoverished atmosphere that supports and amplifies the actors' statements and actions.

Central to the thematic concerns raised by *Sirkus Anjing* are the changing conditions of life for the socially marginalized in urban Indonesia. The performers complain of the difficult current living circumstances, of how they fear going astray in the markets and wonder about their place amidst the garbage and the harshness of Indonesian society. They dream of escape and worry about being driven mad. Even love, as in the comic scene described above, is eventually ensnared in the binding ropes of an uncaring society: the young lovers are thrown into the claws of the market system. Parallel to Sae's critique of the ways the media create confining biographies and images of how Indonesians should define their identities, Kubur's piece also contrasts dreams of the consumerism inundating ordinary Indonesians with the basic needs of food and shelter. Yet here it becomes evident that Kubur's piece is more socially specific than much of Sae's work. *Sirkus Anjing* centers completely on representing the socially marginalized in distinction to *Pertumbuhan di Atas Meja Makan* or *Biografi Yanti*, which, though sympathetic and often taking up themes of the lower classes, nonetheless tended to approach the problems from a much more philosophical, universalizing point of view. Similarly, Kubur's style, though resembling Sae's in its non-narrative form of presentation and often disjunctive leaps from one utterance to the next, still maintained a certain thematic and social coherence: the stressful lives of the urban poor on a stage resembling a gathering place for the marginalized. Further, as noted above and in confirmation of Dindon's statements, the language is taken from and relates to the impoverished everyday urban surroundings. Therefore, the work seemed less puzzling than Sae's most avant-garde performances, yet powerful and innovative in its exploration of just the sort of kampung milieu from which Kubur's members hailed and which many other Indonesian theater groups sought, less successfully, to represent. In a way, Dindon's longing for authenticity achieved a measure of success. Ironically, though, Kubur's work needed to move away from the older popular entertainment forms most familiar to kampung residents in order to create a new form derived in part from high art avant-garde experiments—most prominently those of Sae. In a way, this fusion throws the idea of authenticity into a new light: as the product of a group grounded in a certain milieu but in dialogue with new and foreign concepts and practices. The authentic is not something pure and possessed in static fashion It is the product of a group in a particular social context responding to stimuli, both internal and external, in a way that in a relative sense can be said to be its own.

Kubur continued its efforts to represent the lives and perspectives of Jakarta's lower-class residents in its next work, *Tombol 13* (*Topeng Monyet Bola Plastik*), staged four years later after another long process of exploration. For this performance Kubur returned to the Taman Ismail Marzuki's Teater Arena, and, predictably, the group received more extensive media coverage in the major newspapers and magazines (*Tempo, DeTik, Kompas, Media Indonesia, Republika*) than for *Sirkus Anjing*. Newspaper descriptions of *Tombol 13* noted the way in which the entire Taman Ismail Marzuki Teater Arena became a set: the interior walls of the arena performance space were wrapped in black cloth; broken hunks of concrete with iron rebar protruding were scattered about the edge of the stage and in the seating area; the chairs had been removed and piled against the walls, forcing the audience to sit on mats in the midst of black sand scattered about the floor. Upon entering, audience members were greeted by the din of banging on iron (Tejo 1994bc; Dewanto 1994). So reminiscent of a harsh urban wasteland, this set thus set the mood and theme for much of what followed.

According to print media reviews, *Tombol 13* opened with a woman (played by Sheila Hamzah) intoning, "We chase one another day and night, although my genitals are torn, my entrails are shattered" (Kita berkejaran siang malam, meski kelaminku robek, meski jeroanku ringsek). This opening was followed by five men chattering deliriously, convulsing, and rolling and falling on their backs. One asks, "Where is the time for my liver, where is the time for my genitals, where is the time for my heart?" (Hatiku mana jam? Kelaminku mana jam? Jantungku mana jam?) Thereafter comes a series of scenes in which five men and one woman seek their own names, use chairs to act out various scenes suggestive of contemporary political and social relations, and finally attempt to attack an iron wall that oppresses them.

The *Tombol 13* section of *Trilogi Besi* appears to follow much of what the reports describe fairly closely. This section opens with Sheila Hamzah reciting the lines "We chase one another day and night..." in a slow and quavering high-pitched voice, whose eerie vibrato is reminiscent of ritual singing. As she dances around the stage, several men appear and one of them begins to ask about where the time is for his various body parts—his brain, heart, and eyes. His voice is strangely choked; his movements come in jerky fashion. He stands on one of the metal drums and repeats a word that sounds like *sekam* (imprison, suppress), *sekap* (imprison, close, cover up) or *sekat* (isolate, close, block up). Yet whichever word he repeats, since the meanings of all three generally suggest incarcerating, suppressing, or closing off, it conveys the sense of a society of closed horizons and controlled human association. As he repeats his words in a growling voice, the bodies of the other men twitch convulsively on the ground, seeming to respond to his snarl. He then invites the men to "enter" and one sticks his head between the growling man's legs, which promptly close tightly around his neck. Calling for weapons to be brought to him, the man works his way out of the growling man's leg-vice. The others are writhing even more frantically on the ground. A third man rises and warns, "Look out! Don't eat with soldiers!" The growling man invites the men around him to "Eat!" and then, after caressing the head of each, shoves them away. They crawl back to him as if in worship. The growling man commands them to "Sekap," and they take up chairs, which they begin to aim like guns. The woman from the beginning of the play chants "Men! Men!" and sprays water into their mouths. The men then begin to squeak like monkeys, while the growling man repeatedly begs them to stop. They debate back and forth and the woman leads his followers away, feeding them as they continue to make monkey sounds. The growling man eventually wins his followers back. Moving acrobatically with chairs and barrels, the growling man and his followers continue to mimic shooting guns, and they talk of throwing a long party. After another episode of conflict with the woman, one actor relates that he has found "promises in the garbage." Another recites a strangely poetic passage about souls torn out, cursing himself and asking how long it has been since they have been turned into pig farm manure.

Three of the men, now sitting on chairs, announce their desire to buy televisions, radios, and newspapers, and they begin to elaborate their dreams of consumerism. Simultaneously, they struggle with others who are trying to crawl out from beneath the chairs on which they are sitting. Finally, the three men manage to escape from beneath the chairs and they drag two of the men who had been sitting on the chairs along with them. They begin to kick their behinds with a gentle paddling motion, while the growling man, still sitting on his chair, shouts "Sekap!" The growling man and the two other "sitting" men force the three others back beneath the chairs. The growling man again takes up his chair and rattles it like a machine gun. The woman re-emerges and talks of "thousands of tigers with different kinds of fangs." The growling man and his followers cower beneath their chairs. She declares that the tigers will pounce and asks, "Then what will become of you?" (Terus kau jadinya apa?). The men all slowly rise and stand hunched over, with the chairs wrapped around them like shackles or restraints that deform their bodies. They slowly disentangle themselves and begin to dance and chant. They appear to be working up the courage for something (as one shouts, "Can't do it, must, have to now!"). They decide they must destroy an iron wall, so they charge, but all of them collapse after running against it. One says, "What street is this that blocks my view?" The growling man urges them to find the courage to try again, but they are repulsed once more. The woman describes them as whining children. She screams that they should have clearer goals and give up impossible dreams. They begin to search, but the growling man, who seems to have lost his way, declaims: "And sleep has made me resent dreams, the night, stars, the moon, the sun, department stores,

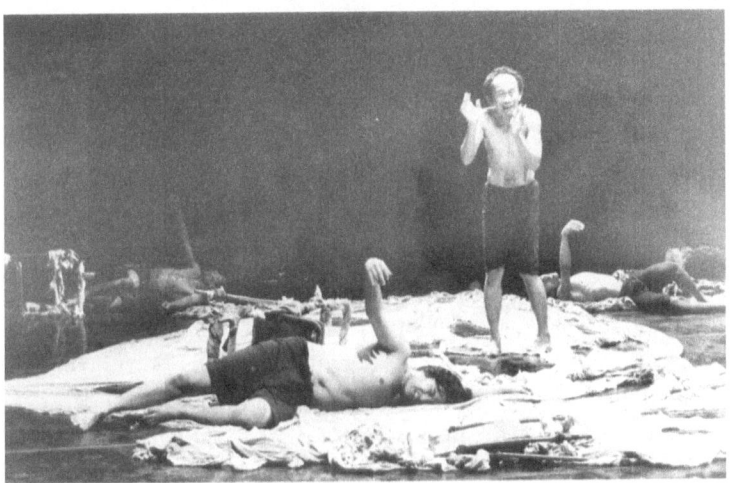

Fig. 4.12. Teater Kubur, *Tombol 13* (1994). Andi Bersama playing the "growling man" stands at right-center. Photo courtesy of *Kompas*.

radios, televisions, newspapers, all of which are swarming with excited pilgrims. Those tombs are tearing our faces to shreds."[34] The others totter about as the woman again chants her opening piece. They move to the edge of the performance area and collapse.

I have described the recreated versions of *Sirkus Anjing* and *Tombol 13* contained in *Trilogi Besi* at some length in order to provide a clear picture of Kubur's work in lieu of published scripts or easily accessible recordings of their performances. *Tombol 13* is rich in allusions to New Order Indonesia circa 1994. To be sure, there is some repetition and overlap of imagery and theme with the earlier *Sirkus Anijng*—most particularly in the portrayal of consumer dreams as incongruent with the reality of Jakarta's under-classes. Yet there are several striking new themes: a gender divide between men and women; the relationship between leaders and the led; and the presence of the military and its contribution to the construction of a violent, militarized society. All of these themes arise repeatedly in the course of *Tombol 13*. Much as in *Sirkus Anjing*, *Tombol 13* makes use of one prop as a multivalent symbol, in this instance, chairs rather than the metal drums of the earlier work.

The opening and closing of the play are framed by the woman who sings of continually chasing through life as though wounded. This frame underscores an important theme, one that connects both to the men's struggles to control and overpower others and to fight against the iron wall that blocks their vision and to their lack of ability to realize the consumer dreams that the media continually project. As a result, the growling man's final soliloquy recounts how the mass media and department stores are "tearing our faces to shreds." Yet the play is also about power relations. Early on the growling man attempts to control the other men, drawing them into his leg-vice grip and feeding them. In return, they bow down to him. This set of actions appears to represent a system of patron-client relations, but it is one rife with violence and tied to the image of the military character of the New Order state. When invited to eat, the men are warned not to eat with soldiers, but one man trapped in the vice-grip of the growling man's legs calls for weapons to be brought to him, and at several points the men use the chairs to mimic firing weapons.

Furthermore, as his frequent calls of "Sekap" suggest, the growling man is obsessed with control and suppression. All of this action is linked to the growth of consumerism and the gaps in wealth between the rich and the poor, as can be seen in the scene of the three men sitting on chairs dreaming of conspicuous consumption while trying to keep another trio from crawling out from underneath their chairs. The idea that the wealthy can consume as they do only by riding on the backs of the poor is thus given a physical representation through the deployment of chairs and the struggle of the actors for position on and around them. The chairs also resonate with the notion of elected representatives, since the Indonesian word for seats in parliament is similar to "chairs" (*kursi*). This association ties notions of the exploiting wealthy to those who have gained elected or appointed positions in government.

This system of control and exploitation is challenged sporadically by the woman who provides water for the men and whose chiding "Men!" critiques the growling man's authority by suggesting that his coercion and threat are an all-too-male manner of organizing society. Yet her intervention also provides sustenance for the men and turns them into squeaking monkey-like characters. The play thus suggests that any system in which a leader has such complete control over the daily needs of

Fig. 4.13. Teater Kubur, *Tombol 13* (1994): Chairs, Militarism, and Power. Photo courtesy of *Tempo* Magazine.

followers is bound to deform the humanity of those concerned. Still, at several points in the piece, the woman appears to challenge and disrupt the growling man's plans and thus raises the image of a serious gender division within Indonesian society.

Finally, the play is, after all, also about the fate of the urban poor and marginalized. This theme is suggested by the costumes—again, denim shorts for the men and plain black tops and pants for the women. However, it is also made clear in the scenes in which leaders promise food and water to potential followers and in the inability of the men, ultimately, to attain the consumer dreams with which they have been indoctrinated. In this light, the relationship of the growling man to the other men also symbolizes the formation of localized groups of thugs, *preman*, from the ranks of the nation's less prosperous, hinting at the way militarization of New Order society works its way down into the kampung. Such a result stems from the lack of real economic development for the under classes, something alluded to in the remark that many promises are to be found in the garbage. *Tombol 13* thereby embodies a profound and disturbingly dystopian view from below of the economic progress achieved by Suharto's New Order.

Conclusion

In a way never achieved by Teater Sae, Teater Kubur was able to combine avant-garde performance styles and aesthetics with a simpler, more direct representation of the struggles of the urban poor, in order to create powerful and disturbing performances that received significant attention from the media and intellectuals alike. Yet the efforts of these two groups were part of an emerging avant-garde scene linked to many NGOs, which opened its performance spaces to workers theater and other less traditional theater performances. Thus, the avant-garde scene was not only critiquing New Order society from the perspectives of society's marginalized in the work of its most powerful theater groups, but was also actively extending its facilities to theater groups emerging from other social strata. In fact, even members of avant-garde theater companies were engaging with such groups in different ways. Teater Sae's Margesti S. Otong and, to a lesser extent, Teater Kubur's Dindon were two of those who found another way of linking theater to the needs of Indonesia's poor. Margesti, Boedi Otong's wife and Sae's leading actress, became involved in the formation of one of the leading workers' theater groups in the greater Jakarta area. Dindon, for his part, offered his encouragement and some theoretical support for workers' theater efforts, while assisting well-known actress, director, and playwright, Ratna Sarumpaet, in mounting a play about the murdered worker activist, Marsinah. Their efforts and those of the NGO activists and factory workers who took part in the rise of Indonesian workers' theater during the 1990s created a web of theatrical relations that once again demonstrated the growth of the new, extended socio-cultural *jaringan* around modern theater in the 1985–98 period. Those relations with the NGO activists and factory workers who took part in the rise of Indonesian workers' theater during the 1990s are the subject of chapter 6.

At the same time that Margesti, Dindon, and Ratna Sarumpaet were becoming involved with workers' theater and themes, another avant-garde group, Teater Payung Hitam, was developing some of the themes taken up by Sae and Kubur and turning them in the direction of an increasingly pointed and direct criticism of the Indonesian political system. The changes in tone evident in Payung Hitam's work of the mid-1990s illustrate suggestively the fact that a considerable segment of modern theater workers and groups were now more actively probing and challenging the New Order's system of censorship and control over the arts. Given Payung Hitam's origin and home base in a post-secondary performing arts academy, it also points toward the rising wave of bolder, more aggressive attitudes and critiques launched by the new student movement of the 1990s. In order to better understand how these changes were transformed into theatrical material, we now turn to an examination of Teater Payung Hitam's genesis and seminal work during the 1994–97 period.

Chapter 5

THE LIMITS OF *BAHASA INDONESIA* AND TEATER PAYUNG HITAM'S "THEATER OF PAIN"

Crisis of Representation of the Nation and Political Allegory

In early October 1996, Indonesia's Directorate of the Arts (under the General Director of Culture in the Ministry of Education and Culture) initiated a national modern theater festival with the idea, according to one of the festival's judges, of presenting "a map of Indonesian theater that had its roots in Indonesian culture" (Leak 1996). In fact, the festival's organizing committee had instructed participating groups to use "local color" elements as part of their performances (Oemar 1996). Ironically, the play singled out for most of the attention in media reports and in the essays submitted for a special theater criticism competition sponsored by the leading Bandung newspaper, *Pikiran Rakyat*,[1] was an adaptation of Austrian writer Peter Handke's *Kaspar* by the Bandung group Teater Payung Hitam. It featured very little local color or elements of traditional Indonesian performance.

Payung Hitam's *Kaspar* had been generating interest and excitement since its first performance more than two years earlier. It was first staged in September 1994, only three months after the government had banned three leading news magazines, thereby signalling the end of its own brief flirtation with increased political "openness" and engendering a series of outraged protests. *Kaspar* focused on how the Indonesian language formed particular kinds of Indonesian subjects. In so doing, it also yoked the notion of national language to the government's recent censorship and attempts to control public discourse. It thereby signalled that the nation itself was in crisis. This sense of crisis was attested to by the fact that the national language, Bahasa Indonesia, long taken as a symbol of national unity in an archipelagic nation where many ethnic groups scattered across thousands of islands also possessed their own distinct local languages, was being harshly judged in an openly political way in Payung Hitam's striking and celebrated work.

Kaspar thereby marked a turning point in modern avant-garde theater. It harnessed some of the techniques and themes of avant-garde theater to more specific commentaries on particular political events, rather than to the highly philosophical critiques of social conditions constructed by groups like Teater Sae or the metaphoric portraits of the conditions of a particular social class, such as offered by Teater Kubur. This ramping up of direct political criticism, though still carefully maintaining room for variant interpretations in accordance with both the dominant modernist aesthetic and lingering fears of censorship, nevertheless represented the fact that modern theater groups had been becoming increasingly frustrated with New Order society and bolder in their criticism. The end of openness, rather than silencing this mounting anger, served to increase the determination of many modern theater practitioners to speak more openly and directly about the failings of the New Order.

In a different manner than Teater Sae, Teater Payung Hitam's most memorable performances after 1994 attempted to problematize the verbal language of Indonesian state and society, presenting it as an instrument of power and a trap for would-be reformers, as sound and fury signifying little but its own existence as a political cudgel to stupefy, drown out, and silence others, and as incapable of giving voice to the pain of Indonesians' everyday existence and their frustration with national politics. In short, by thematizing the problems of the national language, Payung Hitam's work was also thematizing a crisis in the representation of nation on the modern theater's stages. Still, Payung Hitam's history differs from than that of other contemporary avant-garde groups like Sae and Kubur. Payung Hitam developed its distinctive style from within the government-funded academic arts institution, Akademi Seni Tari Indonesia or ASTI (Indonesian Academy of Dance), later renamed Sekolah Tinggi Seni Indonesia or STSI (Indonesian Advanced School of the Arts). Through its leader and director, Rachman Sabur, it also had some roots in one of the pioneering realist theaters of the Sukarno and New Order era, the Studiklub Teater Bandung (STB). Payung Hitam's roots are thus much more uniformly planted in the soil of the high art national culture and theater aesthetic ideology detailed in chapter 1 than most of the other groups discussed in previous chapters. Throughout its long journey to national recognition, Payung Hitam always held firmly to the modernist and universal humanist idea of art (and theater) as continual exploration and experimentation. Payung Hitam's leader, Rachman Sabur, even eschewed characterizations of Payung Hitam's work as "political theater" (teater politik) (Field Notes 13 August 1997), claiming that his group did not "engage in politics." Such statements not only conveyed the ideological fear of political polarization of the arts (an idea that had imprinted itself heavily on post-1965 Indonesian theater and national culture), but also served as a kind of survival mechanism in the shadow of a regime that frequently banned theater productions and had a low tolerance for "political" art. Additionally, this attitude embodied the general idea many Indonesians had of politics as a dirty business from which other spheres of life, especially the arts, had best keep their distance.

Still, the 1990s were a time of sharpening dissatisfaction with the New Order regime among the educated middle-class, which was then growing in size and social importance. As we have observed, this dissatisfaction also precipitated the collaboration of a variety of non-government organizations with peasants, and, as we will see in the next chapter, with industrial workers to empower such constituencies and raise their awareness of their rights in the face of frequent injustice. As Aspinall has noted, beginning in the late 1980s, student opposition to the New Order regime was also growing and becoming more aggressively vocal. As the 1990s wore on, it spread from private university campuses to the more heavily constrained state universities. Increasingly, student activists directly criticised President Suharto and his family and also the military. Other students researched living conditions among peasants, workers, and other groups and contributed to consciousness raising and mobilization efforts among such groups, even as their own consciousness changed by what they discovered in such ventures (Aspinall 2005, 116–44). All of this activity focused anger toward Suharto, but more generally, toward the corruption, collusion, and nepotism that appeared to be among the main causes of the increasingly rapacious "accumulation by dispossession" undertaken by the political and economic elites.

At such an historical juncture, a trend within national theater ideology came increasingly to the fore. It held that theater should play a socially critical role, expressing key issues of concern to Indonesians and pointing out the flaws of government and society alike, perhaps even speaking on behalf of society's marginalized. Though Sabur refused to accept characterizations of Payung Hitam's brand of theater as political, his group nonetheless exemplified the socially committed side of Indonesia's modern national theater simply by expressing its concerns with what group members saw "happening around them" (Field Notes 13 August 1997). Sabur was a particularly sensitive observer of the politics of Indonesian society. Later, the group was also influenced by the participation of some of its members in the student protest movements of the last decade of the Suharto era. And it was precisely the group's balancing act between devastating representations of Indonesian politics and society and its highly experimental and stylized performances that excited and captivated critics and audiences in the waning years of Suharto's rule. Payung Hitam's work, then, displays the growing frustration of the educated middle-class. It provides us with a glimpse of the structure of feeling within these circles in the media and the arts that laid some of the groundwork for the collaboration between theater workers and industrial workers as well as for the struggles against New Order censorship recounted in the next two chapters.

Bandung as a Site of Theater and Payung Hitam's Early Years

Bandung, the capital city of West Java located in the mountainous Parahyangan (or Priangan) region only a couple of hours by train or automobile from Jakarta, has a long and significant history of modern theater. In 1958, one of Indonesia's best-known pioneering modern theater groups,

Studiklub Teater Bandung (STB), was founded in the city by Jim Lim (Jim Adhi Limas), Suyatna Anirun, and a number of their friends (Tjitrosoewarno 1993). Established in the era of realism in modern national theater, STB established a strong reputation for its realist adaptations of Western dramas, such as Tennessee Williams's *The Glass Menagerie* (1960), Anton Chekhov's *Uncle Vanya* (1961), and Wolf Mankowitz's *The Bespoke Overcoat* (1962) as well as Indonesian contemporary works like Kirjomulyo's *Penggali Intan* (The Diamond Miner, 1960). Yet STB did not limit itself to staging works according to Western-style realism. As Saini K.M. has noted, during this period, STB also experimented with elements of traditional theater in both Western and contemporary Indonesian works. Most notably, Saini recalls that the production of Misbach Yusa Biran's *Bung Besar* (Comrade Big Shot, 1960) employed elements of the West Javanese popular theater form, *longser*, although mixing a satirical realist play with folk theater elements at that time was apparently not only harshly criticized but also created something of a scandal. A production of *Hamlet* directed by Lim in 1964, according to Saini's recollections, made use of gamelan and Cirebon mask dance (Saini 1999).[2] Jim Lim left Indonesia to study in Paris in 1967, but STB remained active and highly visible in modern Indonesian theater under the direction of Suyatna Anirun, who until well into the 1990s continued the pattern of mixing realist productions with adaptations of various plays utilizing elements of traditional performance.

In addition to STB, other lively experiments with modern theater were occurring in Bandung during the early New Order. For instance, in 1965 Jim Lim founded a second theater group, Teater Perintis, that mounted at least two productions of absurdist theater—Ionesco's *Rhinoceros* (1965) and Camus' *Caligula* (1966). The late 1960s and early 1970s in Bandung also witnessed the rise of the so-called underground theater or theater *mbeling* (disobedient, insubordinate) led by the flamboyant Remy Sylado (Yapi Tambayong). According to Nandi Riffandi, Sylado's theater mbeling was a part of the '60s generation ethos in Indonesia (Field Notes 16 August 2001). And in fact, Sylado quickly gained a reputation as an iconoclast. His best-known plays, *Messiah II* and *Genesis II* (both circa 1972), intended as counter-versions of some of Christianity's central sacred texts, demonstrated this tendency with outrageous portrayals of Christ or representations of magic and ritual, including "bewitched" young women climbing onto the stage and taking off their blouses. However, such provocative theater did cause some problems. Sylado was questioned by the police because of the "unadorned" or "bare" qualities of his theater (*Tempo* 12 August 1972).

Bandung was also the site of a number of universities, including the prestigious ITB (Institut Teknologi Bandung) and one of the New Order's performing arts schools, ASTI Bandung (Akademi Seni Tari Indonesia—Indonesian Academy of Dance), whose theater department was founded in 1978. One of the key figures in its founding was Saini K.M. (Ismet 2004). Saini, who was an instructor at ASTI Bandung from 1973 to 1989 and later became ASTI's director (1989–95), was one of the leading playwrights of the New Order a tireless promoter of modern theater and, later, a strong supporter of a modernized revival of the West Javanese traditional theater form, *longser*. Saini's original dramas won a number of prizes in playwriting competitions sponsored by the Dewan Kesenian Jakarta (Jakarta Arts Council) between 1973 and 1981, and his oeuvre supplied STB with at least two dramas for production, *Geusun Ulun* (1982–83) and *Panji Koming* (1985). In the 1980s, ASTI facilitated a number of productions by its students and faculty under its own aegis, and this ASTI group also performed works by Saini K.M. (*Ken Arok*, 1987) as well as works by foreign writers (e.g., Bertolt Brecht's *Puntila*, 1988), in both Bandung and Jakarta. Since 1980, the prolific cultural observer and writer, Jakob Sumardjo (Pusat Data & Analisa Tempo), who wrote one of the most comprehensive histories of modern Indonesian theater published to date (Sumardjo 1992), has also been associated with ASTI.

Bandung, thus, was a fertile site for modern theater productions and culture. As additional proof of this legacy, in the late 1980s and early 1990s, new groups appeared in Bandung and began to gain both local and national recognition, among them Kelompok Payung Hitam (later Teater Payung Hitam or Black Umbrella Theater) under the direction of Rachman Sabur and Teater re-Publik, led by the playwright, director, actor, and perceptive theater critic Benny Yohanes. Later, the rise of these groups would be followed by the emergence of yet another promising company, Laskar Panggung (Stage Battalion). Of these new groups, Payung Hitam established itself most firmly as a seminal avant-garde theater company throughout Indonesia, especially with its 1994 production of *Kaspar*. Yet Payung Hitam had been actively mounting productions since 1983, and it is worth taking time to recount briefly the genesis of the group and the background of its leader, Rachman Sabur, before proceeding to a discussion of the 1990s performances for which it is most widely known.

Rachman Sabur was born in 1957, to parents who held an abiding interest in the arts. His mother had been an amateur theater (*tonil*) actress during the Dutch colonial era, and his father worked for a former Dutch electronics firm, which facilitated the young Sabur's viewing of many films (Arcana 2004, 141). His parents also often organized evenings of Cianjuran-sung poetry at their home (Ismet 2004, 95). During his middle-school years, Sabur himself began writing poetry, but, failing to gain entrance into a desired university's literature program, he entered the Akademi Sinematografi Bandung (Bandung Academy of Cinematography). Through a friend studying at ASTI, Sabur became interested in the theater, and in 1979, he switched to ASTI's theater department. Following his completion of a bachelor's degree program (*sarjana muda*) in theater at ASTI Bandung, an indication of Sabur's talent and breadth of interests came when he decided to continue his education at the STSI (Sekolah Tinggi Seni Indonesia, Indonesian Advanced Arts School) in Surakarta, Central Java. There he obtained an artist's degree in dance composition (Arcana 2004, 141). Eventually, Sabur was recruited by his alma mater to teach acting and theater.

While studying at ASTI, Sabur honed his acting skills at STB with the comic roles in which Suyatna Anirun cast him in adaptations of Ben Jonson's *Volpone* (Karto Loewak 1982) and Eugene Ionesco's *Rhinoceros* (Badak-Badak 1985). He also took part in the ASTI Bandung house productions of the late 1980s, including playing Puntila in the Bandung performance of Brecht's play, *Puntila*. Another of his leading roles was in a staging of Carl Zuckmayer's *Der Hauptmann von Köpenick* (Kapten dari Kopenick), co-sponsored by ASTI and Liga Teater

Bandung together with the Goethe Foundation and under the direction of German director, Jorg Friedrich (Ismet 2004, 97). All of this experience gave Sabur a solid grounding in the world of modern national and international theater as well as in the aesthetic ideologies of the Indonesian national theater.

As he was gaining valuable training in the realist and text- and dialogue-oriented theaters produced by STB and ASTI Bandung, Sabur also joined with others to found Kelompok Payung Hitam in 1982. In its early years Payung Hitam focused chiefly on mounting productions of Indonesian plays, such as Putu Wijaya's *Dag Dig Dug* (Racing Heartbeat, 1982), *Aduh!* (Ouch!, 1983), *Aum* (Roar! 1985), and *Bila Malam Bertambah Malam* (As Night Waxes Full, 1988), Saini K.M.'s *Ben Go Tun* (1986), D. Djayakusumah's *Bebek-Bebek* (Ducks, 1988), and Arifin C Noer's *Orkes Madun* (Madun Orchestra, 1989) and *Darim Mencari Darim* (Darim Searching for Darim, 1989, 1991, based on Noer's drama *Kucak-Kacik*) as well as Sabur's own *Tuhan dan Kami* (God and Us, 1987). During these years, according to Sabur, Payung Hitam devoted most of its efforts to Indonesian works, which were linguistically closer to group members. Sabur also led his actors on observation visits to rougher parts of Bandung in preparation for a number of plays portraying the lower rungs of society (Field Notes 13 August 1997). The choice of scripts also indicated a tendency for Sabur and Payung Hitam to choose dramas that related to actual problems faced by Indonesian society.

A landmark production in 1991, *Metateater: Dunia Tanpa Makna* (Metatheater: World without Meaning), however, helped shift Sabur and Payung Hitam's orientation in a different and more stylistically radical direction. By all accounts, *Metateater* was an unusual performance work. Critics and observers could compare it only to Rendra's improvisational pieces of the late 1960s, the so-called *Minikata*, which used minimal verbal language, and to Sardono's modern dance performance, *Meta-Ekologi* (1979).[3] Newspaper reports and reviews are partial and often confused about what happened as part of the performance. I cannot, therefore, hope to describe adequately the performance of *Metateater*. What is obvious is that this particular piece helped Sabur and Payung Hitam develop several key stylistic elements and themes to which they would return when mounting their most acclaimed and original performances throughout the 1990s and into the first decade of the twenty-first century. It is therefore appropriate to note several general details about how *Metateater* was constructed and conceived.

First, the work was a collaborative effort by an especially talented and diverse group of Bandung arts figures: Herry Dim was an artist and stage designer; Harry Roesli and Aat Soeratin were composers associated with the Depot Kreasi Seni Bandung, though Roesli had long collaborated in other theatrical productions by Putu Wijaya's Teater Mandiri; Sabur and his actors were from Teater Payung Hitam; and local artists included Maman Noor and Arahmaiani (who was replaced by Diyanto in later performances). Dim, one of the driving forces behind the performance, explained that the group had wanted to create a kind of "complete" or "perfect" (*paripurna*) theater, in which all of the elements were equally free to explore their own expressive potential, and not simply be subordinated to supporting the actors and the story (GG 1991). For example, while Payung Hitam's actors moved about the stage, dressed in loin-cloths and carrying branches above their heads, Dim projected a series of slides onto the white backdrop, beginning with photographer Herman Effendy's slides of masks and people wearing masks and ending with images of a defoliated tree. At the same time, Maman Noor and Arahmaiani painted large canvases to the right and left of the stage, and Roesli and Soeratin's electronic compositions created a soundscape for the entire event.

A number of commentators noted that the acting, music, painting, and projected slides all seemed to be engaged in a dialogue or a unified effect (Sudradjat 1991; Muchyatim 1991), while others felt they often failed to create a coherent whole (Rachmat 1991; Budiman 1991; Burdansyah 1991). In an interview on Radio Mara, Dim, Sabur, and Roesli explained that their intention was to "return theater to its own complexity. Theater should be more complex than just telling a story. It should speak, but not only with words and sentences, rather through events, movement, music, sets, and all elements. In reality this represents an ancient (*purba*), primitive form of theater whose traces we can still see in the rituals of worship to the rice goddess, for example" (GG

1991).[4] Further, they explained that the structure of the performance was highly unconventional. The reporter for *Pikiran Rakyat* who covered the collaborators' radio interview paraphrased their comments as follows: "No one element is simply in a supporting role to the others. All are involved in a form of dialogue that is unique and intensive. Each of them stimulates the others and responds to the others. For example, an actor will not undertake a certain act if the set design doesn't stimulate him or her with a particular artistic effect, and music will not respond with a particular musical effect, and so on" (GG 1991).[5] Finally, the creators suggested that they were rejecting the tendency to put art into neat, separate boxes and to relegate art narrowly to the duty of providing understanding. They asserted that *Metateater* would not provide "understanding, but rather experience and enjoyment according to the background of each audience member" (GG 1991).

Two things here are important for understanding Payung Hitam's future development. First, the collaboration with artists from a variety of fields enriched Sabur's concept of the possibilities of performance. As Sabur himself admitted, working with Roesli, Dim, and others on *Metateater* had been difficult, since there were many conflicts regarding specific ideas. But, he added, he had learned a lot about using sets, music, and movement, things that contributed to Payung Hitam's own performances throughout the 1990s. Sabur had been especially impressed with Dim's sets and backdrops on which slides had been continually changing, almost like a film (Field Notes 16 August 1997). Second, the distrust of verbal language as a dominant medium for achieving understanding (in a narrow, highly story-oriented sense) would also become a recurring, if not to say, central theme in Payung Hitam's most celebrated works. In *Metateater*, this theme was noted and elaborated by newspaper reviewers who recognized that "words no longer mirror reality" or that words had become a kind of pollution that poisoned Indonesians (*Kompas*, "Eksperimen yang Bukan Titik"; Sudradjat 1991). Reviewers likened its sentiments regarding the New Order's manipulation of the Indonesian language to those of Afrizal Malna and Sae.

Yet there was also a third dimension to the ideas of the creators of *Metateater*. Not only was it of great significance for Payung Hitam's orientation, but it also resonated with the avant-garde work of Jakarta-based groups like Sae and Kubur. In describing the play's intended theme, they argued,

> First, it is meant as a satire towards our surroundings and a life that is already so profane and secular that it has virtually no spiritual dimension. Togetherness and loyalty are increasingly left behind, replaced by greed in chasing after rank and piling up wealth. Sensitivity and solidarity towards one's fellows find no place because they go against economic logic; human conscience and feelings are not in accord with the logic of industry and modern technology which must be profitable, effective, and efficient. We're now faced with a world which becomes increasingly meaningless. (GG 1991)[6]

Sae, Kubur, and Payung Hitam all shared a feeling of anomie in the face of the New Order's repressive politics and coldly aggressive crony capitalism, but *Metateater*'s creative group showed distinct differences in formulating some of the causes of their alienation. Sae saw social structures and discourses—an inhumane urban environment, the straitjacketing of human identity, and media-generated images of human life—as key factors while Kubur viewed economic and political structural factors—poverty and degraded living conditions, the gap between consumerist dreams and the struggle of the poor to meet everyday survival needs, and the militarization of society—as crucial. In 1991, Payung Hitam and its collaborators in *Metateater* seemed to target more individualized moral decay within a modern rationalized economy. They viewed a perceived loss of spirituality and solidarity with fellow human beings, a mania for efficiency, and greed for wealth and position as central to the disappearance of meaning in contemporary Indonesian life. By stressing the world of the rationalized economy and in pinpointing individuals' pursuit of wealth and position at the expense of social solidarity as root causes of the problem, *Metateater*'s creators betrayed more middle-class and elite formulations. This stance would change as Payung Hitam's observation of politics became more focused on the failings of the Suharto regime during the 1990s.

Finally, as one reviewer noticed, as in the work of Sae and Kubur, there were no main characters, no linear storyline, and no dialogue between the characters. All these were replaced, the reviewer argued, with the language of movement. These features would also be important in a number of Payung Hitam's later works (Sudradjat 1991).

In the years just before and immediately after Payung Hitam's collaboration in *Metateater*, Sabur and the group began to work more frequently with Western dramatic scripts of various kinds from Yeats and Eliot to Camus and Beckett. According to Sabur, this step was consciously undertaken for purposes of comparison and for the discipline of the exercise, but also to see if Payung Hitam could bridge the cultural gap (Field Notes 13 August 1997). This was perhaps a positive development for Sabur, who, because he daily had to teach a defined and restricted curriculum at ASTI (which had changed its name to STSI-Bandung by the mid-1990s), derived great pleasure from exploring other possibilities with Payung Hitam. Accordingly, he stressed that theater is a continual process of exploration and learning (Field Notes 30 July 1997; 2 August 1997; Sabur 2004, 116-121). In fact, Sabur once confided that he felt some affinity for Dindon and Teater Kubur since both he and Dindon saw theater as a process that never ends (Field Notes 2 August 1997). It was during this period of work with Western scripts that Sabur approached Peter Sternagel, director of the Bandung Branch of the Goethe Foundation, to inquire about receiving support for a production of Peter Handke's *Kaspar Hauser* (Field Notes 10 August 1999). The assent of Sternagel and the Goethe Foundation led to one of a seminal series of theatrical performances of modern Indonesian theater and rocketed Payung Hitam into the national spotlight.

Kaspar *(1994)*

Payung Hitam's first staging of *Kaspar* in 1994 occurred just months after the banning of three prominent weekly news magazines that had reported on political conflict within the government. The play, originally by Austrian writer Peter Handke, illustrates the ways in which individuals are integrated into particular regimes of social behavior through learning language norms. Yet the timing of Payung Hitam's staging of the work, its sets, linguistic references, and oblique hints of the banned newspapers give it a very specific contextual meaning. Thus, in contrast to works like *Metateater*, which showed Payung Hitam to be exploring directions similar to other avant-garde groups, *Kaspar* announces Payung Hitam's shift toward a social criticism commenting on specific contemporary events.

Handke's play is based on the story of a man discovered to have been isolated since birth from contact with other humans, who is suddenly released into human society and must learn to speak German and to interact with other human beings. The play begins as Kaspar, garishly dressed, moves clumsily onto a stage filled with unarranged furniture and other props. Prompter voices begin to speak to Kaspar, telling him that he already has a sentence with which to begin to explain himself and to differentiate himself from animals. Each time Kaspar encounters an object on the stage, he utters the sentence "Ich möcht ein solcher werden wie einmal ein andrer gewesen ist."[7] (I want to be a person like somebody else was once.) The prompters proceed to tell Kaspar what he can do with a sentence—differentiate things, bring order to disorder, place it between him and objects, give examples, and so on. Gradually, Kaspar is encouraged to speak in simple normative sentences that leave no room for questions, stories, or other disturbing possibilities. In the monologues of Kaspar and his prompters, the normative language is tied to images of a conformist, respectable life. An intermission follows during which members of the audience—whether they remain in the auditorium or go to the lobby—are subjected to a series of fragments of official speeches mixed with recordings of the prompters' instructions to Kaspar. Only here in the text of Handke's *Kaspar Hauser* is a more direct connection established between everyday language and the world of power relations and politics outside the theater. When the second act commences, Kaspar reverts from being well adjusted and normal to having a lapse of faith in what he has learned previously, and as the play ends he retreats into his own private language once again.

Payung Hitam's restaging of *Kaspar* re-contextualizes Handke's play as one in which Kaspar is conditioned to become an Indonesian citizen through the norms of New Order Bahasa Indonesia usage. The set itself, designed by well-known Bandung artist Tisna Sanjaya announces the Indonesian setting in its use of a large billowing backdrop onto which the red and white colors of the Indonesian national flag are occasionally projected. This "Indonesian-ized" backdrop is further elaborated by a metal, cage-like latticework. The stage space is also delimited by barbed wire, as if the stage were the site of a prison. A number of newspaper reviews found the set an accurate reflection of current conditions in Indonesia (*Independen* 10 September 1994; Asikin 1994). This perception in itself suggested the anger of many middle-class Indonesians toward the recent censorship of the mass media.

Payung Hitam's Kaspar learns his language by repeating the utterances of a loudspeaker perched atop a pole on the stage. Another indication of the specific Indonesian contextualization of Handke's work was found in the particular words uttered, especially by the loudspeaker-prompter that attempted to instruct Kaspar on how to speak proper Indonesian. The pronouncements of the loudspeaker are full of the key words of the New Order: *kebebasan, penindasan, kekuasaan, keteraturan, larangan* (freedom, oppression, domination, orderliness, bans), indicating at least a partial identification of the loudspeaker-prompter with the government's official discourse. Similarly, other scenes connect the specificity of Indonesia to the play's central ideas of the power of language to shape human identity and to oppressively enforce desired ways of behaving. For example, after failing to make his body "conform" to the shape of a trolley, Kaspar runs to an iron booth and opens the door, releasing a flood of tin cans. The prompter tells him, "By opening the iron booth you have entered a system of rules, sounds, sentences." Later, when Kaspar has begun to protest, noting that he hears "sentences become power" and that power can make sentences "hurt," he runs to seal himself off inside the booth. Four other figures begin hammering on the booth, and when Kaspar complains about the pain the pounding inflicts on him, the four line up, each with a fist clenched in the air and stomping out a martial rhythm, while the prompter utters a list of things forbidden—becoming angry, discussions, crying, talking nonsense, protesting. It is as if Kaspar's protest earns him only the hammering assault of punishment inflicted by a militarized society at pains to force him to conform and thereby prevent further dissent. Later prompter pronouncements declare the danger of demonstrations and, again using rhetoric common during the New Order, threaten Kaspar, telling him he deserves to be "watched" (*diawasi*), "suspected" (*dicurigai*) and even "exterminated" (*ditumpas*).

Payung Hitam's production also has Kaspar learning Indonesian by reading scraps of newspaper that contain headlines related to current Indonesian events. These headlines are, in part, a nod to the banned news magazines. They begin to introduce a counter-discourse into Kaspar's identity formation, since most hint at government corruption, the persecution of critical public figures, or other political problems. Yet Payung Hitam also contrived to have the overhead speaker/prompter act as more than simply the voice of official discourse. It clearly states that even as he learned, through repeating its sentences, that there is order in the world, Kaspar also came to understand that many rules led to disorder and much disorderliness needed to be put in order. Through this echoing of the New Order's mania for order (ironically juxtaposed to the notion that there are many rules that lead to disorder), Payung Hitam's play casts the New Order's system itself as a cause of disorder. As Kaspar begins to protest, he articulates a number of common complaints that Indonesians of the time might have made about the New Order, including the perception that its officials bend many rules, that it allows many injustices to occur, that it is suspicious of free expression and art, and that it tosses truth into the garbage. Yet Kaspar's statements are usually crafted to express these complaints without tying them specifically to the New Order. Because the complaints he voices are also common in Indonesia, however, the audience can understand them as a reference to their own lives. Finally, Kaspar rebels against the arbitrary "order" to which he has been conditioned to conform, and, in so doing though he means to liberate others, he realizes he has merely formulated new rules and norms. At the end of the play, as the overhead speaker/prompter screams that red and white (almost certainly an allusion to Indonesia's flag) are blackened, he relapses into silence.

Clearly, a radical distrust of the ability of the New Order's Bahasa Indonesia to articulate a more liberating identity and social system, even when the regime's critics use the language, is at the heart of Payung Hitam's staging of *Kaspar*. Added to this, the very idea of the play—that subjects are formed and deconstructed according to linguistic norms and social coercion—hints at the arbitrary nature of Indonesian (or perhaps any) subjecthood and so negates the possibility that subjects thus constituted could possess a natural, individualized, or essential cultural foundation. Still, even in *Kaspar*, one can detect the beginnings of Payung Hitam's attempt to formulate an alternative language, which might express the pain of living under the New Order without becoming trapped in the norms of New Order language.

Payung Hitam's *Kaspar* is distinct from the best-known performances of Sae and Kubur in that, though minimal, it does have a distinct story to tell. Yet, since the plot is relatively thin, the audience's attention is focused on the physical performance of Tony Broer, the actor portraying Kaspar. In a tour de force of physical, comic acting, Broer created numerous humorous moments by interacting with the variety of tin cans and metallic objects that seemed to represent the cacophony of sounds from which Kaspar attempts to form orderly language as well as the sound and fury of social choruses of conformity. Broer wore cans on his feet and head, which occasionally became stuck; he tried to scratch himself even though his hands were covered with cans, and even did a tap dance with cans on all of his hands and feet. Such acting, full of difficult, painful, and humorous contortions, required an acrobatic athleticism that came to symbolize Kaspar's spiritual struggle with language and its formal rules. The most stunning example comes near the play's beginning. The loudspeaker/prompter has already ratified the wisdom of Kaspar's single sentence "Aku ingin menjelma seperti orang yang telah pernah ada" (I want to be a person like somebody else once was), as a means of helping him conform. While Kaspar repeatedly, and with many different speeds, tones, and stresses, says these words, Tony Broer is in the process of crawling over and grappling with a metal, trolley-like framework as though literally trying to fit his body to the normative shape of the trolley. In so doing Broer creates a physical representation of, or literally, embodies Kaspar's conceptual struggle to form himself according to a set mould, to become "a person like somebody else once was." Yet Kaspar's endeavors to make his body conform do not succeed as easily as do his efforts to pronounce the normative sentence he has been given. At the end of this sequence, he

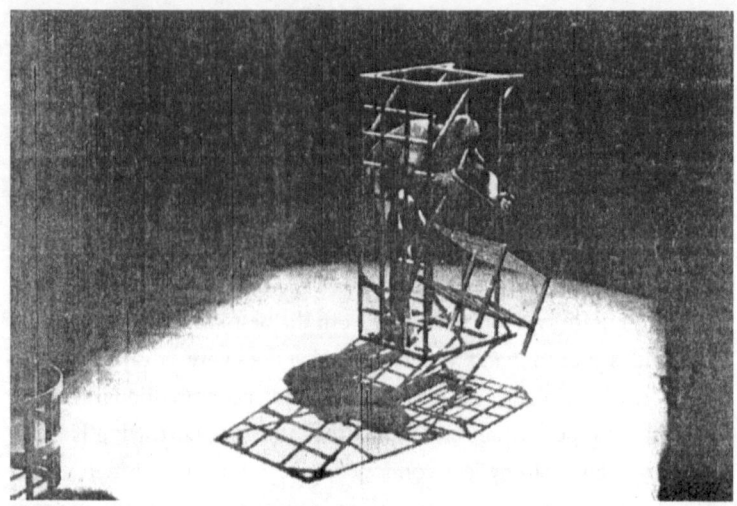

Fig. 5.1. Payung Hitam, *Kaspar* (1996). Kaspar tries to fit himself onto the existing framework of a trolley. Photo courtesy of Blontank Purwoko.

dismounts and falls into the darkness beyond the spotlight, eventually returning to overturn the trolley before continuing, in other ways, to master language and to conform. Such a performance offers glimpses of the potential power of society to shape bodies as well as minds and language. But Kaspar's failure also suggests the possibility that the physical existence of the body may ultimately offer a force of resistance against such social conformity.

With such gestures, Payung Hitam's work comes closer to that of Teater Sae during roughly the same period. But again, Payung Hitam makes the idea of bodily expressiveness part of the realm of the directly political. The dangerous potential of finding a non-verbal, physical language is highlighted in a highly self-referential passage that hints at games of hide and seek with New Order government censors. The verbal text of Payung Hitam's *Kaspar* acknowledges this attempt to create a different language, a body language that exists outside the bounds of New Order Indonesian, when the loudspeaker-prompter voice states: "Don't move too much. Don't speak through symbolic movements. You must speak with words. With sentences.... You must speak verbally. Verbally so that everyone will know what you want."[8] The desire of the system to have all citizens

Fig. 5.2. Payung Hitam, *Kaspar* (2003). Kaspar and the Automaton-like figures of industrialized modern society. Photo courtesy of Teater Payung Hitam.

use language as a simple, clear, entirely instrumental means of communication evokes the idea of government censors frustrated with the symbolic, physical dimensions of performance, which evade the surveillance of scripts. However, it also echoes the fear, articulated several years earlier by Sabur and the other creators of *Metateater*, of the relentless, single-mindedly instrumental economic and industrial logic of modern society that negates human feeling and solidarity because of the all-consuming pursuit of profit, efficiency, and effectiveness.

Yet Payung Hitam went even further in its critique of the New Order. At one point in the performance, Broer/Kaspar recites several ditty-like lines: "Because of frequent oppression, at the very least the people become victims. Power is happy about it. Painful, yes, it hurts." (Karena sering penindasan paling tidak rakyat korban. Kekuasaan suka-suka. Sakit, iya sakit.) He also articulates lines contrasting those who have been silenced to those who live the good life—who laugh and whose mouths bubble over with empty words. Finally, at a point just before his own attempt to formulate rules, which precipitates his collapse, Kaspar argues, "Rather than sitting in chairs, rather than living far from society, we should change things" (Daripada duduk di kursi, daripada hidup jauh dari masyarakat, seharusnya kita mengadakan perubahan). These statements, scattered throughout the play, when juxtaposed to one another form a persistent attack on the gap in wealth between elites and ordinary Indonesians, as well as on the way in which the elites do little to change things, while at the same time stifling criticism.

Indeed, because of its experimental form, abstract philosophical theme, its severely attenuated, generalized story line, and its fragmented, disjunctive criticism of the government, *Kaspar* seemed able to avoid any form of censorship. When asked about the dangers of presenting social and political criticism, Tony Broer commented that while "direct political expression could be dangerous, good Indonesian directors and groups were only spurred on to find more creative ways to express what they wanted to convey" (Field Notes 2 August 1997). However, whether or not the New Order apparatus recognized the strong condemnation of contemporary conditions offered by the play, the critics saw it as highly relevant to Indonesian conditions of the mid-1990s (*Independen* 10 September 1994; Asikin 1994; Purnawady 1996; Yohanes 1996). In confirmation of the play's relevance and expressive power, Payung Hitam was invited to perform the play several times over the next two years,[9] including appearances at two major festivals. Its performances were widely noted and acclaimed by the mass media. *Kaspar*, as a representation of the crisis faced by Indonesians in defining their identities in a social context strongly controlled and over-determined by the New Order government, had struck a strong chord with the theater community and media, particularly in the wake of the 1994 news magazine bannings.

The inclusion of such themes in the play shows Payung Hitam moving toward a more strongly structural political critique and away from its earlier tendency to highlight individual moral failings within the context of a greedy and unfeeling industrial system. The central premise of the play, that language determines consciousness and social behavior, already suggests the power of social and linguistic structures to shape and oppress individuals. And though Kaspar's rebellion still signals trust in individual moral and political choice, it too is triggered both by the critical side of the loudspeaker/prompter's pronouncements and by Kaspar's reading of the newspaper headlines, leading once again to a sense of his being thoroughly enmeshed in a social circuit of relations and processes. Even his failure hints at the power structure within language and society: in formulating counter rules, Kaspar creates something of a mirror image of that against which he has tried to rebel.

One final element of Payung Hitam's *Kaspar* was also crucial in the future trajectory of the group's work: the piercingly loud cacophony of pounding on iron booths, banging tin cans, and the ominous electronic music composed by Harry Roesli, once again collaborating with Payung Hitam. As one of its main elements, this soundscape had a tendency to assault the audience's senses and to inflict a degree of pain, if not of terror. It added to the tension and impact audiences felt. The rising crescendo of this pain seemed to mimic audibly the overload of political oppression and injustice that many Indonesians saw around them. In such a way, the play also mimicked the process producing the rising discontent of many Indonesian intellectuals, students, middle-class members, as well as peasants and workers. As Payung Hitam's lead actor, Tony Broer, became more involved in student politics, which took on an increasingly anti-Suharto cast in the second half of the 1990s,[10] and as Sabur himself became more concerned about the militarization of Indonesian society (Field Notes 10 August 1999), Payung Hitam's depictions of the pain of living under the New Order became even more pronounced.

Teater Musik Kaleng *(1996)* and
Merah Bolong Putih Doblong Hitam *(1997)*

The next original piece performed by Payung Hitam was the January 1996 Jakarta Taman Ismail Marzuki production of *Teater Musik Kaleng* (Tin Can Music Theater). *Teater Musik Kaleng* announced its theme through signs, painted on corrugated metal roofing sheets positioned on the sides of the stage. They proclaimed, "Democracy is not yellow-ization, green-ization, or red-ization!" a clear reference to the colors of the three official parties vying in the upcoming 1997 elections, as well as a reference to how the parties' official colors were being used in the campaign. The stage itself featured a row of industrial metal barrels or drums, reminding audiences of the use of such drums in the Surakarta version of *Kaspar* performed the previous July. Eleven actors continuously pounded out varied rhythms (Zal 1996), while Deden Doblo and Tony Broer, who stalked about the stage in a black suit and a red jacket with white pants, respectively, "dialogued" by shouting out "merah putih" (red and white) and "hitam" (black). This call and response pattern conveyed a sense that Indonesia's national colors were stained black or soiled (Lubis 1996). At one point, an actor shouted out: "Our democracy is a word that sounds piercingly loud, today it's shouted out, tomorrow it's forgotten" (Demokrasi kita adalah kata yang nyaring bunyinya, hari ini teriak besok lupa). Another actor added: "Our democracy is an empty tin can, cans scattered here and there." At another moment, the actors lifted the tops of the drums to reveal a series of prohibitions (Zal 1996). The performance's point was clear enough: Indonesian democracy was a terrorizing experience where parties proffered little else but deafening noise, slogans, and empty words. In *Teater Musik Kaleng*, the Indonesian language played only a minor role, serving only to indicate a harsh and empty noise. The music of Indonesian election campaigns was here represented as a deafening cacophony without much real meaning for most Indonesians. This statement was startlingly direct, and Payung Hitam's increasing daring marked the growing anger and resistance of the national arts community, for theirs was not the only such performance. Harry Roesli and the Depot Kreasi Seni Bandung had earlier taken up the theme of political corruption in a musical performance piece touching on the Bapindo scandal (Pracoyo 1996). At roughly the same time, Emha Ainun Nadjib (now working with a new group of collaborators), workers' theater groups, as well as Ratna Sarumpaet's Satu Merah Panggung, as we shall see in chapter 7, were also becoming increasingly bold both in their stage productions and in their resistance to government control of performances.

Payung Hitam's next original piece was *Merah Bolong Putih Doblong Hitam* (Red Has a Hole, White Torn, Black, 1997). Staged only a few months after the general elections of 1997, the performance paralleled many Indonesians' growing outrage at the government's crude manipulation of the electoral process to close off any real democratic possibilities. The context for the performance and its interpretation thus included the July 1996 *Sabtu Kelabu* (Grey/Dark Saturday) incident, in which supporters of opposition PDI party leader Megawati were violently evicted from their central party headquarters and thereby finally removed from party leadership by pro-government forces. The government party's subsequent electoral victory was one of its largest electoral majorities ever. Though less politically direct than *Teater Musik Kaleng*, or even *Kaspar*, its critique of Indonesian society was nonetheless even more striking, and possibly more devastating, than the group's earlier cacophonous ode to New Order national elections. *Merah Bolong* continued Payung Hitam's relentless critical evaluation of the national language. Going even further than *Kaspar*, the group continued to explore the alternative possibilities for the body to speak—particularly about human pain, which, as Elaine Scarry has noted, is an "internal experience" that strongly resists language (Scarry 1985, 3–4). Yet as the piece demonstrated, the dilemma of paramount importance to Payung Hitam continued to be how to speak about what the group's members were feeling.

During the group's three-day early August run of *Merah Bolong* in Solo, Central Java, Rachman Sabur explained to me that he sometimes felt he needed to find a new language because Indonesian, especially the language of politics, had been manipulated to such an extent by those in authority that the meaning of many words had changed, and it was difficult to believe in them any more. Often, he felt, talking about contemporary politics produced only a string of clichés and people had had more than their fill of such language. Furthermore, Sabur remarked that if one were to speak too directly about Indonesian political issues, it sometimes would make one too sick-at-heart. The particular words he used were *sakit hati* (Field Notes 30 July 1997; 2 August 1997). *Sakit* is the Indonesian word for illness, but also for pain. Thus, the burden Sabur and his group bore was a double one—finding a new language that would be beyond or outside the norms, compulsion, conformity, hypocrisy, and manipulation of contemporary official Indonesian and speaking out about something painful without directly touching on the cause of the pain itself. Interestingly, by this point in time, the government's power of censorship was casting less of a shadow over Payung Hitam and other groups, given public media campaigns against recent censorship of theater, coupled with the surging frustration of many theater workers. As we have seen, Payung Hitam's work also became more direct and sharply critical during the mid-1990s. Thus, Sabur's reluctance to talk directly about politics in *Merah Bolong* should not be seen as motivated principally by fear of censorship, though it may still have been a consideration.

As Elaine Scarry has argued, intense pain is language-destroying. It reduces articulate verbal language to groans and screams, sentience to blinding agony (Scarry 1985, 4). Sabur's reluctance to speak directly about Indonesian political issues suggests an emotional and psychological correlate to the effects of physical pain Scarry describes. Yet in *Merah Bolong*, Sabur and Payung Hitam nonetheless attempted to give voice to that pain, to project this internal feeling onto the physical world in order to make it manifest for others. Rather than talk directly about political issues, Payung Hitam's elegant and powerful solution to this problem was to dramatize their own sense of pain through fashioning a metaphoric stage setting in which that pain, rather than seeking to express itself in words, would present itself embodied in the movements and voices of the actors as well as in the interactions of the actors and the audience with the harsh and threatening set. In effect, the performance was built upon a vocabulary and grammar of physical threat and bodily pain. Furthermore, the particular way in which the set became metaphor implied that the space in which this language of threat and pain existed was that of late New Order Indonesia.

The stage itself evoked a harsh and threatening environment. Large stones hung from ropes immediately in front of the three audience sections at the front and to the left and right of the arena-style stage. Six more such stones hung at the back, as though delineating the far boundaries of the performance space. These rocks were sent swinging on several occasions, providing real obstacles for the actors to negotiate and creating an obvious, fleeting, but repeated element of suspense in a performance with very little plot tension. The stage was also set with several figures made out of smaller stones on the floor beneath the large stones hanging at front, right and left. The actors strode or stumbled through these scattered stone bodies during the course of the performance, almost heedlessly destroying the human shapes (thus implying a lack of regard for human beings) and spreading rocks across the floor of the arena stage. An additional pile of red stones, to which a bucket of white stones was added in the first scene, was foregrounded at stage right. Taken altogether, this landscape of rocks and stones created an impression of a hard, barren, and threatening terrain. In part, this stage terrain as metaphor gave the performance its sense of cohesion.

Consisting of a bare series of narratively independent scenes, the performance itself had even less plot than *Kaspar*. For a little over one hour, *Merah Bolong Putih Doblong Hitam* presented a group of masked figures laboring through a harsh and dangerous landscape strewn with stones of all sizes. The figures dodged stones swinging on ropes, had gravel rained down upon them, rolled in and walked over sharp rocks, engaged in a rhythmic industrial ballet like assembly-line automations, gave offerings for a fallen comrade, attempted to communicate, watched one another warily, and buried a fallen member of their group. In a series of scenes without plot, characters interacted carrying out seemingly arcane and Sisyphean tasks, such as filling buckets held rigidly on their heads with rocks and dumping them, or grieving for one another.

Yet despite this lack of plot, nearly all of the scenes were also linked by the physical enactments of suffering and pain and by the metaphoric set dominated by rocks and stones. From the very onset, the costumes worked to emphasize both the physical features of the actors and their embodied suffering. All of the actors wore black shorts with suspender-like shoulder straps, thus leaving their upper bodies, arms, and lower legs bare and visible. Since there was no verbal dialogue, the main focus of the performance was on the performance's action, and its action was often caricatured or, at the least consisted of highly exaggerated representations of extreme physical exertion and exhaustion. The figures on stage staggered, stumbled, or walked with an exaggerated swaying motion, often hunched over and laboriously bobbing their heads up and down.

Other aspects of the costumes and acting signified physical suffering and through it often emotional and psychological suffering as well. All of the actors donned white masks whose expressions were uniformly frozen in squinting eyes, raised eyebrows, and down-turned frowns and grimaces. They spoke no words, but often sighed, moaned, groaned, and wept, at times with their bodies shaking. Elements of this physical vocabulary of pain were combined to powerful effect in many scenes. For instance, in one episode a figure, with two buckets attached to a yoke carried across his shoulders (Tony Broer), endures for a minute or more a (literally) physically punishing downpour of gravel from above the stage. In this particularly remarkable embodiment of pain and suffering, the actor writhes and thrashes, shrieking, screaming, and rolling over scattered rocks as gravel pours down on him. Watching such a scene, it is difficult not to flinch, for the actor does not really need to act since he undoubtedly is experiencing actual pain.[11] In another scene following the collapse and apparent death of this same figure near the end of the play, a second figure comes near the corpse, looks it over, then scratches and pulls at his own hair, shakes his head, takes agitated steps as though confused about where to go next, shakes convulsively (and thereby rattles the yoked buckets he is now carrying, thus adding a disturbing, percussive sound to the signification of emotional suffering), then shrieks, screams, and stamps his feet. In this scene, the second figure's emotional and psychological suffering is also rendered through physical acts and gestures as well as through non-verbal sounds.

In an interview given in the week following the performances of *Merah Bolong* in Solo, Rachman Sabur declared, "We terrorize the spectators so that they feel the pain or the burden of the problems currently confronting us."[12] This statement echoed the well-known motto of the older generation theater figure, Putu Wijaya, an important innovator with whose work Sabur and Payung Hitam were familiar, having staged at least four of Wijaya's plays. Putu had long spoken of his theater as one that subjected the audience to "mental terror" in order to push them to think in new and critical ways about their lives and what they were witnessing on the stage. Wijaya's brand of theater constantly tried to surprise the audience and at times push them to sensory overload.[13] Payung Hitam's attempt to terrorize the audience is somewhat different. Indeed, *Merah Bolong* contains at least two elements that work to threaten the audience, yet the threats, though possibly shocking and challenging the audience to think harder about what is happening, also work to draw them into an identification with the pain that Sabur and Payung Hitam felt was confronting all

Fig. 5.3. Payung Hitam, *Merah Bolong, Putih Doblong, Hitam* (1997).
Photo courtesy of Y. Harisinthu.

Indonesians. In the opening scene, a lone figure sets into motion the three stones suspended with ropes directly over the front, left, and right sections of the audience. As the stones begin swinging in long arcs, passing close to the first tiers of seats, members of the audience start to flinch and laugh nervously, as if worried the stones might come loose or strike someone. Some among the audience are thereby pulled into the atmosphere of threat evoked by the performance. Secondly, as mentioned previously, the recognition of the *real pain* experienced by some of the actors in particularly surprising and brutal scenes further shocks some in the audience and elicits startled reactions.

As indicated in Sabur's statement about terrorizing the audience, the goal of at least partially drawing the audience into the experience and emotional field of the performance in turn draws our attention back to the "modernist" position of much national Indonesian art theater. As detailed in chapter 1, this theater is part of a national culture whose practitioners, theoreticians, and institutions in large part consist of an intelligentsia from predominantly middle-class and elite ranks. Their identity is based on a commitment to modernity and thus is generally opposed to elites who represent the old, "feudal" aristocracy, along with its reconstructed sense of traditional values. Since the early decades of the twentieth century and the beginnings of the Indonesian nationalist movement, much of this nascent, modern national culture was therefore devoted to defending the ordinary people against the injustices of a system often upheld and perpetuated by native, aristocratic bureaucrats. It thereby legitimated itself through proving its sympathies and relevance. This sense of social and political commitment, yoked to desires for "modernization," "democratization," and "free expression," has long been a hallmark of a number of spheres of national culture, such as art theater, literature, music, and cinema.

Thus, Sabur's statement about the need to terrorize the audience signals a kind of desperation about whether or not that theater really can contribute to a process of positive change or can communicate effectively with its audience, or that its audience truly wants to be part of such a process of change. At the same time it clearly marks Sabur's and Payung Hitam's participation in the national culture's discourse, and practice, of social commitment. Though struggling to find a language with which to speak, Sabur and Payung Hitam did indeed want to be involved in a public discussion of current problems. To this end, the group added further elements to its stage set in *Merah Bolong*, suggesting a context for and metaphorizing the bodily pain it represented. Taken together, these elements suggested that Indonesia was the space for all this suffering, a connection made all the more clear from the use of the red and white stones.

Given the events of the previous year, Sabur had intended these stones to symbolize the government-manipulated Indonesian Democratic Party (whose official color was red) and those citizens who comprised the "White Group" (or refused to vote in the elections on the principle that it would merely legitimize a bad process) (Field Notes 2 August 1997). Together, they constituted a symbol of democratic opposition within Indonesian politics. The possible coalition of these groups could be read in the dumping of the white stones on top of the the pile of red ones at the beginning of the performance, while the government's suppression of such opposition was expressed in the construction and destruction of the red and white stone figure just prior to the play's final "burial" scene. This last scene is in turn linked to the destruction of the "opposition" by the defiantly clenched fist of resistance which emerges from the mound of red and white stones (now mixed ominously with black) under which the corpse is buried.[14]

In an interesting twist on the post-colonial desire of both the New Order government and the mainstream of national theater practitioners to cultivate a sense of connection with tradition, Payung Hitam's *Merah Bolong* suggests the crisis of the nation in one additional way. If the absence of discernable traditional elements in *Kaspar* announced a turning away from the compulsion felt by government and theater workers alike to embrace tradition, *Merah Bolong*, in a sense, goes one step further by mobilizing tradition to reverse the logic with which traditional cultural elements had been employed in the previous three decades as distinct markers of a uniquely Indonesian identity. *Merah Bolong*'s single use of traditional culture ultimately remains separate from the national tradition because it tenaciously clings to an identity that, in its ethnic cultural specificity, is separate from that of the national. Ironically enough, the

Figs. 5.4 and 5.5. Payung Hitam, *Merah Bolong, Putih Doblong, Hitam*. Buried Struggle (5.4) and Destroying a stone effigy (5.5). Photos courtesy of Y. Harisinthu.

search for an alternative language had also led Rachman and his group to incorporate a Sundanese song about grief into the performance. However, in *Merah Bolong*, only hummed fragments of the melody remain. In other words, a re-engineered fragment of tradition becomes one means for critiquing the inhumanity of the New Order's political and social process of modernization. *Merah Bolong* mobilizes this Sundanese dirge not to celebrate the ethnic diversity of Indonesia's populations or to proudly assert a specific ethnic tradition within that unified national community. Thus it does not code the performance as uniquely Indonesian. Rather, following the logic of Sabur and his group's concerns about Bahasa Indonesia, the Sundanese lament is summoned into this strikingly modern, experimental play to give voice to feelings that can no longer be voiced by the formal, official national language.

Merah Bolong's alternative language was designed to speak more genuinely about the pain the group was feeling and, though to a much lesser extent, to avoid censorship, Nonetheless, the metaphoric nature of the performance also presented a particularly fertile opportunity for variant interpretations that led back to thoughts of the nation's dilemma. Indeed media reviewers came to a variety of conclusions about the meaning of *Merah Bolong*: the colored stones portrayed the electoral parties and the process of democracy; the actions of the actors depicted the lives of the marginalized and workers; the whole piece represented both the futility of life and a nationalism that was fragmented (Lubis dan Ramelan, *Gatra* 16 August 1997, 110; *Kedaulatan Rakyat* 5 August 1997; Tammaka 1997). Felicitously, the red and white colors Sabur had chosen to represent the potential oppositional forces were also the colors of the Indonesian flag, a fact which, surprisingly, given the constant working of red and white in Payung Hitam's previous works, had not consciously entered Sabur's mind as he and his group were creating *Merah Bolong* (Field Notes 2 August 1997). Given this coincidence, beyond the specific political references Sabur and his group intended the performance to suggest, there is a possible broader connotation to *Merah Bolong* that may account for some of the nuances of the reviewers' variant interpretations. If the harsh, stone-strewn set is seen as a metaphor for Indonesia, the work's emphasis on bodily physicality can be read both as a representation of actual physical harshness of the life endured by Indonesians as well as a metaphoric projection of the psychological pain many Indonesians experienced as a result of existing social and political conditions. The physical actions of the actors—struggling from one scene to the next with groans and sighs, weeping, swaying and staggering, falling and being assaulted with downpours of gravel, shouldering large stones and being knocked about by swinging stones, or raising fists of defiance from burial mounds—all of these present a language of physicality and suffering inscribed in a harsh landscape in order to speak of the pain of being Indonesian in the 1990s in a more suggestive, emotionally powerful way than could be accomplished with words alone.

Still, as the various reviewers' interpretations noted above suggest, many Indonesians found a need to put the meaning of the performance into clear words. One report appeared to show that even Rachman Sabur, paradoxically, seemed unable to resist the desire to achieve a more transparent linguistic articulation of the crisis his group's piece attempted to embody. An article in the weekly tabloid *Adil* seemed to be paraphrasing Rachman asking the following question about *Merah Bolong*: "Can our nationalism be justified when human rights and justice steadily deteriorate?" (Ma 1997). It is not completely clear whether Sabur himself said this or it was simply a reporter/reviewer putting words into Sabur's mouth. In any case, that such questions were being asked in the language of contemporary international political discourse demonstrated the mounting boldness of the opposition to New Order business as usual.

Conclusion

The 1990s performance work of Payung Hitam, situated securely within the aesthetic ideology of most modern national theater, was nonetheless remarkable for several reasons. First, it showed the movement of the modern theater in an increasingly critical political direction (a fact that will be even more evident in the next two chapters). Payung Hitam's plays radiated an urgency, a need to speak about Indonesia's social and political problems as well as a complementary need to emphasize that urgency to the audience through various techniques of pain—from hammers pounding on metal and the crashing of tin cans, to loudspeakers and ominous electronic music to the riotous cacophony of drum barrel rhythms and chanted slogans to the menacing swinging of large stones, the rain of gravel, and bodies moving painfully through a jagged, rocky landscape. Second, the group gathered acclaim and praise from two constituencies—aesthetics-conscious modern theater workers and critic/reviewers and a media eager to report on social and cultural phenomenon that showed a critical stance towards contemporary social and political problems. These compliments reflected both the general sharpening of political attitudes and willingness to entertain more politically critical works within the arts community, but also suggested how Payung Hitam negotiated between the dominant strands of the aesthetic ideology of modern national theater and popular social pressures for relevance and criticism of the existing system. Increasingly harsh in representations of Indonesian language, society and politics, yet always preserving a measure of interpretive ambiguity (through generalizing or metaphoric devices, coupled with compelling set designs and soundscapes, athletic and physically expressive acting, carefully arranged and choreographed blocking within scenes, and the measured rhythm of scenes that sustained interest in the overall performance), Payung Hitam satisfied both aesthetes and those interested in social and political commentary. Finally, like Teater Sae with its fragmented and often abstract philosophical language (language that isn't pleasant to read—*bahasa yang tidak enak dibaca*) and Kubur with its equally fragmented but rugged *kampung* mutterings, ravings and curses, Payung Hitam engaged in an intensive reworking of the notion, and uses, of language in its most celebrated works of the 1990s, from *Metateater* to *Kaspar* to *Teater Musik Kaleng* and *Merah Bolong*.

Yet Payung Hitam again differed from both Sae and Kubur in terms of its social genesis and grounding. Given its base in a performing arts academy environment, Payung Hitam's members were faculty and students from chiefly more affluent middle- and upper-class families, and its orientation, though avant-garde, was much more comfortably situated within the main currents of modern national theater aesthetics. In its engagement with the crisis of representation of the nation and the alienation and anomie that accompanied the final years of the New Order, Payung Hitam focused on a loss of human solidarity, on how language shapes social consciousness and being, on the issue of elections and democracy and their perversion, and on a highly metaphoric representation of the harsh, stoney environment of national life. In its choice of subject matter and the style of its presentations, though subjecting actors and audience alike to pain and terror, Payung Hitam was both less fragmented and post-modern than the highly intellectual Sae at the levels of theme and coherence of particular performances and less linguistically and socially rough-edged than the kampung-based productions of Teater Kubur. Payung Hitam's brilliant works of the 1990s thereby mediated between radical avant-garde techniques and a modern theater tradition that most often pitched the tenor and themes of its works to the educated middle class in a less fragmented form that conveyed relatively clear issues, though leaving room for multiple interpretations in its choice of formal devices and its layering of themes.

Though Payung Hitam shows how the leading modern theater groups were becoming increasingly politicized, its particular brand of interrogation of the Indonesian language and the stylistic vocabulary of performance it developed kept it from a head-on confrontation with the New Order state. Other groups, however, were unable to avoid such a confrontation. In the 1990s, several workers' theater groups arose in the greater Jakarta region to provide information and promote solidarity and consciousness-raising among industrial workers in Indonesia's burgeoning factory sector. These groups inevitably ran afoul of a government security apparatus concerned to quash any hint of communism and anxious to ensure that Indonesia's competitiveness in the arena of foreign investment in industrial production was not harmed by an insubordinate working class. The construction and development of such theater, given the prevailing hostile environment as well as the way it helped forge wider *jaringan* (networks) among theater workers and NGO activists from different social classes, is the subject of the next chapter.

Chapter 6

WORKERS' THEATER AND THEATER ABOUT WORKERS IN 1990S INDONESIA

In September 1994 the Satu Merah Panggung theater group had staged Ratna Sarumpaet's *Nyanyian Marsinah: Dari Bawah Tanah* (Marsinah's Song: From Beneath the Earth) for close to capacity crowds five nights running in the Arena Theater of the Taman Ismail Marzuki (*Kompas* 22 Sept. 1994). At a time when interest in labor issues was high and taking as its point of departure the 1993 rape and murder of an East Javanese worker and labor activist, Marsinah, Sarumpaet and Satu Merah Panggung hoped to attract a mainly middle- to upper-class audience by staging the play in an increasingly commercial TIM. Yet, knowing that Indonesian industrial workers had already been creating their own theater for several years prior to the performance of *Nyanyian Marsinah*, Satu Merah Panggung was also aiming to draw this potentially new audience of industrial workers to the modern theater by keeping the prices at a relatively low Rp. 5000 per ticket (Sabur 1994). The play's organizers had also worried that the authorities might not allow the play to be performed, given the sensitive nature of its material. Even so, NGO activists who witnessed the play were often highly critical of the view of workers it presented.

Less than nine months later, in early 1995, the Indonesian Workers' Theater's (TBI) performances of its original play, *Senandung Terpuruk Dari Balik Tembok Pabrik* (Song Buried behind the Factory Wall), scheduled for May 13 and 14 also at Taman Ismail Marzuki, were banned by the Head of the Jakarta regional government's Socio-Political Directorate. In essence, the Directorate Head, R. Bagus Suharyono, felt that the play portrayed elements inappropriate to Indonesia, exaggerated social tensions between workers and owners, and threatened national stability (*Kompas* 1 and 5 June 1995; *Republika* 1 June 1995; *Merdeka* 1 June 1995).

The growth of workers' theater and the interest shown by middle-class Indonesian intellectuals and artists in workers' issues, symbolized by the media notoriety the Marsinah case generated as well as by Sarumpaet's play, indicated a growing movement for social change in Indonesia that was constructed, in part, through theater. Yet the tensions noted in the two examples cited above also point to the difficulties faced by theatrical resistance to the New Order regime. Sarumpaet's and Satu Merah Panggung's play demonstrated gaps, both economic and aesthetic, between workers and the middle-classes, while also showing disagreements among the regime's critics—here artists and NGO activists—over how art might best serve social change. The case of TBI, with its attempt to stage its newest play at the preeminent middle-class arts venue in Jakarta, and the government's response hint at the ways in which workers and artists were attempting to form alliances in the face of strong government surveillance and repression.

This chapter examines the growth of Indonesian workers' theater and theater about workers as one sign of the budding alliance between middle-class and elite artists, activists, and industrial workers. It also tracks the New Order government's mounting anxiety about the growth of both workers' theater and the alliances being forged through it and surrounding it. Yet the growth of these alliances or *jaringan* (networks) was not an unproblematic, easily unified resistance to aspects of the New Order state's regime of social and cultural control. As John Brenkman has argued, works of art and culture, too, are the product of complex "material-social practices." These practices consist of humans interacting within relations of domination and contestation intertwined with artistic forms, techniques, conventions, and concepts (1987, 59–76). As in the previous chapters, in tracing the growth of Indonesian workers' theater, I will demonstrate how these cultural productions, by and about workers, took shape in the *articulation* (the *jointing* together) of the diverse and sometimes conflicting interests of a variety of groups—workers, middle-class artists, NGO activists, the media, and the state—into specific material-social practices. These practices were thus formed through the association, collaboration, and conflicts of these groups, all of which are structured by relationships of dominance, subordination, contestation, and genuine desires for more egalitarian ties.

I will begin by briefly reviewing the social background of workers' theater and then discuss the origins and first productions of the two most prominent theater groups. Then, using the experience of Teater ABU, I will illustrate in detail the tensions that arose among artists, workers, and NGO activists in the creation of this form of theater. The media closely followed such theater, and media reviews and analyses indicate how workers' performances were viewed through middle-class lenses, lenses that influenced the development of workers' theater. In addition, the media reviews are evidence of growing interaction between middle-class activists, writers, artists, and workers. Middle-class artists eventually produced a rejoinder to workers' theater in the form of Ratna Sarumpaet's play, *Nyanyian Marsinah*, and I will note both that play's engagement with and differences from the performances of the worker groups. Furthermore, I will show how the repressive power of an authoritarian government was clearly inscribed in the discourses and practices of workers' theater. Of particular importance here are the public debates from 1989 to 1996 about the appropriate goals and aesthetics of workers' theater as well as government attempts after March 1994 to cast it as a marginal, illegitimate activity within New Order society.

LSMs (NGOs) and Labor in Indonesia

In the mid-1980s, the New Order government faced an economic crisis induced by the collapse of prices on the global oil market. Attempting to replace dependency on declining oil revenues with an export-oriented industrialization strategy, the government began to liberalize investment laws and at the same time tighten controls on labor in anticipation of the industrialization push (Bourchier 1994b, 53; Hadiz 1994, 66–67).

During the same period segments of the small but culturally strategic and growing middle-class (professionals, lower-level bureaucrats and military, and small business people) were becoming increasingly restive in relation to the authoritarian structure and economic corruption of the New Order. Some groups within this middle-class formation had developed a critique of the New Order's development strategy during the 1970s, claiming that it benefited foreign capital and its local collaborators at the expense of the masses. These middle-class critics, mainly students, formed grassroots development-oriented non-government organizations (NGOs) or *LSMs* (*Lembaga Swadaya Masyarakat*/social self-help institutes) (Eldridge 1990, 506–7; Lev 1990, 33; Robison 1986, 156–68). In the 1980s, these LSMs began to shift from simple community development projects to a combination of actual projects and consciousness-raising and rights mobilization activities.

By the late 1980s, a number of non-governmental organizations had come into being to press for increased democracy and more egalitarian distribution of wealth. Some of these LSMs began to serve workers in ways that the tightly controlled, official government union could or would not. Since they were not officially involved in labor union organizing, such groups could bypass constraints imposed on would-be independent unions. LSMs like Yayasan Sisbikum and Yayasan Perempuan Mardika in Jakarta and Yayasan Annisa Swasti in Yogyakarta concentrated on founding worker educational groups and self-help cooperatives and associations (Hadiz 1993, 194–95).

At the same time, several bold efforts were made in the 1990s to launch new, independent trade unions (Bourchier 1994b; Hadiz 1993, 194–97). As export-oriented industrialization quickened in sectors such as garment, shoe production, electronics, rattan processing, and packaged food, wildcat strikes and other industrial actions also increased. Such actions took place even though these sectors predominantly employ women who are young, unmarried, possessed of only a low level of education, and often inculcated with a strong respect for patriarchal authority (Wolf 1996; Dewi 1995; Mather 1983).[1] The explanation for this increase in labor unrest, in large part, lay in the fact that working conditions were often harsh and arbitrarily determined by factory owners, while wages remained low—often below the state-mandated minimum daily wage pegged at a level sufficient to fulfill only 60 percent of a worker's minimum daily needs (Hadiz 1994, 68–69).

Teater Buruh Indonesia and Teater ABU

Workers' theater emerged shortly after the appearance of LSMs dedicated to assisting workers. Throughout the 1980s, a number of Indonesian grassroots LSMs had already experimented with theater as a means for building solidarity, increasing confidence, and conscientizing peasants, students, and scavengers (see chapter 2). Between 1988 and 1991, as the New Order government began proclaiming a new policy of greater political openness (*keterbukaan*) that ran parallel to its economic liberalization, groups like *Yayasan Sisbikum* (Saluran Informasi Sosial dan Bimbingan Hukum/Foundation for the Channeling of Information and Legal Guidance) in Jakarta and *Yayasan Annisa Swasti* (*Yasanti* or Private Sector Women's Foundation) in Yogyakarta, Central Java, also began to feel role-playing techniques were more effective means of informal education for workers than lectures (Thamrin 1996, 27; Tejo and Witdarmono 1995; Sirait 1994).[2]

According to Sisbikum director Arist Merdeka Sirait, his foundation's initial approach, which included regular information sessions with workers about workers' rights, negotiation strategies, and general social analysis, did not encourage workers to participate actively. These methods only reinforced the "culture of silence" cultivated by the worker's subordination as low-paid factory laborers. Theater—in the form of role-playing—was more helpful in stimulating workers to voice their concerns and understand the issues they faced (Thamrin 1996; Tejo and Witdarmono 1995; Sirait 1994). At the urging of workers participating in role-playing workshops, in mid-1989 Sisbikum helped found the Teater Buruh Indonesia (TBI or Indonesian Workers' Theater) (Tejo and Witdarmono 1995).

For three months, a well-known poet and theater figure, Remy Sylado, was engaged to train the first group of TBI members in acting, direction, management, make-up, and dramaturgy. Later, an idea for a script was generated and Sri Murwaty, one of the workers who had previously been involved in organizing an earlier women factory workers' theater group, was chosen director (Conroy 1997).[3] Entitled *Pengalaman* (Experience), TBI's first play was rehearsed for roughly three months prior to performance and staged on November 19, 1989, at the Galaxy Theater in Cisalak near Bogor. The piece presented the difficulties workers faced when seeking work. Those who found factory jobs often received sub-standard wages, while those who did not were forced to work as pedicab drivers, itinerant traditional medicine peddlers, and in other economically precarious occupations. The factory workers, disappointed about their wages, fantasized about becoming directors of their plants (Indrayati and Wahyuni 1991; *Kompas* 27 Nov. 1989).

In its first three years, Teater Buruh Indonesia performed five times, staging a total of four different plays.[4] It most often performed to sell-out crowds of between 1000 and 1400 workers from the greater Jakarta area, typically presenting a thirty- to forty-five-minute play along with programs of popular music genres, such as *dangdut* and *calung*[5], and in at least one case, a comedy act. The group had no permanent members, and there were few holdovers from one production to the next. Simply finding money for transportation and time to attend practices was, and remains, difficult. Workers who were unable to continue often recommended a replacement from among their friends (Tejo and Witdarmono 1995). Most productions involved about thirty workers, and scripts were generated from discussions about current problems in the factories (mostly garment, textile, and electronics). Some of the workers' experiences were then acted out, written down, compiled, and turned into a rough story line by Arist or someone else assigned to lead the production. This synopsis was returned to the workers who fleshed out the story through improvisations (Sirait 1994). Themes included the arbitrary treatment of workers by management, the firing, without severance pay, of pregnant workers and workers who question factory decisions, sub-minimum wages, forced overtime, the difficulties of women workers in obtaining stipulated menstrual-period time off, the reduction of health, food, and transport stipends, and workers' poor living conditions (*Kompas* 27 Nov. 1989; Sabur 1990; *Kompas* 9 June 1991; Indrayati and Wahyuni 1991; *Berita Buana* 23 Dec. 1991).

As the media noted, TBI's performances drew enthusiastic responses when staged for worker audiences in factory areas such as Cisalak, Bogor, and Tangerang. Frequent jokes, vocal audience rejoinders to key scenes or statements, and the use of popular music to invite workers to join in dances at the end of the evening created a lively, popular theater-style dynamic.

TBI was indeed successful in connecting with its target audience, yet the turnover rate of the group's members from one production to another indicates that this success was not easily won. Furthermore, though media descriptions of TBI's creative process gave the impression of effortless collaboration between LSM activists and workers, a careful reading of the reports on TBI's early performances also suggests that subtle differences of vision existed among the main participants in this theater.

Sisbikum's Arist Sirait, singled out in the media as the group's mentor, maintained that TBI's theater offered a medium for communication and exchanging information as well as raising the workers' awareness of their rights and responsibilities while allowing them to develop their talents (Sabur 1990). In a report covering a later play, (*Lauk-Lauk Janji* [A Side Dish of Promises], June 1991), Arist and Suzanna, an LSM activist who directed the play, simply emphasized theater as a means of "raising awareness" (*Kompas* 9 June 1991).

Arist raised another key point: this theater was by workers, about workers, and *for* workers (Indrayati and Wahyuni 1991). In December 1991, he rejected suggestions that TBI should perform in TIM, claiming that TBI's theater was just for workers and that taking it to TIM would sever the group from its workers' context (*Berita Buana* 1991). On the other hand, Remy Sylado, the poet-trainer of TBI's first cohort, was usually quoted commenting on TBI's activities in relation to "high" art. Sylado described his difficulties in conveying artistic material to the workers "given their varying levels of education," but he defended their efforts by comparing TBI to California's El Teatro Campesino, which he noted had gone from humble beginnings to an international reputation (*Kompas* 27 Nov. 1989; *Kompas* 9 June 1991). The implication was that even these workers, lowly as they presently seemed in terms of artistry, could one day become accomplished.

Not surprisingly, members of the LSM community who watched TBI's plays were more concerned about the group's ongoing contributions to a workers' movement than they were about its artistic growth. Perhaps following the June and August 1991 performances of *Lauk-Lauk Janji*, in which workers protesting their firings regain their positions, a number of LSM activists claimed that TBI had resorted to an "escapist happy ending." They maintained that TBI's plays would do better to end with questions that provoked reflection and a desire to pursue the issues further. TBI members responded to such criticisms by stating that the play showed their reality: though oppressed at work, they could still be happy and relaxed at home. Yet Arist Merdeka Sirait stated that as a result of these criticisms, later plays did become more critical (Sirait 1994). And in fact, *Hitam Menunggu Putih* (Black Waiting for White), performed only six months later in December of 1991, has a darker ending, one in which workers striking for better wages are accused of creating instability and are threatened with dismissal if they refuse to sign a work agreement drawn up unilaterally by the factory owner.

Statements of workers about the value of workers' theater echoed those of their LSM collaborators. By portraying their everyday conditions of life, theater helped them to exchange thoughts and communicate with their friends in a focused and direct manner as well as to tell other workers about their rights and the applicable government regulations. In addition, they emphasized that theater work helped build confidence among worker-members to demand their rights and allowed them to release pent-up frustrations (*Kompas* 27 Nov. 1989; Sabur 1990; *Kompas* 9 June 1991; *Berita Buana* 23 Dec. 1991). Thus, theater was important to workers not simply for building solidarity or for education and consciousness-raising, but also for personal growth and emotional health. Both of these latter, it could be argued, are also absolutely necessary for strengthening a workers' movement.

However, the disagreement between external LSM activists and TBI members over TBI's "escapist happy endings" indicates a possibly more fundamental difference of perspective, one carried into the formation of workers' theater practices. If LSM activists preferred to see TBI's productions geared entirely toward providing information and producing what they perceived to be the proper and necessary attitudes for workers involved in a germinal workers' movement, many workers seemed to derive other satisfactions from their theater work—the pleasures of association, recreation, and relaxation. This difference was supported by the incorporation of performance-ending dances into TBI's theater programs and the interest of former TBI members in gathering all past and current members together for a combined TBI reunion and showcase of its repertoire (Sirait 1994). Arist was clearly aware of these pleasures but commented about them as though they were simply a side benefit of TBI's existence. Nor were such issues explored in depth in media coverage.

These subtle tensions are absolutely crucial to understanding how workers' theater, as a material-social practice, is an articulation of varied interests. Given support, guidance, and long-term stability through the participation of Sisbikum, TBI took up the task of informing Jakarta-area industrial workers of common problems and current rules and regulations. It thereby undertook work that the LSM community saw as essential to building a strong movement capable of defending workers' rights and fighting for their well being. However, as Sisbikum had already discovered, in order for TBI to succeed in this mission, it had to appeal to fellow-workers through more than a dry lecture. TBI's solution was not simply to give public voice to complaints with which all workers could identify, but to address workers' needs for release, pleasure, and association by incorporating those complaints into a particular performance style and structure whose key elements included straight-forward stories, humor (especially jokes about and allusions to official hypocrisy), an atmosphere that allowed for and encouraged audience rejoinders, performance-ending dances, and accompanying music and comedy routines. The tension between the intersecting, though not completely congruent projects, needs, and visions of middle-class LSM activists and workers resulted in the construction of a cultural form that could be seen as an attempt to resolve those tensions. Yet it was an attempt that remained *in process* and subject to modification, as the disagreement over "escapist happy endings" indicates. Moreover, this tension became more acute in the development of a second workers' theater group, Teater ABU.

Formed in mid-1992, Teater ABU (ABU, or Aneka Buruh, All Kinds of Workers) was conceived by the Yayasan Perempuan Mardika (The Independent Women's Foundation), an LSM providing support for industrial workers, with a special emphasis on women and gender issues.

One of YPM's staff had worked with Yayasan Sisbikum and was convinced that theater was a potent organizing and educational tool for workers. Still, YPM's plans to use theater differed in one significant respect from Sisbikum's model. In contrast to TBI's limited use of Remy Sylado as initial artistic trainer for TBI, YPM contracted with Margesti S. Otong, the leading actress in the avant-garde Jakarta theater troupe, Teater Sae, to provide ongoing training and direction for its workers' theater (Gumeulis 1994). Margesti's pivotal role in the consolidation and development of Teater ABU produced a group that was more aesthetically focused than Teater Buruh Indonesia. She also gave ABU stronger ties to the middle-class high arts community.

Lacking knowledge about the workers whose artistic efforts she would be facilitating, Margesti began by simply holding personal discussions with interested workers in order to create an open atmosphere and to help her understand the workers' hopes and expectations for the project. She concluded that the workers needed to "actualize" themselves as complete human beings, something the rigid routines and hierarchical organization of the factories did not allow. As a seasoned avant-garde actress, Margesti also brought her own particular training, perspective, and social network into the process. During months of personal bonding, confidence-building, and basic exercises in performance skills and group dynamics, she took members of Teater ABU to see middle-class urban theater at the Taman Ismail Marzuki and Bulungan using YPM's support funds. Further, the group held workshops in poetry reading and a number of members even entered competitions (M. Otong 1993, 2). Margesti also took a personal role in designing the group's sets. As a result the sets, props, and forms of ABU's plays displayed a more artistic orientation than Teater Buruh Indonesia's simple, minimally realistic stages.

To be sure, there were similarities. Like TBI, the roughly twenty members of Teater ABU also generated the themes for their plays through group discussions, and many were similar to those broached by TBI—authoritarian treatment of workers by factory management, arbitrary firings, low wages, menstrual leave, and forced overtime (Gantra 1993; Tejo 1994a). As with the performances of Teater Buruh Indonesia, ABU's audiences were drawn mostly from greater Jakarta's working-class population (Tejo 1993a; Tejo 1994a; Dahana 1994; M. Otong 1994). And like Teater Buruh, ABU's early performances encouraged lively interactions with audience members, eventually flowing into a participatory dance at the end of the evening (Dindon 1993; Laksana and Ginanjar 1993; Tejo 1993a; Teater Abu 1993a).

Yet the script materials and venues of ABU's first play indicate some differences. *Nyanyian Pabrik* (Factory Song) was crafted around a series of poems by prominent Indonesian poets and segments of Arifin C Noer's well-known play, *Kapai-Kapai* (Moths), which the worker-members of ABU had chosen as representative of their feelings and problems (M. Otong 1993, 2; Dindon 1993). Their "Factory Song," therefore, was not built in precisely the same way as Teater Buruh Indonesia's scripts, but relied upon "serious literature" (M. Otong 1993, 2). These works were then combined with songs and a sequence of dynamic dances based upon the popular *jaipongan* form. Following this poetic dramatization of the problems of factory life, the performance ended with a raucous enactment of police breaking up a demonstration and a dance to popular dangdut music in which audience members were invited to participate.

A second contrast lies in the locations of ABU's performances. *Nyanyian Pabrik* was first staged on 19 January 1993 at the urban studio of well-known theater figure Ratna Sarumpaet, a friend and supporter of Margesti's efforts as a fellow female theater director/facilitator. The performance was attended not only by workers, but by members of the avant-garde arts community as well. ABU's second performance of the piece occurred less than three weeks later in the factory-district studio of a Bandung artist and again was attended by a mixed crowd of artists and workers.

Another difference between the two groups, perhaps a result of YPM's attention to women's issues, was the inclusion in *Nyanyian Pabrik* of the theme of supervisors' sexual harassment of workers. A final interesting divergence was the fact that both Margesti and ABU members stressed that building members' self-confidence and opening an avenue of "self-actualization" were ABU's chief accomplishments. In contrast to TBI's main focus on education and dissemination of information, ABU put more emphasis on developing the individual human potential of its members (Gantra 1993; Tejo 1993a; M. Otong 1994; Sutrisno and Wijiono 1994).

This contrast owed much to Margesti's approach. Noting the workers' lack of confidence and difficulty in expressing themselves, Margesti chose to familiarize them with middle-class theater and poetry readings to stimulate their own creative efforts. Paraphrased by *Editor*'s Maman Gantra, Margesti implied that such familiarizing boosted their confidence (Gantra 1993; see also M. Otong 1993)). A middle-class, high-art aesthetic education thus figured as a key element in her idea of workers' self-actualization, although Margesti's interest in popular culture, such as jaipongan, also entered the equation (M. Otong 1994).

The ABU workers cited some feelings about their creative production that were similar to those of TBI members. ABU's worker leader, Sutrisno, called *Nyanyian Pabrik* an expression of reality and saw it as a way for workers to let out their frustrations. Others talked of the importance of airing grievances about lack of health subsidies, forced overtime, and low wages. Yet ABU members put greater emphasis on the personal growth and emotional release the theater process had facilitated for them. Some stated that ABU's productions helped them better understand their own problems and that their participation in ABU had given them more self-confidence. In the program for their first performance of *Nyanyian Pabrik*, "brief notes" by ABU members had already stated their desire for self-development:

> The world of the factory is like a world that imprisons us as human beings. From day to day we always do the same tasks, things which only require parts of our body, our hands, for example, or our legs.
>
> Now we have a theater group that we formed to make use of our minuscule amounts of free time. Within this group we feel we can speak and think as well as undertake explorations as complete human beings. What we mean is, our brains and feelings can also contribute a little to these explorations. (Teater ABU 1993b)[6]

Another significant difference was manifested in statements ABU workers made about their purposes, for example, describing one of the

Fig. 6.1. Teater ABU, program for Bandung Performance of *Nyanyian Pabrik*.

aims of *Nyanyian Pabrik* as informing society or revealing the problems to a "broad audience" (*khalayak luas*) (Tejo 1993a; Laksana and Ginanjar 1993). In contrast, those involved in TBI insisted that its plays were aimed at workers alone.

ABU's striking performance style and the modest amount of critical media excitement engendered by *Nyanyian Pabrik* registered in the attitudes of reporters covering TBI's next play, *Bercanda Dalam Duka* (Joking amidst Sorrow) in late 1993. They also seemed to have affected TBI's style. *Bercanda Dalam Duka* opens with a plea to workers to help a comrade whose hands have been badly mangled in an industrial accident. In appealing to his fellow workers, the injured worker, Gunen, tells his story: GUNEN: "Listen to what my new problem is... I, y'know, reported to the factory t'get compensation for the medical costs. But the factory turned around and said: 'We don't have to pay you anything, you lost your hand because you were careless, so you were the liable one, it was your responsibility,' they said. Of course, I was confused. A problem like this is a handicap for the rest of my life."[7]

In the context of jokes, slips of tongue that play on the meaning of official phrases, and songs, the workers discuss their low wages, prohibitions on their organizing activities, factory safety, forced overtime, menstrual leave, and democracy. As the discussion unfolds, the workers dispense information about various laws that help or further oppress them and also begin to formulate a meeting protocol by which they can make orderly decisions. In contrast to TBI's previous plays, there is very little plot. The entire play projects the feeling of a spontaneous discussion among industrial workers, punctuated by several songs and harassment from factory guard characters.

The staging also departed from TBI's previous pattern: the group displayed a folksy *sampakan* style in which performers fluidly move from acting their parts to playing music and back again. Despite this gesture towards a more artistic style of folk theater, at least one reviewer compared *Bercanda Dalam Duka* to ABU's *Nyanyian Pabrik* and found TBI's production less intimate with its audience and less polished. Unnamed TBI sources promised changes (Tejo 1993b).

LSMs and Aesthetics

This germinal concern with the aesthetics of workers' theater and the slight but real pressure to adjust to such concerns points to a growing interest in workers' culture among members of the middle-class media and arts community following the emergence of Teater ABU. Yet ABU's decidedly "more artistic" productions, the expenses involved in taking its members to see urban theater performances, its venues, and mixed working- and middle-class/arts audiences had begun to make the LSM sponsors uneasy. This sense of unease was registered in YPM's pamphlet, "Strive for Workers' Theater," which described YPM's connection to Teater ABU and the group's early experiences. The pamphlet questioned the use of the works of middle-class poets in ABU's plays and suggested that ABU needed to perform more in public and working-class venues rather than in "middle-class theater show places" (Yayasan Perempuan Mardika 1993?). The same pamphlet declared that ABU's members had "not yet been able to make a change in their interests as workers through their theater work" and questioned whether ABU was yet able to "meaningfully convey workers' interests" (Yayasan Perempuan Mardika 1993?).

YPM's Linda Gumeulis felt that the group should contribute to the workers' movement by taking an active part in campaigns on specific issues. She had regularly attended practices and provided support and suggestions. When ABU resumed activities in July 1993, five months after *Nyanyian Pabrik*, Linda was asked not to attend in order to let the group see what it could develop on its own. Later Linda began to appear at ABU's practices once more, but members were reluctant to hear her out about the need for ABU to present current issues in the workers' movement, such as the freedom to form unions independent of government control. Linda felt that the time was right for such a campaign. The independent SBSI[8] was struggling for official recognition, and, in June of 1993, the United States government had initiated a review of Indonesian labor practices and threatened to suspend Indonesia's preferred trading partner status if improvements were not made (Human Rights Watch/Asia 1994, 41–42).[9] Yet ABU's workers complained of being too tired after practice to discuss such things and were evasive when Linda countered by suggesting they hold discussions prior to practice. YPM began to be concerned that under Margesti's guidance ABU was shifting its emphasis away from being part of a workers' movement and moving toward artistic development (Gumeulis 1994).

If YPM was concerned about the direction of ABU, members of ABU had also become concerned with YPM's style of support. According to

Margesti, ABU members felt insulted by YPM staff, whom they perceived to be arrogant and bossy (M. Otong 1994). ABU members also resisted shaping their themes to conform to Linda's suggestions. They argued that they could just as legitimately deal with other issues (Gumeulis 1994).

This series of events revealed a set of tensions similar to those evident in Arist's refusal to consider taking TBI to perform in TIM or in his statements that TBI's theater was by, for, and about workers. Unlike TBI, however, ABU was unable to resolve the conflict with its LSM collaborators/sponsors. Margesti's central presence in ABU, in contrast to TBI's artistic guidance by Arist and other LSM activists, created a dynamic in which two sets of aims clashed. On one side was Margesti's notion, readily subscribed to by many ABU members, that theater was a means for individual and group self-actualization. This concept did not ignore the immediate issues of the lives of ABU's worker-members, but sought to embody them in a performance generated through aesthetic experimentation and creative growth. The result had been a workers' theater that was both enjoyable for workers and intriguing to the arts community. Yet desiring to see ABU contribute immediately and continuously to current issues, YPM argued that ABU's brand of theater was not sufficiently utilitarian for the workers' movement and hinted that ABU might be keeping workers from realizing their true interests.

Such conflicts bred distrust and contributed to the cancellation of ABU's second performance in the kind of venue YPM ostensibly favored—the public square of a local Jakarta neighborhood. YPM refused to give Margesti money to pay local security officials a key administrative expense. As a result, in early February 1994, ABU's second performance, *Mentok*, was inserted at the last moment into the interstices of the annual Jakarta Youth Theater Festival at Bulungan. ABU assured wary police censors that of the two possible meanings of the word "mentok," the title referred to "ducks" and not to a "dead end" (M. Otong 1994; Tejo 1994a; Purnasatmoko 1994; Widyawan 1994). Again, ABU's script was not constructed solely from its members' experiences, but based loosely on a "serious" play by D. Djajakusuma (Dahana 1994, 99). There were four major characters: a worker accused of theft from her factory, the factory's owner, a government union representative asked to adjudicate, and a lawyer representing the worker. The play ended with workers protesting what they perceived to be the union representative's unfair decision, followed by police sirens, the chaotic dispersal of the protest, and a lone worker waving an Indonesian flag with the wind of his breath. Perhaps because of the constraints of the more formal Youth Theater Festival venue, ABU's *Mentok* seemed to depart from previous workers' theater performances by not concluding with a mass dance.

Stylistically, ABU mixed traditional popular theater with a modern urban stage script and venue: the play included symbolism, ritual elements, aspects of street troupe performance, children's songs, and the use, by the four principle actresses, of simple colored masks, as well as their conscious identification with the clown characters of the traditional Javanese shadow theater (Tejo 1994a; Dahana 1994; Widyawan 1994). ABU's typically "mixed" audience was even more striking for *Mentok*. Informed about ABU's projects as a part of Margesti's campaigns to raise extra funds for the group, established theater community figures such as Arifin and Jajang C Noer and Nano and Ratna Riantiarno attended and lent their moral support (Tejo 1994a).

Once again, there was extra emphasis put on women in *Mentok*. The four main roles were all performed by women, and these characters engaged in behavior uncharacteristic of supposedly demure Javanese females, either in the factory or in traditional theater. They engaged in wild dancing, recited down-to-earth verses, and displayed masculine performing style of the clowns. Hatley argues that such assertive cheekiness, with ABU's men providing musical accompaniment, mocked both New Order gender ideology and factory behavioral controls (Hatley 1994a, 22).

While media reviews demonstrated that the critics and the arts community were divided in their evaluation of the play's merits, members of ABU, along with Margesti and Linda Gumeulis, all expressed disappointment with the result. Two ABU members told me that they preferred *Nyanyian Pabrik* to *Mentok* because the first play had been more spontaneous (Sutrisno and Wijiono 1994). In a similar vein, Margesti stated that the Bulungan venue had felt too "exclusive" (M. Otong 1994). Characteristically, Gumeulis remarked that attention to artistic details was clearly important to Teater ABU because issues need good packaging, but that *Mentok* had appeared to put artistic concerns before workers' issues (1994).

Even so, following the performance of *Mentok*, when asked why they participated in theater, ABU's members also articulated an agenda of pleasure—one rarely covered by the media or LSM spokespeople in relation to TBI or ABU. One worker told a reporter, "We too need to play, right? We need to communicate, brother." Another worker stated that "Basically, brother, I like getting together with friends from other factories, especially since it's more pleasant doing theater together than holding a discussion."[10] Only *Prospek*'s Setiaji Purnasatmoko took extended notice of such comments, arguing that workers' lives were claustrophobically constrained, thus making their desires to play and to have contact with the "world outside" all too natural (Purnasatmoko 1994). In a way, the workers' comments and Purnasatmoko's analysis run parallel to those of Margesti, who argued that theater's main value for workers was as a kind of "self-actualization." Yet Margesti had focused on aesthetic education, confidence-building, and performance. A different set of emphases was contained in the workers' statements: namely, that play and pleasure and an opportunity for social recognition through communication with a broad public are part of the process of becoming complete humans.

The Media and Middle-Class Aesthetic Ideology

News coverage of workers' theater performances mediated between workers' theater and a wider reading public (including the arts community) dominated by middle-class values. Newspaper and magazine reports about TBI and ABU were crucial to this wider public's attempt to understand this new theater and fix its place within Indonesian social and cultural practices. The media thereby constituted a key forum for broad discussions about the proper aesthetics for workers' theater.

A central component in constructing an understanding of workers' theater for a broader public was the manner in which media reviews/reports granted particular kinds of authority to the various participants.

For instance, in the early coverage, workers were likely to be cited with regard to details of their productions and their lives as workers or for their motivations and feelings about involvement in theater. In reports about TBI, while LSM activists were quoted describing details of the group's operations, in addition, they were even more likely to be sources of political analysis and information about the purposes of TBI. LSM activists—mainly Arist Merdeka Sirait—thus occupied a crucial analytical position in the public discussion.

In contrast to the coverage of TBI, stories about ABU gave significantly little space to representatives of the LSM (YPM). Rather, Margesti or arts community figures were frequent sources. Like the workers, Margesti was the source for many details about the production process, but she was also cited much more often than workers about matters of aesthetics, the arts world, and the psychology of workers engaged in theater. Thus, in the coverage of ABU, people from the arts community replaced LSM activists as the main analytic informants. As detailed in the previous section, there were serious differences between the views of LSM activists and members of the arts community (as represented by Margesti) about the purpose of workers' theater. Consequently, ABU's style and publicly stated aims contributed to the growth of a debate about the aesthetics and goals of workers' theater.

In order to better understand the source of these differences, as well as the way in which the media responded to workers' theater, it is necessary to reiterate briefly a part of the aesthetic ideology dominant in the world of modern Indonesian theater, as discussed in chapter 1. This aesthetic ideology places a high premium on formal/technical experimentation and on the elaboration of presumed universal human values through the exploration of individual psychology or through archetypal, surreal, fragmented, or multi-layered narratives or compositions (Foulcher 1987; Tickell 1987; Foulcher 1993; Asmara 1995). In addition, many artists and theater practitioners avoid addressing politics too directly in their writings and performances. In part, this reluctance responded to the political polarization of the early 1960s when cultural groups aligned themselves with competing political parties and often experienced pressure to make their works conform to particular political issues (Foulcher 1986, 114–15).

In part, it was also a concession to the restrictive reality of New Order public discourse.

At the same time, New Order practitioners of modern theater sought to create a communicative new theater style that could be called distinctively Indonesian—one that was moving away from Western psychological realism and Aristotelian unities (Asmara 1995). To that end, these New Order innovators endeavored to adapt folk and traditional theater forms to fit their own experimental framework. Despite some resulting turns towards a more broadly communicative, popular theater and despite its often antagonistic position towards the New Order state, the world of modern Indonesian theater continued to be dominated by an emphasis on formal experimentation, universal values, and the avoidance of political messages deemed too direct or partisan.

The reporters who covered workers' theater and who played a significant part in shaping public discourse about it often seemed to be writing with this aesthetic ideology of theater as a basic assumption. Invariably, when attempting to explain the significance of workers' theater, reporters wrote in a mixed language that slipped over from objective detailing of facts and quoting of sources into the authoritative, evaluative language of a critical discourse. Such articles resorted to the language of aesthetic expertise (the norms of art) and "common sense" to buttress evaluative authority. For example, in 1990 Syah Sabur of *Suara Pembaruan* wrote of TBI's performance of *Di Mana Aku Berpijak*: "This performance, if analyzed according to the norms of art, would certainly collapse and seem worthless. . . . To watch this performance, which was staged through the maximal efforts of about 30 workers from various factories in Depok and Cimanggis, one has to be prepared beforehand, especially with a deep knowledge of their lives."[11]

Most of these articles sought to support TBI's efforts by stating that the plays proved that theater was not only for expressing artistic ideals, but could also be a means for raising awareness (e.g., *Kompas* 1989). Yet, in defending workers' theater they inevitably also resorted to a "common sense" discourse about art, noting that such performances *could* not and should not be compared to aesthetically refined performances at TIM (*Kompas* 27 Nov. 1989 and 9 June 1991; Sabur 1990; Indrayati and

Wahyuni 1991; Gantra 1993; Laksana and Ginanjar 1993). One pair of reporters argued that this type of theater had to be seen as part of a social process and as an event that created an intimate relationship with its audience. Sympathetically, but nonetheless patronizingly, they characterized TBI's plays as expressions "from below," staged "as is" (*apa adanya*). The pair went on to state that Remy Sylado's artistic theories were no longer important for TBI. In their view, art was not the essential matter, but rather how to bring workers' problems to the stage (Indrayati and Wahyuni 1991). Similarly, a report covering ABU's *Nyanyian Pabrik* in Bandung commented: "Therefore, it's not particularly relevant to evaluate this performance in technical or aesthetic terms. That's because it contained a number of events which could not be judged successfully using such frames of reference"[12] (Laksana and Ginanjar 1993).

As these examples demonstrate, rather than challenging the criteria of middle-class aesthetics, the media attempted to separate art with aesthetic values from art as a part of social and educational processes. The lack of formal and technical sophistication characterizing TBI's early productions, coupled with the group's realist approach and its close connection to specific social sectors and issues, indeed seemed to place workers' theater outside the aesthetic norms of modern, middle-class theater. Still, the very details that reporters/reviewers noted about workers' theater—questions about how to bring workers' problems to the stage, its aims of education and consciousness-raising, its function as an emotional outlet, and the performances' ability to generate camaraderie and a participatory atmosphere—raised the possibility that workers' theater was a new form that required a different aesthetic. As distinct from middle-class theater's borrowing of narrative strategies, acting gestures, and staging techniques from traditional theater in order to indigenize modern theater and expand its non-realist, experimental possibilities, workers' theater incorporated the populist spirit of many popular and traditional forms. Rather than searching for universal values, workers' theater embraced the local, specific issues of its primary audience and did so in a way that allowed the audience to join in the fun. This "intimacy" was then joined with modern notions of theater as an educational medium.

It is not that this theater cannot be compared to performances in TIM, but rather that despite the reporters' obvious sympathies, middle-class theater is still seen as the sole norm of good theater. Thus, the reporters end by abandoning sole proprietorship over the term aesthetics to a particular kind of theater practice and aesthetic experience. Workers' theater, both in its educational and solidarity-creating functions within a workers' movement and its role as a creative and emotional outlet for the workers themselves, is relegated to the status of a sociological artifact whose context must be understood.

This line of argument, taken up so unanimously by reporters sympathetic to workers' theater and dedicated to convincing a middle-class readership of the value of workers' theater, was pitched so as not to disrupt middle-class notions about serious art. By locating workers' theater outside good art, rather than as an alternative capable of seriously challenging middle-class notions of art, this strategy allowed middle-class supporters to maintain their concepts of aesthetics unchallenged. As a result, middle-class sympathizers could retain feelings of superiority toward the unfortunate workers whose art did not quite "measure up." The value of such theater is thus reduced to its functions as social statement or protest, categories that serious art can claim to present more effectively through its command of aesthetics and technique. The media, however sympathetic, can therefore be seen as *mediating*, from a middle-class-dominated perspective, between TBI and a middle-class public.

This discussion shifted subtly with the entrance of ABU. As with TBI's early plays, although reporters found the style of *Nyanyian Pabrik* amateurish, they also held that it wasn't relevant to judge ABU in terms of aesthetics and technique. ABU's members were praised for finding time and energy for theater and for successfully creating theater that dissolved the boundaries between performance and audience (Gantra 1993; Laksana and Ginanjar 1993). Furthermore, Margesti's involvement resulted in a more visible response from the artistic community to ABU than to TBI's early productions.

Dindon, Teater Kubur's leader and someone well acquainted with Margesti, saw in the play an expression of the workers' desire "to become human beings." In an article written for *Media Indonesia* a week after the performance of *Nyanyian Pabrik*, Dindon argued that the success of ABU's play lay in its cathartic effect. Through expressing their frustrations, then ending the performance in a celebratory dance with the audience, the workers could reclaim their complete humanity and negate the fragmenting nature of factory production. Dindon's view thus implied that art is both therapy and, following Marcuse, a fundamental act of resistance against an unhealthy society, whose capitalistically organized productive imperatives compartmentalize people, alienating them from the breadth of experience that signifies a complete human being. Yet at the end of his article Dindon, too, broached the issue of the aesthetic value of workers' theater. Repeating the truism developed by reporters, Dindon saw ABU's point of departure as a commitment to raising awareness, with aesthetics occupying a position of secondary importance. Nevertheless, he asserted that aesthetic development. in time, would equal the group's consciousness-raising mission, since aesthetic growth was a logical consequence of ABU's pursuit of art as "self-actualization" (Dindon 1993). Like Margesti, Dindon implied that aesthetic development and human growth were inseparable and that aesthetics and politics could go together.

Other cultural workers struck a different note. The artist Moelyono, himself engaged in using graphic art as a means of raising the awareness and self-confidence of women workers in the factories of the East Javanese port of Surabaya, responded to reports of ABU's performances with an opinion piece about workers' art in the 4 April 1993 edition of *Kompas*. In contrast to Dindon and Margesti, Moelyono argued that while it might temporarily be necessary for artists to work together with workers, artists should not let their artistic ideology become a burden for workers. "A democratic attitude needs to be built patiently and continuously, let the workers find themselves through the artistic process," he added (Moelyono 1993).

Media coverage of the next two workers' theater productions, TBI's *Bercanda Dalam Duka* (September 1993) and ABU's *Mentok* (February 1994), began to use *Nyanyian Pabrik* as the measure of good workers' theater. Some observers and reviewers found both of the more recent works to be less intimate with their audiences and marred by the strained efforts of the workers to be artistic (Tejo 1993b; Tejo 1994a; B. Otong 1994).

Others praised ABU for striving to increase artistic complexity, mobilize folk and other techniques that preserved a fluid atmosphere between audience and performers, and use Javanese children's songs to lighten an otherwise grim script (Dahana 1994; Widyawan 1994). Although still no set of clear ideas about the exact aesthetics of workers' theater had emerged, in the wake of ABU's *Nyanyian Pabrik*, the media, too, was now divided about whether or not increased attention to aesthetic development resulted in a more powerfully expressive form of workers' theater.

Ratna Sarumpaet and High Art Theater about Workers

Given rising interest in workers' theater in the second half of 1994, it was no coincidence that members of the middle-class arts community produced a play dealing with labor issues. When I visited Indonesia in the summer of 1994, many artists voiced disappointment with the New Order government's continued censorship of the arts. In their comments, this frustration was often linked to broader frustration about the commercialization of culture and society as well as the glaring differences in wealth and opportunity. That June this dissatisfaction had been heightened with the sudden government-ordered revocation of the publishing permits of three of Jakarta's leading newsweeklies.

In response to the brutal murder of Marsinah in early 1993 and to the general atmosphere outlined above, Ratna Sarumpaet staged her play, *Nyanyian Marsinah: Dari Bawah Tanah* (Marsinah's Song: From Beneath the Earth. The play's title was later changed to Marsinah: Nyanyian Dari Bawah Tanah.) in September 1994. Though not workers' theater, *Nyanyian Marsinah* was clearly a rejoinder to the practices of workers' theater. As noted before, Ratna had supported Margesti and ABU and was sympathetic to workers' issues. Yet she felt that workers' theater was limited by the workers' narrow education. In workers' theater, she maintained, one got the impression that workers had unrealistically become "too intelligent," that NGOs often dictated which issues the workers should present, and that the effectiveness of workers' theater in communicating with other workers was doubtful. Ratna stated that this kind of theater only wore out workers and exposed them to being fired. In her view, artists could contribute more effectively to the workers' cause (Sarumpaet 1994b).

Nyanyian Marsinah drew extensive media coverage and its near capacity crowds included government officials, international diplomats, NGO activists, and some workers (Oei 1994; *Kompas* 22 Sept. 1994; *Citra* 26 Sept.–2 Oct. 1994; Rizal 1994). Given the government's decision to revoke the licenses of the three news weeklies, along with the banning of an art exhibition dedicated to Marsinah in Surabaya, East Java, in mid-1994 (*Harian Terbit* 12 Sept. 1994), Ratna admitted to the media that she wasn't sure whether the play would be allowed to go on. Further, she confessed that the sensitive political nature of its material made it extremely difficult to secure financial backers. In early 1994, the trial of nine people accused of conspiring to murder Marsinah had raised even greater controversy after it was revealed that a number of the accused had been tortured by police in order to obtain confessions (Human Rights Watch/Asia 1994, 52–56). Ratna was often quoted as adding that the play did not manipulate or "exploit" the case because it did not actually take up the specific details of the events surrounding Marsinah's murder, but rather used Marsinah as a symbol for injustices that could befall absolutely anyone in Indonesia. She called for Indonesians to reflect on these issues (*Pos Kota* 11 Sept. 1994; *Jawa Pos* 12 Sept. 1994; *Harian Terbit* 12 Sept. 1994; *Republika* 13 Sept. 1994; Sabur 1994; *Nova*, n.d.; *Kompas* 22 Sept. 1994).

Set in the "afterlife," the play is dominated by a series of debates between several deceased souls. In the course of heated arguments with a former judge and a once powerful government official/businessman simply identified as the Third Man, a "Prominent Figure" (*Tokoh*) whose awful fate bears a clear resemblance to that of Marsinah rages against the injustice of New Order society. These debates are juxtaposed with poetic interludes and two extended scenes based on the problems of contemporary factory workers. If the debates and the workers' scenes touch on a number of current issues in painfully direct fashion, the poetic interludes introduce an evocative, philosophical, and metaphorical framework for understanding the "larger context" (and perhaps for placating the censors by stylistically insulating the more sensitive references).

The play sharply criticizes New Order society and the rhetoric that legitimizes it. It does so by representing New Order social and economic development as egotistical and male-dominated, enabled by the sacrifices of women, children, and the weak. In this representation, the oppression of women and their response to it takes center stage, turning the Marsinah surrogate, the Prominent Figure, into a symbol of women's angry desire to fight back. The wrathful Prominent Figure is, however, contrasted to other women: the Judge who sees no use in opening old wounds and a mother who suppresses her own anguish over widespread social oppression and injustice. Many of the play's most important arguments, the majority of which outline how current conditions should be faced, take place between these women.

The theme of gender relations is central to how the play makes sense of the problems of New Order society. In one of the play's early poetic sequences. the lack of democracy and women's oppression begin in the home, we are told by the mother, also a symbol of the nation (Sarumpaet 1994a, 4–6, 64–65[13]). There men dominate women instead of working together with them (8–11). The worker scenes are also characterized by the domination of ordinary female workers by male officials and guards (12–21). In the wider Indonesian context, development is presented as a male project from which chiefly men benefit. This reality is illustrated by the three male businessmen/politicians with whom the Prominent Figure debates (43–60), as well as in the scene where the worker, Kuneng, is betrayed by her man, when he signs over their house and land to a developer, then leaves with the money (28–30).

A second key theme, as in so much contemporary dissident middle-class literature and theater in Indonesia, is the suffering of the ordinary people and the poor. In response to one of the businessman/politician's remarks that everyone must sacrifice to bring Indonesia into the ranks of the advanced industrial nations, the Prominent Figure retorts that it is usually the poor who must sacrifice the most and that they have already sacrificed enough since the time of the revolution (51, 53). The Prominent Figure herself comes from poverty and has struggled to survive (5–6, 46, 50, 67, 71, 74). Scenes representing the life of workers (12–21) and discussing development (30–35, 46–60) underscore how poor Indonesians are repeatedly the victims, rather than the beneficiaries, of the nation's "progress."

It is important to note, however, that the portrayal of the workers and poor in *Nyanyian Marsinah* is marked by a clear ambivalence. As already stated, Ratna felt that workers' theater was not particularly effective and that artists could do more for them. In one newspaper article about the play, Ratna was quick to point out that she didn't want to blindly defend the workers. She argued that workers had their faults too. They needed to discipline themselves and increase their knowledge, improve their skills, and not be prone to giving up so easily. To avoid simply glorifying the workers in the play, Ratna commented, she introduced the characters of the judge and the third man (government official/businessman) to allow them to convey a different point of view (Sabur 1994). This last statement suggests that Ratna's remarks in part conform to a pattern of New Order public oppositional discourse in which dissidents must demonstrate their objectivity lest they be dismissed or judged dangerous. Similarly, Ratna's assertion that the play is not too politically partisan also tries to situate the play within the middle-class literary and theatrical aesthetic ideology previously outlined. Yet Ratna's personal comments also indicate that she truly believes much of what the article reported her as saying.

How does this ambivalence manifest itself in the play? On the one hand, *Nyanyian Marsinah* features militant, daring workers like Itut, who is bold enough to stand up to male factory officials in the lengthy factory scene, and the Prominent Figure. Yet the play also insinuates that workers and the poor are partly to blame for current conditions because neither they nor the middle-class resist the schemes of the powerful (31, 35). Thus, militants are lonely exceptions to the general lack of spine among the working- (and middle-) class. Elsewhere, however, workers and the poor are described as helpless and powerless (23, 30), much like children and women who are crushed, co-opted, or abandoned by a cruel New Order society (1–2, 10–11, 30, 55). They are without options before the power of the state: coerced to leave their land, to work for low wages, and to keep silent (29–31, 33–35, 45, 49, 57–58).

Still, the Prominent Figure and Itut do resist. But it is precisely the form of their resistance that seems to pose one of the same problems Ratna felt characterized workers' theater: The leaders of *Marsinah*'s workers are incredibly articulate and daring in confronting factory owners. Furthermore, rather than stating concrete situations and needs, as happens in TBI's and ABU's plays, Ratna's worker spokeswomen often abstract their experiences, presenting them on a philosophical or highly general level. When a factory official interrogates Itut about why the workers have assaulted another official, Itut launches into a highly poetic discourse on "hunger as a motivation" (17–21). The Prominent Figure is even more brilliant.

If the Prominent Figure is Marsinah, then she is a Marsinah created in the image of a modern, middle-class-style intellectual. The play valorizes the individual human quest for knowledge (6, 46), and the Prominent Figure glorifies the intellectual probity of scientists as servants of humanity (52). The Prominent Figure is also characterized as someone who continually questions (62). Structurally, in a series of one-sided debates, the Prominent Figure is pitted against government and middle-class figures such as the three bureaucrats and the judge. She proves to be highly articulate and relentless in demolishing their arguments. Furthermore, she engages and pleads with the middle-class professional figure of the judge and at one point at least she addresses the audience directly, suggesting that the play's primary aim is winning the hearts and minds of the professional middle-class with its indictment of New Order oppression, corruption, and development. Her role in the play is thus a dual one with respect to middle-class audience members. By virtue of her resemblance to an idealized middle-class female intellectual, the Prominent Figure allows middle-class audience members to imagine themselves as defenders of the weak, while at the same time she urges them to take up that position, to become more like her.

Ratna's research into Marsinah's life and her contact with Teater ABU gave her material that may have aided her in constructing the situations presented in the play's worker scenes. (She required members of her company to read some eighty pages of clippings on the case [Sabur 1994; *Jawa Pos* 12 Sept. 1994].) Yet, the play also incorporates several social issues that had only recently begun to be tackled in workers' theater in a manner much more specific to workers' lives—the nature of New Order "development," men's general domination of women, the state of the justice system, and the rule of law. *Nyanyian Marsinah* presents these issues as much more general, socio-structural problems, thus transforming Marsinah into a metaphor for diverse kinds of oppression.

In intellectualizing Marsinah, as well as in broadening her discourse to encompass all the problems of contemporary Indonesia, Ratna's play transmutes the specific nature of workers' problems into generality, embedding the worker scenes in a general debate about individual human greed, the lust for power, the desire for truth and justice, and the need to survive. The play even ends on a highly philosophical and religious note, posing questions about fate and the relationship of individuals to God. Though this strategy seeks to avoid government censors, it is also consistent with a common theme in modern, "serious" Indonesian literature and theater: that good art presents universal human values. In short, Ratna's play aims to speak for the working class, a task it accomplishes admirably in many ways, but in so doing, it replaces the voice of the worker with a voice that, eloquent and impassioned as it is, is nonetheless different.[14] Symptomatic of persistent tensions between the arts community's notion of aesthetics and LSM desires for a more transparently committed art, one review of the play reported that several LSM activists attending the last night's performance felt that the play was fatalistic and that the Prominent Figure was too submissive in surrendering her fate completely to the Almighty (*Citra* 26 Sept.–2 Oct. 1994).

Government Pressures

Beginning with TBI's first play, various participants had spoken of the group's activities as though imagining the unseen surveillance of the New Order government apparatus. For instance, at the time of TBI's first performance in 1989, Remy Sylado, TBI's former trainer, stated that it was more positive for workers to be protesting through theater than in the streets (*Kompas* 27 Nov. 1989). In a country where protest is often viewed as disruptive or dangerous, his comment hints at a listener who is especially concerned about workers taking up forms of public political action. This is born out by Arist Sirait's remarks following TBI's 1990 play. Arist maintained that people would not be likely to take offence if criticism came in theatrical form (Sabur 1990). If Arist's argument was later proven wrong, it nonetheless demonstrates how people involved with TBI were already attempting to counter possible negative views from those with the power to censor and ban. An important part of such defensive arguments was stressed by Arist and Suzanna during 1991 when they maintained that the plays were based on the workers' own experiences and created by the workers themselves. Such statements asserted that the plays were highly realistic and authentic, while also working to circumvent possible accusations that LSM activists were manipulating the process for their own ends (Indrayati and Wahyuni 1991; *Berita Buana* 23 Dec. 1991). When interviewed about the 1991 performance of *Lauk-Lauk Janji*, one TBI worker similarly argued that theater was better than other media, such as a speech, because the ideas were mediated by the actors, not directly delivered to an audience by an orator. Such mediation allowed the emotions of the spectators to be better controlled (*Kompas* 9 June 1991). Here, too, we can detect the worker speaking for the unseen ear of intelligence units. The power of the government to affect workers' theater was given credibility, perhaps unintentionally, by the run-up to TBI's December 1991 performance. Whether it was because the police bureaucracy was simply inefficient, was waiting for an appropriate "payment," or was beginning to discern a threat, TBI had been forced to postpone its play for several days while waiting for the apparatus to issue a permit (*Berita Buana* 23 Dec. 1991).

Following ABU's February 6, 1993, performance of *Nyanyian Pabrik* in Bandung, one worker, perhaps responding to a reporter's question, also displayed an awareness of potential state censors when he asserted that the play had no political aim, but was just a way to release frustrations (Laksana and Ginanjar 1993). The worker's concern was well founded. Some fifty workers from Majalaya had attended the performance, and when a wildcat strike occurred in a Majalaya factory a few days later, authorities questioned the artist at whose studio the performance had taken place (Laksana and Ginanjar 1993). Margesti was also questioned with regard to the strike. YPM's Linda Gumeulis, too, was called to the local military headquarters, but her interrogation centered more on YPM's activities than on Teater ABU (M. Otong 1994; Gumeulis 1994).

Indeed, as the number of industrial strikes increased and organizing for the SBSI independent union began to gain momentum, the New Order security apparatus seemed to be casting a more suspicious eye towards workers and workers' theater activities. This can be illustrated by looking at some of the dialogue of TBI's September 1993 play, *Bercanda Dalam Duka* (Joking amidst Sorrow), as well as in comments made by Arist to a reporter/reviewer in conjunction with the play's performance. *Bercanda Dalam Duka* took up the theme of the draconian labor regime enforced by government and factories alike that had limited workers' ability to fight for better conditions, and even to gather:

SARINAH: Is there anything that's not forbidden? Just talking...
GROUP: Is forbidden!
GENDANG: Demand your wages...
GROUP: Given the sack!
SARON: To organize...
GROUP: Emasculated!
SURTI: To gather together like this...
GROUP: A secret meeting!
SAONAH: So what isn't forbidden, Nen...
GUNEN: You can laugh to your heart's content! (All break out into laughter). As long as laughter is still permitted.[15]

In a review of the play published in the *Kompas* daily, the increased pressure being brought to bear on workers' theater and the workers' movement as a whole by the government was revealed in the comments of Arist Merdeka Sirait. In the exchange between Arist and a *Kompas* reporter, Arist denied the play had a "political" aim. Instead, he countered, TBI used theater as a medium for transformative education, raising awareness, and disseminating information. He admitted that obtaining the performance permit had taken time, but maintained that all had gone smoothly once organizers had convinced the concerned government offices that the play didn't "reek of politics" (*Sinar Pagi* 8 Sept. 1993). Arist concluded: "Of course, what is there to get upset about in the desire to dialogue like this? You know, it's like they said in the performance, 'We have to state our opinions. We shouldn't just have to listen; on the contrary, we should be heard as well. That way we're all happy . . . '"(Tejo 1993b).[16]

Perhaps as a result of the brighter international spotlight thrown upon New Order labor practices by the U.S. review begun earlier that year, the Indonesian security apparatus seemed content to allow TBI to perform. The situation changed dramatically following the U.S.'s suspension of its review in February 1994. Freed from this international pressure, the Indonesian government found an excuse to begin a more comprehensive crackdown on labor in the Medan incident of April 1994.[17] The New Order's targets soon came to include workers' theater groups.

Following ABU's February 1994 production of *Mentok*, tensions between Teater ABU and YPM had developed into a serious rift. With workers' issues becoming more sensitive in the wake of the Medan riots, Margesti was advised by friends to suspend ABU's activities temporarily. As a result, ABU did not perform for over a year (M. Otong 1994).

In the early months of 1994, TBI released a cassette containing ten songs composed by Arist Sirait and sung by members of TBI. The collection, *Marsinah: Bersatulah Buruh Indonesia* (Marsinah: Indonesian Workers Unite), expressed a number of workers' grievances—no security against dismissal, sub-standard wages, young workers' difficulty in providing for their families—and called for worker solidarity in struggling for justice and adequate pay. There were also songs celebrating Marsinah and decrying government officials who make empty promises.

The government seemed to become aware of the cassette's existence rather slowly, responding only several months later. General Banurusman, national commander of the police, ordered the cassette withdrawn from circulation on July 4 because it "could incite workers." Some reports conveyed the government's usual rhetoric of terror, including statements that the songs contained social criticism that *exploited* the circumstances surrounding Marsinah's death and thus could create social unease and disturb national stability. Following the ban and a fruitless search of music stores in East Java, the government took no further immediate action (*Republika* 4 July 1994; *Surya* 4 July 1994; *Pos Kota* 4 July 1994; *Pos Kota* 5 July 1994). Nonetheless, it was clear that workers' theater could only expect increased surveillance and pressure in the future.

Change of Strategy: 1995–1996

Both TBI's *Bercanda Dalam Duka* and ABU's *Mentok* gave evidence of thematic attempts to link workers' issues to those of the broader middle-class. TBI's play touched on issues of democracy as they related to workers' need to make their complaints known, while *Mentok* touched on the issue of legal practice and justice for workers. From a middle-class high art perspective, Ratna Sarumpaet's *Nyanyian Marsinah* had knit workers' issues into a play about universal values. All of these plays as well as the debate about workers' theater and aesthetics are concrete evidence of the ways in which workers, LSMs, journalists, and middle-class artists were attempting to form alliances and explore the possibilities and limits of such alliances through the construction of material-social practices—in this case, theater.

Indicative of continuing debates over the uses and aesthetics of workers' theater and culture, in a March 12, 1994, *Kompas* analysis of TBI's cassette, H. Sujiwo Tejo suggested that the songs on *Marsinah: Bersatulah Buruh Indonesia* were ineffective in the current environment. Tejo reasoned that with the increasing prominence of public demonstrations (*unjuk rasa*) as vehicles for the expression of workers' grievances, workers' theater was no longer their sole expressive outlet. Furthermore, he added, demonstrations were more "real" (*nyata*) than theater, making theater seem pale and less effective. Tejo advised workers' theater to take up more complex issues, ones that couldn't easily be expressed on banners and placards, such as comparing the amount businesses spent on bribery to the amount (purportedly far less) they spent on workers' wages (Tejo 1994d). Tejo had argued consistently that workers' theater should not attempt to imitate middle-class theater. His critique of the cassette revealed that he did not view workers' theater as a valuable and alternative cultural form, but mainly as a malleable instrument for advancing the workers' struggle. Even so, his suggestion that the groups take up more complicated issues also begged the question of whether the "familiar" form of workers' theater, which he had defended as essential to maintaining a bond between workers' theater and its audience, might not also have to change and become more complex.

Indeed, in the first half of 1995, there were signs that the Jakarta workers' theaters were adjusting their strategies and attempting to initiate a new stage of social dialogue. The Indonesian arts community had grown increasingly weary of New Order censorship. This frustration manifested itself in the 1995 May Declaration issued by roughly forty prominent literary figures, including Ratna Sarumpaet, which represented present conditions for the arts as a continuation of those during the much maligned, fractious early 1960s (Junaedi 1995; Pracoyo et al. 1995; Putera et al. 1995).

As recounted at the beginning of this chapter, in scheduling the May 13 and 14 performances at TIM in 1995 (which subsequently were banned by the government), Teater Buruh Indonesia was attempting to further engage the middle-class, and especially its frustrated arts community, in a more intensive dialogue. Clearly, the event was partly intended as another intervention in the debate about whether workers' theater was for workers' education and networking or whether it should be judged from an artistic point of view. In the program printed for the scheduled May 1995 performances, Arist Merdeka Sirait emphasized that Teater Buruh's aim was not to create art, but rather to give workers a medium for discussion, debate, and education. He invited the urban middle-class to watch the performance of *Senandung Terpuruk* and urged the arts community to debate with Teater Buruh its viability as an alternative kind of theater as well as to discuss how workers' problems could be solved by everyone working together (Sirait 1995, 3–4). Ironically, Teater Buruh was now seeking to perform in the very middle-class venue whose appropriateness for workers' theater Arist had rejected five years earlier.

At this juncture, R. Bagus Suharyono and Jakarta's Socio-Political Directorate imposed the first banning order on a workers' theater performance, as described at the beginning of this chapter. TBI did not simply concede defeat, however. The group cannily refrained from protesting the TIM ban until its show could at least be performed on the 15th at their usual venue, the Galaxy Theater in Cisalak, Bogor.

Fig. 6.2. Program Cover for TBI's *Senandung Terpuruk*, 1995.

The banning of TBI's performance at the Taman Ismail Marzuki signaled the next step in the government's attempt to crack down on workers' theater. However, the government banning did not discourage TBI. In fact, it chose to fight back in at least two ways: through seeking other venues in the following months and through the courts. In chapter 7 I will describe the content of the play and present the details of these struggles as part of my examination of the battle theater workers waged against government censorship of theater. The important point here is that in the course of their struggle with the state censors, TBI did in fact manage to engage in something of a dialogue with middle-class critics of the government as well as participate in legal battles that resembled concurrent media challenges to the state's power to grant and withdraw publishing licenses.

As TBI found opportunities to perform *Senandung Terpuruk* outside its regular Galaxy Theater venue (LBH offices, Studio Oncor, Parahyangan University), middle-class arts community figures continued to comment on the group's work. The performance at Oncor generated an enthusiastic if predictable discussion, in which some of the artists criticized the group for not paying much attention to the aesthetic, artistic aspects of the performance, while the workers insisted on being true to their experience (Ayu Ratih 1995). Interviewed after the performance, Arist again tried to counter government claims by stating that theater didn't need to be banned because the workers were just performing their real conditions—presenting things that happened among the workers, like the Marsinah case. He added that TBI's play was not abusive towards the government and echoed Remy Sylado's earlier argument that creating theater was positive in contrast to demonstrating (*Jayakarta* 1 September 1995).

Writing for *Media Indonesia Minggu*, Djadjat Sudradjat defended workers' theater in the aftermath of the government banning. Sudradjat cited Arifin C Noer's notion of theater as something that "always creates human connections" in order to argue that workers' theater was better than demonstrations, for it sought human ties rather than drove people into polarized camps. This argument was directed at both the government and those segments of Indonesian society (including portions of the middle-class) who, while sympathetic to workers' plight, might well be concerned about visible public demonstrations as potential sources of disorder.[18] Sudradjat defended TBI's alternative model by concluding that those who privileged aesthetics shouldn't be angry with

TBI, but should learn to become "democrats" in a variety of spheres (Sudradjat 1995). His argument thus followed a direction pioneered by Moelyono two years earlier, which incorporated middle-class political ideals, such as tolerance and democratic behavior, to argue that workers' theater as a distinct practice had every right to exist. Plurality in theater was becoming discursively tied to the legal political aspirations of dissident segments of the middle-class. These linkages were reinforced by TBI's legal challenge to Suharyono's decision. TBI's lawsuit tactically joined workers' struggles to those of middle-class journalists using the courts to contest the New Order press bans of June 1994. It thereby helped put the issue of "rule of law" (*negara hukum*) more prominently on the public agenda.

By mid-1995, the dispute between YPM and Teater ABU had precipitated the group's splintering into two separate Teater ABU troupes. One, centered in Tangerang, the industrial city just west of Jakarta, was closely aligned with and funded by YPM, while the other, no longer funded by YPM, remained connected to Margesti (Field Notes 16 August 1997). Strangely, Linda Gumeulis now echoed the approach of Margesti and some of the ABU members in commenting that Teater ABU (Tangerang) had chosen a different path than TBI, one that placed more emphasis on artistic aspects. In contrast to YPM's early doubts, Linda now stated: "As a result they can perform amidst artists and the middle-class in formal venues.... Performing in that kind of place is useful in that it continuously keeps workers' tragedies in public focus" (Tejo and Witdarmono 1995).[19] In fact, the Tangerang Teater ABU had performed a new piece, *Kesaksian* (Bearing Witness), in June of 1995 to another "mixed" audience of workers, legal aid activists, and unionists at the Jakarta Legal Aid Institute. However, while Linda spoke of ABU's ability both to raise awareness and develop artistic presentation, ABU workers began to sound more like TBI members, stating that the importance of their theater lay in communicating about their experiences, their rights, and current regulations. The performance itself was much simpler than ABU's previous efforts, though it still bore elements of the artistic style Margesti had encouraged, including a ritual of solidarity in which the group sang patriotic songs and held hands with audience members while kissing the national flag.

On this occasion Margesti, too, though not involved in the Tangerang group's production, was nonetheless asked to comment on the rival Teater ABU. Out of solidarity, Margesti took a broadly democratic tack in her explaination of the value of ABU's activities, emphasizing that she was only helping the workers to express themselves and show that anyone could engage in artistic production (Suriaji 1995).

Both TBI and the Tangerang ABU seemed to agree on one key point. The shift in strategies, articulated by the LSM sponsors, shows that activists had begun to think that raising the consciousness or self-confidence of workers was not enough; in order to successfully pursue their specific struggles, workers needed an alliance with segments of the urban middle-class. Still there were two different positions on this question. While Arist attempted to portray TBI's theater as an alternative to high art that needed to be seen on its own terms, YPM argued that ABU could appeal to the middle-class through artistic form—suggesting a single norm of theater which workers could master in order to satisfy middle-class tastes.

At the same time, other workers' theater groups emerged in the course of 1995. In September the Sanggar Pabrik (Factory Studio)—sponsored by the struggling, still officially unrecognized independent union, the SBSI (Serikat Buruh Sejahtera Indonesia or Indonesian Prosperous Workers' Union)—announced its formation. Five days after Sanggar Pabrik's first performance on the 16th of September was prevented by the refusal of the police to issue a performance permit; the group complained to the National Human Rights Commission. On that occasion, Sanggar Pabrik performed a part of its play *Surat Cinta Bagi Marsinah Di Sorga* (Love Letter to Marsinah in Heaven) for members of the Commission. In late October they again performed the piece on the TIM grounds for a pro-democracy rally organized by several pro-democracy youth groups. Unlike Ratna Sarumpaet's play, Sanggar Pabrik's work did offer a reconstruction of the events surrounding the death of Marsinah. The group was scheduled to perform again in mid-May 1996 at the offices of the Legal Aid Institute in downtown Jakarta (Basri 1995; *The Jakarta Post* 30 October 1995; *Republika* 19 Sept. 1995; Pijar 1995; *Pijar-KDP* 1995).

BUBUTAN, TABUR, and Middle-Class Aesthetics

A further sign of alliance building between artists and workers came in January 1996 when a group of Jakarta region poets and workers formed an artistic community called "Tangerang Workers' Culture" (Thamrin 1996, 26). As a loose network of workers' cultural groups under the acronym BUBUTAN (*Budaya Buruh Tangerang* or Tangerang Workers' Culture), its members' activity included theater, poetry, painting, and later, music. A key figure in this development was a worker poet, Wowok Hesti Prabowo, one of the community's early official leaders and its most consistent advocate and spokesperson. According to Prabowo, even prior to the founding of TBI there had been factory support in Tangerang for leisure activities, such as sports and theater. He added, however, that factory-sponsored theater activities were performed mainly for Independence Day celebrations and the sponsoring factories strictly limited their themes to lighter fare. BUBUTAN had formed only after Prabowo's dismissal from the post of Personnel Manager at PT Berlina Plastik, ostensibly for showing too much support for an employee strike action (Field Notes 16 August 1997). Wowok's response to his firing was to announce a fifty-day period in which he would refuse to speak, in protest for arbitrary treatment he felt he received as well as the generally poor living conditions for workers in Indonesia—low wages, laws against freely organizing unions, the threat of firing for strike actions, and the rising cost of living (*Media Indonesia* 13 July 1995; Amin, Sambodja, and Nurhanafiansyah 1995). BUBUTAN grew as a result of solidarity connected to Wowok's protest and included several worker theater groups, most prominently TABUR, Teater Detik, and ABU Tangerang. Given a high interest in writing and a large number of worker-poets within the network, BUBUTAN also set up the Institut Kesenian Tangerang (Tangerang Arts Institute) with well-known literary figures such as Ahmadun Y. Herfanda, Eka Budianta, and Diah Hadaning as instructors, thus creating further linkages between workers and established middle-class writers. Wowok proudly asserted that BUBUTAN had not been established under the aegis or initiative of any LSM, and therefore was neither manipulated nor told what to do (Field Notes 16 August 1997). Still, given the participation of several established, middle-class writers in the Institut Kesenian Tangerang, it is likely that some elements of middle-class arts aesthetics were presented to and influenced worker poets and theater workers.

Possibly the most active theater group in the BUBUTAN network was TABUR (Teater Buruh—Workers' Theater) which had performed as many as ten times by 1997, mostly for groups of workers. The group had performed in a former church building in Tangerang and had also received some support from the Jakarta Bishopric's office to publish, in modest pamphlet format, two of its play scripts, *Impian Diantara Cerobong Asap* (Dreams among the Smokestacks, 1995) and *Bag Big Bug* (1996), both of which were written by a worker-member of BUBUTAN named Igor. Yet despite its busy performance agenda, TABUR and other Tangerang groups had received little media attention compared to groups like TBI and ABU. Wowok felt this neglect allowed them to fly under the radar, avoiding conflicts with the government, even though there had been one incident during the staging of a BUBUTAN festival of workers' poetry to formally launch the network when security forces surrounded the area. The festival had been allowed to continue, however, after authorities were convinced that such an activity posed no danger to the state (Field Notes 16 August 1997).

In these two scripts, the style developed by Igor and TABUR is not only characterized by rather minimal story/plot, but it also has little to do with introducing specific government regulations to a worker audience. To be sure, a very abbreviated story is presented in scattered scenes, but these story fragments are interspersed with scenes of mimed symbolic action (a long journey at the beginning of *Bag Big Bug*), musical interludes with accompanying movement by the performers, and scenes in which characters make declamatory statements about such issues as worker indecision, the need to take a stand (*Impian*), why God has allowed such conditions to occur, the labeling of workers as troublemakers for anything they do other than following orders, and rhetorical questions about workers' identity and whether people are destined to become workers or a social process compels some to seek employment in the factories (a process that can be changed).

Thematically, *Impian Diantara Cerobong Asap* is focused on the desires of a key character, the son/worker (Anak/Buruh I), to serve the struggle of workers through art. His mother initially scoffs at her son's dream, but eventually comes to defend him in the face of his worker-father's scorn. The mother and father engage in a debate about whether life as an artist will allow him to earn a secure living and whether as parents they should lovingly support his aspirations. In the closing scene, the son/worker, angry at his father's uncertainty, attempts to prove himself by reading his poetry at a worker gathering. In the middle of his reading, he is arrested and taken away by security operatives. His sister ends the play by uttering the words "Dilemma, dilemma," leaving the play doubly open-ended. We are left to wonder what the son's fate will be as well as to ponder how workers might deal with the existential and strategic conflicts the play introduces.

The play's focus on the aspirations of the son/worker to become an artist-poet seems self-referentially to embody the aspirations of the BUBUTAN network itself. In early January 1997, a number of BUBUTAN writers, including Wowok Hesti Prabowo and Dingu Rilesta, took part in a *Sidang Puisi* (Poetry on Trial), in which they argued for the legitimate place of workers' poetry within the field of Indonesian literature (Komunitas Sastra Indonesia and Pusat Dokumentasi Sastra H. B. Jassin 1997). Several years later, Wowok confided that a number of workers' theater members in Tangerang hoped to parlay their theater training into modest television soap opera acting roles and thus, a possible avenue out of factory work (Field Notes 13 August 2001). Wowok stated that though he had always encouraged BUBUTAN members to develop their artistic potential and though their independence from LSMs allowed them to create art about whatever topics they deemed fitting, he also took pains to remind worker-artists that they had a responsibility to their fellow workers and the workers' struggle (Field Notes 16 August 1997). Igor's play appears to take up this problematic and to resolve it by showing how the son/worker dedicates his artistic efforts to improving the workers' lot:

> MOTHER: You're going to rebel! Who you going to rebel against, your mom?
> SON: Among others, but mainly against myself. Physically, my body may be a tiny worker's body but my soul and spirit shouldn't be stunted.
> MOTHER: So what will you do?
> SON: What's clear is I want change.

MOTHER: Are you up to it?
SON: Just wait till I've really become an artist.[20] (7–8)

In another scene the son is more specific about the meaning of his rebellion when he confronts his fellow factory workers:

SON: How long will you go on dreaming while the sun climbs higher in the sky. Where is your will to struggle? Are you going to let injustice and arbitrary power go on partying right in front of our very eyes?
THEY: Sure, you talk real smoothly about injustice . . . talk about arbitrary power . . . talk about the meaning of the struggle . . . but we're sure that it's nothing but slogans. Let it be, let it go . . . all of that has long been the tradition in our country anyway.
SON: You're all worthless! You surrender to your circumstances so easily, you lose heart so easily and so easily you forget the meaning of the struggle. Where, where is your solidarity as workers?[21] (9)

Yet the play remains on this generalized level, never presenting more than an image of the son/worker being arrested for reciting his poetry to workers. It never builds a plot around specific worker grievances or strategies for obtaining better working conditions. It does, however, offer scenes in which the characters are able to make jokes referring to contemporary political issues, such as corruption and the practice of bribing officials with an envelope full of money in exchange for required permits, tight government permit regulations for social activities, and the New Order government's assertions (at the time) that there were subversive "Formless Organizations" (*Organisasi Tanpa Bentuk* or OTB), an accusation that became the butt of much activist mockery.

Bag Big Bug continues this generalized style of approaching worker issues, but draws closer to a critique of state rhetoric and detention/interrogation practices, along with statements about workers' common humanity. In this play, workers mount a demonstration. As a result, several workers are detained and the last half of the play presents an interrogation/torture session as security operatives question and occasionally hit the detained workers. However, the interrogators' work is interrupted by the appearance of a group of workers who turn the tables on them, surrounding and cornering them. The play ends with one of the workers arguing that violence is not the solution. Instead, both workers and security forces must behave more humanely in order to struggle together for a better nation.

At one point, when rejecting the label of "subversive" for workers who want to improve their conditions, one of the workers states: "Hey... don't go along with those who say subversive. If you dare to speak up they call you subversive... if you all get together, subversive.... We only want to ask questions, and, anyway, as human beings we have the right to ask questions (7)."[22] Here, as in a number of other instances, the play foregrounds the notion that the workers share a common humanity with others. Furthermore, the final scene, in which a worker asks the security commander to make the journey together—to struggle together—hints at a utopian national unity of common interests that abolishes oppression.

All of this suggests that TABUR's plays are designed with both the government and its critics in mind. On the one hand, in order to appeal to a government concerned with any form of opposition, the play is crafted to stress a desire to avoid violence and to work together for a better national future. Nonetheless, it urges security officials to avoid violence and oppressive tactics and criticizes hegemonic public discourses that cast the workers in the role of a constant source of disturbance. On the other hand, the play appeals to the government's critics by underscoring the common humanity of workers and showing how the security apparatus abuses human rights. Thus, TABUR's plays of the mid-1990s can be seen as both attempting to avoid government suspicion and to enlist the support of middle-class intellectuals. As if to highlight the latter point, there are even a few similarities at the level of both theme and form between Igor's scripts and Ratna Sarumpaet's *Marsinah: Nyanyian Dari Bawah Tanah*. Both refrain from presenting the same kind of harsh details of workers' factory experiences, opting instead for more general appeals to common human values. Similarly, both intersperse episodes of declamation and general discussions of abuses of power with scenes representing some aspects of the reality of workers' lives. TABUR's plays ultimately contain more of a sense of folk humor and everyday working-class language than Ratna's work. It remains unclear as to whether there was any contact between Ratna and Wowok or members of Tabur, or if Tabur members had seen Ratna's *Marsinah* play. Yet the common elements shared by the two sets of works suggest that Igor's TABUR scripts were crafted with some sense of middle-class aesthetics in mind, possibly prompted in part by the association of middle-class poets with workers' arts groups within BUBUTAN. Such formal similarities and thematic strategies of alliance-building mark the plays of BUBUTAN's most active workers' theater group as representative—in their own, distinctive way—of the general, alliance-building dynamics of other workers' theater groups of the 1995–96 period.[23]

Continued Resistance

By mid-1995, the circumstances did not appear at all favorable to the continuation of workers' theater. Both TBI and Sanggar Pabrik had suffered government censorship and had become embroiled in protracted legal disputes challenging the censors (see chapter 7). Elsewhere, increasing repression of the Indonesian pro-democracy movement was seen in the government's manipulation of the Indonesian Democratic Party's (PDI) leadership election (Fennel and Leahy 1996; Robison 1996) and its crackdown on pro-democracy and labor groups following the 27 July 1996 riots (sparked by its own efforts to evict followers of deposed PDI leader Megawati Sukarnoputri from the PDI's Jakarta offices [Human Rights Watch/Asia 1996]). These repressions provided still more evidence of the government's desire to stifle all serious criticism and opposition. Nonetheless from 1995 to 1998 workers' theater and cultural groups bravely struggled to continue their activities.

Margesti's Teater ABU performed briefly for an Independence Day celebration in Kampung Melayu in mid-August (Fillion 1995), but in the autumn of 1995 YPM was dissolved due to internal conflicts, making the rival Tangerang ABU's continued existence extremely precarious (Andriyani 1996). In early 1996, in the politically progressive cultural magazine, *Media Kerja Budaya*, Margesti wrote an impassioned plea urging workers' theater groups not to emphasize their anger at unjust treatment, but to redirect their energies toward positive attitudes and strategies (M. Otong 1996).

The productions of the Margesti-led ABU following its Independence Day piece in August 1995 did indeed point to a new direction. As with their initial production of *Nyanyian Pabrik* (Factory Song), this ABU group's plays were performed chiefly at private theater venues, such as Ray Sahetapy's Studio Oncor and Rendra's Bengkel Teater stage, although one performance took place on the grounds of a factory. The main change was in the thematic material. As Margesti explained to a Jakarta *Post* reporter in 1996:

> "I don't want to get trapped in a cliché about workers' theater performances tending to exploit the bad treatment they suffer," said Margesti, the director. "It's too predictable: the classic conflict with the employer ends with the workers losing their jobs," added Margesti, who is an actress.
>
> "This time I asked them to share various aspects of their life which reflect being a worker with all the consequences. It still includes the typical topics, such as low wages, the empty promises of their employers for health allowance, and the long working hours. Yet it also opens up other facets of their life, such as how becoming a worker can affect their love lives." (Minarti 1996)

Starting with the workers' own experiences, as recorded in their personal letters, Margesti and script-writer Adinda Luthfianti created scripts for *Rembulan Terbakar* (The Burning Moon) and *Sesa'at Rasa* (A Fleeting Feeling) in 1996 and *Mesin Baru* (The New Machine) in 1997, with themes of personal human experiences taking a more prominent place. For example, and as hinted at by Margesti's statement cited above, the theme of workers' love lives was taken up centrally in both *Rembulan Terbakar* and *Sesa'at Rasa*. In the latter play, this theme is expressed most poignantly in a poem sung in the style of Javanese *macapat*:

> The sky always grows suddenly dark
> Amidst the roar of factory machines
> Seizing feelings in the name of Love
> And I'm in the midst of the roar

> A thousand steps away from home
> Hoping the world supplies color
> I get to know the color of industry
> I give myself over to human desire
> The pulsing of love always tempts
> I view myself in the mirror seeking meaning
>
> What does love mean, what do I mean, what does it mean to enjoy
> What ability do I have to find meaning
> What I understand is that life must know its proper place
>
> There are many walls that separate
> And people are busy creating social classes
> Till the right to love and be loved has perished
> We pull ourselves together again and give in
>
> The sky always grows suddenly dark
> Amidst the roar of factory machines
> There is no love without manipulation
> And we are inside it. (Luthfianti and Margesti 1996, 3)[24]

In this song the dreams and frustrations of the mostly female workers are vividly represented in particular relation to the rhythm of factory work, which makes time for love or for thinking about the meaning of one's life rare and elusive. This theme is linked to the various social barriers and divisions that force industrial workers into circumstances that cause love to perish, a loss workers must simply accept as unavoidable. The theme of social divisions is further elaborated in relation to family life and children in ABU's 1997 production of *Mesin Baru* (New Machine). In the midst of several song and movement pieces, two ABU actors also portray the wives of an industrial worker and a factory owner whose statements are juxtaposed to stress both human similarities and class differences:

> RIGHT: I'm an ordinary woman with an identity card as insurance wherever I go, in case something happens in the course of my life's journey.

LEFT: I'm an extraordinary woman with no identity card and my husband's position always functions as an I.D. card when something happens along the way.
RIGHT: I raise my child with nothing but prayers, without money so that she grows into a long list of I.O.U.s.
LEFT: I raise my child in line with the trendy purchases I make at the supermarket, so that she grows into a fashion leader.
RIGHT: My husband is only a factory worker who has never seen a year pass without participating in a demo for higher wages.
LEFT: My husband wears a jacket and tie and any minute he's prepared to fire anyone who demonstrates...
RIGHT: Nights in the rainy season are full of longing for my husband who always dreams of a nice house.
LEFT: Nights in the rainy season are for new loves who await me outside our home.[25] (Luthfianti and Margesti 1997)

Ironically, as can be seen from these passages, by exploring such facets of workers' experience as love and family circumstancies—rather than regulations and day-to-day oppression on the factory shop floor—ABU's work began to take on a much more pointed social analysis than the plays of TBI, Sanggar Pabrik, or TABUR. But clearly, the thrust of these comparisons from *Mesin Baru* is also intended to emphasize the workers' typically human aspirations for children, home, and a decent living and to suggest that the gap between the two women is somehow connected to, perhaps even a cause of, the fact that the factory worker's family cannot fulfill those typical desires. Yet there do not seem to have been significant problems with the censors, as if topics of love and family aspirations among workers, along with performing in smaller venues, caused ABU's productions to be of less concern for the security apparatus.

Curiously, though the thematic approach to workers' lives was new, the group's style returned to ABU's earliest production, *Nyanyian Pabrik*, in stressing song and movement over dialogue. *Rembulan Terbakar*, for example, featured dangdut, and rap songs, marches and ballads (Minarti 1996). *Mesin Baru* featured lively songs, with a number of women dressed in grey uniforms moving in unison and creating per-

Fig. 6.3. Teater ABU, *Mesin Baru* (1997). Photo courtesy of Titi Margesti.

cussive effects with kitchen implements. Short bits of dialogue in *Sesa'at Rasa* and *Mesin Baru* were interspersed with music, song, movement, and broadly sketched-demo-action scenes. These works have almost no narrative content, resembling instead cabarets with highly coherent themes.

BUBUTAN too was active during this period. As mentioned above, TABUR performed *Bag Big Bug* several times in 1996. Then, in January 1997, Wowok Hesti Prabowo, Dingu Rilesta, and other BUBUTAN poets helped organize the *Sidang Puisi* and, on 10 August 1997 at Studio Oncor, they put on a show of poetry and drama (featuring TABUR performing *Bag Big Bug*) in conjunction with an exhibition of workers' paintings (Field Notes 9 August and 16 August 1997). Again, like ABU's productions, which stressed the common human aspirations of workers, BUBUTAN's and TABUR's activities, as detailed above, continued to emphasize workers' general human aspirations and the desire for their art to be considered as a legitimate alternative to high art products in the construction of Indonesian national culture. During 1997 TBI also began to create and rehearse a new play, *Bila Saatnya Tiba* (When the Time Comes). It was scheduled for an audience of workers and activists at Oncor Studio in late 1997. However, local military authorities banned the

Fig. 6.4. Teater ABU, *Mesin Baru*. Photo courtesy of *Kompas*.

play, accusing it of disturbing national stability. As a result, the play was never allowed to be performed (Conroy 2006, 131–32).

Conclusion

Workers' theater and theater about workers in 1990s Indonesia provide clear examples of the complex manner in which an alliance of resistance to the New Order state's labor policies and its policing of cultural activity was being constructed through and around theater. They also demonstrate the ways in which cultural forms represent the articulation of diverse interests and discourses into specific material-social practices. These practices, simultaneously embracing the cultural and political realms, arose out of the desires of workers and LSM activists to engage in a pleasurable and effective form of education, one that could help raise workers' consciousness and advance their movement for greater rights and prosperity. Emerging in the late 1980s and early 1990s, at a time when both workers and broad segments of the middle-class were dissatisfied with the restrictions of New Order society, workers' theater became one arena for seeking common ground, building alliances, and attempting to give their concerns concrete representations that could capture the imagination of particular public constituencies.

The various actors engaged in the construction of workers' theater, workers, LSM activists, and performing artists were seldom on equal footing in such practices, however. LSM activists and artists, given their analytic and organizational abilities as well as their easier access to greater financial and logistical resources, were usually better able to provide leadership and continuity. Consequently, the forms these groups took were greatly dependent upon the visions and competencies of such figures as Margesti, Arist, or Wowok and the middle-class artists involved in the BUBUTAN network. The different visions of activists and artists with regard to the methods and goals of workers' theater, symbolized by these contrasts, caused internal group tensions in some cases. Yet, both LSM activists and artists saw the relations of production as necessarily democratic and collaborative and helped to inject tolerance and democracy into public evaluations of workers' theater.

Still, workers themselves were far from passive in shaping their own theater. They were the catalysts for the transfer of role-playing techniques into actual performances in 1989. They generated the themes for their plays. Furthermore, their desires for emotional release, association, and pleasure led to the specific styles of TBI's and ABU's performances—styles that allowed for audience participation and included ample humor, music, and dancing. An additional motivation for some workers, as Wowok suggested in 2001 in connection with TABUR, was that many had joined BUBUTAN's theater groups hoping to escape from factory work by launching a modest television acting career. This tendency may have inclined TABUR and other BUBUTAN groups to imitate middle-class high art theater more closely than ABU or TBI, and it may also account for the group's self-referential focus on workers' artistic aspirations in *Impian Diantara Cerobong Asap*.

Media reviews and commentaries and the dominant middle-class ideology of modern art thus also exercised a gravitational pull on the development of public discourses about workers' theater and its subsequent development. At the same time, middle-class artists were also powerfully attracted to workers' struggles, both in offering support to workers' theater and in Ratna Sarumpaet's play about Marsinah. Government pressure, particularly from mid-1994 on, also shaped the development of workers' theater. As bans became more frequent and the pressure on the workers' movement increased, TBI, ABU, and the newer Sanggar Pabrik and BUBUTAN/TABUR all sought to forge stronger links with the middle-class. The themes of workers' theater had already begun moving in this direction in TBI's and ABU's productions of late 1993 and early 1994, incorporating ideas of democracy and justice important not only to workers' struggles, but also pointing toward possible common ground with a larger segment of the middle-class. In several ways, TABUR's plays even resembled Ratna Sarumpaet's framing of worker issues. Margesti's ABU, after 1995, also changed its themes to incorporate more universal human concerns, such as love and family relations, though ironically sharpening its critique of unequal class relations in the process.

Forged in this intersection of interests, events, and pressures, both workers' theater and Ratna Sarumpaet's *Nyanyian Marsinah* illustrate the complex processes by which social relations work themselves out in particular cultural practices and products. These practices and products in turn generated responses and linked themselves to practices in other spheres: for example, middle-class journalists' attempts to use the courts to further notions of the rule of law and the broad movement for democracy (as will be seen in chapter 7). Yet given these linkages between workers and sections of the middle-class in developing a wider democratic space in Indonesia, perhaps the most troublesome aspect of workers' theater during this period was the relative subordination of the worker-performers to their LSM and arts community facilitators. This subordination is paralleled by the failure to generate an aesthetics of workers' theater that situated the form as a viable alternative to middle-class theater with its dominant aesthetic ideology, but instead left it outside aesthetics, thus rendering it a cultural charity case or mere sociological artifact. These problems of workers' theater highlighted structural inequalities that were in turn embedded in the Indonesian democracy movement as a whole. Overcoming these problems seems a prerequisite to building a truly democratic culture and ultimately a democratic society.

Despite these problems, however, the democracy movement and the social alliances constituting it gained political momentum in the last few years of Suharto's New Order regime. Theater played a modest yet significant role in building and sustaining that movement. In addition to the ways in which theater contributed to building new social alliances, created new paradigms for understanding life and challenging the New Order and its social and aesthetic ideologies, the censorship battles between 1990 and 1997 offer compelling evidence of theater's contribution to the pro-democracy opposition within Indonesia, an opposition prepared by groups and practices such as those described in previous chapters. The final chapter details the processes through which theater struggled against censorship on the national stage.

Chapter 7

STAGED OPENNESS

Theater and Censorship in Indonesia's 1990s Era of Keterbukaan

On August 16, 1990, Indonesia's President Suharto suggested in an official speech that the nation was ready for increased political openness (*keterbukaan*). Less than two months later, however, the Jakarta police abruptly closed down Teater Koma's political satire, *Suksesi*. The ensuing years witnessed a series of performances by Emha Ainun Nadjib and Komunitas Pak Kanjeng, the Indonesian Workers' Theater (Teater Buruh Indonesia), the SBSI labor union-sponsored Sanggar Pabrik (Factory Workshop) group, and Ratna Sarumpaet's Satu Merah Panggung (One Red Stage) all suffering bans. Still, as the decade wore on, the New Order government became less able to defend its censorial actions in the face of increasingly confident and aggressive critics from the arts community and other sectors of the middle and working classes. The intimidating, silencing authority of the New Order government was visibly eroding.

Aside from its concerted efforts to control, remodel, adapt, and appropriate traditional genres of performance for purposes of social control, tourism, and economic development (Hatley 1990, 333–35; Hough 1992, 1–19; Hatley 1994b, 229–38, 254–57; Widodo 1995; Sears 1996, 233–65; Yampolsky 1995), Suharto's Indonesia had a long record of banning modern, Western-derived theatrical performances stretching back to at least the early 1970s. Those plays whose banning was reported widely in the national and local media were almost certainly not the only works proscribed. Many more were quietly being ordered or negotiated off the stage, or failing even to get off the censor's desk.¹ Yet suddenly in the 1990s, after twenty-five years of New Order rule and censorship, the banning of theatrical performances and poetry readings began to be subject to sustained public criticism and even spirited resistance.

Seen in this light, the debates and struggles surrounding state censorship of contemporary, Western-derived Indonesian theater permit us another angle from which to observe clearly the decline of the New Order regime and the rise of the pro-democracy movement. Beginning in the late 1980s, the New Order regime began to flirt with the idea of "openness" (*keterbukaan*) in public political discourse in order to neutralize both widespread social criticism and the restiveness of powerful sections of the military. In order to chart the way in which the government attempted (and ultimately failed) to control the meaning of keterbukaan with respect to modern, Western-derived theater, I will look in detail at the five cases of banning mentioned above since they span the 1990–98 period when the concept of openness was put forward in public discussion. An investigation of this sort will afford us insights into why the New Order eventually lost its grip on power.

What was immediately at stake in each of these instances of banning was the free, direct expression of specific issues (and in one case, the parody of the highest government figures) that the government deemed too sensitive (or insulting). In comparison to earlier modern national theater, the style of these plays was much more aggressive: variously mocking or angrily accusing the government and society of an array of wrongs. One element of my argument, therefore, is that the New Order objected both to the specific topics and the more direct style of the performances in question, preferring instead that any criticisms be as veiled and in as suppliant a mode as possible. That the plays were also linked to audiences representing newly emerging, threatening constituencies within society, or in one case to a particularly charismatic, highly visible public critic of the government, provided further reason for the government to have acted as it did.

Another important strand of my argument will show how critics of the Suharto government, both from outside and within, used the debates as one discursive site to pry open the doors to a wider democratic space within

Indonesian society or as a way to gain an advantage over rival factions within the government. What emerges from an examination of the New Order's bans and attempts to control and shape this form of theater during the 1990s is the fact that such public clashes introduced another opportunity for an array of middle-class and activist critics to reiterate wide-ranging ideas on a number of issues—from freedom of expression to good governance, transparent legal codes and the rule of law, economics, and democracy. Similarly, dissatisfied factions within the government attempted to ride the appeal of such issues to advance their own agendas. The social struggle over banning momentarily made theater one important arena for shaping the trajectory of a growing pro-democracy discourse within Indonesia, and at the same time, provided early signs of the increasing fragility of the Suharto regime. After all, the struggles against and debates about banning were at root struggles over the power to delineate both the limits and the style of public discourse in New Order Indonesia. And such power flows from, as well as facilitates the maintenance of, social and political legitimacy.

In this respect, one important theme embodied both in the texts and performances of the plays, as well as in the public debates and actions which followed the bannings, is the idea that the New Order regime was outside the bounds of community values and national law. I will demonstrate the way in which this discourse sharpens and changes over the course of the five most publicized banning incidents of the 1990s. The New Order's inability to follow its own laws perhaps became the most prominent theme of the campaigns against government banning of theater (and by extension, discussions, and other mass activities), providing a connecting issue between struggles for freedom of expression on the stage and the broader pro-democracy movement within late New Order Indonesian society.

Elite Conflict and Middle-class Dissent: Indonesia enters the 1990s

As described in chapter 1, beginning in the late 1980s, as Suharto dealt with a restive military and a growing industrial sector that called forth a increasingly militant industrial workers' movement, sections of the middle-class, for a variety of reasons, were also gradually becoming more assertive. For example, in 1989 middle-class intellectuals mounted successful opposition to the military-backed notion of the integralist state and argued for political liberalization (Bourchier 1997). As a result, by 1990, the need to open the Indonesian economy to more foreign investment was complemented by insistent calls among small and medium-sized entrepreneurs for regularization of business practices (Robison 1992, 82) and, in the civil sphere, for broader freedom of expression and association and the "rule of law" (Lev 1990, 35–37; Chua 1993, 148–56).[2] This incipient pro-democracy movement was expanding to encompass other groups as well. NGOs staffed by mainly middle-class activists and intellectuals were forging new links with peasants and workers; and a new breed of student activists, mainly from lower middle-class and rural backgrounds, was reaching out to similar groups as well as radicalizing the student movement (Aspinall 2005).

At roughly the same time, speculation about how much longer President Suharto could maintain his grip on power and about the possible scenarios for presidential "succession" emerged ubiquitously in public discussion. Parts of this discussion were likely fuelled by a serious rift developing between Suharto, his family, and his closest associates on the one hand, and large sections of the military officer corps (whose political power the president had been steadily curtailing for almost a decade) on the other. Led by former long-time Suharto ally, Benny Moerdani, the military "dissidents" covertly encouraged some student protests (Aspinall 1995, 34–36) and supported demands for more political openness and equitable economic growth (Vatikiotis 1993, 142–43). The military fraction in parliament was especially prominent in helping to air these issues, supplying additional pressure for Suharto to react with his own statements about the need for openness in 1988 and 1989 (Aspinall 1999, 214). In order to outflank the military, Suharto sought to claim the moral high ground by lecturing prominent Chinese businessmen about the need to promote social equality (Vatikiotis 1993, 157). His call for more open discussion in August 1990 can be seen as a related maneuver—playing to the disaffected intellectuals and members of the middle-class, which, due to Indonesia's generally high rate of economic growth, had been expanding steadily during the late 1980s.

1990s Theater, Democratization, and Censorship Patterns

Seen in the context of these social trends and tensions, modern national theater and attempts to control it in the 1990s underwent a number of crucial changes. First, there was a tendency for a number of groups to attempt to confront particularly sensitive issues (Teater Koma's *Suksesi* [succession politics]; Komunitas Pak Kanjeng's *Pak Kanjeng* [peasant land evictions]; TBI and Sanggar Pabrik [industrial workers' problems]; Satu Merah Panggung's *Marsinah Menggugat* [workers' issues, social justice]). In most cases, these themes were also inscribed in forms, which broke with the New Order's dominant notions of aesthetics and social behavior. Form and content were interlocked in aggressively critical expressions difficult for the New Order government to digest. Secondly, middle-class commentators and arts critics became more critical and assertive as the decade wore on, often challenging the statements and explanations of government bans. Third, the arts community itself, often divided by personal and group rivalries as well as genuine disagreements about the fit between art, aesthetics, and political commentary, closed ranks during the decade and found a new solidarity. This united front provided less room for the government to obtain partial validation from cultural workers themselves. Fourth, in the face of more aggressive criticism, and in an attempt to appear more sympathetic to middle-class concerns, while simultaneously endeavoring to maintain control of the situation, the Suharto group within the government and security apparatus officials on the frontline of banning conflicts seemed to grope about for acceptable ways of justifying the bans. With each succeeding incident, government officials appeared to become less confident and more shamefaced. Attempts to generate a kind of official *Pancasila* aesthetics were scattered and seemed unconvincing, alternating as they did with retreats to a rather different position—that of the security approach to managing society. Fifth, this situation was certainly intensified by frictions within the regime, resulting in perceptions of incoherence, if not incompetence. After virtually every publicized case of banning in the 1990s, pronouncements by government officials that such incidents would not occur again were followed embarrassingly by another ban. Both Suharto group spokespeople, trying to convince the middle-class of the sincerity of the government's proclaimed openness, and rival faction military figures, championing openness in order to curb the Suharto group's power, frequently made statements or even promulgated rules with which in the end the regime found it could not comply.

A sixth change was in the nature of the media's engagement with the incidents. Staffed in part by former student activists, the press was often sympathetic to pro-democracy issues, even more so after the 1994 revocation of the press licenses of the prominent newsweeklies *Tempo*, *Editor*, and *DëTik* (Heryanto 1996, 250). Increased journalistic attention to and support for pro-democracy issues manifested themselves in changes in the way banning was covered, substantially contributing to shaping the public debate. If the 1978 arrest of Rendra had been covered chiefly as a matter for discussion by members of the arts community, reporting of the bannings in the 1990s distinguished itself by the frequency with which reporters sought commentary from an expanding cast of characters, including representatives of legal aid associations, journalists, ex-generals, parliamentarians, and members of the National Human Rights Commission.

This dramatic expansion of "expert" commentators served to magnify the problem of theatrical bans, enlarging the scope of the incidents by linking them most specifically to questions of the rule of law and using them to illustrate the ways in which the government seemed a regime unable to conform to its own regulations. The combative legal challenges, that workers' theater groups mounted in opposition to the banning of their work added significant momentum to this turn in public discourse. These legal cases, brought by workers in concert with middle-class NGO activists, served to connect working-class issues to those of the middle-class as well as cementing the links between theatrical struggles and those of other middle-class constituencies, such as journalists, who similarly had been bridled and taken the government to court. The momentary formation of a tentative inter-class alliance, in part through resistance to theater bannings, constituted a seventh change in the landscape within which new tradition theater operated. In such ways, the struggle for freedom of creative expression in modern national theater became an important piece of the overall pro-democracy struggle.

I will now proceed to the details of five celebrated cases of banning in the 1990s in Indonesia. By dividing my discussion into four main areas, I will be able to bring the points just raised into clearer focus. The four areas to be covered are (1) an examination of the themes and plots of the plays as well as the circumstances in which they were performed and banned; (2) the changes in the attitudes, actions, and criticism of the arts community towards the banning; (3) the role of the press and the joining of banning to other issues, as well as the impact of the workers' theater lawsuits; and (4) the disarray and growing defensiveness of the government.

More Direct Themes, Aggressive Styles, and Banning Contexts

Teater Koma, headed by N. Riantiarno, had gained a large and loyal following among the middle-class during the 1980s with its lively modern theater that combined slangy Jakartan jargon, transvestite actors and roles, earthy humor, social criticism, and Broadway style songs. In 1990, in the midst of the context of growing middle-class assertiveness, intra-regime friction, and the resulting proclamations of keterbukaan, outlined above, Koma decided to stage Riantiarno's latest play, *Suksesi* (an Indonesianization of the word "succession" as well as the name of one of the play's central characters). In this play an aging ruler, King Bukbangkalan, spreads rumors that he is dying in order to see how those around him will plot to succeed him and to learn who is in fact most fit to become the next king. Much attention is given to the king's children, three of whom control huge, diversified conglomerates and are awash in excess capital. Two of these children also harbor ambitions to succeed their father. As the play unfolds, together with several other parties (including a group of generals), they jockey to gain the best position to succeed the aging monarch. But in the end, it is the king's ruthless elder daughter, Suksesi, who outwits her father and captures the throne, as a confined and chastened Bukbangkalan broods helplessly in a cell.

On the thematic level, *Suksesi* attempted to engage with the notion of keterbukaan by proposing a more open and democratic public discourse. But the play also contained other themes that clearly made the

Suharto regime nervous, if not angry. The wealth and corruption of several of the king's children, whose attributes evoke immediate association with Suharto's sons and daughters, are painted with broadly caricatured strokes and stand in sharp contrast to the poverty of the ordinary people, who are described as worrying primarily about basic necessities. The problem of dynastic succession is equated with a "law of the jungle" situation in which only the strongest and wiliest survive—hardly the New Order's preferred self-depiction as protector of order and stability. This theme carries over into the play's conservative critique of the first family. The king realizes his inability to be a good father has led to his children's lack of familial solidarity. On his children's part this has evolved into ruthless deviation from socially expected gender roles within their own families. Here the play also suggests that the Suharto family itself and, by implication, New Order society are unable to conform to the regime's ideology of *kekeluargaan* (familiality) and the idea of harmony attached to it.

Yet it was not simply these themes that led to the banning of the play. The themes were intertwined with a particular style whose features were even more important in contravening the norms of taste and content the New Order had been endeavoring to impose on public discourse since the mid-1970s. In the years just prior to 1990, Suharto and other top officials had warned that openness must not violate Pancasila. Public discourse (including theater), they maintained, should not create tensions among ethnic groups, races, religions, or classes (suku bangsa, agama, ras, antar-golongan or "SARA"). In one formulation, Suharto even added that it should not harm the interests of the government or other families. These qualifications of openness were combined with a general concept of the necessity of deference to authority and extreme politeness and sensitivity in launching criticism. Derived from ideas of Javanese culture reconstructed during the New Order, this concept was supported legally by colonial-era style statutes that punish anyone "for publicly expressing what the regime arbitrarily defines as hatred, insult, or hostility towards the incumbent authorities" (Heryanto 1996, 260–61).

Koma challenged many of these notions. First of all, the play parodies the first family in a shockingly obvious manner, presenting it as a site of

Fig. 7.1. The cast of Teater Koma's *Suksesi* (1990). Photo by Desmaizal Zainal, courtesy of N. Riantiarno and Ratna Riantiarno/Teater Koma Documentation.

familial chaos rather than harmony and stability. Further, the king is seen as a bad father, who carelessly engages in power contests over the possibility of succession merely to test his own cunning and power, while his children are venal, unscrupulous, and obscenely wealthy. Its language, in a similarly direct fashion, burlesqued the public-speaking style of the president and his close associates in one scene by peppering the speech of the king's eldest daughter with characteristically inappropriate or excessive use of words like *daripada* (rather than) and *maka* (therefore). The play also deals irreverently with the shadow theater tradition, mixing it with elements of more vulgar theater forms as well as anachronistically combining *wayang*-esque kings and princesses with business conglomerates, oil tankers, and characters named after Hollywood films. *Suksesi* clearly violated the unwritten code of New Order theater by presenting its political criticism in a direct, aggressive, caricatured, and emotive style that had more to do with Broadway and traditional Indonesian folk theater than it did with the *halus wayang* world that figured so prominently in New Order imaginations.

The play began its scheduled two-week run on September 28, but was closed down by police order prior to the October 9 performance. The banning of *Suksesi* was echoed one month later by further banning of the first of a poetry reading by Rendra and a subsequent Teater Koma restaging of its 1985 classic hit, *Opera Kecoa* (Cockroach Opera). Since these bans followed so closely on the heels of Suharto's major statement calling for openness, they elicited growing distress and anger, if not exactly surprise, from the Indonesian cultural community and its supporters. These bans became landmark examples of New Order censorship, cases which both showed the emerging cracks in the foundation of New Order authority and set the general pattern and direction for future clashes as the decade wore on.

Following the 1992 elections, Secretary of State Moerdiono again tried to cultivate better relations between the arts community and the government. At a seminar organized by Teguh Karya's Teater Populer in Jakarta in October 1993, he guaranteed that there would be no more banning of artistic performances (*Kompas* 2 February 1994). However, less than four months later (February 1994), censorship struck once again. Police and military authorities in Surabaya refused permission for a new play, *Pak Kanjeng* (the main character's name), by charismatic Muslim poet and outspoken social critic, Emha Ainun Nadjib. This denial occurred even though the play had previously been performed in Yogyakarta and Solo in November 1993. The permit for the Surabaya staging was refused at virtually the last minute after the play's local promoters had endured more than a month of permit application procedures, applying to at least five government offices. Police told organizers that the play's performance should be postponed indefinitely given recent social conditions in East Java (*Surya* 1 February 1994).

Briefly, *Pak Kanjeng* involves three actors all playing the same peasant character who is about to be evicted from his land so that developers may build a factory and a golf course. As the play progresses, the three Pak Kanjengs, as though symbolizing different sides of a single person struggling to resolve his own doubts, commiserate and argue with one another. While the work offers sharp censures of the New Order, to a certain extent the nature of this divided character diffuses the criticism of the government as well as prevents Kanjeng himself from appearing to be simply a suffering saint of the ordinary people (*rakyat kecil*).

At key points, however, the play touches forthrightly on well-known instances of official greed and abuse of power. For instance, though then Minister of Information and Chairman of Golkar (the regime's electoral vehicle) Harmoko was not named, references to reporters who can get rich and hold stock in many publications (if only they become minister in charge of the mass media) make clear who is being criticized.[3] Suharto himself is also targeted for criticism rather explicitly. While describing the traitorous, independence-era history of "Den Beine,"[4] the official who has worked to evict him and his neighbors, Kanjeng One complains: "This is the kind of human being who's risen to become a leader! He acts as though he's the one who's done the most, presenting his face as though he's the grandfather of development, clutching thousands of the people's skulls in his hand, he sews, he strings them together into a historical accessory!"[5] (Nadjib 1993, 30). The nod to Suharto's oft-repeated epithet as Father of Development (*Bapak Pembangunan*), here given a gruesome twist, would have been difficult for any Indonesian to miss. This image is tied to the play's presentation of development (*pembangunan*), claimed by the regime as the centerpiece of its legitimacy, as primarily a process whereby the little people and the poor are divested of their rights through deception, intimidation, and brutal coercion (5, 17, 30–32, 38). One of the Pak Kanjengs comments that the powerful seem to plan to impoverish the people while greedily lining their pockets with profits (3, 30–32, 38). The play contrasts this sorry state of affairs with an image of the ordinary people who have faithfully served the nation and who are the true owners of the country and its wealth (2–3). Kanjeng becomes a symbol of the *rakyat kecil*, stating that he was once loved during the independence struggle, but has not been valued during the New Order and is ignored by the media (18).

Pak Kanjeng, like *Suksesi*, presents duplicity as the very prerequisite of getting ahead and holding power in New Order society. Those who want to survive and rise to the top, according to the Kanjengs, must bend with the wind and master the art of becoming yes-men to the leaders (25). Again, as in *Suksesi*, Nadjib's play shows a penchant for mocking official rhetoric, sarcastically situating several of the government's clichés of censorship and development within a discussion of duplicity:

KANJENG ONE:
I certainly wouldn't be so bold as to conclude that all leaders are duplicitous. But it would also be hard for me to deny that duplicity is one of the absolutely primary requirements for the principle of leadership. But assuming that's so, couldn't we at least find a kind of duplicity that's a little bit good, that's not so obvious. That's it, a duplicity *with educational value*....

KANJENG TWO:
A duplicity that's *free and responsible*, the duplicity of the *well rounded, complete Indonesian human being* ...[6]

Duplicity is connected with being a *priyayi* (aristocrat, civil servant). The Kanjengs ascribe negative characteristics to priyayi: they are cast as bootlickers, cowards, and oppressors (21, 30, 32), members of a group that seeks to stigmatize any opposition by branding them as disruptors and rebels (17). Further, Pak Kanjengs Two and Three suggest that the New Order government is like an internal colonizer, duplicating the methods of Dutch rule (35, 36). If Riantiarno's *Suksesi* undermined New Order pretensions to an aristocratic ideology and a set of tastes by comically mixing the wayang world with competing and disparate cultural forms and discourses, *Pak Kanjeng* opts to denigrate the same ideology frontally through its dialogue. As a partial prescription for positive change, the play proposes democratization—here seen as the public's right to speak out and to disagree with what the government proposes (34).

Yet, there is still another difference between *Suksesi* and *Pak Kanjeng*. *Pak Kanjeng* offers an image of the New Order regime, with its reconstructed version of priyayi ideology, as a violator of an assumed norm of community solidarity and egalitarianism. Such an image echoes discourses of radical populism tied to various forms of Islamic and left-nationalist political currents prevalent in Indonesia from 1910 to 1950 (Shiraishi 1990;

Williams 1990). It also suggests many Indonesian regime critics' and some NGOs' insistence on the importance of reducing socio-economic disparities in the name of Pancasila ideology's principles of social justice (Morfit 1986, 49; Chua 1993, 152; Eldridge 1995, 21, 218). In so doing, the piece points an enraged, accusing finger at the New Order regime as betraying one element of its own self-proclaimed ideology.

As mentioned above, the authorities maintained that they were not banning, merely postponing the performance because of concern the play might inflame volatile social conditions in East Java. The sources and proofs of volatility were identified as the recent burning of a place of worship in Pasuruan, the shootings of several villagers in a land dispute near Nipah in Madura, and the 1993 murder of labor activist Marsinah (*Kompas* 2 February 1994). However, the play may also have been targeted for banning as part of a government drive begun in early 1994 to roll back "openness" and silence opposition, thereby assuring that Suharto's power would remain unchallenged prior to the 1997 DPR elections.[7]

The next episode in the 1990s struggle over censorship of theater took place on rather different terrain, that of workers' theater. Here again, context was of vital importance, since the banning of pieces by two workers' theater groups, TBI (Teater Buruh Indonesia/Indonesian Workers Theater) and Sanggar Pabrik (Factory Workshop) occurred at an historical juncture in which the New Order government was concerned to control labor in order to ensure a competitive edge for foreign investment. Yet it was also a moment when middle-class artists and cultural workers were becoming ever more frustrated with New Order censorship and control of culture, resulting in their May Declaration of 1995 denouncing the nation's conditions for artistic production (detailed in the next section).

To reiterate some of the key points about the social significance of the first of these productions, as related in the previous chapter, at almost precisely the same time as the May Declaration of leading arts figures was being announced, the oldest of Indonesia's workers' theaters, the Teater Buruh Indonesia, attempted to create a dialogue with potential sympathizers from the arts and NGO communities by scheduling its latest production, *Senandung Terpuruk Dari Balik Tembok Pabrik* (Song Buried behind the Factory Wall) to be performed on the stage of the Taman Ismail

Marzuki in downtown Jakarta on May 13 and 14, 1995. Given middle-class journalists and theater critics' sympathetic but paternalistic reaction to previous workers' theater productions, TBI's leader, Arist Merdeka Sirait, clearly intended to use the event to raise the issue of workers' theater as a legitimate alternative cultural form designed for education and consciousness-raising among workers. The program for the production stated his hope that everyone working together could solve workers problems. The prospect of a growing alliance between workers and elements of the middle-class likely gave the regime cause for concern.

Senandung Terpuruk differed from TBI's previous less plot-oriented production, *Bercanda Dalam Duka* in that it was longer (1.5 hours) and was built around a more typical narrative. The play offers a straightforward story about the travails that female workers face in daily factory work and life. The play opened by representing the cramped living conditions of a group of female workers, then followed them to their work in a garment factory, showing how they are interrogated and examined when requesting menstrual leave or asked to resign if they are found to be pregnant. In seeking to defend three pregnant friends who are fired, the major character, Marsih (whose name resembles Marsinah), also loses her job and is forced to complain to the Department of Labor. But the department's decision goes against her, suggesting that there is no justice for workers in the current system. The play ends by concluding that the workers must continue their struggle.

The moment of dialogue Arist had hoped for in writing his introduction to the performance program was, however, not to occur in the form Sirait and members of TBI had imagined. Indonesian government officials once again intervened to stop a theatrical performance by denying TBI the necessary permit. Among a number of other reasons which I will outline below, government officials and documents denied the permit on the grounds that the actors, all workers, had to be replaced. That this requirement was included in the banning rationale suggests that the government had begun to see workers' theater itself as a threat, one crossing the boundaries of what it considered acceptable art. The idea of workers performing their own stories was cast as a potential source of instability and, therefore, was simply not allowed (*Kompas* 26 May 1995; *Pos Kota* 10

Sept. 1995). The New Order's security approach and its aesthetics, which strove to separate politics from art, here found a common nexus.

Just a few months later (August 22), Sanggar Pabrik, a theater group sponsored by the officially unrecognized workers' union SBSI (Serikat Buruh Sejahtera Indonesia—Indonesian Prosperous Workers' Union), had obtained a permit from the South Jakarta police to perform their play, *Surat Cinta Bagi Marsinah Di Sorga* (Love Letter to Marsinah in Heaven), on September 16 at a South Jakarta Youth Arena. Suddenly, only one day before the scheduled performance, representatives of the police informed the group that the play could not be performed. The reason given was that since the group's headquarters were in Utan Kayu, East Jakarta, it should have gotten the permit from the Greater Jakarta police rather than from South Jakarta, where the performance was to take place (*Kompas* 18 Sept. 1995; *Republika* 19 Sept. 1995).

In addition to the government's general fear of workers' theater, Sanggar Pabrik's play certainly presented controversial material. It bore a title which included the name of the murdered worker/activist from East Java and through a collage of brief scenes suggested a possible narrative of and motives for Marsinah's murder. The piece portrays workers as constantly in fear, dehumanized and controlled like robots by owners sporting handphones, ties, and suits. Building upon widespread public suspicions, the play shows a group of sturdy men (often a euphemism for soldiers) who set out to silence worker protests in Porong Sidoarjo (the location of the actual factory involved in the Marsinah incident) and who end by dragging the lifeless form of a woman worker across the stage. Since operatives of the security apparatus were widely suspected to have carried out the actual murder, this production was bound to irritate.

Unlike Ratna Sarumpaet's landmark 1994 play that, in taking Marsinah's death as its thematic point of departure, nonetheless tended to elevate Marsinah into a symbol of universal suffering and oppression in New Order Indonesia, Sanggar Pabrik's play about this working class martyr kept close to the concrete specifics of the lives of industrial workers. However, like Ratna's earlier play, *Surat Cinta Untuk Marsinah Di Sorga* tapped into broader pro-democracy sentiments within Indonesian society. Sanggar Pabrik's worker characters, by asking to be valued as humans (and not mere means of production) and to be given a living wage, were crying out for what are often argued to be universal rights—justice, economic security, and a better life.

The final highly publicized banning case occurred two years later in the course of Ratna Sarumpaet and Satu Merah Panggung's performance tour of *Marsinah Menggugat* (Marsinah Accuses) in late 1997. Once again, Ratna had taken up the figure of Marsinah, this time for a one-hour monologue in which the circumstances of Marsinah's death are narrated much more forthrightly than in her previous Marsinah work. Offering as its central device the figure of Marsinah as a spirit looking back on her death, the play links her tragedy to a number of current social and political topics. Indicative of the growing boldness of modern theater workers and surpassing Sanggar Pabrik's presentation of the same incident, a speculative version of Marsinah's torture and rape is narrated in harrowing detail.[8] Men wearing heavy boots, possibly soldiers, are intimated to have been responsible. Further, the New Order is directly characterized as a sick society in which capitalists rake in profits with bloodstained hands. Aside from the theme, surely a source of concern for the security apparatus, Ratna's *Marsinah Menggugat*, like her earlier piece, is emotionally charged with a visceral, fiery anger that is stylistically embodied in a frequently accusatory delivery. Again, a modern theater work was violating both the thematic and formal norms of New Order aesthetics.

Successfully performed in the Javanese cities of Jakarta, Tegal, Tasikmalaya, Solo, Yogyakarta, Jember, Malang, and Semarang, the tour was nonetheless plagued in several locales by the presence of security apparatus contingents or mysterious obstructions. Finally, in late November and early December, performances of the play were prevented in Surabaya, Bandung, and Bandarlampung in Sumatra. The resulting debate in the media, which coincided with an additional banning of a Sanggar Pabrik play, revealed a deepening erosion of public trust in the authorities as well as the inability of the government any longer to direct the debate.

Thus, a review of these five cases suggests that the banned works all raised politically sensitive issues not only by violating norms of taste and style by presenting these themes quite directly, but also by their angry, sarcastic, or painfully realistic modes of presentation. Further, given the juncture of public dissatisfaction with the government and the tentative alliance between middle-class intellectuals, workers, and others, the New Order was now trying to paint the very idea of workers' theater as an affront to its desire to keep art and politics safely distant from one another.

Unification of the Arts Community and Sharper Criticism

In October 1990, the arts community unanimously expressed its regret at the banning of Riantiarno's and Koma's *Suksesi*. However, indications of *Suksesi*'s transgression of New Order theatrical taste can be found in the reactions of a number of arts world figures who dismissed the play as "too obvious," vulgar, even pornographic. These statements, based upon modern ideas of serious art and aesthetic values, fit well with the unwritten tastes and values of the New Order for public discourse. Yet some members of the arts community were highly critical of the government, insisting that if authorities felt that theater violated any law, a response should be rendered through the judicial process and not by police fiat (Bodden 1997a).

Given this kind of division within the arts community, Riantiarno's own response to his play's fate seemed cautious. He insisted that he had only tried to produce a work consistent with the new atmosphere of openness in which people were encouraged to be creative and not to fear differences of opinion. While Riantiarno stressed above all that he only portrayed the existing reality, he also showed signs of the combativeness to come from the arts community by disputing dominant aesthetic norms, maintaining that *halus* (refined) and *kasar* (crude) were relative categories. Furthermore, he hinted that these categories might be irrelevant in judging what was good art, citing Aristophanes and *Petruk Dadi Ratu* (Petruk Becomes King) of the wayang tradition as prime examples of crude masterpieces (*Tempo* 20 Oct. 1990).

The succeeding bans on Rendra's poems and Koma's next production quickly caused the arts community to drop the issue of aesthetic quality and close ranks. Their new focus became simply the arbitrary nature of government banning. As had cinema producers fifteen years earlier, some called for clear guidelines. Others, such as Goenawan Mohamad, sharply attacked the power of the police to ban as ridiculous. Neither was the arts community cowed by the interventions of powerful ministerial-level Suharto allies such as Minister of Information Harmoko and Coordinating Minister for Security Sudomo. Instead, a large contingent of cultural workers took their case to the legislature and eventually met with Sudomo, who seemed to grant permission, however grudgingly, for the banned works to be performed (Bodden 1997a).

In 1994, *Pak Kanjeng* playwright Emha Ainun Nadjib angrily contested his play's Surabaya banning. Having gotten wind of the impending ban, on January 31 Nadjib and several of his collaborators[9] issued a press release bluntly insisting that the play was a realization of the pure values of Pancasila, not those of a reduced or manipulated version. The release further alleged that refusal to permit performance of *Pak Kanjeng* meant the Indonesian people's human rights, the nation's freedom of expression, and promises of democracy and political fairness couldn't be guaranteed by those obligated to uphold them—i.e., those in power (Rahardjo et al. 1994). In this early statement, as in its play, the *Komunitas Kecil Pak Kanjeng* (Pak Kanjeng's Little Community) had painted the government as duplicitous and manipulative. By doing so, and by citing censorship as one more proof that the government did not protect its citizens' rights, it had struck at the government's vulnerable spot, namely, its desire to win the hearts and minds of the middle-class by portraying itself as a liberalizing force that upheld the rule of law. With such a discursive move, the banning debate began more clearly to shift the focus of blame away from considerations of a work's propriety and the individual creator's "mistakes" or motives and point instead towards the behavior of the government.

Following the official announcements of the postponement, Nadjib's own response was equally combative. He ridiculed the authorities' attempted distinction between "postponement" and banning and decried the bureaucracy as irrational. He refused to revise the script and denied that his play would ignite social flare-ups, commenting instead that it would help calm things down by inviting critical reflection on the problems it raised (*Jawa Pos* 1 February 1994; *Republika* 1 February 1994; *Surya* 1 February 1994).[10]

Nadjib and his colleagues received strong support from both the Surabaya and Jakarta Arts Councils, who demanded that the authorities provide clearer explanations for the banning and the government's general policy in the arts (*Republika* 3 Feb. 1994; *Surabaya Post* 4 Feb. 1994). But as a key sign of the shifting discursive terrain, more members of the arts community began voicing increasingly critical comments about the government. Cultural commentator and academic Ariel Heryanto felt the security apparatus was out of touch with social change and that the ban would only result in a loss of credibility for the government (*Republika* 2 February 1994). Salim Said of the Jakarta Arts Council was one of many commentators who foregrounded the fact that the ban seemed to contradict Moerdiono's statement[11] of October 1993 that such bans would not occur again. Said bluntly declared that this incident demonstrated the government's incoherent handling of the permit process (*Kompas* 3 Feb. 1994). Tapping into growing discussions of human rights, validated by the establishment of the National Human Rights Commission less than a year earlier (Human Rights Watch 1994, 122), playwright, director, and poet Ikranegara also accused the government of violating the *cultural rights* of cultural workers under the U.N. Universal Declaration of Human Rights, to which the Indonesian government was a signatory (*Republika* 4 Feb. 1994). Later interventions, including meetings between cultural workers and legislators in East Java to discuss the banning (*Surabaya Post* 2 March 1994) and Ariel Heryanto's call for the complete abolition of the permit system for mass gatherings, including theater (*Kompas* 13 Feb. 1994), occurred in early March.

When the police attempted an apparent face-saving compromise, telling promoters they would allow the play's performance but adding that the play should be revised, Nadjib remained unmoved. He flatly refused the police's grudging permission, stating that he would not revise his script and didn't feel safe given the attitude of the apparatus—that is, he felt that the authorities were not honest nor well-intentioned. He went on to state that they were hypocritical in claiming that the play only criticized, since it offered a straightforward solution, but one the authorities hardly wanted to hear since it might hurt their interests (*Republika* 5 Feb. 1994).[12]

Fig. 7.2. T-shirt printed by Komunitas Pak Kanjeng after the Surabaya banning. The shirt reads: "Loving Pak Kanjeng is Forbidden."

Following the banning of *Pak Kanjeng* and ongoing harassment of Nadjib and Rendra in April and May 1994[13], three leading newsweeklies were shut down by government order in June of the same year. This last government action led to large and sustained demonstrations in many cities throughout Indonesia. By May of 1995, the mounting frustrations of cultural workers crystallized in a May Declaration, authored by Rendra, Nadjib, the recently banned *Tempo* magazine's Goenawan Mohamad, and Arief Budiman, and signed by about forty prominent cultural figures. Timed to commemorate the 1964 Sukarno era's outlawing of the

Cultural Manifesto, the May Declaration condemned the New Order's interference in cultural matters and claimed that contemporary conditions were as bad as those prevailing during the much maligned, fractious early 1960s (Junaedi 1995; Pracoyo et al. 1995; Putera et al 1995).

This was the juncture at which the banning of two workers' theater groups' plays occurred. As though taking their cue from the end of their own play, which urged workers to continue their struggles, TBI fought back even more tenaciously than Nadjib and the *Komunitas Pak Kanjeng*, if somewhat less flamboyantly. Rather than submit to Suharyono's conditions, TBI went on the offensive, suing the Jakarta Socio-Political Chief in the special courts (PTUN) established to hear cases brought against the government (*Kompas* 1 June 1995; 5 June; 18 July; 25 July; 1 Sept.; *Jayakarta* 18 July 1995; 8 August; 1 Sept.; *Media Indonesia Minggu* 23 July 1995; *Merdeka* 8 Aug. 1995; *Jakarta Post* 8 Aug. 1995; 1 Sept.; *Pos Kota* 1 Sept. 1995; *Republika* 1 June 1995).

Yet TBI also pursued an even more audacious line of resistance. Along with the scheduled performances at TIM on the 13th and 14th of May, the group had also arranged to perform on May 15th at their usual venue, the Galaxy Theater in Cisalak, Bogor. TBI strategically delayed publicly protesting the TIM banning in the hope of salvaging the Galaxy performance, but obtaining a permit for the latter was hardly a simple matter. Having already demanded revisions and issued a performance permit, the local security apparatus rescinded its permission, claiming the play was intended to fan the flames of the workers' emotions. When 1000 ticket-holding workers arrived only to find the theater doors locked, the organizing committee met with local police once more, ultimately convincing them to allow the play to go on (*Harian Terbit* 16 May 1995). Then, while its case against the government was being heard in the courts, TBI found several other occasions to perform. The first was at the Jakarta LBH (Legal Aid Institute) offices (*Harian Terbit* 2 Sept. 1995). A second occurred when TBI was invited to perform on August 30 for a group of artists at Studio Oncor, a haven for experimentation in theater and the arts (*Jayakarta* 1 Sept. 1995; *Media Indonesia* 3 Sept. 1995). A third occurred on September 30 in Bandung at Parahyangan University (*Harian Terbit* 2 Sept. 1995;

Kompas 15 October 1995; *Jakarta Post* 10 December, 1995). Plans for two performances in Solo on September 23 and 24, however, also met with police bans.

TBI's manner of resistance apparently provided the model for Sanggar Pabrik as well. Like TBI, Sanggar Pabrik decided to take the responsible authorities to court. Similarly, they also found opportunities to perform: part of the play was presented to the National Human Rights Commission on September 21 (*Kompas, Merdeka, Suara Pembaruan, Pos Kota* 22 Sept. 1995), while the entire piece was performed in the courtyard of the Taman Ismail Marzuki for a commemoration of the 1928 nationalist "Youth Oath" on October 28 (*Kompas* 29 Oct. 1995), at the IAIN (State Islamic University) Sunan Kalijaga in Yogyakarta on November 18, and at the Gajah Mada University Literature Faculty Auditorium in Yogyakarta on November 19 under the title *Tabir* or "Screen"(*Bernas* 20 Nov. 1995).

Though the media seemed to query few members of the cultural community about these bans (preferring instead to solicit reactions from lawyers and members of the National Human Rights Commission[14]), there were some indications that the established cultural community was in solidarity with worker groups who had suffered bans. For example, as mentioned above, Ray Sahetapy's experimental performance space, Teater Oncor, was opened to Teater Buruh Indonesia for a performance of *Senandung Terpuruk* in late August 1995, even while their case was being reviewed by the courts (*Media Indonesia* 3 Sept. 1995). Commenting on the withdrawal of the permit for Sanggar Pabrik's work, playwright and novelist Putu Wijaya ironically called for "reflection" on the seeming government confusion about how the permit system should work (*Bisnis Indonesia* 24 Sept. 1995), while Rendra invited Sanggar Pabrik to perform on his Bengkel Studio stage (*Swadesi* 26 Dec.–1 Jan. 1996).

During the debates following the banning of Ratna Sarumpaet's *Marsinah Menggugat* in late 1997, the consolidation of the arts community, along with its growing anger and boldness towards the security authorities, became even more apparent. After the first prohibition of the piece in Surabaya, a group calling itself Jakarta Artists' Solidarity demanded that the police respect the rights of free expression as guaranteed in the 1945

Constitution. Since the 1945 Constitution represented the key point of reference for New Order claims to uphold the rule of law, these demands served to point out the gap between legal foundations and government actions. The statement dovetailed with the way in which the broader community critical of the Suharto regime had been expanding the banning debates to focus on New Order abuses of human rights and to portray the regime as outside the law (see next section). Representative of the cultural workers' growing boldness, however, was their novel request that the police apologize for their actions (*Suara Pembaruan* 3 Dec. 1997).

The greater literary community was also less wary of offending the authorities. Reacting unsympathetically to the security apparatus's efforts to prevent a further performance of the play at the Archipelagic Writers' Conference in Kayutanam, West Sumatra, A. A. Navis, the respected West Sumatran writer, stated bluntly that the banning of the performance of Ratna's play in West Sumatra by the security apparatus meant the apparatus didn't really understand local culture. He said that it was the banning itself that had created problems, not the play (*Kompas Online* 10 Dec. 1997). A few days later, in response to the criticism launched against the play by Edi Sediawati, Director General for Culture in the Ministry of Education and Culture, a group of prominent cultural figures, including Goenawan Mohamad and Arief Budiman, issued a statement to the press questioning Sediawati's logic and demanding that she officially withdraw her comments. The statement then proceeded to call on all artists to defend Indonesian's constitutionally guaranteed rights of free expression (*Kompas Online* 18 Dec. 1997).

Sarumpaet's response to the furor was a firmly stated desire to be able to speak freely in Indonesia. She also countered the criticism of officials like Sediawati by contesting the government's long-standing efforts to brand politics as off-limits to art:

> Is there anything about human existence which doesn't have a political quality to it? ... My aspiration as an artist is to express the results of my reflections and observations about our daily life. To be able to speak about society without being allowed to discuss politics would be an astonishing feat. Even more so in the case of Marsinah.[15]

With Ratna's statement, the arts community had challenged one of the central pillars of New Order arts ideology.

Between 1990 and 1998 then, the arts community came together with a tighter solidarity than ever before to support the rights of theater workers (and others) to freely express their opinions. Closely related to this newfound solidarity was a tendency to debate and even to deride, with mounting anger and assertiveness, government rationales for preventing performances. This momentum became intertwined with a thematic expansion in the discussion surrounding the debates. Here, the role of the media, and especially the print media, was decisive.

Media Coverage and the Expanding Social Arena

Coming as it did so shortly after Suharto's much publicized call for increasing public openness, the banning of Riantiarno's *Suksesi* raised a minor storm of media coverage. The incident and debate about it were followed at length in newspapers like *Kompas* and *The Jakarta Post* and served as the focus of major features in magazines such as *Tempo, Editor,* and *Jakarta-Jakarta*. The press's approach was quite different from that taken when Rendra was arrested for reading poetry in 1978. In the earlier case, *Tempo* had canvassed only the opinions of cultural workers, including the government's representative, Minister of Education and Culture Daud Yusuf, himself a painter. For the *Suksesi* debates of late 1990 and those following later bannings, the media sought out a much wider range of figures for commentary. This set of commentators, mostly critical of the government's actions, included members of the press, New Order dissidents, and military officers and ex-officers. The emergence of this last group, whose statements were characterized by an emphasis on the need for openness and democracy, was indicative of tensions between the Suharto group within the government and those sections of the military who resented the way the president had been tightening his control over the armed forces. The press was also sensitive to the entrance into the debate of members of the government's own political party, Golkar, who sought to use President Suharto's call for openness as ammunition to condemn the banning. All these interventions worked to place theater in an arena of legal procedure that elicited questions of good governance, democratization, and openness.

This trend continued during the *Pak Kanjeng* banning debate of 1994, when parliamentarians and members of the National Human Rights Commission were again prominent commentators. Former police general Rukmini, then a member of the National Human Rights Commission, made an especially salient contribution to the debate, seconding Ikranegara's call to respect cultural rights and adding that respect for human rights was also enshrined in the 1945 Indonesian Constitution (*Republika* 4 Feb. 1994). With this appeal to constitutionality, the debate about banning began to take a significant turn.

The authorities also came under attack for continuing harassment of Nadjib and Rendra in the first half of 1994, as noted above.[16] Supported by Adnan Buyung Nasution and Mulyana W. Kusuma of the Indonesian Legal Aid Institute, Nadjib, and Rendra held a press conference on May 10 during which they echoed Ariel Heryanto's suggestion that the permit system be eliminated. In their remarks, the four broadened the discussion to include a condemnation of the requirement to obtain permits for any public gathering. According to Kusuma, such regulations were unconstitutional, violating the rights of free expression and association contained in the 1945 constitution (*Wawasan* 11 May). New Order dissidents and cultural workers were now more aggressively casting the government as the lawbreaker.

This tack was further extended in the legal challenges of permit denials that Teater Buruh Indonesia and the Sanggar Pabrik brought against the government in 1995. Here, the press moved discussion mainly into the area of legal rights, government regulations and procedures, with members of the legal profession, local legislators, and members of the Human Rights Commission becoming the central commentators.[17]

Still, there were other dimensions to the workers' theater cases. Both *Surat Cinta Bagi Marsinah Di Sorga* and TBI's *Senandung Terpuruk*, once banned by the authorities, became occasions for legal aid activists, students, and members of the National Human Rights Commission to publicly dispute the government's banning rationales (which were seen as arbitrary and contrary to the concurrent initiative to simplify the permit process described below) and to assert the need for openness, democracy, and even the abolition of the permit system for performances and mass gatherings.[18] Subsequent performances of both plays were sponsored most prominently by student groups and middle-class arts figures. Additional performances were directed at the National Human Rights Commission. With theater serving as the arena, expanding linkages were being forged between segments of the middle-classes and industrial workers. The decisions by both TBI and Sanggar Pabrik to take the authorities to court were something no previous middle-class modern group that had suffered a banning had yet done (despite the fact that such possibilities had been discussed). Their actions linked workers' rights to those of the recently banned news magazines, since *Tempo* was also litigating the revocation of its publishing permit.

Remarkably, both court cases at least partially vindicated the workers. The decision in the TBI/*Senandung Terpuruk* case was rendered in mid-October by a panel of judges headed by Benyamin Mangkudilaga, famed for his earlier decision in favor of *Tempo*. Though the court's decision in the TBI case did not award the workers a clear victory, it nonetheless cast further doubt on the ability of the government apparatus to conform to its own rules and procedures. The decision essentially stated that the court could not accept TBI's complaint because the banning decision by the Head of the Jakarta Socio-Political Directorate was not a final, legally binding decision. The court held that only the police could make a decision in permit cases. On the other hand, the court also pointed out that the Head of the Socio-Political Directorate had absolutely no legal authority to make a decision on permits nor could he revoke the recommendations of the other bureaus involved. Ultimately, the judges found R. Bagus Suharyono's actions to have no legal basis, something which the leading Indonesian daily, *Kompas*, highlighted in its headline: "The Head of the Jakarta Regional Socio-Political Directorate Violated the General Principles of Good Government" (Kaditsospol DKI Salahi Asas Umum Pemerintahan yang Baik, 17 Oct. 1995). Other newspapers echoed the same sentiment.

The debate seemed to subside with the promulgation in late December 1995 of the government's Section 510 Joint Field Instructions freeing theater performances and most meetings from the need to obtain a permit. Evidence of a positive turn might have been found in the stunning court victory of Sanggar Pabrik's lawsuit in May 1996. In the court's decision, the Kebayoran Baru district police were found to have acted arbitrarily in canceling the permit at the last moment. Arguing that the accused had had ample time to ask the plaintiff to redirect their permit through the proper office if indeed such actions were required, the court ordered the police to pay Rp.1.7 million (about US $800 at that time) to Sanggar Pabrik as compensation (*Kompas* 14 May 1996; *Merdeka* 14 May; *Target* 21–27 May).

Then, in the run-up to the 1998 MPR session at which Suharto was expected to be selected for yet another five-year term as president, censorship of theater began again. When Ratna Sarumpaet's *Marsinah Menggugat* was banned in late November and early December 1997, public debate soon targeted the fact that the banning contravened the Joint Field Instructions of December 1995 (*Kompas Online* 29 Nov. 1997). On December 1, Hendardi of the Legal Aid Institute added this incident to a list of events, including the police mishandling of the murder of Udin (an investigative reporter in Yogyakarta), which he felt were causing Indonesians to lose confidence in the police (*Suara Pembaruan* 1 Dec. 1997). The National Human Rights Commission condemned the banning for violating the right to freedom of expression, even more so because police gave no clear reason for the action (*Kompas Online* 2 Dec. 1997).

Amidst the evident anger and defiance of cultural workers, Clementino dos Reis Amaral of the Human Rights Commission, finding it difficult to believe that the police couldn't conform to the government's own regulations, declared the banning a violation of the law (*Kompas Online* 9 Dec. 1997). Subsequent reporting only confirmed the impression that the regime was outside the law. After a meeting with the representatives of the national police headquarters, Assistant Chair of the National Human Rights Commission, Marzuki Darusman, stated that the police affirmed their adherence to the 1995 Joint Field Instructions and had explained the banning of Sarumpaet's plays as the result of "miscommunications" (*Kompas Online* 2 Jan. 1998). Sarumpaet's legal counsel, the Legal Aid Institute's Bambang Wijoyanto, welcomed the statement by the police that they would comply with the Field Instructions. Nevertheless, relating that the organizing committee in Bandarlampung had been terrorized in an effort to force them to cancel the performance, he doubted their assertion that miscommunications had been at fault.

Government Disarray

As noted previously, the authorities closed down *Suksesi* only on the twelfth night of a scheduled two-week run. That *Suksesi* was performed for eleven nights before being banned was already peculiar, since all plays still had to be submitted to censors well ahead of time in order to receive the required performance permit. Typically, this requirement meant that theatrical banning occurred before the players ever had the opportunity to step before the footlights. This discrepancy suggests either that local police authorities were confused about the extent of keterbukaan intended by the president or that there was opposition to the banning from within the state apparatus—perhaps the military.

From the very beginning, the police appeared unable to find a single persuasive rationale with which to explain their banning action. Subsequently, they provided conflicting explanations, thus allowing critics to contest their reasons more easily. The commander of the Jakarta Metropolitan Police, M. H. Ritonga, told the press that the ban was a result of procedural violations and had nothing to do with politics. The official written statement issued by the police, however, offered three reasons for stopping the play's run: first, the performance deviated from the script submitted for police review prior to granting a performance permit; second, the play was non-educational and presented a false picture to the audience; and third, the idea for the story was not taken from the traditional (*pakem*) wayang stories and therefore indicated an intention to influence the audience about things that were untrue.[19] The statement said that the ban had been applied to preserve public order (*Kompas*, Oct. 11, 1990, 1). Contrary to Major General Ritonga's express denial, the official written statement indicated that there were indeed political considerations involved.

In contrast to the official reasons issued by the police, Minister for State Apparatus Efficiency Sarwono, Minister of Culture Hasan, and State Secretary Moerdiono attempted to legitimize the banning through arguments about aesthetics and taste, echoing some of the artists' criticisms that openness required high artistic expression and that Koma's *Suksesi* was just rowdyism. Similarly, they stressed that artists had to be sensitive to society's norms. When critics remained unconvinced, however, Secretary of State Moerdiono revealed something of the regime's anxiety about losing the battle for the hearts and minds of the middle-class by pleading for Indonesians to be patient about the realization of democracy (*Kompas* 22 Oct. 1990).

In reaction to the furor created by the succeeding bans on *Opera Kecoa* and Rendra's poetry, new government spokespeople emerged, both of them close associates of President Suharto. Between them, they attempted to reinforce the authority of the government's preferred style for public discourse, including theater. Minister of Information Harmoko denied that the banning tarnished openness and warned artists that creative freedom must stay within the limits of Pancasila and national cultural values. Coordinating Minister for Security Sudomo stated that creative criticism should be objective, not personal, and that it should observe decency and use polite language (*The Jakarta Post* 3 Dec. 1990; *Kompas* 12 Dec. 1990). Throughout the course of the three bans, the government tried to insist that it was not restricting openness. Yet to maintain such an argument they nonetheless had to restrict the meaning of openness, qualifying it with words such as "responsible," "Pancasila," and "in accord with national values." However, government rationales often did not correspond to those of the police but shifted from aesthetics to morality to national values and back to aesthetics. The government seemed in disarray and ill-prepared for a debate about theater censorship.

When a cultural workers' delegation protested before the DPR and visited his office to discuss the banning issue, Minister Sudomo finally struck a partially conciliatory pose in recommending that performance of the banned works be permitted. Still, he insisted that writers must strive to write better, more polite works, and, when criticism absolutely had to be made, provide positive solutions to the problems. While the government had not exactly surrendered, in the face of mounting criticism, it at least tried to appear flexible.[20]

Perhaps as a result of the minor debacle surrounding the *Suksesi* banning, continuing divisions within the military, and generally expanding resistance among the middle-class, the Suharto group's attempt to reassert

Fig. 7.3. A *Kompas* story from 12 December 1990 features Coordinating Minister for Security Sudomo meeting with a cultural workers' delegation including from right, N. Riantiarno, W.S. Rendra, and Noorca Massardi. The headline accompanying the photo read: "Coordinating Minister for Security: Artists may criticize, as long as they do so responsibly." Photo courtesy of *Kompas*.

the repressive power and ideological hegemony of the New Order in theater as well as in politics in early 1994 was hobbled from the start. During the *Pak Kanjeng* incident, the authorities seemed determined to avoid any hint of censorship, insisting that they were merely postponing the play. However, both the local regional police headquarters and the East Java military command[21] also attempted to delegitimize the play's author and subordinate him to their control. They suggested that before permission could be granted the script needed to be revised and refined (*diperhalus*) in order not to cause social tention to flare-up (*Surya* 1 February 1994; *Jawa Pos* 1 February 1994). This requirement clearly demonstrated that the case was not, in fact, a simple postponement, but rather an effort to censor and redirect cultural production.

However, few members of the government openly defended the banning after Nadjib ridiculed the security apparatus's suggestions of revision and attempts to distinguish between postponement and banning. In the face of the subsequent combative barrage of public criticism. Feisal Tanjung,

Commander in Chief of the Armed Forces, felt it necessary to deny that ABRI had had anything to do with it; he even declared that there was nothing to worry about in the play (*Bernas* 3 Feb. 1994).²² When confronted with media questioning and delegations of protesting students, Commander of the East Java Brawijaya Military Command, Haris Sudarno, either denied responsibility (*Jawa Pos* 3 Feb. 1994) or pleaded, "Give us some time and don't be too quick to say *Pak Kanjeng* was banned." Only East Java governor, Basofi Sudirman, was willing to state unequivocally that he supported the action. This situation left regional police spokesmen to take the brunt of public criticism, though they maintained that the decision had been taken in full consultation with the army's social-political wing and the Regional Council for Coordinating National Stability, Bakorstanasda (*Jawa Pos* 3 Feb 1994.; *Kompas* 3 Feb. 1994).

With students in Surabaya delivering letters of protest to Polda headquarters, the Governor of East Java, and the Brawijaya Regional Military Command (*Jawa Pos* 3 Feb. 1994) and with the arts councils of Jakarta and Surabaya demanding that the authorities provide explanations about the banning and government policies towards the arts (*Republika* 3 Feb. 1994; *Surabaya Post* 4 Feb. 1994), the pressure seemed to become too great for the government. On February 4 several newspapers reported that the promoters had met with the regional police command and had obtained an agreement that the play could be performed some two to four weeks later. The spokesperson for the promoter group also revealed that the commander of the regional police had appealed to the play's author to make the script "more objective." This suggestion meant that the criticisms in the script were permitted, but that solutions should be provided and the positive side of development should also be shown (*Kompas* 4 Feb. 1994; *Jawa Pos* 4 Feb. 1994; *Surabaya Post* 4 Feb. 1994). These suggestions seemed to echo and advance Sudomo's admonitions from 1990, raising again the kernel of an idea about what might constitute a regime-approved "Pancasila realism."

Eventually, after Nadjib had refused police suggestions for revision, prominent central government officials were once again brought into the debate. State Secretary Moerdiono endeavored to deny that the *Pak Kanjeng* ban invalidated his October statement (*Republika* 11 Feb.), while Major General Hendropriyono, military commander of the Jakarta region and head of the regional Council for National Stability, reaffirmed the security apparatus's prerogative to censor in order to avoid instability (*Republika* 11 Feb. 1994). The government thus sought to hold the line on the security approach rationale for banning theater, though its critics were beginning to dismantle such arguments.

By the time of the banning of Teater Buruh Indonesia and Sanggar Pabrik's plays in 1995, public sentiment against government banning had been further heightened by harassment of Nadjib and Rendra, the banning of the three newsweeklies, and the 1995 May declaration. It was thus an especially inauspicious juncture for additional censorship. As in the case of *Pak Kanjeng*, government officials sought to deny that they were banning the play, insisting that the play could still be performed if it conformed to certain conditions. In explaining the reasons for the ban, R. Bagus Suharyono, Head of the Jakarta regional government's Socio-Political Directorate, declared that the play and the name of the theater group contained a word—'*buruh*' (worker)—which had suspicious political connotations and was no longer appropriate in New Order Indonesia.[23] Suharyono stated that the play's content exaggerated problems of antagonism between workers and owners.[24] Before the play could be given permission, he stated that the group needed to replace the word buruh and change the theme and story. As discussed previously, a government coordinating committee, meeting to consider TBI's permit request, had even decided, that in order to obtain a permit the worker-performers had to be replaced! Suharyono felt that the play should focus more on the unity of the nation, and he confided to reporters that if plays treated issues such as the national struggle or other themes promoting patriotic feelings, he would certainly grant performance permits. In general, the reason for bannng the play was that it might threaten national stability (*Kompas* 1 June 1995; 5 June 1995; *Republika* 1 June 1995; *Merdeka* 1 June 1995). Going even further than Sudomo or the Surabaya police and military spokespeople, Suharyono justified his banning decision on the basis that the play gave a false picture of reality. He then provided the most extensive description yet of a possible, officially prescribed art doctrine, namely, that plays should present a more positive picture of reality and promote patriotism. By stipulating that the worker-performers needed to be replaced, the government suggested that it saw workers' theater itself as a threat.

Possibly stemming from the extensive criticism of its rationale for the TBI banning, the police's publicly stated reasons for the banning of Sanggar Pabrik's *Surat Cinta Bagi Marsinah* were strictly procedural. Yet even here, the reasons put forward seemed flimsy and indefensible. Another court case ensued.

Whether as a result of mounting social pressure around the permit issue or possibly the desire on the part of the Suharto group to win the support of the middle-classes, the Indonesian government began to explore ways to resolve the permit controversy as early as September 1995. Prior to the Sanggar Pabrik banning, Coordinating Minister for Security Susilo Sudarman had announced that new rules for simplifying the permit system were being promulgated. Rather embarrassingly, while the banning of Sanggar Pabrik's play was being discussed in the newspapers, Justice Minister Utoyo Usman stressed that permit requirements for religious, social, and cultural meetings would be abolished, while political meetings would only require written notice to the police (*Kompas* 19 Sept. 1995; *The Jakarta Post* 19 Sept. 1995; *Kompas* 20 Sept. 1995).

In late November 1995, even Syarwan Hamid, then the army's Assistant Commander of Socio-Political Affairs and part of the pro-Suharto army leadership, felt obliged to enter the discussion. Responding to the much reported difficulties that Riantiarno and Teater Koma encountered before finally obtaining a permit for their December 1995 play, *Semar Gugat* (Semar Accuses), Hamid called on the security apparatus to restrain itself from knee-jerk banning or automatic assumptions about theatrical performances (*Kompas* 26 Nov. 1995). In late December, just two months after the court decision in TBI's lawsuit, Defense Minister Edi Sudrajat[25] and Interior Minister Yogie S. Memet issued field instructions for the implementation of Section 510 of the legal code. These instructions modified the section in question, stating that many types of meetings and activities—including theater—no longer needed a permit. The police did not even need to be informed about theater performances. However, many social commentators, including Abdurrahman Wahid of the Nahdlatul Ulama and Hendardi of the Legal Aid Institute, remained skeptical, arguing that the government could still find loopholes in the field instructions (*Gatra* 6 Jan. 1996, 70–71; *Tiras* 11 Jan. 1996, 64).

The decisions rendered in the workers' theater court cases further delegitimized the government's practices. Together with the Joint Field Instructions of December 1995, these decisions seemed to signal an end to theatrical banning under the New Order. Though the Suharto government was on the defensive regarding theater and mass gathering permits, and in a number of other spheres, it was still a powerful adversary. Proof came in the form of its efforts to destabilize the leadership of the Democratic Party of Indonesia under Megawati Sukarnoputri, coupled with the "Dark Saturday" storming of PDI party headquarters in downtown Jakarta on July 26. Obviously, the state was still deeply troubled by any elements outside the control of its formal apparatuses.

The Suharto government's retreat on the issue of performance permits also began to appear less certain by 1997. In fact, as early as late 1994, with Ratna Sarumpaet's cancelled second round of performances of her play, *Marsinah: Nyanyian Dari Bawah Tanah*, suspicions arose that the government was experimenting with a more covert form of censorship. Sarumpaet related that after initial performances of the play in September and October, the funding for a subsequent series of performances in Jakarta, Surabaya, and Padang had mysteriously been withdrawn (Field Notes 22 & 24 Aug. 1997). By August of 1997, there were other indications that the government was still not obeying its own regulations. Members of SBSI associated with the Sanggar Pabrik reported that they still needed to request permission from the police for their cultural performances despite the government's official instructions easing the permit system (Field Notes 24 Aug. 1997). Though the New Order seemed embarrassed, even pressured, into announcing new rules for performances, a number of cultural workers still harbored suspicions that the security apparatus continued to prevent the dissemination of works it deemed threatening. This suspicion was validated when TBI was not allowed to perform its newest play in September of 1997 (Conroy 1997, 1) and when Ratna Sarumpaet's new Marsinah play, *Marsinah Menggugat*, was banned in peculiar circumstances in November and December of the same year.

The case of *Marsinah Menggugat* is particularly revealing of this new shape to the dynamics of censorship during the final years of the Suharto regime. Though the piece was successfully performed in several Javanese cities, security officials had shown up en-masse at the Jakarta opening and the Tasikmalaya performance. During the course of the play's tour through Java, a series of mysterious events also dogged Sarumpaet. In Solo, following the failure of the local security apparatus to prevent the performance, the lights mysteriously went out and the play had to be performed with improvised torch lighting. At other venues the doors to the buildings were found locked or threats of demonstrations were received. Sarumpaet claimed that the security apparatus was behind all of it (*Kompas Online* 27 Nov. 1997; *Tempo Interactive* 10 Jan. 1998). Events in Surabaya in late November 1997, when Sarumpaet attempted to perform *Marsinah Menggugat* in conjunction with a regional Islamic conference, lent credence to her beliefs and provided a glimpse of the security apparatus's new but ineffective covert strategy for banning theater.

Police showed up hours before the show was scheduled to go on, surrounding the building and informing Sarumpaet that there would be no performance. Initial reports on November 26 had the police asserting that there was no permit for the performance, yet the organizing committee countered that it had conveyed its request for permission to the police well in advance (*Kompas Online* 27 Nov. 1997). Next followed accusations that the organizing committee had backed down because the local Socio-Political Directorate threatened to withhold funding for the concurrent conference. The organizing committee denied this assertion, relating that, in fact, an official with the directorate had offered them money if they would cancel the performance, a request to which the committee refused to accede (*Kompas Online* 29 Nov. 1997).

Despite a fierce barrage of public condemnation, the security apparatus seemed far from apologetic. On December 6, security forces risked an international incident by showing up in armored vehicles to block a performance of *Marsinah Menggugat* at the French Cultural Center in Bandung, West Java. The director of the cultural center, Jean Pheline, attempted to dissuade the police, reminding them that cultural events no longer needed police permission. Furthermore, Pheline added that since the performance was to occur in the French Cultural Center, which supposedly was not subject to Indonesian police authority, he was considering filing an official protest with the French Embassy. Undeterred, the responsible police commander insisted that the actions were in accord with Section 510 of the criminal code and that a performance permit was therefore required. Though blocked from entering the Cultural Center complex, a sizeable crowd decided to create an impromptu cultural event by reading critical poetry in the adjoining street. Jajang C. Noer, widow of the late Arifin C Noer, even defied the police by jumping over the fence onto the Cultural Center grounds, remarking angrily, "As an Indonesian citizen, it's an insult to be prohibited from watching a cultural performance in my own country" (*Kompas Online* 7 Dec.).

Confronted by a growing chorus accusing the security apparatus of being unable to follow its own rules, National Chief of Police Dibyo Widodo fell back on the old, tired security approach reasons to justify the banning. Widodo claimed the implementation of the 1995 permit instructions depended on the circumstances at the place of performance. He claimed the police took preventative actions in order to avoid threats to public order and safety. Echoing aspects of Widodo's statement, Edi Sediawati, noted dance scholar and Director General for Culture in the Ministry of Education and Culture, entered the fray on December 13. Sediawati advanced once more the old argument about the separation between art and politics by insisting that the banning of *Marsinah Menggugat* was not repression of the arts because the play contained political messages that could cause public unrest and chaos. In reiterating elements of the New Order's hegemonic ideology about public discourse and art, she called for politeness and called upon artists to be sensitive to society's norms about what could and couldn't be done. Sediawati implied that plays such as Sarumpaet's constituted prior judgment of a legal case still in question, and she held that this was best left to the legal system (*Kompas Online* 15 Dec. 1997).

Such arguments, however, were either ignored or brushed aside by public critics of the regime. Public anger mounted with an additional banning of Sarumpaet's play in Bandarlampung, and the denial of a permit to Sanggar Pabrik at roughly the same time (*Kompas Online* 18

Dec. 1997; *Tiras* 12 Jan. 1998). The National Human Rights Commission meanwhile intervened to request explanations from the security apparatus, and, as related in the previous section, when police explained the banning as a result of "miscommunications," Sarumpaet threatened to take the government to court once again.

Evidence that the security apparatus found itself further than ever on the defensive came from National Police Chief Dibyo Widodo. After reiterating that the police only banned a play if they thought it would create a disturbance or be dangerous in a particular region, he ended with the plea, "Don't keep bashing us [the police]. We too are among the nation's children who participated in seizing our independence" (*Tiras* 12 Jan. 1998). The government now appeared completely unable to direct public debate, having recourse only to covert methods of banning, discredited justifications, contradictory affirmations of respect for regulations and laws, and complaints about the unfairness of public criticism.

The dynamics of this process, the fluid relationships among theater workers, the media, students, dissident intellectuals, workers' theaters, the security apparatus, and rival factions within the government, once again demonstrated the complex processes involved in the production and reception of modern national theater in Indonesia. Yet the struggles against New Order theater censorship also illustrated how theater could play a visible role in the process of democratization. Though the New Order still had not collapsed by the beginning of 1998, the signs of a rapid decay in the regime's public legitimacy were unmistakable. As the foregoing analysis has shown, the style of theater performances, the mode of government banning, and the increasingly angry public debates about them during the 1990s, both foreshadowed and contributed to Suharto's fall in May of 1998 as well as to the concurrent eclipse of the military's public image and political power.

CONCLUSION

The resistance of modern national theater workers to the New Order's power was only a part of larger social processes then in motion, yet it also represented a clear continuation and heightening of a very specific antagonism that had long existed between the independent Indonesian state and those involved in contributing to the construction of a modern national culture. This resistance began to increase in the 1980s with the efforts of several groups of theater workers to engage in joint practices with peasants, Muslim youth, and workers respectively. At the same time, avant-garde troupes of modern national theater workers challenged the dominant, pervasive narratives of nation and individual identity by representing the torment, agony, and anger of urban alienation in the late New Order. Such efforts of social community building, empowerment, protest, and challenging of dominant ideologies and frames of understanding culminated from the mid-1990s on (though preceded by a few scattered, exceptional works like Teater Koma's *Suksesi*) in a wave of increasingly direct and angrily critical works that openly questioned the New Order's aesthetic norms and voiced bitter criticism of the prevailing political and social system and its leaders.

In public debates over several highly visible cases of government censorship, theater workers were able to forge discursive alliances with journalists, legal aid advocates, dissident politicians, military figures, and industrial workers. These alliances helped identify key areas of common interest in the realm of civil and human rights. By so doing, they also contributed to the pro-democracy movement that eventually played a role in ousting Suharto from power in May 1998.

Yet major problems in the pro-democracy and Reform movements can also be seen in tensions faced by grassroots theater and workers' theater practitioners, as well as in the relatively small audiences for most avant-garde performances. Here, the issues of aesthetic ideologies, taste, and *noblesse oblige* (the sympathetic yet patronizing attitude of the elites and middle-class intellectuals toward the majority of less well-off Indonesians) are central. Such socio-cultural divisions produce both a desire for an alliance and create unequal relations of power and differing perspectives on the themes and uses of a theater jointly created by disparate parties. Thus, one of the most important aspects of the politics of theater in Indonesia is precisely the gap in expectations about the purposes and aims of theatrical activity, which existed among high arts modern theater workers, NGO activists, peasants, industrial workers, and other involved constituencies of participants and spectators. This gap was embodied in the continual attempts by grassroots theater workers to find more effective ways to use their practices in conjunction with peasants and in the strains among artistic theater practitioners, NGO activists, and worker performers in workers' theater troupes. In the Yogyakarta-based Islamic theater of 1989–91, a parallel set of tensions is also visible in interactions among government officials, stricter members of the Muslim community, and the performers mounting the actual productions. Similarly, the aesthetic and thematic tensions in the work of avant-garde groups also illustrate both the expressive power and the limits of Indonesian modern national theater's ideology and practice. Though willing to express social concerns and criticisms in their work, they nonetheless adhered to high art notions of performance and venue, disdaining "shallow" political statements. Groups like Teater Sae or Teater Payung Hitam failed to gain wider audiences even though they attracted much attention from specific middle-class audiences, including other arts and theater practitioners, NGO activists, and journalists, and thereby exercised considerable influence on a newer generation of modern theater practitioners and helped build alliances within the pro-democracy movement. They mainly gave voice to frustrations and criticism, without being able to consciously offer alternative visions. Even

Teater Kubur, more firmly connected to its Kampung Kober lower-middle-class roots and a somewhat wider audience, was caught in much the same dilemma. Its productions were primarily intended to represent a sense of the reality of Jakarta's socially marginalized. Despite its impressive tours to other sites and cities in Java, the group has never gained a large mass following outside that of its own *kampung*, appealing mainly to intellectuals and other modern national theater workers.

Yet despite the limitations and socially telling dynamics of their work, all of these groups contributed to a general social critique of the New Order that, for their specific and at times overlapping constituencies, helped construct, support, and sustain resistance to the Suharto regime and contributed to its eventual overthrow in May 1998. Those groups still in existence—Teater Kubur, Teater Payung Hitam, workers theater groups—carried the momentum of the long struggle against the Suharto regime into their work of the post-May 1998 Reform period. And indeed, some of the social alliances forged earlier continued to operate as well during the new era.

For instance, in August 1999 the NGO Kontras, which had formed to advocate and pursue justice on behalf of the families of a number of student activists abducted in the waning months of the New Order, sponsored a production of Seno Gumira Ajidarma's *Mengapa Kau Culik Anak Kami* (Why Did You Abduct Our Son?), a powerful piece consisting of a series of dialogues between the father and mother of a fictional abducted activist. Commercial sponsors of the production consisted mainly of print media and radio stations. Similarly, Ratna Sarumpaet restaged her *Marsinah Menggugat* in the same month in conjunction with JEJAK: Human Right Investigation for Truth and Justice. The production was part of a campaign to seek justice for Marsinah, and the program for the production also announced the other events in the campaign and featured advertisements from a plethora of radio stations and several of the major print media in Jakarta. In addition, in the program's acknowledgments page, JEJAK thanked leading figures from the once-banned, now revived *Tempo* magazine and several prominent NGO activists as well as cultural institutions. These productions, then, clearly showed the continuing nexus of media, NGO, and artistic involvement in productions about social issues.

Yet, at the Jakarta productions of these shows that I attended at TIM, audience numbers were relatively small, and only one year after the Reform period had begun, it seemed as though the critical political theater had lost some of its drawing power in the capital city. Such productions may have still elicited considerable excitement in provincial cities. For example, the original anti-militarist piece *Tiang Setengah Tiang* (Flag at Half Mast) staged by Payung Hitam in Makassar in September 1999 painted callous electioneering and military violence and intimidation as part of an exasperatingly New Order-like Reform-Era national canvas. With its previously unimaginable representations of military violence, *Tiang Setengah Tiang* symbolized the new freedom of expression for which Indonesia's modern theater workers had helped fight, even if many agonizing social realities remained much the same as before.[1] Similarly, Ratna Sarumpaet's play about the ongoing separatist conflict in Aceh, *Alia, Luka Serambi Mekah* (Alia: Wound of Mecca's Veranda 2000–2001) was able to draw large crowds in Bandung and Aceh as well as in Jakarta. Still, it seemed as though a change was in the air. A number of friends involved in the theater said that in the new, freer environment of the Reform Era, people could more easily get political news and commentaries from the media, so that theater no longer seemed as singular or powerful a vehicle for social commentary and political criticism as it had only a few years before.[2]

In some situations, the alliances formed around theater in the 1990s were also dissolving. From 1999 on, workers' theater no longer seemed to capture as much attention from the media. It is possible that many members of the elites and middle-classes felt that such inter-class alliances were no longer as urgent after the removal of Suharto, long seen by some (Aspinall 2005, 76) as the greatest obstacle to democracy. The internal tensions highlighted previously between the participants also played a role in altering the landscape of workers' theater. In 2000, TBI split with Yayasan Sisbikum and Arist precisely over imbalances of power and control between NGO organizers and worker performers (Conroy, 2006). Margesti and Wowok undertook to organize a festival of workers' culture in 2001, but Teater ABU, due in large part to the personal life circumstances of its leader, Margesti, gradually moved away from a central focus on workers issues to a broader focus on gender issues and issues of concern to women.

After moving to the semi-rural Parung Panjang area outside Tangerang, Margesti began to become more involved in the lives of local housewives and other residents, who soon came to form a substantial part of ABU's membership.

In fact, with Suharto gone, it seemed to become more difficult for the opposition to rally around a single or unified set of goals, a fact made even more complex by the introduction of regional autonomy laws in 2001 which gave considerable independence in economic and local political affairs to the regions (Bain 2005, 6; Hatley 2008, 194). Yet new causes emerged in the theater as well as the wider society. The trauma of New Order violence spurred the creation of a number of works, including Seno Gumira Ajidarma's *Mengapa Kau Culik Anak Kami* mentioned above. Margesti's turn to productions more centered on women's issues is indicative of another such trend. Women's NGOs have taken a lead in funding and co-producing theater about women and their concerns in the Reform Era. Women's NGO activists and theater workers have banded together to form loose alliances for purposes of producing plays ranging from *The Vagina Monologues* to an adaptation of Nawal El Sadawi's *Woman at Point Zero*, and most recently, a play based on the character Nyai Ontosoroh from Pramoedya Ananta Toer's Buru Tetralogy of novels. In Makassar, too, a coalition of NGOs, including two dynamic women's NGOs, funded a production by a leading local group, Teater Kita Makassar, which highlighted issues of violence against women (Bodden 2007b). Elsewhere, a growing number of women have appeared as writers, performers, and directors, as demonstrated by Barbara Hatley's recent work (2007). In addition, since 1999 Lena Simanjuntak has collaborated with a variety of NGOs to create grassroots theater of empowerment productions together with several women's groups, including sex workers in Surabaya, plantation workers and housewives from North Sumatra, displaced Acehnese women, HIV sufferers, and domestic workers. These efforts, though not directly connected to the work of the Central Javanese grassroots theater movement of 1980–94, nonetheless mark the continued relevance of such theater practices for many in Indonesia (Field Notes March 2007).

Payung Hitam, too, has partially switched from performance pieces centered on national politics to a concern with environmental destruction and deforestation, especially in their 2004 production, *Relief Air Mata* (Relief of Tears). Other newer avant-garde groups, such as the Yogyakarta-based Teater Garasi, have attempted to look to the traumas of colonialism, in interaction with cultural and ethnic identity, for the causes of Indonesia's present-day malaise. This soul-searching also located trauma in Javanese pre-colonial traditions and was related to feelings of disappointment with reform. It appeared to suggest that something in the historical social construction of ethnic and national identities may have played a role in Indonesia's continuing inability to create a more just society (Bodden 2007).

Though the themes may be changing, it seems clear that Indonesia's modern national theater remains committed to raising pressing issues and giving voice to some of those who otherwise have a difficult time being heard. Whether such theater will be able to compete for the attention of wide and diverse social audiences in the face of a growing plethora of modes of mass entertainment and private pleasure seeking seems uncertain. Thus, questions of the politics of contemporary Indonesian theater, its themes, styles, and relations to its audiences, remain central to the future vitality of this cultural form. In the new neo-liberal, post-1998 era in Indonesia, in which private companies continue to wreak havoc on the lives of many fellow-citizens,[3] surely, part of the answer to that question lies in modern theater's ability to bridge the gap, in background, aesthetic assumptions, cultural training, and social relations, between high arts theater practitioners and the large numbers of ordinary Indonesians to whom modern theater does not yet speak with intimacy and passionate urgency.

GLOSSARY

Adiluhung—a concept of art which valorized court art and refinement. It holds that art should be removed from gross physical reality, should not stimulate base desires, and should be seen as a service to a ruler.

Asas Tunggal—The Sole Foundation. This formulation was most prominent in the New Order Government law of 1985 that the state ideology, *Pancasila*, should be the sole philosophical foundation for all social organizations in Indonesia.

Bag Big Bug—1996 TABUR workers' theater play written by Igor and dealing with workers' protests, police detention, and interrogation of demonstrators.

Banyolan—Popular Javanese joking and comedy routines.

Bedug—drums used in the Surabaya performance of *Lautan Jilbab*. Traditionally suspended horizontally in a mosque to summon Muslims to prayer.

Bercanda Dalam Duka—a Teater Buruh Indonesia play performed in 1993 which deals with the issue of compensation for disabling injuries sustained at work, and which may have adopted a less narrative form in response to the success of Teater ABU.

Biografi Yanti Setelah 12 Menit—Teater Sae play produced in 1992 which continued the group's exploration of post-modern themes and techniques while representing more complex notions of family, identity, and politics than traditional narratives or biographies seem able to offer.

Buruh—Indonesian word for manual laborer. The New Order regime of General Suharto tended to avoid use of this word, viewing it with some suspicion and regarding it as associated with the banned Communist party and notions of labor linked to the radical industrial unions of the

Sukarno era (1950-1965). The New Order preferred the more general term, *pekerja* (worker).

Dagelan and dagelan mataram—Comedy routine, the dagelan mataram was a joking style specific to the Yogyakarta region of Central Java. In dagelan mataram, a thing which can not be openly discussed is replaced by an elaborate comic metaphor which suggests it without actually calling it by its name.

Dajjal—a play written by Agung Waskito and first performed in 1989 by Sanggar Shalahuddin under Waskito's direction. Using the apocalyptic figure of the evil temper (dajjal) appearing at the end of the world, the play views New Order society as dominated by irreligious "western" values, greedy, materialistic, foolishly arrogant, and oppressive towards ordinary Indonesians.

Dakwah—Islamic proselytization or consciousness-raising.

Dangdut—a kind of popular music beginning in the mid-1970s which combines Indian and Middle-Eastern sounds with an earlier form of Indonesian popular music, Melayu, and western style rock and roll using amplified guitars.

Demang—a district administrator.

Desa binaan—term used to describe a village under guided development. The guidance was usually provided by the government, though at times non-government organization workers also thought of villages where they were involved in developmental or cultural projects in the same paternalistic terms.

Gedongan—people living in large houses close to the main streets and their cultural milieu

Halus—refined, of high aesthetic quality.

Impian Diantara Cerobong Asap—A 1995 play by Igor and TABUR centered on the ambitions of a young factory worker to contribute to the growth of a workers' movement through his poetry.

Ijtihad—the right of Muslims to interpret the meaning of the scriptures.

Jahiliya—the pre-Islmaic era in the Arabian peninsula. Considered by Muslims to be a time of ignorance and sin in which immorality and skewed values were rampant.

Jaipongan—a popular modern, tradition-based music and dance form created in West Java in the 1970s. This form was taken up popularly, peaking in a *jaipongan* dance craze during the 1980s.

Jaringan—network. Here, used to describe the web of connections and relations between elite theater practitioners and groups they helped construct their own kinds of theater, as well as between all these theater groups and the media, politicians, and other social groups in the broad pro-democracy movement.

Jilbab—the head-covering, similar to the habits worn by nuns, that covers the hair and ears while leaving the face uncovered, and which became an important symbol of modern Muslim women's identity in New Order Indonesia.

Kampung—a rural village or lower/lower middle class slum in larger cities.

Kasar—"crude," used to describe rude or rough behavior, or less refined and often, more popular forms of art

Kaspar—a Teater Payung Hitam adaptation of a Peter Handke play, first staged by Payung Hitam in 1994. The play's theme—the ways in which language forms identity and is a form of social control—resonated closely with resentment of government censorship and control of the media, especially in the light of the recent banning of three leading news weeklies.

Kecapi—a boat-shaped zither of West Java.

Kekeluargaan—"familiality" or family relations. This term was used during the New Order to suggest the ordained pattern for all social relations and was often employed to circumvent calls for a more liberal democratic political system with greater human and political rights by evoking the notion of society as a harmonious family in which everything could be peacefully settled through respect for one's seniors and close consultation.

Keluarga Sakinah—play written by Emha Ainun Nadjib and directed by Agung Waskito, the play was first performed at the 42nd Congress of the Muhammadiayah organization in December 1990, and employed a large number of local Muslim schoolgirls in its production, as well as members of Teater Jiwa, a group formed by Waskito.

Kesatria—a "knight." A word suggesting the ideals of a Javanese male aristocrat who should be dispassionate in performing his duties, faithfully serve the kingdom (or nation), protect the weak, and not expect fame or material reward for his efforts.

Keterbukaan—"openness." This word was used by both the Suharto group within the New Order government, and its rivals and opponents beginning in the late 1980s and continuing on into the early 1990s. Keterbukaan was a key phrase in public discussions of politics and referred to the perceived need for Indonesian society to become more liberal ("open").

Ketoprak—a form of popular theater originating in the second half of the nineteenth century in Central Java, where it is most commonly performed. It took as its chief material the legends and histories of the great Javanese kingdoms of the past, though other material such as Chinese legends, western fairy tales, and middle eastern tales might sometimes be performed as well.

Komunitas Pak Kanjeng—a group that formed around Emha Ainun Nadjib and the core members of the production of the play, *Pak Kanjeng*, which was particularly active in opposing the prohibition on the play's performance in Surabaya in February, 1994.

Konglomerat—name for the huge Indonesian corporations which became prevalent during the 1980s and which owned businesses in many sectors of the economy.

Kyai—an Islamic scholar, often running an Islamic boarding school in many parts of rural and urban Indonesia.

Lautan Jilbab—a play written by Emha Ainun Nadjib and first directed by Agung Waskito and performed by members of Sanggar Shalahuddin, a Gajah Mada University campus-based Islamic cultural organization. First performed in 1988, the play was mounted several times over the next three years, always drawing large audiences, sparking much interest among Muslim arts observers and receiving significant media attention.

Lekra—(Lembaga Kebudayaan Rakyat) A left nationalist cultural organization that often worked closely with the Indonesian Communist Party (PKI) from 1950–1965. Long vilified as having persecuted non-communist arts figures in the 1963–1965 period, the group strongly supported the policies of President Sukarno, held a radically egalitarian nationalist vision of politics, and believed that art was always imbued with particular political views and ideologies.

Lembaga Swadaya Masyarakat—(LSM) Non-government organizations or Social Self-help Institutes, these organizations were often dedicated to small scale development projects to improve the lives and economic conditions of Indonesia's less well off citizens. Other groups engaged in legal aid or advocacy work.

Lenong—a type of popular theater prevalent in the early twentieth century in the environs of Dutch Batavia (present-day Jakarta).

Ludruk—A form of popular theater originating in East Java in the late nineteenth and early twentieth centuries. It was considered to be a theater of the urban lower classes which took as its primary material the perils and rewards of adapting to life in the city. A significant feature of traditional *ludruk* was the fact that men played all the roles, including those of female characters.

Madzhab—One of four schools of Islamic jurisprudence.

Malaikat—An angel.

Marsinah: Nyanyian Dari Bawah Tanah—A 1994 play by Ratna Sarumpaet and performed by her company, *Satu Merah Panggung* with Ratna herself in the lead role. Takes the issues of government corruption, abuse of human rights, and gender inequities as its key themes. The name Marsinah in the play's title recalls the name of a labor activist/factory worker from East Java who was brutally raped and murdered in 1993. Her story became the inspiration for the play, parts of which suggest that Marsinah is the model for the play's lead character.

Marsinah Menggugat—A 1997 monologue written and performed by Ratna Sarumpaet which takes up more directly Marsinah's life, murder, and the subsequent perceived judicial coverup, when several workers at the factory were coerced into confessing involvement in her murder. Several performances of *Marsinah Mengugat* were banned in the second half of 1997.

Merah Bolong Putih Doblong Hitam—A 1997 Teater Payung Hitam production created by Rachman Sabur and members of the group. The set for *Merah Bolong* consisted of gravel painted red and white, many small stones, and larger stones suspended on all sides of the stage by ropes. This was meant to suggest the harsh environment, especially for democracy, in late New Order Indonesia.

Mesin Baru—A 1997 production by Teater ABU which contrasted the lives of factory owners/managers and ordinary workers.

Metatheater—A 1991 multi-media theater production in Bandung involving Teater Payung Hitam, set designer and artist Herry Dim, composers from the Depot Kreasi Seni Bandung, and artists Maman Noor, Arahmaiani, and Diyanto.

Nyanyian Pabrik—Teater ABU's inaugural performance in 1993, featuring dance and song with text taken from the works of a number of poets as well as Arifin C Noer's play, *Kapai-Kapai*.

Ombak-Ombak—An Arena Teater play written by Indro Gunawan, Fred Wibowo, and others and first performed at the 1981 people's theater workshop at Parangtritis, Central Java. Performed several times thereafter, the play deals with the efforts of the youth of a poor Central Javanese coastal village to come to grips with their village's poverty and their own lack of fulfilling options for creating a brighter future.

Opera Kecoa—A play written by N. Riantiarno and first performed by Teater Koma under Riantiarno's direction in 1985. The play represents the lives of a marginal urban community struggling to avoid displacement by a government development scheme. Prominently featuring a transvestite character, as well as several prostitute roles, the play's planned second production, in preparation for a Japanese tour, was banned in late 1990.

Pak Kanjeng—A 1993 play by Emha Ainun Nadjib performed by Joko Kamto, Butet Kartarejasa, and Novi Budyanto. It took the forced displacement of Javanese peasants from their land as its central theme. The play's planned 1994 production in Surabaya was banned.

Pancasila—Indonesia's official national ideology. It has five principles: belief in one supreme God; a just and civilized humanity; the unity of Indonesia; democracy guided by inner wisdom in the unanimity arising out of deliberations among representatives; social justice for all Indonesian people.

Pembangunan—"Development." This word served as something of a government mantra during the New Order era. The successes of the New Order in promoting economic development served to legitimate the regime.

Peranakan—Indonesians of Chinese or mixed Chinese descent who had lived for some generations in Indonesia and who had acculturated themselves to local society.

Pertumbuhan di Atas Meja Makan—A Teater Sae play written by Afrizal Malna and performed in 1991. The piece took up themes of censorship, the role of intellectuals in public life, and the inability of language to express our most intense feelings in a fragmented, montage-like style.

Pesantren—Traditional Muslim boarding schools.

Pesta rakyat—Concept used by Fred Wibowo in characterizing how theater should allow the masses to express themselves, take the side of the people's own interests, be the voice of conscience and reason, and not differentiate between the protagonist and the audience.

Polemik Kebudayaan—1930s polemic, occurring most famously in the pages of the journal, Pujangga Baru (Poedjangga Baroe). This polemic was primarily concerned with establishing the best basis for the new national culture, and its arguments often focused on whether this new culture should imitate the West, or draw on Eastern culture as its chief source.

Priyayi—Javanese bureaucratic servants, initially of the Javanese kingdoms, later of the Dutch colonial administration. Though these positions were not hereditary, there was a strong continuity of family members in many cases.

Qori—Members of the chorus in Lautan Jilbab and other Islamic plays by the Yogyakarta group in which Emha Ainun Nadjib was a pivotal figure. Originally, this term referred to a male Quranic reader.

rakyat (kecil)—The people; "little" people, or ordinary people when modified by "kecil" (little).

Sampakan—A style of folkish national theater in which cast members fluidly move back and forth between the stage and the orchestra, and which makes extensive use of clown figures and humor. The term comes from a particular kind of gamelan music usually played during quick-paced marching or battle scenes.

Samroh—An Islamic genre of music and dance from the Jakarta region, usually performed by a women's chorus after the birthday of the prophet Muhammad.

Sandhyakala Ning Majapahit—A play written by Sanusi Pané in 1932 and often performed in school pageants and nationlist youth gatherings. A section of it appears in Afrizal Malna's script for Teater Sae's 1991 performance *Pertumbuhan di Atas Meja Makan*.

Sanggar Shalahuddin—An Islamic student organization of the Yogyakarta Gajah Mada University campus which was instrumental in initiating a theater production in collaboration with Emha Ainun Nadjib and Agung Waskito in 1988, and whose members constituted much of the cast for some of the performances of 1988 and 1989 which initially generated much enthusiasm for Islamic theater and aesthetics.

Satria—A "knight." One of the castes in Hinduism, the image of the *satria* was retained in Javanese ideology as an ideal model of the proper way for a *priyayi* or bureaucratic aristocrat to act.

Satu Merah Panggung—A modern theater group based in Jakarta. Led by playwright and actress Ratna Sarumpaet.

Senandung Terpuruk Dari balik Tembok Pabrik—A 1995 TBI play about the lives and struggles of factory workers whose performances at the Taman Ismail Marzuki were banned, but which was later performed in several other venues thereafter in defiance of the authorities.

Sirkus Anjing—A play developed by Dindon WS and Teater Kubur and performed in 1989–1990. The play focuses on the lives of Jakarta's under classes and their alienation from the urban, consumerist milieu growing up all around them.

Suksesi—A 1990 ply written by Riantiarno and performed under his direction by Teater Koma. The play deals with the machinations of a ruthless king whose daughter outwits him in a struggle for power. The play was banned in October 1990 part way through its run.

Surat Cinta Bagi Marsinah di Sorga—A 1995 play by the workers' theater group, Sanggar Pabrik, which took the murder of Marsinah as its central material. The play was banned by Jakarta police, though the group found other opportunities to perform all or part of the play, and eventually won a lawsuit against the police ban.

Taman Ismail Marzuki—The performing arts center in downtown Jakarta, viewed as the premiere venue for theater productions during the 1970s and early 1980s.

Teater Musik Kaleng—A Teater Payung Hitam performance piece negatively representing the elections in Indonesia as a deafening cacophony without real meaning.

Teater Rakyat—Grassroots theater practices designed to encourage ordinary Indonesians to create plays based on their own life situations and to give participants confidence in their own abilities.

Tirakatan—A night vigil or meditation vigil, used in the early 1970s to protest government policies and corruption.

Tombol 13 (Topeng Monyet Bola Plastik)—A 1994 play constructed by Dindon WS and Teater Kubur, the piece continued Kubur's exploration of the alienation of urban lower classes, while adding significant new themes such as gender issues and the militarization of society.

Topeng—Literally, "mask," the word denotes both masks used to conceal identities as well as several traditional performance genres which involve either a single or many masked dancers.

Tumbal—A 1985 play written by Fred Wibowo and performed by Arena Teater, it takes up the issue of the skewed development between cities and villages in Indonesia.

Ulama—An Islamic scholar.

Umat—The community, especially members of a religious community, most commonly used in relation to Islam.

Wayang golek—Popular rod puppet theater of West Java. Thought to have its origins in the nineteenth century, this form takes as its most frequent material the lives and adventures of the heroes of the Mahabharata epic. The role of the clowns has grown considerably in recent years.

Wayang kulit—The shadow puppet theater of Central-East Java, and Bali. Existing since as early as the first millenium of the current era, this form has undergone many changes with distinct differences in performance between Javanese and Balinese versions. *Wayang kulit* still remains popular with large sections of the population. Its most common material is the lives and adventures of the heroes of the Mahabharata epics. There is currently extensive experimentation occurring with this form.

Wayang wong—A theater using human dancers to portray the same story material as that of Wayang kulit. The movements of the dancers often reflect the movements of Wayang kulit puppets.

Zikir—A repetitive chant in praise of Allah, often consisting of the 99 names of Allah.

Appendix

Short Biographies of the Major Theater Writers, Directors, Actors, and Organizers

Fred Wibowo

Actor, writer, and director. Joined Arena Teater under the leadership of Yasso Winarto in 1964. Became leader of the group in 1969 when Winarto left for Jakarta. Studied communications, radio, television and film at Saint Gabriel's College, Hatch End, London. Beginning in 1971, he became manager of Studio Audio-Visual PUSKAT, Yogyakarta. He directed and helped produce numerous educational videos while managing PUSKAT. Attended a grassroots theater workshop in Manila and upon his return began to move Arena Teater in the direction of a more active political engagement in support of people-centered development. Has also written numerous television scripts. In recent years, he has acted occasionally in film.

Emha Ainun Nadjib

Born on 27 May 1953 in Jombang, East Java. Studied at the Pesantren Gontor, and finished his secondary school in Yogyakarta. Joined the Persada Study Club under the leadership of Umbu Landu Paranggi while briefly attending Gajah Mada University in Yogyakarta. Participated in grassroots theater workshop in the Philippines in 1980, then went on to attend the International Writing Program in Iowa City USA (1984), and was invited to take part in poetry festivals in Rotterdam (1984) and West Berlin (1985). Became actively involved with

Teater Dinasti in Yogyakarta from the early 1980s till 1988, writing several plays for the group. Wrote regular columns for *Masa Kini* and other Yogyakarta newspapers. From 1988 to 1991, involved in Islamic theater efforts centered on Yogya. He has published many volumes of poetry, essays, columns, and novels. He travels frequently, giving talks on contemporary social and religious issues, and regularly holds large cultural gatherings monthly at Padang Bulan in East Java.

Boedi S. Otong

Born in Bandung on 28 August 1957. Son of a well-placed Sundanese family, he was active in Arifin C Noer's Teater Kecil in the mid-1970s. Helped train original Teater Sae members, then played a key role in reforming the group in 1977. Won awards for Best Director and Best Artistic Design in the Jakarta Youth Theater Festival three years in succession (1981–83). Collaborated with writer Afrizal Malna on a series of highly acclaimed productions in which Sae's pioneering, experimental form was developed (1983–84; 1989–93). Moved to Switzerland in the late 1990s and has continued to perform in experimental theater in Europe, returning regularly to Indonesia.

Titi Margesti Ningsih

Born in Bandung, West Java, on 21 August 1959. Active in theater since 1977. Won award as Best Actress in Jakarta Youth Theater Festival of 1978. Married Teater Sae director Boedi S. Otong. Performed in productions of acclaimed theater director Teguh Karya and choreographer Sardono in 1987. Performed in all of Sae's major productions between 1987 and 1993. Began working with industrial workers under the group name Teater ABU in 1993 and has continued to lead and direct Teater ABU until the present.

Afrizal Malna

Born in Jakarta on 7 June, 1957. Graduated from secondary school in 1976 and enrolled in Driyarkara Higher School of Philosophy beginning in 1981 as a special student. Won the Golden Windmill award sponsored by Radio Netherlands Wereldomroep in the same year. Collaborated with Boedi S. Otong and Teater Sae as scriptwriter for its seminal experimental performances of 1983 and 1984 and 1989 through 1993. Has written several collections of poetry, short stories, and a novel. Also active in the Urban Poor Consortium (c. 1998–2002) and involved in independent video production from 1998 on.

Zainal Abidin Domba

Born in Pekalongan, Central Java, on 14 April 1957. Joined Teater Sae in 1979 and won awards as best actor two years running in the Jakarta Youth Theater Festival (1982–1983). Leading actor for Teater Sae throughout the 1980s and its highly acclaimed series of performances of the 1990s. He has since gone on to success and public recognition as a television and film actor.

Dindon W. S.

Born in Jakarta on 10 August 1959. The son of a father who enjoyed theater and the arts, Dindon became involved in theater in East Jakarta in 1979 by joining Teater Adinda. Joined Teater Sae in 1980 and acted in most of the group's performances from 1980 to 1984. Participated in an all-Southeast Asian Theater Festival in Manila in 1982 with Teater Sae, and briefly attended the Driyarkara Higher School of Philosophy. Acted with Teater Kecil from 1984 to 1988. Founded Teater Kubur in 1983 and with this group won Jakarta Youth Festival awards for best director, best artistic design, and best group three years in succession (1986–1988). Gained increasing recognition for himself and Kubur beginning with the experimental performance of *Sirkus Anjing* (1989) and *Tombol 13* (1994). Has continued to direct Teater Kubur in various experimental pieces up to the present, as well as serving as a member of the Jakarta Arts Council's (Dewan Kesenian Jakarta) Theater Committee.

Arist Merdeka Sirait

Born on a tea plantation in Simalungun, Pematang Siantar, North Sumatra. Son of a plantation school teacher, Arist grew up playing with migrant Javanese children of plantation workers. His father stressed education, and Arist went to university, graduating with a degree from the faculty of Law. After spending several years trying to build a career as a musician in hotels near Danau Toba and Padang Sidempuan in North Sumatra, he moved to Jakarta and became involved in an NGO urban mission, active in informing industrial workers in the greater Jakarta area of their rights. Was sent to study in South Korea and the Philippines (1986–87), and upon his return to Indonesia, established a legal aid and advocacy foundation for workers and farmers, Yayasan Sisbikum. Through Yayasan Sisbikum, helped found TBI and guided it until conflicts between Sisbikum and the worker-members of the group caused TBI to break with Sisbikum. Has also been a strong advocate for regulating and protecting child laborers, and helped found Kompak, an NGO that struggles for the rights of child laborers.

Wowok Hesti Prabowo

Born in Purwodadi, Grobongan, Central Java on 16 April 1963. After finishing secondary school he moved to Surabaya, where he operated a factory laboratory for two years. Eventually, he moved to Tangerang and found employment as a factory worker. Became the head of the local government-controlled union at the factory and personnel manager at the PT Berlina factory but was fired for being too sympathetic to the workers (according to factory management). Finished his tertiary education in the Faculty of Textiles, Chemical Technique at the Sheikh Yusuf Islamic University in Tangerang. Formed the Komunitas Buruh Tangerang (BUBUTAN) along with Dingu Rilesta in the early 1990s, and has consistently promoted and supported workers' cultural activities in the Tangerang area. He has published several volumes of poetry.

Ratna Sarumpaet

Born in Tarutung, North Sumatra on 16 July 1949. Her parents were politicians in pre-New Order Christian political parties but did not raise Ratna for a life in politics. Studying architecture at the University of Indonesia in 1969, she saw a production of one of Rendra's plays and decided to devote herself to theater. Soon thereafter she joined

Rendra's Bengkel Teater and after a time, set off to direct on her own. Financed by her husband, she mounted productions of Omar Kayam's *Rubaiyat* and Shakespeare's *Romeo and Juliet* and *Hamlet*. From 1976 until 1989, Ratna stopped performing theater though she continued to work in television and film. Following her return to theater, her productions maintained a clear focus on women's issues and included her two Marsinah plays (1994, 1997) as well as a play about conditions in Aceh, *Alia, Luka Serambi Mekka* (2000), and *Jamila and Sang Presiden* (2006), which dealt with the issue of trafficking in women. Ratna has been head of the Jakarta Arts Council, and has been a strong supporter of women in the modern theater, helping organize various events and festivals of women's theater.

Rachman Sabur

Born in Bandung, West Java on 12 September 1957. Born to parents with a strong interest in the arts, Rachman displayed an interest in the arts from an early age. As a youth he wrote poetry and attempted to enter a literature faculty when first applying to university. However, after failing to gain such admittance, he entered the Akademi Sinematografi, but soon switched to ASTI-Bandung's Theater Department (1979). Following completion of a Bachelor's degree in theater at ASTI, he obtained an Artist's degree in dance composition from STSI-Surakarta, Central Java. Returned to teach in the theater program at ASTI Bandung. Has performed with STB, ASTI-Bandung's in-house productions, and has directed many plays and performances of his own group, Teater Payung Hitam, since 1982. He has also directed studio productions for STSI (formerly ASTI)-Bandung and for the Bandung Station of National Television. Has given workshops and performances, sometimes with Payung Hitam, in Japan, Thailand, Australia, Germany, and Canada.

Tony Broer

Joined Payung Hitam in 1988 and participated in over thirty productions for the group over the next twelve years, including the signature role of Kaspar in several versions of Payung Hitam's most acclaimed work. Has traveled to Australia, Germany, and Japan. In 2000, took part in a joint Japanese-Indonesian production, *Whalers of the South Seas*, in which he played a leading role. Has since joined the theater program at STSI Bandung as an instructor.

N. Riantiarno

Born on 6 June 1949 in Cirebon, West Java. Has been active in theater since attending secondary school in Cirebon. After finishing secondary school, studied at the Indonesian National Theater Academy (ATNI) in Jakarta and the Driyarkarya Advanced School of Philosophy. Joined Teguh Karya's Teater Populer in 1968. Helped found Teater Koma in 1977, and became the group's chief playwright and director, while his wife, Ratna Riantiarno (née Madjid), worked as the group's publicist, promotor, and main actress. The group rose to fame with its trilogy portraying the lives of slum dwellers and transvestites, *Bom Waktu* (Time Bomb, 1982), *Opera Kecoa* (Cockroach Opera, 1985), and *Opera Julini* (Julini's Opera, 1986), and by 2001 Koma had mounted 93 stage and television productions. Riantiarno was a five-time winner of the dramatic script-writing contest sponsored by the Dewan Kesenian Jakarta (Jakarta Arts Council), 1972–75 and 1998, and has won awards for his television and film scripts as well. He has worked in the media for the news and feature magazine *Zaman* (1979–86) and helped found another magazine, *Matra,* in 1986. He has also directed a film and, more recently, written and published several novels.

Notes

*Chapter 1: The Modern National Theater and
the Indonesian New Order State*

1. Since the most extensively studied elites are the Javanese *priyayi*, and since Javanese elites have had such strong political and cultural influences on the development of Indonesian national culture, especially since independence, I have argued previously (Bodden 2007a) that examining the effect of Dutch colonial and educational policies on them is an important means of understanding the way in which national culture developed in partial antagonism to the Indonesian state. To be sure, some non-Javanese elites may have had quite different perspectives on culture and art, while others, such as the Malays, possessed cultural ideologies which, though not precisely the same, had many points in common with those of the Javanese *priyayi*. Still, through Dutch education and the growing influence of Javanese culture on national culture, I would argue that intellectuals' and modern theater workers' views on art increasingly came to be shaped by a combination of conservative Dutch bourgeois and *priyayi* or similar traditional aristocratic values and aesthetics. For evidence of Malay elite culture's similarities to Javanese *priyayi* systems for signifying social and aesthetic value, see Milner on Malay culture (2008, 65, 195, 238). It also seems likely there is substantial overlap between Malay literary aesthetics and theory and those of the Javanese courts, particularly in the sense that beauty, *indah*, should be orderly and that literary works should possess moral or educational value that often can only be discerned by a superior act of cognition of a hidden beauty or truth (Braginsky 2004, 243–60).

2. This phrase that has so often been interpreted to mean that day-to-day politics of the Communist Party (the PKI) would dictate the content of artworks was in fact interpreted in different ways by leftist cultural

workers. Some indeed attempted to follow the Party's political line as closely as possible in their works. Others argued that the phrase simply acknowledged that the political context always conditions, to varying extents, the form and content of artworks and that no artworks escape some form of political shaping or statement, no matter how subtle or indirect.

3. Bourchier 1997. It is perhaps indicative of the rising power of the new Indonesian middle-class that the attempt to install integralist notions of the state was blocked in the late 1980s at roughly the same time that Indonesian postmodernism began to emerge.

4. In Raymond Williams's *Marxism and Literature*, "structures of feeling" are defined as a kind of social feeling and thinking of lived experience or proto-ideology not yet able to be articulated in an organized sense, that most often are manifest in periodic general changes of style—language, dress, manners, building, the forms and conventions of literature, music and so on. See Williams 1977, 130–35.

5. To be fair, Riantiarno's Teater Koma should be recognized as a group that has always included in its work a measure of social criticism. This criticism became sharper and more directly political, causing the group to run afoul of the security and censorial apparatus, precisely at the beginning of the 1990s when Suharto publicly called for increased openness, and when the middle-class, according to Heryanto's analysis, began to become restless under the constraints of the New Order's corporatist authoritarianism (see chapter 7). Thus, Riantiarno and Koma are interesting in the world of theater for two reasons: they represent the rise of a more commercially oriented middle-class culture but at the same time also lead the way in expressing some of the key general social and political concerns of large segments of that class.

6. These theaters are Padepokan Bengkel Teater Rendra (1988), Teater Oncor (1989), Teater Dalam Gang Tuti Indra Malaon (1993), and Teater Utan Kayu (1997).

7. For more information on Bentang's operations and objectives, see "Penerbit Bentang Budaya," *Media Kerja Budaya*, 1 (Nov. 1994): 30–33.

8. However, it must be noted that this is not the case with all Indonesian postmodernists. Cultural critic Nirwan Dewanto, for example, saw "the market" as a source of salvation from the feudal-bureaucratic strictures that govern New Order society. Dewanto attributed to the market the positive virtues of encouraging competition, negotiation, experiment, quality control, and openness. Those who didn't accept the market were only those who live in the world of the "palace" (*kerajaan*), he wrote (1995).

9. This permit application process also applied to many other activities aiming to attract large audiences/public participation, such as seminars, meetings, and the like.

10. A number of informal conversations with friends from the theater community suggested that certain plays were withheld from performance for fear that they wouldn't be passed by New Order censors. Others preferred to cast their criticisms in the form of an allegory or *pasemon* using actual or quasi-historical stories so as to create a cognitive distance with contemporary conditions. Another method was to write a script based on topics that did not relate to public politics but which could be seen as containing analogous relations—such as stories of power and domination within a family.

11. This also suggests a key difference between theater and the print media as well, since print media risked considerable financial loss, along with unemployment for a large group of regular employees, if they were to be closed temporarily or have their publishing permit withdrawn.

12. That the modern theater was not a reliably lucrative venture during the 1970s and early 1980s was also partly due to the deeply ingrained resistance within the arts community to seeing their work as a commercial product. Long linked closely to the staunchly anti-commercial artistic ideology of modern high art literature, artistic activity was seen by many as something divorced from the tainted world of money and finance. Evidence for such attitudes can be found in Goenawan Mohamad's watershed 1973 essay, "Sebuah Pembelaan Teater Indonesia Mutakhir" (A Defense of the Latest Indonesian Theater), esp. pp. 100–22 (Mohamad 1980, 91–142), where Mohamad discusses the organic relationship of modern theater workers to their audiences as well as the disdain of older Western-influenced theater practitioners and some contemporary critics toward modern groups' use of humor in their performances, that in the opinion of such critics was inserted simply to attract larger audiences. Also, revealing of these attitudes are articles in the magazine *Tempo*, "Teater Djalan Buntu Atau Didjalan Normal" (Theater at a Dead End or Theater on a Normal Course, 12 Aug. 1972, 32–38) and Cholid et al., "Bisnis Malu-Malu Kucing" (18 Mar. 1989, 104, 106). For a clear signal of continuing resistance among arts practitioners to viewing modern theater as an economic venture, see Putu Wijaya's 1996 essay, "Pelacuran Teater" (Prostituting Theater) in which the author vigorously urges other theater workers to "prostitute theater," to take up the challenge of "the market" and to find ways to popularize theater with paying audiences (Wijaya 1997, 368–78). Anti-commercial attitudes began to be undermined during the New Order, but the real rush to the "market" did not gain momentum until the second half of the 1980s (Cholid et al. 1989 [*Tempo*, 18 Mar.], 104–6). Again, see Goenawan Mohamad 1980 "Sebuah Pembelaan untuk Teater Indonesia Mutakhir" in *Seks, Sastra, Kita*, 91–142. (Jakarta: Sinar Harapan,). Mohamad argues that during the late 1960s and early 1970s, the

management of the Taman Ismail Marzuki encouraged all forms of performance, thus creating conditions in which modern practitioners not only saw one another's work but also the performances of a variety of older traditional kinds of theater. One of the most important lessons that the modern theater workers such as Arifin C Noer and Rendra learned from the older traditional forms was that such older forms worked to create an intimacy with their particular audience. This realization launched a number of new tradition theater workers on an exploration of traditional theater, elements of which they consciously incorporated into their own practice. It also encouraged them to think differently about the relationship of theater to its audience and eventually to imagine a more viable new tradition commercial theater.

13. For instance, organizers of the planned Feb. 1994 Surabaya performance of Emha Ainun Nadjib and Komunitas Pak Kanjeng's play, *Pak Kanjeng*, had to seek permission or recommendations from the following: (1) Permit to use building; (2) Surabaya Department of Education and Culture (*Depdikbud*); (3) Head of the County Police for South Surabaya (*Polres Sursel*); (4) the District Office of the East Javanese Department of Education and Culture (*Kanwil Depdikbud Jatim*); (5) the Police Chief of East Java (*Kapolda Jatim*); and (6) the Commander of the 5th Military region/Brawijaya Command (*Kodam V/Brawijaya*) (*Kompas*, 2 Feb. 1994). Presumably, the provincial military and police commanders were required to vet this particular permit because of the notoriety of the play's author, Nadjib, as well as for contextual reasons that I will discuss later.

Regulations for obtaining a performance permit also varied according to the composition of the group involved. A Teater Buruh Indonesia (Indonesian Worker's Theater) performance permit, granted in Bogor but not in Jakarta in 1995, required the group to submit its request to the following desks: (1) Jakarta Area Cultural Office (*Dinas Kebudayaan DKI*); (2) Jakarta Area Tourism Office (*Dinas Parawisata DKI*); (3) Jakarta Metropolitan Region Police (*Polda Metro Jaya*); (4) the Jakarta Socio-Political Directorate (*Direktorat Sosial-Politik DKI Jakarta*); (5) The Jakarta Regional Military Command (*Kodam Jaya*); (6) the Area Labor Resources Office (*Kanwil Tenaga Kerja*); (7) the Labor Resources Office (*Dinas Tenaga Kerja*); (8) the Jakarta All-Indonesian Workers' Federation Branch (*SPSI—Serikat Buruh Seluruh Indonesia—DKI*); and (9) Social Guidance (*Binsos*) (*Jayakarta*, 27 May 1995).

Chapter 2: Grassroots Indonesian Theater

1. Those groups include the KTRI (Kelompok Teater Rakyat Indonesia or Indonesian People's Theater Group), Emha Ainun Nadjib and Teater

Dinasti, a group around theater activist Indro Gunawan, ITRJ (Institut Teater Rakyat Jogja or Yogya People's Theater Institute), Kelompok Pinggiran in Solo, and Yasanti (Yayasan Annisa Swasti or Private Sector Women's Foundation).

2. These ideas are articulated as part of Brecht's "Kleines Organon für das Theater," sections 20–25 and 35–52.

3. Wibowo and Arena materials were my main sources of information on the Tanen Pakem project. Unfortunately, I was unable to solicit firsthand accounts from the villagers involved to gain their impressions of the workshop and related events. This fact certainly influences my narrative of the project and should be taken into account.

4. The Indonesian reads:
> Jali: Ini pengadilan masyarakat, pak. Hakimnya pilihan penguasa tertinggi negara.
> Boying: Astaga! Apakah saudara semua ini fungsionaris negara yang berhak menunjuk hakim?
> Ola: Lho dalam negara demokrasi, penguasa tertinggi negara kan rakyat. Nah kami semua ini kan rakyat.

5. This information is based on personal conversations with Fred Wibowo and a number of his associates both from Arena Teater and from Studio Audiovisual PUSKAT. Also information comes from three pre-publication manuscripts given to me by Wibowo that contain the theoretical justification and practical instructions for the kind of theatrical practice that Arena seeks to create in its grass-roots activities, i.e., the *Pesta Rakyat* (People's Festival). The socio-political court cases of Mario Kaplun, developed for Latin American radio stations that asked the listeners to act as jurors, were also known to Arena members who recorded them as dramas in 1983. Thus, it is highly likely these cases also inspired Arena's own version of "courtroom" drama (Van Erven 1992, 192).

6. The courtroom frame is evident in Brecht's *Lehrstücke* (Teaching/Learning Plays) such as *Die Maßnahme* (1930) and *Die Ausnahme und die Regel* (1930) but also in his later works such as *Das Verhör des Lukullus* (1938–39) and *Der kaukasische Kreidekreis* (1943–45).

7. The Indonesian reads:
> Maya: Mengapa keadaan desa kita dibandingkan kota terlampau jauh bedanya?
> Wasa: Aku tak tahu. Mungkin ada teman-teman yang tahu?
> Kelompok Semua (Koor):
> Tidak, kami tak tahu
> Kami kan petani biasa-biasa saja
> Yang patuh dan setia

Kepada yang berkuasa
Kami terus berusaha
Mengolah nasib sebisanya
Tanpa banyak prasangka
Meski hidup tetap menderita.

8. This series of choral statements is reminiscent of two aspects of Brechtian theater. The terse summary of who the peasants are and how they fit into the social structure is very similar to the way in which characters introduce themselves in Brecht's *Die Maßnahme*. Secondly, the way in which Maya and Wasa pose questions, which the Koor then refutes through argumentation, is similar to the debates involving choruses in *Das Badener Lehrstück vom Einverständnis* and *Die Maßnahme*.

9. The term *desa binaan* means "village under development," a term that also suggests a certain amount of paternalistic control by someone or some institution that must guide the development, much as the New Order government did with its various *"Binaan"* and *"Pembinaan"* projects. Here, the implication is that Indro and his group were guiding the village's development. This, too, hints at the ways in which inter-class collaboration is fraught with tensions, including those produced by differences in education and social status, and those resulting from the fact that even the regime's critics and opponents had, to some extent, absorbed some of its patterns of viewing and ordering social relations.

10. As Hatley has noted, the government did use a kind of teater rakyat to promote some of its programs and messages. Yet this theater was quite different from the grassroots theater pursued by Arena and the other groups discussed in this chapter. It was usually conceived and performed by middle-class and elite cultural workers in an idiom thought to be closer to popular entertainment, rather than by ordinary Indonesians themselves. Similarly, its emphasis on conveying government messages was at odds with the grassroots theater goal of empowering ordinary people to create and perform plays about their own problems (Hatley 2008, 136–39).

11. *Dangdut* is a popular, commercialized music blending Middle Eastern, South Asian, and Indonesian sounds, and using modern amplified instruments such as guitars together with traditional flutes. Its themes are most often love, although Rhoma Irama, the star who first popularized, if not invented, the genre, has created many songs that focus on Islamic faith and social issues.

12. The original Indonesian would read: "Dalam konteks ini dialog yang perlu dikembangkan untuk interaksi sosial yang demokratis itu haruslah berupa lambang-lambang, kodifikasi atau bahasa yang mereka kenal. Selain bahasa verbal seni rakyat adalah lambang-lambang yang

sering lebih efektif dan secara tepat dapat mengungkapkan dan mengekspresikan maksud mereka..."

13. "Teater rakyat bukan untuk revolusi, tetapi untuk menciptakan tatanan dunia yang baru berdasarkan persaudaran, perdamaian, keadilan."

Chapter 3: Asas Tunggal *and Laughter in the Mosque: Indonesian Islamic Theater on the National Stage*

1. See cover notes to 1992 printing of Emha's *Indonesia Bagian Dari Desa Saya* (Yogyakarta: Sipress).

2. The collection was published in 1989, but the cycle was first written in 1986.

3. Emha Ainun Nadjib, *Syair Lautan Jilbab* (Yogyakarta: Sipress, 1989), p. 1. The Indonesian is as follows:

Dan mereka bernyanyi:
Kekasih, Ya Kekasih!
Kalau mula dan akhir kita satu
Kenapa harus begini lama berburu!

Kalau dulu dan kelak kita sama
Untuk apa bikin jarak yang maya
Kalau Engkaulah asal-usul hamba
Kenapa harus menantiMu sampai gila

4. The Indonesian is as follows:

Buku-buku pelajaran memakan kami
Tontonan dan siaran melahap kami
Iklan dan barang-barang jualan menggiring kami
Panggung dan meja-meja birokrasi mengelabui kami
Mesin pembodoh kami sangka bangku sekolah
Ladang-ladang peternakan kami sangka rumah ibadah
Mulut kami terbungkam, mata kami menangis darah
Hidup ialah mendaki pundak orang-orang lain...

5. It should be emphasized here that Brenner also feels that there are limits to the self-empowerment this act might signify for individual women. A number of the stories she recorded regarding decisions to don the *jilbab* included accounts of peer and sibling pressure.

6. Here I use the capitalized and italicized form, *Jilbab* to denote Nadjib's synechdochic use of the word to designate those who wear the garb. I thus use the uncapitalized and italicized word, *jilbab*, to denote the actual article of clothing itself.

7. Barbara Hatley provides additional information on Jamaah Shalahuddin and its ties to the UGM student community as well as to Emha

Ainun Nadjib in her *Javanese Performances on An Indonesian Stage: Contesting Culture, Embracing Change* (Singapore: Asian Studies Association of Australia and NUS Press, 2008), pp. 149–50.

8. The reported figures are as follows: Yogyakarta, 10–11 Sept. 1988, 5,000 (Waskito 1988); Ujung Pandang, 9–10 Aug. 1989, 9700 (*Kedaulatan Rakyat*, 20 Aug. 1989); Madiun, 27–28 Apr. 1991, 35,000 (*Jawa Pos*, 29 Apr. 1991; Surabaya, 12–13 Aug. 1991, 10,000 (*Suara Indonesia*, 14 Aug. 1991).

9. As evidence that Nadjib had good reason for making such a change, less than a year later he was accused by a group led by several well-known modernists from Yogyakarta of writing poetry full of "polytheism" (*menserikatkan Tuhan*). Nadjib's poetry was said to contain the same spirit as the "negative" teachings of famous Sufi martyrs Al Hallaj and Syech Siti Jenar, and he was accused of "personifying" God. Though the complaint and the scheduled "hearing" were later cancelled, this incident is suggestive of the tensions existing within Indonesian Islam between modernists and more traditional Muslims (*Panji Masyarakat*, 22 Jul.–1 Aug. 1989, 25; *Panji Masyarakat*, 11–20 Sept. 1989).

10. *The Koran*, translated by N. J. Dawood (London: Penguin Books, 1990) 264.

11. Comments such as these appeared in the following newspapers: *Fajar*, 10 Aug. 1989; *Pedoman Rakyat*, 10 Aug. 1989; *Kedaulatan Rakyat*, 20 Aug. 1989; *Jawa Pos*, 8 Apr. 1991. See also the *sambutan* (greetings) of the committee and other figures in the program for the Surabaya performance of the play titled "Pagelaran Drama Kolosal *Lautan Jilbab*" (Surabaya: Organizing Committee, 1991).

12. The Indonesian is as follows:
> PENARI 1: Menari juga ndak dilarang lho Mas Penyair. Pernah ada seorang sahabat Rasul, saking gembiranya mendengar indahnya untaian kalimat Nabinya, ia lantas mendendang-dendangkan puisi dan tak sengaja menari-nari. Rasul tidak melarang, bahkan tersenyum dan menyukainya.
> PENYAIR: Tapi ini di Indonesia lho Dik. Harus hati-hati. Kalau di Masjid, jangan tertawa, jangan bertepuk tangan, apalagi menari-nari.

13. "Seperti kita sepakati bersama, Masjid harus kita budayakan. Masjid harus kita jadikan tempat yang menyenangkan, yang menarik hati dan merangsang rasa cinta semua Remaja Masjid terhadap kehidupan yang segar dan bermutu.

"Masjid adalah ujung tombak dakwah. Masjid harus mampu mengungkapkan suara indah ajaran Allah, yang lebih indah dibanding segala keindahan. Masjid tak boleh membosankan, suasananya jangan kering, setiap kegiatannya harus membuat setiap Muslim dan Muslimat merasa krasan di dalamnya, serta membuat kawan-kawan lain yang belum beragama Islam merasa kepingiiiiin banget terlibat di dalamnya."

14. "Soal kesenian Islam saja berdebat ndak habis-habis. Orang lain sudah pada menguasai televisi, panggung, pasar kaset, iklan-iklan di sepanjang jalan, koran dan majalah—mereka masih ribut mencapai definisi kesenian Islam. Gitu kok mau tinggal landas! Menyongsong abad 21! Era industrialisasi!"

15. This general theme haunts the articles covering the performances. For example, in the *Kedaulatan Rakyat* article, "'Lautan Jilbab' Menggetarkan Masyarakat Ujung Pandang" (20 Aug. 1989), the writer remarks that the play's Ujung Pandang performance defeated rock concerts and other popular entertainment by attracting close to 10,000 spectators. Following the Madiun performances, Nadjib stated that "Lautan Jilbab" was intended as an alternative to non-Islamic entertainments, such as discos, cinemas and others (Upacara Sujud Lautan Jilbab, *Jawa Pos*, 29 Aug. 1991). Statements by Nadjib and journalists during the Surabaya performances echoed these sentiments (*Surabaya Post* and *Jawa Pos*, 13 Aug. 1991).

16. *Dajjal* was first staged in Yogyakarta on 3–5 Aug. 1989, then performed in Jakarta's Taman Ismail Marzuki sometime in October of that year.

17. *Wayang Wong* is a traditional type of performance which, like *Wayang Kulit*, takes as its material the stories of the Mahabharata and Ramayana epics, but is acted out by live human actors rather than puppets. Ironically, the actors' movements and stances are modelled on those of the puppets of *Wayang Kulit*.

18. It is of some interest that the initiative to have the play performed as part of the Congress was taken not by Muhammadiyah itself, but also by members of its women's auxiliary, Aisyiyah (*Jawa Pos*, 8 Dec. 1990).

19. The Indonesian is: "aurat dibuka-buka, dibeber-beber di layar bioskop dan dalam majalah . . . "

20. Among the more tell-tale headlines are "5,000 Penonton Tenggelam dalam Lautan Jilbab" (5000 Spectators Sink into the Ocean of Jilbabs, *Pedoman Rakyat*, 10 Aug. 1989); "'Lautan Jilbab' Meledak, Diserbu Lautan Manusia" ('Ocean of Jilbabs' Explodes, Attacked by an Ocean of Humanity, *Fajar* 10 Aug. 1989); "Neno-Emha di 'Lautan Jilbab'" (Neno/Emha in 'Ocean of Jilbabs,' *Jawa Pos*, 8 Apr. 1991); "Neno: syair Ainun Dahsyat" (Neno: Ainun's [Nadjib's] Poems Are Amazing, *Jawa Pos*, 27 Apr. 1991); "'Lautan Jilbab' Diharapkan Meraih 40 Ribu Penonton" (It Is Hoped That 'Ocean of Jilbabs' Will Draw 40,000 Spectators, *Surabaya Post*, 27 Apr. 1991); "Lautan Jilbab di Madiun Dibanjiri Pengunjung" (Ocean of Jilbabs

is Flooded by Visitors in Madiun," *Jawa Pos*, 28 Apr. 1991); "Gito Rollies Membatalkan Show-nya di mancanegara: demi Drama Kolosal 'Lautan Jilbab'" (Gito Rollies Cancels His Shows Abroad: For the Sake of the Colossal Drama 'Ocean of Jilbabs,'" *Jawa Pos, 7 Aug. 1991);* "Emha Komandani Gladi Resik Lautan Jilbab" (Emha Takes Command of the Dress Rehearsal for Ocean of Jilbabs," *Jawa Pos*, 11 Aug. 1991); "Emha Terjun Sebagai Sutradara Kelima" (Emha Enters the Field as the Fifth Director, *Surabaya Post*, 12 Aug. 1991). Other articles which commented upon the huge numbers, compared the performances to rock concerts, played upon the celebrity status of Nadjib or the guest stars, or praised the work as inspiring Islamic art were *Kedaulatan Rakyat*, 20 Aug. 1989; *Panji Masyarakat* 622 1–10 Sept. 1989; *Yogya Post*, 10 Apr. 1991; *Jawa Pos*, 29 Apr. 1991; *Harian Umum Karya Darma*, 1 May 1991; *Surabaya Minggu*, 1st Week in May, 1991; *Jawa Pos*, 12 Aug. 1991; *Memorandum*, 12 Aug. 1991; *Surabaya Post*, 13 Aug. 1991; *Jawa Pos*, 13 Aug. 1991; *Jawa Pos*, 15 Aug. 1991.

21. The number of local *santri* used for the Ujung Pandang performance was ten (*Fajar* 10 Aug. 1989). In Madiun, the number of local performers recruited was approximately 175 (*Jawa Pos*, 8, 26, 29 Apr. 1991). At the Surabaya performances, forty local performers were involved (*Jawa Pos*, 12 Aug. 1991). This feature of the group's work was apparent in other performances as well. Nadjib's play, *Keluarga Sakinah*, was staged with approximately forty Yogyakarta Muslim school children participating in the performance, and his historical play, *Bani Khidlir*, was performed at the Gontor *pesantren* in East Java with fifty of the school's santri performing (*Jawa Pos*, 25 Jun. 1991). Nadjib was explicit in stating his desire that the performances encourage the formation of "new cultural pockets" (*kantong budaya baru*) (*Jawa Pos*, 8 Apr. 1991; *Jawa Pos*, 26, 29 Apr. 1991; *Jawa Pos*, 25 Jun. 1991).

22. *Bedug* are large drums traditionally used to call the faithful to prayers in the mosque. *Samroh* is an Islamic genre of music, usually sung by a women's chorus. At least two reports on the performance noted that the latter element did not seem to fit very well into the overall performance (*Tempo*, 24 Aug. 1991; *Surabaya Post*, 13 Aug. 1991).

23. The *Jawa Pos* paragraph quoting Djody on this point is as follows:

"Ditanya tentang kritik-kritik yang disampaikan lewat puisi-puisi *Lautan Jilbab* itu, Djodi mengatakan bahwa puisi memang cukup tajam. "Pinternya Cak Nun [Nadjib], dia bisa menetralisasi kritik yang tajam itu," katanya."

(When asked about the criticisms contained in *Lautan Jilbab*'s poetry, Djodi said that the poetry was indeed quite pointed. "Cak Nun's [Nadjib's] brilliance lies in the fact that he can neutralize such sharp criticism," he said.)

Chapter 4: Teater Sae, Teater Kubur, and Avant-Garde Performances of Urban Alienation

1. I am defining "lower middle-class" here as those social groups who made their living as small-scale merchants or in the lower ranks of the state bureaucracy, the military, and some professions. Busyra Q. Yoga's narrative of his experience with Teater Sae gives us a sense of the background of many of the group's original members, as well as that of many other youth theater members in Jakarta at that time.

> After failing in the entrance exams for University that year (1975), I decided to prioritize the search for work....
>
> Ever since that, my job was to wait and wait. That is, wait for calls about the applications I'd sent to businesses with openings, or wait for the newspaper to read the ads concerning employment opportunities. At times I grew bored with this and I'd go to another uncle's house in a different part of the city, the Jembatan Besi neighborhood in the West Jakarta area of Grogol. Sometimes I'd stay there for several weeks while waiting.
>
> My uncle in Jembatan Besi had a younger brother named Syukran, who was about my age. He was usually called Kuran for convenience's sake. Like me, his work was also "waiting." One day when I came to stay there, Kuran told me that there was a theater group in the Youth Centre that needed actors. He invited me to go along with him to the theater practices at the Youth Centre in order to fill up the time and chase away our boredom. And I agreed. That was about the beginning of or maybe mid-1976.
>
> There was [as leader of the group] Asril Joni, born in West Sumatra, who was in the process of finding himself. He'd come to Jakarta to try his luck in the midst of the harsh life of the Capital. (Yoga 1994, 1)

2. Another indicator of the group's contingent construction came as it was attempting to rebuild after the performances of its first play, *Dilarang untuk Melarang*. (For more information on this play and the circumstances surrounding it, see elsewhere in this chapter.) Yoga had invited a friend to join the group, and this friend had offered the auditorium in the Jalan Salemba Education and Culture Service Building for practices. Upon arriving, they found an eccentric young man holding theater practices with a group of primary school students. This young man and his charges were also invited to join Sae, and though the young director, Zainal Abidin (also known as Zainal Abidin Domba), did not at first agree as readily as some of his primary school charges, he eventually did consent to join and went on to become Sae's leading actor throughout the 1980s and early 1990s (Yoga 1994, 13–14). Zainal Abidin Domba came from a lower- middle-class kampung

background. His family was involved in selling animals as pets, and Domba helped support himself during his years with Sae by selling birds (Halim HD personal communication, 2008).

3. Born in Jakarta in 1957, Malna had completed only a high school education before entering the work force as an office worker. From 1981 to mid 1983, he studied philosophy at the Sekolah Tinggi Filsafat Driyarkarya in Jakarta as a special student but dropped out without finishing his studies. In 1981 he won an award for a dramatic monologue submitted to a Radio Nederland Wereldomroep competition. Shortly after the time when he and Otong became acquainted, he received an award from the Jakarta Arts Council for his first book of poetry, *Abad Berlari* (A Century Flees) (Malna 1995, 97).

4. See Williams (1989: 37–48) for a discussion of the relationship of European Modernism to the changes in cities and technologies wrought by capitalist society's development from the nineteenth century to the early twentieth century.

5. The proceedings of this discussion were later published in the organizing group's stenciled magazine *Kongko* in 1984.

6. "... bukan bahasa seni: tidak meyakinkan sebagai hasil penghayatan, tapi lebih merupakan cuplikan dari bacaan saja; atau mungkin dari pengalaman hidup, tapi belum mampu dirumuskan menjadi bahasa mengandung penghayatan. Yang muncul baru berupa rumusan-rumusan: kayak aljabar; jadi: sangat kering."

7. "Tapi itulah hanya kata-kata. Sementara yang aku ingini hanyalah diriku sendiri. Diriku yang bersih dari segala peranan."

8. "Sembilan bulan sudah, sembilan bulan sudah jiwaku disimpan di dalam rumah sakit. Dan aku biarkan saja orang-orang mengutak-utik jarum jam di tempat-tempat mereka menghabiskan waktu dengan bekerja. Dan kematian yang berdiam di dalam jarum jam itu, aku biarkan saja perlombaan ekonomi yang kejar-berkejaran di dalam laras senjata bagi tegaknya sebuah industri."

9. "... ke manakah masa depan dari modernisasi akan bertujuan. Dan jelas, itu tidak berada di dalam namaku. Suatu nama yang mencoba melihat bahwa tata perekonomian yang bagaimanakah yang bisa melihat lebih banyak lagi kepada manusia dan alam. Dan bukan suatu perekonomian yang hanya menyembah pada angka-angka. Sedang namaku bukan sebuah agama atau pun sebuah lembaga politik. Dan berlapis-lapis pakaian aku pergunakan hanya untuk menutupi tubuhku yang menyimpan kemiskinan. Suatu masa depan kematian yang dibawa oleh modernisasi."

10. After marrying Otong, Margesti changed her name to Margesti S. Otong.

11. For example, during Sae's 1992 production of *Biografi Yanti Setelah 12 Menit* (Yanti's Biography After 12 Minutes), the group received coverage

in two major news weekly magazines, *Tempo* and *Editor,* as well as articles in a number of dailies. Similarly, its 1993 production, *Migrasi dari Ruang Tamu* (Migration from the Guest Room) was widely reported. The group first performed in mid-May for a small audience of activists and arts figures (approximately sixty) in the South Jakarta Arts Practice Centre before touring to four Swiss and German cities (Zürich, Bern, Basel, Hamburg), then returning to Indonesia for stagings in Jakarta and Solo in mid- and late July. Not only did *Migrasi dari Ruang Tamu* receive coverage from prestigious dailies such as *Kompas* and *The Jakarta Post* but also from the leading weekly magazines *Tempo* and *DeTik.*

12. "Dalam penampilan SAE, suasana berdiskusi sangat dominan. Apakah teater cukup dengan ide? Apakah tontonan sudah merupakan barang kedaluwarsa?... Pementasan SAE kali ini memang ekspresif, tetapi sulit. Ia seperti sebuah esei. Esei yang melelahkan meskipun tidak berarti tidak penting."

13. Here, Malna's and Otong's ideas resemble those of Jerzy Grotowski, the pioneering director of the Polish Laboratory Theater of the 1960s and early 1970s. There is a crucial difference, however. In the 1960s, in an attempt to do away with conventional, socially constructed roles and masks, Grotowski's actors sought to unearth their deepest feelings through generally narrative plays dealing with mythical or archetypal situations. Sae actors, on the other hand, were engaged in excavating their personal realities in the course of preparing for non-narrative installations that took social constructions of identity as their very theme and sought to dismantle traditional myths.

14. In other writings, Malna, like Nirwan Dewanto, argues against talking about modern theater in grand narrative terms—for example, analyzing the state of Indonesian theater. In a 1994 article, "Teater dan Sebuah Indonesia Kecil," Afrizal attacks both modernism and national culture as dominant frames of reference for cultural analysis. Instead, he prefers to talk about the specific history and works of particular groups rather than searching for a large paradigm (Malna 1994a, 17).

15. Curiously, in Malna's text, Camus's Helicon is replaced by Caesonia, as though it were she to whom Caligula speaks in this dialogue. Does this represent an error in the Indonesian translation, or is it, as seems more likely to me, a case of Malna altering the translation of the original text slightly in order to enable it to echo and amplify the central husband-wife structure of the piece?

16. The Indonesian translation of this passage, probably taken from an English translation, reads: "Jika semua orang telah sependapat bahwa perbendaharaan adalah maha penting, maka jiwa manusia tidak penting sama sekali. Hukuman telah dijatuhkan. Dunia ini tidak penting lagi!" It

should also be noted that Malna has spliced together sentences separated in the original by additional dialogue.

17. "Aku bukan pemerintah Kolonial seperti yang dituduhkan oleh Hatta itu, aku juga bukan Sukarno yang aku ucapkan tadi."

18. "Orang terpelajar yang disewa oleh yang berkuasa di dunia adalah penghianat kepada fungsinya."

19. "Halo. Selamat pagi. Bagaimana keadaanmu? Baik-baik. Baik. Saya harap baik-baik. Kamu adalah manusia kebudayaan. Saya pun demikian. Bagaimana? Apa bisa kita mulai sekarang?"

20. "Pendamping dari keluarga yang baik, sukses, moralis, pelindung, beragama yang sama, tidak terlalu tua, kalau perlu memiliki ukuran baju yang sama juga. Pokoknya sebuah percintaan yang sesuai dengan cita-cita nasional dan lingkungan hidup: pertumbuhan, pemerataan, dan pengurasan alam tidak menjadi kontras, yang tidak melawan pembangunan, keberhasilan dan masadepan."

21. "Tetapi tahukah, ibu, bahwa Amir Hamzah telah mati, yang hanya menyerahkan cintanya pada satu orang.... Perkawinan, ibu, kini tidak lebih penting dari orang-orang yang keluar masuk kantor. Mobilitas pertemuan orang yang tinggi dalam kehidupan kota, membuat tinggi pula grafik angka-angka pertemuan dan perpisahan. Jangan sedih."

22. "Tidak ada tikus dalam biografiku, seperti kau selalu mencium bahwa pipiku berbau aluminium."

23. As Barbara Hatley (1994b) has pointed out, some of this anger may have entered the performance through the actors' self-actualization of personal tensions within the company.

24. With a script by Afrizal Malna, *Hamlet Menjelang Pemilu* (Hamlet as the General Election Draws Near) was directed by Busyra and performed in Bandung, Jakarta, and Surakarta (Solo) in late May and early June 1999.

25. The relationship of Kubur to its kampung base is different than most other Jakarta groups but may have parallels with groups in Yogyakarta and Solo, as documented by Barbara Hatley (1990, 1993).

26. "Saya ingin menjembatani gap antara pemain dan penonton, ujar Dindon suatu sa'at."

27. Interestingly enough, Boedi Otong had also expressed reservations about the festival system before Teater Sae went on to enter and win in three consecutive years. Otong's complaint was that art should not be seen as a competitive event (Yoga 1994, 16).

28. "... teater adalah sebuah misteri yang tak pernah habis dan selesai dilacak. Kalau kita merasa selesai dengan peta teater yang sudah ada sekarang ini, menurut saya pandangan itu sangat sempit. Padahal, teater memberikan ruang yang lebih besar."

29. "Pada lakon ini, Dindon berusaha mengungkapkan keluhan-keluhan rakyat kecil dengan menggali situasi yang selalu muncul dari kesumpekan, kekumuhan dan kebisingan kendaraan maupun iklan-iklan yang menggelitik kehidupan masyarakat luas."

30. "Apa yang kami pentaskan kemarin, sekaligus merupakan bahasa kami sendiri. Apalagi, kami berangkat dari situasi yang sangat marginal. Teater Kubur tidak punya penyandang dana atau bos. Kami berangkat dari kemiskinan yang sesungguhnya, yang selalu menentukan kami harus selalu bercerdik-cerdik menggali dari apa yang ada pada diri kami untuk selanjutnya diberi makna.... Saya pikir, Teater Kubur berangkat dari persoalan kita dan masyarakat. Setelah saya dan teman-teman bersentuhan dengan nilai-nilai, kondisi sosial, ekonomi, politik, dan juga sistem di sekeliling kita, saya rasa hal itu yang akhirnya membuat kami merasa sebagai bagian yang tak bisa dilepaskan dari masyarakat. Artinya, apa pun tema yang akan kami angkat, pasti akan berangkat dari berbagai persoalan masyarakat yang terdekat dengan kita."

31. "Kenapa saya tidak memakaikan *make up* pada pemain saya, misalnya, itu karena saya pikir kekuatan ekspresi pemain sudah memberi *make up* yang orisinal. Kalau kami paksakan, maka ketrampilan sang aktor berekspresi jadi terbunuh. Di samping itu, *make up* berarti mengandung pretensi sebagai pemanipulasian nilai kejujuran yang ada."

32. "Tak sedikit para penonton menggerutkan dahi, mencari benang merah repertoar ... "

33. "Menurutnya, ketulusan teman-teman di Teater Kubur dalam mengeksplorasi berbagai persoalan masyarakat, merupakan 'bahan bakar' yang dapat mempersatukannya. "Bayangkan, kalau orientasi kami berteater hanya sebatas pentas, mungkin sudah bubar," tutur sutradara ... "

34. "Lalu tidur membuatku gusar pada mimpi, pada malam, pada bintang, pada bulan, pada matahari, pada departemen store, pada radio, pada televisi, pada surat kabar, semua seru diziarahi orang-orang. Kuburan itu sedang cabik-cabik wajah kita."

Chapter 5: The Limits of Bahasa Indonesia *and Teater Payung Hitam's "Theater of Pain": Crisis of Representation of the Nation and Political Allegory*

1. The writers and titles of the articles were Ipit S. Dimyati, "Belajar Bicara dari Pengeras Suara" (10 Nov. 1996, 2nd Runner Up); Agus S. Sarjono, "Beberapa Kelakar Di Antara Kaleng dan Besi" (3 Dec. 1996, 1st Runner-Up); and Benny Yohannes, "Ketika Bahasa Menjadi Bunyi dan Bunyi Menjadi Orgi" (3 Dec. 1996, Winner). That at least two of these writers were also

from Bandung needs to be taken into consideration. Nevertheless, one of the three special award winners, the Surabaya-based Akhudiat, also wrote about Payung Hitam's *Kaspar* in his article, "Kritik Teater" (3 Dec. 1996). All appeared in *Pikiran Rakyat*.

2. See also his undated article, "Indonesian Theater—Historical Background and Current Trends" posted at http://www.mindspring.com/ ~accra/indoXchange/rendraRef.html under the subsection on "Jim Lim and the Bandung Theater Study Club," though it may have been a production Lim undertook with a different group, since the 35th-anniversary volume of STB does not mention it in its list of STB's performances.

3. For comments of this sort, see Totim Moh. Muchyatim, "Ketika "Metateater Main di TIM: Ternyata Lebih Bebas Daripada Jazz," Bandung Pos, 10 Aug. 1991: 13; Eriyandi Budiman, "Ritus Tentang Geleng Kepala," publication unknown, date unknown (sometime soon after the Feb. 14–16 run in Bandung); and Arie F. Batubara, "Pentas Teater "Dunia Tanpa Makna": Makna Kebebasan," Pelita 24 Feb. 1991.

4. "... mengembalikan teater pada kompleksitasnya sendiri. Teater itu seharusnya lebih kompleks dari sekedar *bercerita*. Ia harus *berbicara*, tetapi bukan sekedar dalam kata dan kalimat, melainkan melalui peristiwa, gerak, musik, set, dan seluruh unsur. Ini sesungguhnya merupakan bentuk teater yang purba, primitif. Yang jejaknya masih bisa kita lihat pada ritus-ritus pemujaan terhadap dewi padi, misalnya."

5. "Unsur yang satu bukan merupakan pendukung bagi yang lain. Kesemuanya terlibat dalam sebentuk dialog yang unik dan intens. Satu sama lain saling memberikan rangsang (stimulus) dan tanggapan (respons). Misalnya saja, pemain tidak akan melakukan laku tertentu, apabila tata artistic tidak merangsangnya dengan efek kerupaan tertentu, musik tidak meresponsnya dengan efek bunyi tertentu, dan sebagainya."

6. "Pertama, ia dimaksudkan sebagai sebuah satir terhadap linkungan dan kehidupan yang sudah sedemikian profan dan sekulernya, sehingga nyaris tak memiliki lagi sisi spiritual. Kebersamaan dan semangat kesetiakawanan semakin ditinggalkan diganti oleh kerakusan mengejar kedudukan dan menumpuk kekayaan. Kepekaan dan solidaritas terhadap sesama tidak mendapat tempat karena bertentangan dengan logika ekonomi, hati nurani dan perasaan kemanusiaan disingkirkan lantaran tidak sejalan dengan logika industri dan teknologi modern yang harus menguntungkan, efektif, efisien. Kita tengah berhadapan dengan dunia yang semakin kehilangan makna."

7. This phrase first appears in the text of *Kaspar* in scene 4 (Handke 1972, 109). In Payung Hitam's Indonesian version, the line as spoken was "Saya ingin menjelma seperti orang yang telah pernah ada."

8. "Jangan terlalu banyak bergerak. Jangan bicara dengan simbol-simbol gerak. Kau harus bicara dengan kata-kata. Dengan kalimat-kalimat.... Kamu harus bicara yang verbal. Yang verbal biar semua bisa mengetahui apa yang maumu."

9. The first staging was in Bandung on the 2–5 Sept. 1994. Succeeding performances occurred nearly a year later in Solo, in Surabaya in July 1996, and at the National Theater Festival in Bandung in October of the same year. Most recently, the play was re-worked yet again for a performance at the Third Art Summit in Jakarta during September 2001.

10. Broer may have experienced some problems in advancing his education in the mid -1990s, possibly as a result of sanctions imposed due to his activism (Field Notes 18 Aug. 2001).

11. And in fact, in a conversation following one performance of *Merah Bolong*, Broer readily admitted that the pain this particular scene caused him was quite intense.

12. "Kami teror penonton agar mereka merasakan sakit atau beratnya persoalan yang kita hadapi sekarang."

13. See Putu Wijaya, *Ngeh* (Jakarta: Pustaka Firdaus, 1997): 387–92.

14. Other instances of solidarity and human sympathy also offered some hope in the midst of this harsh portrayal of Indonesian life: scattering stones on the grave of the dead, attempting to help carry a burden, weeping at the suffering and death of another, and singing a song of grief.

Chapter 6: Workers' Theater and Theater about Workers in 1990s Indonesia

1. Informal conversations I had with a number of workers, LSM activists, and performing artists involved with workers' theater also confirmed that these industries predominantly employ women.

2. *Yasanti*'s efforts at actually staging workers' experiences were abruptly cut short when military units appeared to halt rehearsals (Simon H. T. 1991). However, the group has continued to use role-playing techniques to bring out stories and to build awareness and solidarity in its work with women factory workers (Sari Roh 1994).

3. This earlier women's workers' theater group was called Sanggar Teater Buruh Wanita.

4. The plays and dates for 1989–91 are *Pengalaman* (Experience), 9 Nov. 1989,; *Di Mana Aku Berpijak* (Where I Stand), 2 Sept. 1990, *Lauk Janji-Janji* (A Side-dish of Promises), 9 Jun., and once in August 1991 on the occasion of the visit of a group of Japanese Women's organization activists; and *Hitam Menunggu Putih* (Black Waiting for White), 22 Dec. 1991.

5. *Calung* is a kind of music using a bamboo xylophone.

6. "Dunia pabrik adalah dunia yang seakan-akan memenjarakan kami sebagai manusia. Dari hari ke hari kami selalu mengerjakan hal-hal yang sama, hal-hal yang cuma membutuhkan anggota-anggota tubuh kami, tangan misalnya atau kaki.

"Kami sekarang punya 'kumpulan teater' kumpulan yang kami bentuk untuk memanfaatkan sisa-sisa waktu kami yang sedikit itu. Didalam kumpulan ini kami merasa bisa berbicara dan berpikir serta melakukan petualangan-petualangan sebagai manusia lengkap. Artinya, otak dan perasaan kami sedikit-sedikit juga ikut serta dalam petualangan ini."

7. The Indonesian reads as follows: "Didengerin kenapa Gua lagi susah nih . . . gua kan kemarin lapor ke Pabrik minta penggantian biaya pengobatan. Tapi pabrik malah bilang: 'Tak ada yang perlu dibayar, tanganmu putus itu adalah karena kamu tidak berhati-hati, jadi itu adalah resiko dan tanggunganmu sendiri,' katanya. Saya kan jadi bingung, masalahnya ini kan cacat seumur hidup."

8. The Serikat Buruh Sejahtera Indonesia (SBSI) was a new union organized independently of government control and headed by Mochtar Pakpahan. For more information on the SBSI, see Human Rights Watch Asia, *The Limits of Openness* (New York: 1994): 46–50, 57–76 and David Bourchier, "Introduction" to *Indonesia's Emerging Proletariat*, David Bourchier, ed., Annual Indonesia Lecture Series No. 17 (Clayton, Victoria: Monash University Center of Southeast Asian Studies, 1994): i–v.

9. TBI workers were reported to be aware of the GSP review in September 1993, though they did not raise the issue in *Bercanda Dalam Duka*. When I talked to them in August 1994, a number of TBI members stated that they felt the GSP review had been beneficial to workers, forcing the government and industry alike to respect laws already on the books.

10. The Indonesian reads as follows: "Kita ini kan juga butuh bermain, kita kepingin berkomunikasi, Mas." and "Habis seneng Mas ketemu temen-temen dari lain pabrik, lagian daripada diskusi melulu, Teater lebih enak untuk main bareng."

11. The Indonesian reads: "Pementasan tersebut, bila ditelaah dengan patokan-patokan kesenian niscaya akan tumbang dan tidak bernilai. . . . Menonton pementasan yang dikerjakan sepenuhnya oleh 30—an pekerja berbagai pabrik di Depok dan Cimanggis itu, haruslah berbekal, terutama pemahaman yang mendalam akan nasib mereka."

12. "Maka, tidak relevan agaknya untuk menilai pertunjukan ini dalam kategori-kategori teknik estetik. Karena terdapat sejumlah peristiwa yang akan gagal dinilai dengan memakai kaca mata tersebut."

13. Ratna Sarumpaet, *Marsinah: Nyanyian Dari Bawah Tanah* (Jakarta: typescript, 1994). All further page numbers cited in the text refer page

numbers in this manuscript. Subsequently, the play was formally published by Bentang in 1997.

14. Another striking feature of this fascinating work is the ambiguous nature of the central character—merely called the *tokoh* (Prominent Figure). The title of the play might lead an audience to believe that this Prominent Figure in all likelihood is a representation of Marsinah. Evidence supports this supposition: the Prominent Figure is described as having come from poverty (40, 46) and from the lower classes (49–50). Finally, the ending, in which the judge's description of Marsinah's death is juxtaposed to the Prominent Figure's act of submission to Allah, suggests the connection between the tokoh and Marsinah (72–73). Yet there is also more ambiguous, perhaps even contradictory, evidence. At one point, the Prominent Figure describes an incident very like the Marsinah case as though it happened to a third, different person (55). This blending may simply be the rhetorical device of a debate-seasoned spirit, yet it nicely symbolizes the ambiguity of the Prominent Figure in relation to the real life figure of Marsinah and workers in general.

15. The Indonesian is as follows:

SARINAH: Apa sih nyang tidak dilarang. Ngomong saja . . .
KELOMPOK: Dilarang!
GENDANG: Nuntut gaji . . .
KELOMPOK: Di PHK!
SARON: Berorganisasi . . .
KELOMPOK: Dikebiri!
SURTI: Ngerumpi kayak gini . . .
KELOMPOK: Rapat Gelap!
SAONAH: Jadi apa dong yang tidak dilarang Nen . . .
GUNEN: Ketawa saja lu sepuasnya! (Semua pemain tertawa spontan) Selagi ketawa itu tidak dilarang . . .

16. "Memang apalah yang perlu dipersulit dari kehendak untuk berdialog seperti ini? Toh seperti dikatakan dalam pementasan, 'Kita harus mengeluarkan pendapat. Jangan cuma mendengar, tapi sebaliknya kita harus didengar juga. Jadi sama-sama enak . . . '"

17. Begun as a protest of low wages and poor working conditions, this incident saw tens of thousands of North Sumatran workers resort to frustrated rioting after local officials refused to meet with them on 14 Apr. 1994 (Human Rights Watch/Asia 1994, 57–76).

18. For some comment on the complex politics of the Indonesian middle-class, see Aswab Mahasin's "The Santri Middle-class: An Insider's View," *Prisma* 49 (Jun. 1990): 91–96.

19. The Indonesian at first paraphrases Linda's remarks, then moves to direct quotation: "Mereka lalu bisa pentas di tengah seniman dan kelas

menengah di gedung-gedung resmi.... Pentas di tempat-tempat itu memiliki manfaat untuk terus menghidupkan tragedi buruh."

20. The Indonesian is as follows:

> IBU: Kamu akan melakukan pemberontakan! Pada siapa kamu akan berontak, pada ibu?
> ANAK: Salah satunya, tetapi yang utama ialah pada diriku sendiri. Boleh tubuhku secara fisik sebagai buruh kecil tetapi jiwa dan semangatku tidak boleh kerdil.
> IBU: Lantas apa yang akan kamu lakukan?
> ANAK: Yang jelas akau ingin perubahan.
> IBU: Kamu mampu?
> ANAK: Tunggu saja kalau aku nanti sudah benar-benar jadi seniman.

21. The Indonesian is as follows:

> ANAK: Sampai kapan kalian akan terus bermimpi sementara hari semakin pagi. Dimana semangat juang kalian, apakah kalian membiarkan ketidakadilan dan kesewenangan terus berpesta di depan mata kita.
> MEREKA: Memang, manis kata-katamu bicara tentang ketidakadilan ... bicara tentang kesewenangan ... bicara tentang arti sebuah perjuangan ... tetapi kami yakin bahwa semua itu hanyalah slogan belaka. Biarkan, biarkan..toh semua itu sudah tradisi di negeri ini.
> ANAK: Gombal kalian semua! Begitu mudahnya kalian menyerah pada keadaan, begitu mudahnya kalian kehilangan semangat dan begitu mudahnya kalian melupakan arti sebuah perjuangan. Dimana, dimana rasa solidaritas kalian sebagai kaum buruh?

22. "Hei ... kamu jangan ikut-ikutan latah utnuk mengatakan subversif. Berani bicara dibilang subversif ... kumpul-kumpul subversif ... Kita hanya ingin bertanya, toh kita sebagai manusia punya hak untuk bertanya."

23. In fact, TABUR's and BUBUTAN's relationship to middle-class aesthetics remained troublesome. This tension continued even after the fall of President Suharto in 1998. In 2001, when I asked Wowok why workers theater groups didn't try to develop their own aesthetics, rather than looking towards middle-class arts, he replied that pressure from critics was strong and that workers had to think of aesthetics from the viewpoint of high arts-oriented critics. Otherwise they would be belittled and the workers would lose confidence and feel ashamed. He maintained that many workers joined theater groups with the idea that they could become "artis" and get a bit part in a television serial and thus a ticket out of factory work (Field Notes 13 Aug. 2001).

24. In Indonesian, the poem reads:
    Tiba-tiba langit selalu saja malam
    Di tengah deru mesin-mesin pabrik
    Berebut rasa atas nama CINTA
    Dan aku berada di tengahnya

    Seribu langkah tinggalkan rumah
    Berharap dunia memberi warna
    Ku akrabi warna industri
    Ku ikhlaskan keinginan manusiawi
    Debar-debar rasa untuk bercinta selalu menggoda
    Kupandangi diri dalam cermin meminta arti

    Arti CINTA, arti diri, arti menikmati
    Apa daya tak kudapati arti
    Yang aku mengerti hidup harus tahu diri

    Banyak dinding-dinding pemisah
    Dan orang-orang sibuk membuat kelas sosial
    Sehingga hak mencintai dan dicintai punah
    Kembali berbenah dan hanya bisa pasrah

    Tiba-tiba langit selalu saja malam
    Di tengah deru mesin-mesin pabrik
    Tak ada CINTA tanpa rekayasa
    Dan kami ada di dalamnya

25. The Indonesian is as follows:
    KANAN: Aku seorang wanita biasa dengan KTP sebagai jaminan di mana saja, apabila aku menemukan sesuatu dalam perjalanan hidup ini.
    KIRI: Aku seorang wanita luarbiasa tanpa KTP dan selalu saja Jabatan suamiku berfungsi menjadi KTP ketika menemukan sesuatu dalam perjalanan.
    KANAN: Anakku kubesarkan hanya dengan do'a, tanpa rupiah sehingga ia tumbuh menjadi catatan panjang!
    KIRI: Anakku kubesarkan dengan trend yang kubeli di supermarket, sehingga ia tumbuh menjadi Mode!
    KANAN: Suamiku hanya buruh disebuah pabrik yang setiap tahunnya tak lepas dari demo kenaikan upah.
    KIRI: Suamiku berjas dan berdasi yang setiap menit siap memecat siapa saja yang mendemo. . . .
    KANAN: Malam-malam dimusim hujan adalah kerinduan pada suami yang selalu saja bermimpi tentang rumah bagus.

KIRI: Malam-malam dimusim hujan adalah kasmaran baru yang menanti diluar rumah.

Chapter 7: Staged Openness:
Theater and Censorship in Indonesia's 1990s Era of Keterbukaan

1. Several examples gathered from informal conversations or brief anecdotes in the mass media point to the possibility that the number of theatrical bans is indeed larger than the lists featured in the Indonesian mass media circa 1994 (see, for example, Republika 1994; YLBH 1994, 43–50). For example, Rachman Arge noted that in early 1974, around the time of the Malari riots in Jakarta, the Makassar (Ujung Pandang) security authorities had successfully urged him to cancel a performance of *MacBeth*—a play about an ambitious warrior's illegal seizure of power (*Tempo* 1978, 53–54). In 1978, another year of student protests, a Bandung performance of Teater Koma's *Ma'af, Ma'af, Ma'af* (Sorry, Sorry, Sorry) was banned by local authorities on a technicality (Riantiarno 1990). Saini K. M.'s 1978 drama, *Egon*, was also banned in Makassar and elsewhere according to one theater worker (Field Notes 24 Jun. 1988). An article on the banning of a Teater Gajah Mada performance of Gogol's *Inspector General* from late 1981 briefly mentions another banning incident, that of an unnamed Pirandello play mounted by Azwar A. N. of Yogya's Teater Alam in 1980 (*Tempo*, 12 Dec. 1981, 25). Bandung acquaintances have also informed me that there were several bans of theater in Bandung during the New Order, including the prohibition of one performance of a play mockingly entitled *Jenderal Anjing* (The Dog General) (Diary 15 Sept. 1999). One might add to this list the banning of several poetry readings which were not widely reported, including the prohibition of a reading of a Sutardji Chalzoum Bachri poem in Bandung in either 1989 or 1990 (*Buana* n.d), a ban on two Ikranegara poems about religious tolerance in Surabaya in 1993 (*Republika*, 4 Feb. 1994), and a prohibition on several of Rendra's poems in Bandung in Jan. 1995 (*Republika*, 31 Dec. 1995).

2. For an example of such calls see the remarks of writer and film director Asrul Sani as reported in *Kompas* on Sept. 10, 1990. In a talk on literature in Indonesia, Sani stated: "The growth of art requires freedom of expression in relation to all aspects of human life, so that they can develop as they should. The lack of free expression causes artists to be cut off from human life." Attempts to form new industrial unions in the late 1980s and early 1990s are also indicative of this trend.

3. See discussion of Harmoko's stock holdings in "Sticky Fingers: Harmoko's Business Interests" in *Inside Indonesia* 42 (Mar. 1995): 2–4. Though the article notes that no clear-cut regulation exists governing "con-

flict of interest" issues at the ministerial level, it also suggests that the fact Harmoko acquired shares in 23 different publications during his time as Minister of Information, may be morally dubious, given that he controlled the granting of publishing licenses.

4. This name seems to be a combination of Javanese and German. *Beine* is German plural for "leg," possibly related to the fact that the character who bears the name is evicting peasants from their land, but is also referred to as the servant of other masters. *Den* is derived from the Javanese title for nobility, *Raden*. This last is confirmed by the fact that in the script, *Den Beine* sometimes becomes *Den Bei*, an appellation which could refer to an aristocrat or *priyayi* with a particular rank in the civil service.

5. "Manusia jenis begituan sekarang naik menjadi pemimpin!, berlagak seolah-olah dia yang paling berjasa, unjuk muka seakan-akan ia adalah Mbah-nya pembangunan, menggenggam di tangannya beribu-ribu butir kepala rakyat, dia jahit, dia rentengi menjadi sebuah aksesori sejarah!"

6. The Indonesian reads:

> KANJENG SATU: Saya pasti tidak cukup sembrono untuk menyimpulkan bahwa semua pemimpin itu palsu. Tetapi saya juga sukar membantah bahwa kepalsuan termasuk syarat utama dan terpenting dari prinsip kepemimpinan. Namun seandainyapun demikian, mbok ya dicari kepalsuan yang agak baik sedikit, yang agak kurang kentara. Kepalsuan yang mendidk-lah....
>
> KANJENG DUA: Kepalsuan yang bebas dan bertanggung jawab, kepalsuan manusia Indonesia seutuhnya..."

7. East Javanese governor, Basofi Sudirman, seems to have been a staunch defender of Suharto's political interests. As Heryanto notes, he waged a particularly vigorous and protracted struggle contesting the right of the PDI central board, under Megawati Sukarnoputri, to appoint the leadership of the party's East Java regional branch. He was also the only ranking government official who unambiguously supported the banning action in the early days of the public debate.

8. See the translation of *Marsinah Menggugat* in *Silenced Voices* (*Manoa* 12.1: 155–66). Since I did not personally witness the performances of the first version of *Marsinah Menggugat*, I am basing my remarks on this translation and a later, updated version which I saw Ratna perform in Jakarta in August 1999.

9. This group was exceptionally talented. The statement's signatories included actors Butet Kartarejasa and Joko Kamto, actor/musician Novi Budiyanto, theater critic and writer Indra Tranggono, and social activist and musician Toto Rahardjo.

10. This line of counter-argument taken up by several commentators in addition to Nadjib was expanded to declare that theater had never caused any social "flare-ups" (*Jawa Pos*, 2 Feb. 1994). Indicative of continued fear that the government would brand cultural works as politics, this argument was criticized by Faruk H. T. as conforming to the censor's logic. Faruk felt there was nothing wrong with cultural works having political goals, that is, their criticizing entrenched power (*Jawa Pos*, 6 Feb. 1994).

11. As well as individual commentators, a number of reports also cited Moerdiono's statement. See the relevant articles in *Republika*, 3 Feb. 1994; *Bernas*, 4 Feb.; *Suara Merdeka*, 5 Feb.; *Jawa Pos*, 6 Feb.; *Republika*, 10 Feb.; *Republika*, 11 Feb.; *Surabaya Pos*, 12 Feb. [Wiratmo Sukito] 1994; *Kompas*, 13 Feb. [Ariel Heryanto]; *DeTik*, 2–8 Mar..

12. On Feb. 19, the Pak Kanjeng group went even further, announcing that they would not perform the play again anywhere, since they felt the security apparatus could not be trusted (*Jawa Pos*, 19 Feb. 1994).

13. Nadjib was not allowed to speak on at least one Central Java university campus during May, and a friendly meeting between Nadjib and Rendra at Nadjib's home was broken up by police who claimed that the meeting did not have the proper permit. See, for example, "Emha akhirnya kena 'cekal' juga di Solo" (In the end Emha also banned in Solo), *Wawasan*, 11 May 1994) and "Pandam heran, aparat larang pertemuan di rumah Emha" (The Regional Military Commander is surprised that the security apparatus banned the meeting at Emha's home), *Wawasan*, 10 May 1994.

14. Here, it is also worth wondering if the press did not in some way share the government's opinion that workers' theater was essentially a social or political activity, not a matter of "art," thus obviating the need to ask the opinions of established cultural workers and arts bodies? While this lacuna could also, perhaps, have been due to the fact that the workers' theater cases were being litigated, the lack of symmetry with the variety of commentators in the earlier *Suksesi* and *Pak Kanjeng* cases is still striking.

15. "Apa ada dalam hidup manusia yang tak mengandung bobot politik?... Aspirasi saya sebagai seniman adalah mengekspresikan hasil perenungan dan pengamatan terhadap kehidupan sehari-hari. Kalau saya boleh bicara tentang masyarakat dan tak boleh berbicara politik itu ajaib. Apalagi kasus Marsinah" (*Sinar* 20 Dec. 1997).

16. See coverage in national (*Republika*, *Kompas*) and, especially, regional (*Jawa Pos*, *Bernas*, *Kedaulatan Rakyat* and *Wawasan*) newspapers during May and early June of 1994 for details. In the intervening period, a Surabaya seminar on human rights, whose main guest was to be the outspoken former police general and member of the national human rights committee, Rukmini, had also been banned. Once again, the head of the Surabaya police and Gov-

ernor Basofi Sudirman were the government's point men. For a brief discussion of the Rukmini case, see Human Rights Watch/Asia 1994, 129–34.

17. Not surprisingly, headlines for articles covering the case provide an indicator of this shifting focus. Several examples should suffice: "Rights body blasts ban on workers' play" (*Jakarta Post*, 27 May 1995); "Teater Buruh Dilarang, Mengadu ke Komnas HAM" (*Republika*, 1 Jun.); "Secara Yuridis Istilah Buruh Masih Diakui" (*Kompas*, 5 Jun.); "Anggota Teater Hadiri Sidang PTUN" (*Kompas*, 18 Jul.); "Perkara yang Diajukan TBI Penuhi Syarat" (*Jayakarta*, 18 Jul.); "Kami Berharap Persidangan Berlangsung fair" (*Merdeka*, 8 Aug.); "Sanggar Pabrik akan Ajukan Tunutan ke-PTUN" (*Republika*, 21 Sept. 1995); "Theater sues police over performance ban" (*Jakarta Post*, 19 Jan. 1996).

18. See the comments about the TBI banning made by various parties in "Rights body blasts ban on workers' play" (*Jakarta Post*, 27 May), "Dilarang Pentas 'Senandung Terpuruk'" (*Jayakarta*, 27 May), "Ban on performance deplored" (*Jakarta Post*, 1 Jun.), "Secara Yuridis Istilah Buruh Masih Diakui" (*Kompas*, 5 Jun.). In the Sanggar Pabrik case, see the remarks of Hendardi, Rukmini and the Letter to the Editor from the Bandung-Sanctus Thomas Aquinas Branch of the Indonesian Catholic Student's Organization in "Pencabutan Izin Pentas Dinilai Mengada-ada" (*Kompas*, 19 Sept.), "Police Forbid Workers' Play" (*Jakarta Post*, 19 Sept.), "PMKRI Protes Pembatalan Izin Pentas Teater Sanggar Pabrik" (*Merdeka*, 20 Sept.), and "*Surat Cinta Untuk Marsinah* Dipentaskan di Komnasham" (*Kompas*, 22 Sept.).

19. The term *pakem* is most frequently used in relation to *wayang* plays. Its introduction into the debate indicates the importance of elite Javanese values as nationalized norms.

20. For a more detailed account of *Suksesi*, its banning, the prohibition of Rendra's poems and *Opera Kecoa*, and the public debates constituting the aftermath of these incidents, see Bodden 1997a.

21. Here the role of the press was crucial. They quickly revealed that the regional police had requested advice on the permit from the central police headquarters in Jakarta. The Central Headquarters had left the decision to the local Polda (regional police) command, which, apparently feeling as though it were holding a political hot potato, had then asked the advice of the regional army command headquarters, the Kodam V/Brawijaya. The regional army command, while giving its recommendation to the police, also felt it possessed sufficient authority to inform the play's promoters that the play should be postponed even before the local police were willing to make such a statement (*Jawa Pos*, 1 Feb. 1994). The regional police spokesperson quickly denied that the play had been banned: "Who banned it? We didn't ban it, we only postponed it," he declared (*Surabaya Pos*, 1 Feb. 1994). The Brawijaya regional army command, in contrast, adapted a paternalistic,

authoritative air in suggesting that if the script were first refined, it could again be submitted for consideration (*Republika*, 1 Feb. 1994).

22. This was in marked contrast to official statements of Try Sutrisno, Tanjung's predecessor, during the Koma bannings. Then Sutrisno had called Koma's and Riantiarno's plays "excessively free" (*Kompas*, 7 Dec. 1990, p. 1 & 8).

23. The word buruh means "laborer" or "worker," carrying the connotation of manual or coarse physical labor. It has been discursively linked by the New Order to the militant labor activism of organizations affiliated with the proscribed Indonesian Communist Party (PKI) and to class analysis, which was also forbidden in New Order Indonesia. An alternative term, *pekerja*, is much more neutral, connoting all workers who are paid wages to do specific work.

24. Conroy (1997, 32) also writes that in another source Suharyono went so far as to claim that the word *terpuruk* from the play's title had connotations of oppression and that this was inappropriate because "since the inception of the New Order regime, there are no longer any oppressed persons in the Indonesian community."

25. It is of some interest that Sudrajat is the figure who finally issued the decision. Long considered to be in the military professionalist camp, Sudrajat was allied with those officers and ex-officers in conflict with the Suharto group. Sudrajat appears to have felt that the military's turn towards Islam, signified by the Feisal Tanjung, Hartono, and Syarwan Hamid leadership, and the subordination of the military beneath the government's Golkar party, were tarnishing the army's image by making it seem sectarian and partial, rather than a "neutral" leader and protector of the nation as a whole. As a result, during the 1995–96 period now under discussion, he championed a more broadly based nationalism, probity, and democracy within New Order society. See Honna 1999, pp. 90–115.

Conclusion

1. Alarmingly enough, Ratna Sarumpaet's 2000–2001 production of *Alia: Luka Serambi Mekah* (Alia: Wound of Mecca's Veranda), which took up the issue of military operations in Aceh (as did a Payung Hitam piece of roughly the same period, *DOM*) and was performed in Aceh and elsewhere, did appear to experience censorship in 2002. When the play was filmed for television, its actual broadcast was suddenly subjected to an "indefinite postponement" by the national television network, TVRI, at the request of the Army's office of public relations (*Sinar Harapan* 2002). Such occurrences raised the spectre of censorship once again, though incidences of government banning had greatly decreased since 1998.

2. Hatley notes the same feelings among theater workers (2008, 193).

3. See, for example, the Newmont Mining case in North Sulawesi (*Inside Indonesia* 80, Oct-Dec 2004, 3; and *Inside Indonesia* 82, April–June 2005, 3) and that of Lapindo Brantas in East Java (Holm 1996). More recently, see also Jim Schiller, Anton Lucas, and Priyambudi Sulistyanto, "Learning from the East Java Mudflow: Disaster Politics in Indonesia," *Indonesia* 85 (Apr. 2008): 51–77.

Bibliography

Ahmed, Leila. 1992. *Women and Gender in Islam*. New Haven: Yale University Press.
Aji, Arwinto Syamsunu. 1988. "Pementasan 'Kapai-Kapai' Teater Kubur." *Sinar Pagi*, 18 April.
Amin, Nazir, Asep Sambodja, and Nurhanafiansyah. 1995. "Jika Wong Cilik Protes." *Sinar*, 15 July, 89.
Anderson, Benedict.1992 [1983]. *Imagined Communities*. London: Verso.
———. 1990. *Language and Power: Exploring Political Cultures in Indonesia*. Ithaca: Cornell University Press.
Andriyani, Nori. 1996. "Myth of the Effective Little NGO." *Inside Indonesia* 46 (March 1996): 22–23.
Appiah, Kwame Anthony. 1996. "Is the Post- in Postmodernism the Post- in Postcolonial?" In *Contemporary Postcolonial Theory*, edited by Padmini Mongia, 55–71. London: Arnold.
Arcana, Putu Fajar. 2004. "Sabur, Percaya Kepada Bahasa Tubuh." In *Teater Payung Hitam: Perspektif Teater Modern Indonesia*, edited by Rachman Sabur, 139–42. Bandung: Kelir.
Asikin. 1994. "Karya-Karya Pasca Pembredelan." *Forum Keadilan* III.12 (29 September): 31.
Asmara, Cobina Gillitt. 1995. "*Tradisi Baru*: A "New Tradition" of Indonesian Theatre." *Asian Theatre Journal* 12.1 (Spring): 164–74.
Aspinall, Edward. 2005. *Opposing Suharto: Compromise, Resistance, and Regime Change in Indonesia*. Stanford, CA: Stanford University Press.
———. 1999. "The Indonesian Student Uprising of 1998." In *Reformasi: Crisis and change in Indonesia*, edited by Arief Budiman, Barbara Hatley, and Damien Kingsbury, 212–38. Clayton, Victoria: Monash Centre of Southeast Asian Studies.
———. 1996. "The Broadening Base of Political Opposition in Indonesia." In *Political Oppositions in Industrializing Asia*, edited by Garry Rodan, 215–39. London: Routledge.

———. 1995. "Students and the Military: Regime Friction and Civilian Dissent in the Late Suharto Period." *Indonesia* 59 (April): 21–44.

Assariroh, Nadlroh. 1994. Personal Communication.

Aveling, Harry. 1981. "Introduction." In W. S. Rendra, *The Mastodon and the Condors*, v–xxvii. Calcutta: Writers Workshop.

Ayu Ratih. 1995. Personal Communication.

Bain, Lauren Halligan. 2005. *Performances of the Post-New Order*. PhD diss., University of Tasmania.

Barton, Greg. 1994. "The Impact of Neo-Modernism on Indonesian Islamic Thought: The Emergence of a New Pluralism." In *Democracy in Indonesia: 1950s and 1990s*, edited by David Bourchier and John Legge, 143–50. Clayton, Victoria: Monash Centre of Southeast Asian Studies.

Basri, Agus. 1995. "Sebuah Pentas di Komnas HAM." *Gatra*, 30 September.

Batubara, Arie F. 1991. "Pentas Metateater 'Dunia Tanpa Makna': Makna Pembebasan." *Pelita*, 24 February.

Bawantara, Agung and Yayan Sopyan. 1994. "Setelah Setahun Menggeluti Kursi." *DeTik*, 16–22 February.

Bennett, Susan. 1990. *Theatre Audiences: A Theory of Production and Reception*. London: Routledge.

Boal, Augusto. 1985. *Theatre of the Oppressed*. New York: Theatre Communications Group.

Bodden, Michael. Forthcoming. "How to Make Foreign Plays Speak to Indonesian Audiences: Universalism and Postcolonial Identity in Indonesian Modern Art Theatre." In *The History of Translation in Indonesia and Malaysia*, edited by Henri Chambert-Loir.

———. 2007a. "'Tradition,' 'Modernism,' and the Struggle for Cultural Hegemony in Indonesian National Art Theatre." *Indonesia and the Malay World* 35.101 (March 2007): 63–91.

———. 2007b. "Languages of Traumas, Bodies, and Myths: Learning to Speak Again in Post-1998 Indonesian Theatre." In *Arts, Popular Culture and Social Change in the New Indonesia*, edited by Michael Leaf, 119–51. Vancouver: Consulate General of the Republic of Indonesia in Vancouver and Institute of Asian Research—Centre for Southeast Asian Research, University of British Columbia.

———. 2002. "Satuan-satuan Kecil and Uncomfortable Improvisations in the Late Night of the New Order: Democratization, Postmodernism, and Postcoloniality." In *Clearing a Space: Postcolonial Readings of Modern Indonesian Literature*, edited by Keith Foulcher and Tony Day, 293–324. Leiden: KITLV Press.

———. 1997a. "Teater Koma's *Suksesi* and Indonesia's New Order." *Asian Theatre Journal* 14.2 (Fall 1997): 259–80.

———. 1997b. "Utopia and the Shadow of Nationalism: The Plays of Sanusi Pane 1928–1940." *Bijdragen tot de Taal-, Land- en Volkenkunde* 153. III: 332–55.

———. 1997c. "Brecht in Asia: New Agendas, National Traditions, and Critical Consciousness." In *A Bertolt Brecht Reference Companion*, edited by Siegfried Mews, 379–98. Westport, CT: Greenwood.

———. 1995. "Arena Teater and the Brechtian Tradition: Indonesian Grassroots Theater." *The Brecht Yearbook* 20: 153–73.

———. 1993. *Imagining the Audience as Agent of its Own History: Brecht, Grassroots Theater and Representations of Interclass Alliance in the Philippines and Indonesia*. PhD diss., University of Wisconsin.

Borch, Rosslyn von der. 1988. *Art and Activism: Some Examples from Contemporary Central Java*. Asian Studies Monograph No. 4. Adelaide: Flinders University.

Bourchier, David. 1997. "Totalitarianism and the "National Personality": Recent Controversy About the Philosophical Basis of the Indonesian State." In *Imagining Indonesia*, edited by Jim Schiller and Barbara Martin-Schiller, 157–85. Monographs in International Studies Southeast Asia series, no. 97. Athens: Ohio University Press.

———. 1994a. "Introduction." In *Indonesia's Emerging Proletariat*, edited by David Bourchier, i–v. Annual Indonesia Lecture Series No. 17. Clayton, Victoria: Monash University Centre of Southeast Asian Studies.

———. 1994b. "Solidarity: The New Order's First Free Trade Union." In *Indonesia's Emerging Proletariat*, edited by David Bourchier, 52–63. Annual Indonesia Lecture Series No. 17. Clayton, Victoria: Monash University Centre of Southeast Asian Studies.

Bourchier, David, and Vedi R. Hadiz, eds. 2003. *Indonesian Politics and Society: A Reader*. London: Routledge-Curzon.

Bowen, John R. 1986. "On the Politcal Construction of Tradition; Gotong Royong in Indonesia." *Journal of Asian Studies* 45: 545–61.

Bourdieu, Pierre. 1984. *Distinctions*. Cambridge, MA: Harvard University Press.

Braginsky, Vladimir. 2004. *The Heritage of Traditional Malay literature*. Leiden: KITLV Press.

Brecht, Bertolt. 1966. *Der Kaukasische Kreidekreis*, edited by Victor Lange. New York: Harcourt, Brace & World.

———. 1972. *Die Maßnahme*, edited by Reiner Steinweg. Kritische Ausgabe mit einer Spielanleitung von Reiner Steinweg. Berlin: Suhrkamp Verlag.

———. 1975. *Das Badener Lehrstück vom Einverständnis, Die Rundköpfe und die Spitzköpfe, Die Ausnahme und die Regel*. Berlin: Suhrkamp Verlag.

———. 1981. *Die Mutter*. Reinbeck bei Hamburg: Rowohlt Verlag GmbH.

———. 1981. *Das Verhör des Lukullus: Hörspiel*. Berlin: Suhrkamp Verlag.
———. 1986. *Brecht on Theatre*. Trans. John Willett. New York: Hill and Wang.
Brenkman, John. 1987. *Culture and Domination*. Ithaca: Cornell University Press.
Brenner, Suzanne. 1996. "Reconstructing Self and Society: Javanese Muslim Women and the Veil." *American Ethnologist* 23(4): 673–97.
Budiman, Eriyandi. 1991. "Ritus Tentang Geleng Kepala." *Pikiran Rakyat*, n.d.
Burdansyah, Cecep. 1991. "Metateater, Dunia Tanpa Makna." *Pikiran Rakyat*, 20 February.
Camus, Albert. *Caligula and 3 Other Plays*. New York: Vintage.
Cholid, Mohamad, Bersihar Lubis, Aries Margono, Budiono Darsono, and Priyono B. Sumbogo. 1989. "Bisnis Malu-Malu Kucing." *Tempo*, 18 March, 104–6.
Chua, Beng Huat. 1993. "Looking for Democratization in Post-Soeharto Indonesia." *Contemporary Southeast Asia* 15.2 (September): 131–60.
Chudori, Leila and Nunik Iswardhani. 1993. "Sebuah Tempat di Luar Arus Besar." *Tempo*, 11 December, 104.
Citra. 1994. "Gerangan Geram Pada Hakim yang Tak Hakim." 5.235 (26 September–2 October).
Conroy, Rebecca. 2006. *Performing Resistance: Oppositional performance practices in contemporary Indonesia*. PhD diss., University of Newcastle.
———. 1997. "The Subjugated Subversive in the Aesthetic Space: a case study of Teater Buruh Indonesia." B.A. Thesis, University of Newcastle.
Craven, David. 1999. *Abstract Expressionism as Cultural Critique: Dissent During the McCarthy Period*. Cambridge: Cambridge University Press.
Crouch, Harold. 1988. *The Army and Politics in Indonesia*, revised edition. Ithaca, NY: Cornell University Press.
Dahana, Padhar Panca. 2001. *Ideologi Politik dan Teater Modern Indonesia*. Magelang: IndonesiaTera.
———. 1994. "Teater Buruh dan Wek-Wek." *Tempo*, 19 February, 99.
Dasmarinas, Jules. 1988. "Artists From Other Lands Came and Sang Our Songs." *Makiisa* 1, No. 1 (First Quarter): 19–40.
Dewanto, Nirwan. 1996. "Kebudayaan Indonesia; Pandangan 1991." In *Senjakala Kebudayaan*: 13–53. Yogyakarta: Bentang.
———. 1995. "Seni, Birokrasi, Pasar." *Media Kerja Budaya* 2: 45–47.
———. 1994. "Teater Kubur di Teater Arena." *Tempo*, 19 February, 98.
———. 1992. "Rangkaian Kolase yang Cemas." *Tempo*, 12 December, 94.
Dewi, Kumara. 1995. "Indonesia Women Worker." *Inisiatif*, Special Edition Aug.–Sept.: 71–82.

Dhofier, Zamakhsyari. 1980. "Islamic Education and Traditional Ideology on Java." In *Indonesia: The Making of a Culture*, edited by James J. Fox, 263–71. Canberra: ANU Research School of Pacific Studies.

Dindon. 1993. "Aku Ingin Jadi Manusia: Teater Abu." *Media Indonesia*, 26 January, 14.

Diponegoro, Mohammad. 1983. *Iblis*. Jakarta: Panjimas.

Djajamihardja, Hidayat. 1986. "Reporting Indonesia: An Indonesian Journalist's Perspective." In *The Indonesian Press: Its Past, Its People, Its Problems*, edited by Paul Tickell: 37–47. Annual Indonesia Lecture Series No. 12. Clayton, Victoria: Monash University Centre of Southeast Asian Studies.

Eldridge, Philip. 1995. *Non-Government Organizations and Democratic Participation in Indonesia*. Kuala Lumpur: Oxford University Press.

———. 1990. "NGOs and the State in Indonesia." In *State and Civil Society in Indonesia*, edited by Arief Budiman, 503–18. Clayton, Australia: Monash University Centre of Southeast Asian Studies, 1990.

Federspiel, Howard. 1973. "The Military and Islam in Indonesia." *Pacific Affairs* 46.3: 406–20.

Fennel, Tom and Joe Leahy. 1996. "Islands of Unrest." *Maclean's*, 19 August, 30–31.

Fillion, Nancy. 1995. Personal Communication.

Foucault, Michel. 1995 [1977]. *Discipline and Punish: The Birth of the Prison*. New York: Vintage.

Foulcher, Keith. 1993. "Literature, Cultural Politics, and the Indonesian Revolution." In *Text/politics in Island Southeast Asia*, edited by D. M. Roskies, 221–57. Southeast Asia series No. 91. Athens: Ohio University Center for International Studies.

———. 1990. "The Construction of an Indonesian National Culture: Patterns of Hegemony and Resistance." In *State and civil society in Indonesia*, edited by Arief Budiman, 301-321. Clayton, Victoria: Monash University Centre of Southeast Asian Studies.

———. 1987. "Sastra Kontekstual: Recent Developments in Indonesian Literary Politics." *Review of Indonesian and Malaysian Affairs* 21.2 (Winter): 6–28.

———. 1986. *Social Commitment in Literature and the Arts: the Indonesian "Institute of People's Culture" 1950–1965*. Clayton, Victoria: Monash University Centre of Southeast Asian Studies.

———. 1980. *"Pujangga Baru": Literature and Nationalism in Indonesia 1933–1942*. Bedford Park, S. Australia: Flinders University of South Australia.

———. 1978. "Image and Perspective in Recent Indonesian Literature." *Review of Indonesian and Malaysian Affairs* 12.2: 1-16.

Keith Foulcher and Tony Day. 2002. *Clearing a Space: Postcolonial Readings of Modern Indonesian Literaure.* Leiden: KITLV Press.

Frederick, William. 1989. *Visions and Heat: the Making of the Indonesian Revolution.* Athens: Ohio University Press.

———. 1982. "Rhoma Irama and the Dangdut Style: Aspects of Contemporary Indonesian Popular Culture." *Indonesia* 34 (Oct. 1982): 103–30.

Freire, Paulo. 1989. *Pedagogy of the Oppressed.* New York: Continuum.

Gantra, Maman. 1993. "Ekspresi Lugu Para Pekerja: Sebuah Teater Persembahan Para Buruh Tentang Nasib Mereka." *Editor* 6.18 (23 January): 89.

Geertz, Clifford. 1960. *The Religion of Java.* New York: The Free Press.

GG. 1991. "Mengembalikan Teater Kepada yang Purba." *Pikiran Rakyat*, 15 February.

Gilbert, Helen and Joanne Tompkins. 1996. *Post-Colonial Drama.* London: Routledge.

Gillitt, Cobina Ruth. 2001. "Challenging Conventions and Crossing Boundaries: A New Tradition of Indonesian Theater from 1968–78." PhD diss., New York University.

Guibault, Serge. 1983. *How New York Stole the Idea of Modern Art: Abstract Expressionism, Freedom, and the Cold War.* Chicago: University of Chicago Press.

Guinness, Patrick. 1994. "Local Society and Culture." In *Indonesia's New Order*, edited by Hal Hill, 267–304. Honolulu: University of Hawai'i Press.

———. 1990. "Forced Into Opposition: Yogyakarta's Kampung People." *Inside Indonesia* 22 (March): 13–15.

Gumeulis, Linda. 1994. Personal Interview. Jakarta. 4 August.

Hadiz, Vedi R. 1994. "The Political Significance of Recent Working Class Action." In *Indonesia's Emerging Proletariat*, edited by David Bourchier, 63–73. Annual Indonesia Lecture Series No. 17. Clayton, Victoria: Monash University Centre of Southeast Asian Studies.

———. 1993, "Workers and Working Class Politics in the 1990s." In *Indonesia Assessment 1993: Labour: Sharing the Benefits of Growth?*, edited by Chris Manning and Joan Hardjono, 186–200. Political and Social Change Monograph 20. Canberra: ANU Department of Political and Social Change, Research School of Pacific Studies.

Hall, Stuart. 1985. "Signification, Representation, Ideology: Althusser and the Post-Structuralist Debates." *Critical Studies in Mass Communications* 2: 91–114.

Handke, Peter. 1972. *Stücke 1.* Frankfurt am Main: Suhrkamp Verlag.

Hart, Gillian. 1986. *Power, Labor, and Livelihood: Processes of Change in Rural Java.* Berkeley: University of California Press.

Hartoyo, Budiman S. 1991. "Samudera Cinta Kasih." *Tempo*, 24 Aug.: 68.

Hartoyo, Budiman S., and R. Fadjri. 1992. "Panggung Swasta di Sekitar TIM." *Tempo*, 14 November, 42.
Harvey, David. 2005. *A Brief History of Neoliberalism*. Oxford: Oxford University Press.
———. 1989. *The Condition of Postmodernity*. Oxford: Basil Blackwell.
Hatley, Barbara. 2008. *Javanese Performances on an Indonesian Stage: Contesting Culture, Embracing Change*. Singapore: Asian Studies Association of Australia and NUS Press.
———. 1994a. "Stage Texts and Life Texts: Women in Contemporary Indonesian Theatre." *Australasian Drama Studies* 25 (October): 17–39.
———. 1994b. "Cultural Expression." In *Indonesia's New Order*, edited by Hal Hill, 216–66. Honolulu: University of Hawai'i Press.
———. 1993. "Constructions of 'Tradition' in New Order Indonesian Theatre." In *Culture and Society in New Order Indonesia*, edited by Virginia Mattheson Hooker, 48–69. Kuala Lumpur: Oxford University Press.
———. 1990. "Theatre as Cultural Resistance in Contemporary Indonesia." In *State and Civil Society in Indonesia*, edited by Arief Budiman, 321–48. Clayton, Victoria: Monash U. Centre of Southeast Asian Studies.
———. 1971. "Wayang and Ludruk: Polarities in Java." *Theatre and Drama Review*, 15, No. 3 (Spring): 88–101.
Hefner, Robert. 2000. *Civil Islam: Muslims and Democratization in Indonesia*. Princeton: Princeton University Press.
———. 1993. "Islam, State, and Civil Society: ICMI and the Struggle for the Indonesian Middle-class." *Indonesia* 56 (October): 1–35.
Herfanda, Ahmadun Y. 1989. "Dajjal dan Fenomena Kesenian Islam." *Kedaulatan Rakyat*, 9 April.
Heryanto, Ariel. 2006. *State Terrorism and Political Identity in Indonesia: Fatally Belonging*. London: Routledge.
———. 1996. "Indonesian Middle-class Opposition in the 1990s." In *Political Oppositions in Industrializing Asia*, edited by Gary Rodan, 241–71. London: Routledge.
———. 1995. "What Does Postmodernism Do in Contemporary Indonesia?" *Sojourn* 10.1: 33–44.
———. 1994. "Postmodernisme yang Mana?" *Kalam* 1: 80–93.
Hill, Hal. 1994. "The economy." In *Indonesia's New Order*, edited by Hal Hill, 53–122. Honolulu: University of Hawai'i Press.
Hill, David. 1994. *The Press in New Order Indonesia*. Perth: University of Western Australia Press and Asia Research Centre of Social, Political and Economic Change.
———. 1987. "Press Challenges, Government Responses: Two Campaigns in 'Indonesia Raya.'" In *The Indonesian Press: Its Past, Its People, Its Problems*,

edited by Paul Tickell: 20–36. Annual Indonesia Lecture Series No. 12. Clayton, Victoria: Monash University Centre of Southeast Asian Studies.

Holm, Chris. 2006. "Muckraking in Java's Gas Fields." *Asia Times Online*, 14 July, http://www.atimes.com/atimes/Southeast_Asia/HG14Ae01.html.

Honna, Jun. 1999. "Military Ideology in Response to Democratic Pressure During the Late Suharto Era: Political and Institutional Contexts." *Indonesia* 67 (April): 77–126.

Hooker, Virginia Matheson. 1993. "New Order Language in Context." In *Culture and Society in New Order Indonesia*, edited by Virginia M. Hooker, 272–93. Kuala Lumpur: Oxford University Press.

Hough, Brett. 1992. *Contemporary Balinese Dance Spectacles as National Ritual*. Working Paper No. 74. Clayton, Victoria: Monash University Centre for Southeast Asian Studies.

Hübner, Zygmunt. 1988. *Theater and Politics*. Evanston: Northwestern University Press.

Human Rights Watch. 1996. "Indonesia: Tough International Response Needed to Widening Crackdown." Vol. 8.8 (August).

———. 1994. *The Limits of Openness: Human Rights in Indonesia and East Timor*. New York: Human Rights Watch.

Hüsken, Frans, and Benjamin White. 1989. "Java: Social Differentiation, Food Production, and Agrarian Control." In *Agrarian Transformations: Local Processes and the State in Southeast Asia*, edited by Gillian Hart, Andrew Turton, and Benjamin White with Brian Fegan and Lim Teck Ghee, 235–65. Berkeley: University of California Press.

Hutcheon, Linda. 1989. *The Politics of Postmodernism*. London: Routledge.

Huyssen, Andreas. 1984. "Mapping the Postmodern." *New German Critique*, 33: 5–52.

Igor. 1996. *Bag Big Bug*. Jakarta: Lembaga Daya Dharma.

———. 1995. *Impian Diantara Cerobong Asap*. Jakarta: Lembaga Daya Dharma.

Independen. 1994. "Mereka Menjauhkan Manusia dari Kemampuan Berbicara." 10 September: 16.

Indrayati, Sri and Sri Wahyuni. 1991. "Dari Bawah Terbitlah Terang." *Tempo*, 22 June: 77.

Inside Indonesia. 2005. "Newmont Knew." (Taken from the *New York Times*) 82 (April–June): 3.

———. 2004. "Newmont Mining and NGOs in Court over Marine Pollution." (Taken from *The Jakarta Post*). 80 (October–December): 3.

———. 1995. "Sticky Fingers: Harmoko's Business Interests." 42 (March): 2–4.

———. 1983. "Rural Workers Down but Not Out." 1 (November): 20–23.

Ismail, Usmar. 1948. *Lakon-lakon Sedih dan Gembira*. Jakarta: Balai Pustaka.
Ismet, Adang. 2004. "Realitias Sosial Politik Dan Teater Nonverbal Pada Karya Rachman Sabur." In *Teater Payung Hitam: Perspektif Teater Modern Indonesia*, edited by Rachman Sabur: 85–115. Bandung: Kelir.
Jameson, Fredric. 1998. "Notes on globalization as a Philosophical Issue." In *The Cultures of Globalization*, edited by Fredric Jameson and Masao Miyoshi, 53–77. Durham: Duke University Press.
———. 1984. "Postmodernism or the Cultural Logic of Late Capitalism." *New Left Review* 146: 53–92.
Junaedi, Nanang. 1995. "Ketika Yang Kuat Itulah Yang Benar." *Tiras* 1.17 (25 May): 61–62.
Kartakusuma, Rustandi. 1974. "Sastra Tanpa Kebanggaan Nasional." *Budaya Jaya* 73 (June 1974): 327–34.
Kershaw, Baz. 1992. *The Politics of Performance: Radical Theatre As Cultural Intervention*. London: Routledge.
Kertaraharja, Kuswandi. 1988. "Sebuah Potret Nasib Wanita Berjilbab." *Berita Buana*, 4 Oct.
"*Kesenian di Luar Pabrik*" 1997. *Tiras*, 3 November, 48–60.
Kidd, Ross. 1979. "Liberation or Domestication: Popular Theatre and Non-Formal Education in Africa." *Educational Broadcasting International*, March: 3–9.
Kidd, Ross, and Mamunar Rashid. 1983. "From Outside In to Inside Out: People's Theatre and Landless Organizing in Bangladesh." *Theaterwork*, Jan.–Feb.: 28–39.
Koentjaraningrat. 1985. *Javanese Culture*. Singapore: Oxford University Press.
Komunitas Sasta Indonesia and Pusat Dokumentasi Sastra H. B. Jassin. 1997. *Sidang Puisi ala KSI atas "Fenomena Penyair Buruh."* N.p.: Typescript, 4 January.
Kompas. 1991. "Eksperimen yang Bukan Titik." N.d.
Kongko. 1984. "Kongko Teater: (Berangkat dari Pertunjukan Teater Sae: 'Teater Hitam Konstruksi Keterasingan')." 1.1 (July): 17–46.
Kratz, E.U. 2000. *Sumber Terpilih Sejarah Sastra Indonesia Abad XX*. Jakarta: Kepustakaan Populer Gramedia.
———. 1986. "Islamic Attitudes Toward Modern Indonesian Literature." In *Cultural Contact and Textual Interpretation*, edited by C. D. Grijns and S. O. Robson, 60–93. Dordrecht: Foris.
Kruger, Loren. 1992. *The National Stage: Theatre and Cultural Legitimation in England, France, and America*. Chicago: University of Chicago Press.
Labad, Lutgardo. 1988. "Philippine People's Culture Across the Seas: The Values of Internationalism in our People's Cultural Work." *Makiisa* 1, No. 1 (First Quarter): 3–10 + 42.

LaBotz, Dan. 2001. *Made in Indonesia: Indonesian Workers Since Suharto.* Cambridge, Massachusetts: South End Press.

Laksana, A. S. and Ging Ginanjar. 1993. "Yang Berteater Dari Pabrik." n.d.

van Langenberg, Michael. 1985. "East Sumatra: Accommodating an Indonesian Nation within a Sumatran Residency." In *Regional Dynamics of the Indonesian Revolution*, edited by Audrey R. Kahin, 113–43. Honolulu: University of Hawai'i Press.

Leak, Sosiawan. 1996. "Eksotisme Peta Teater Indonesia." *Suara Merdeka*, 12 October.

Lev, Daniel S. 1990. "Intermediate Classes and Change in Indonesia: Some Initial Reflections." In *The Politics of Middle Class Indonesia*, edited by Richard Tanter and Kenneth Young, 25–43. Monash Papers on Southeast Asia No. 19. Clayton, Victoria, Australia: Monash University Centre of Southeast Asian Studies.

Liddle, William. 1990. "Indonesia Is Indonesia." In *The Politics of Middle Class Indonesia*, edited by Richard Tanter and Kenneth Young, 53–58. Monash Papers on Southeast Asia No. 19. Clayton, Victoria, Australia: Monash University Centre of Southeast Asian Studies.

Lockhard, Craig. 1998. *Dance of Life: Popular Music and Politics in Southeast Asia.* Honolulu: University of Hawai'i Press.

Lubis, Bersihar. 1996. "Tong Kosong Nyaring Bunyinya." *Gatra*, 20 January.

Lubis, Bersihar, and Kastoyo Ramelan. 1997. "Lalu Batu Bukan Batu." *Gatra*, 16 August: 110.

Lubis, Mochtar. 1984. "Wawasan Sastra." In *Dua Puluh Sastrawan Bicara*, edited by Dewan Kesenian Jakarta, 21–31. Jakarta: Sinar Harapan.

Lucas, Anton. 1997. "Land Disputes, the Bureaucracy, and Local Resistance in Indonesia." In *Imagining Indonesia*, edited by Jim Schiller and Barbara Martin-Schiller, 229–60. Monographs in International Studies Southeast Asia series, no. 97. Athens, Ohio: Ohio University Press.

Luthfianti, Adinda and Margesti S. Otong. 1997. Mesin Baru. Jakarta. Typescript.

———. 1996. Sesa'at Rasa. Jakarta. Typescript.

Ma. 1997. "Ketika Payung Hitam makin ke Depan." *Adil* 44.65 (13–19 August).

McDonald, Hamish. 1980. *Suharto's Indonesia.* Victoria, Australia: Fontana.

McVey, Ruth. 1986. "The *Wayang* Controversy in Indonesian Communism." In *Context Meaning and Power in Southeast Asia*, edited by Mark Hobart and Robert Taylor, 21–51. Ithaca: Cornell University Southeast Asia Program.

Mahasin, Aswab. 1990. "The Santri Middle-class: An Insider's View." *Prisma* 49 (June): 91–96.

Makarim, Nono Anwar. 1978. "The Indonesian Press: An Editor's Perspective." In *Political Power and Communications in Indonesia*, edited by Karl D. Jackson and Lucian W. Pye, 259–81. Berkeley: University of California Press.

Malaon, Tuti Indra, Afrizl Malna, and Budi S. Otong, eds. 1985. *Menengok Tradisi: Sebuah Alternatif Bagi Teater Modern*. Jakarta: Dewan Kesenian Jakarta & Lembaga Studi dan Riset Mahabodhi Indonesia.

Malna, Afrizal. 1995. *Antologi Tubuh dan Kata*. Unpublished manuscript.

———. 1994a. "Kebebasan Baru Dari Teks-teks Tteater." *Kompas* 3 July: 17.

———. 1994b. "Teater dan Sebuah Indonesia Kecil." *Kompas* 6 March: 17.

———. 1992. *Biografi Yanti Setelah 12 Menit*. Unpublished playscript.

———. 1991. *Pertumbuhan di Atas Meja Makan*. Unpublished playscript.

———. 1991. "Teater Ide Dari Menyurutnya Pengaruh Sastra." Unpublished talk given for a discussion on the philosophical dimensions of theater in Indonesia, presented at TIM, 4 May.

———. 1984. *Teater Pengantar Ekstase Kematian Orang-Orang*. Jakarta: Teater Sae.

Massardi, Yudhistiria ANM. 1980. "Amarah di Tengah Gamelan," *Tempo*, 20 December, 38.

Mather, Celia. 1983. "Industrialization in the Tangerang Regency of West Java: Women Workers and the Islamic Patriarchy." *Bulletin of Concerned Asian Scholars* 15.2: 2–17.

Mernissi, Fatima. 1991. *The Veil and the Male Elite: A Feminist Interpretation of Women's Rights in Islam*. Reading, Massachusetts: Addison-Wesley.

———. 1987. *Beyond the Veil: Male-Female Dynamics in Modern Muslim Society*. Bloomington: Indiana University Press.

Mihardja, Achdiat K. 1986 [1948]. *Polemik Kebudayaan*. Jakarta: Pustaka Jaya.

Milner, Anthony. 2008. *The Malays*. Chichester, West Sussex: Wiley-Blackwell.

Minarti, Helly. 1996. "'The Burning Moon' Focuses on Workers." *The Jakarta Post*, 24 March 1996, 9.

Moeljanto, D. S. and Taufiq Ismail. 1995. *Prahara Budaya: Kilas Balik Ofensif LEKRA/PKI DKK*. Bandung: Mizan and Harian Umum Republika.

Moelyono. 1993. "Buruh dan Kesenian." *Kompas*, 4 April.

Mohamad, Goenawan. 1993. *Kesusastraan dan Kekuasaan*. Jakarta: Pustaka Firdaus.

———. 1980. *Seks, Sastra, Kita*. Jakarta: Sinar Harapan.

———. 1973. "Sang Penyair dan Sang Panglima." *Tempo*, 24 November, 13–15.

Morfit, Michael. 1986. "Pancasila Orthodoxy." In *Central government and Local Development in Indonesia*, edited by Colin MacAndrews, 42–55. Singapore: Oxford University Press.

Muchyatim, Totim Moh. 1991. 'Ketika "Metateater' Main di TIM: Ternyata Lebih Bebas Daripada Jazz." *Bandung Pos*, 10 August.
Nadjib, Emha Ainun. 1993. *Pak Kanjeng*. Unpublished play script.
———. 1992. *Indonesia Bagian Dari Desa Saya*. Yogyakarta: Sipress.
———. 1991. "Lautan Jilbab." Unpublished play script.
———. 1989a. *Lautan Jilbab*. Yogyakarta: Sipress.
———. 1989b. "Problema Utama Kesenian Kita." *Kedaulatan Rakyat*, 3 Sept. 1989.
———. 1988. "Naskah Teatrikalisasi Puisi Lautan Jilbab." Unpublished play script.
———. 1984a. *Sastra Yang Membebaskan*. Yogyakarta: PLP2M.
———. 1984b. "Dinasti: Dari Budaya Jamaah Sampai Ayat-Ayat Kesenian." *Horison*, June 1984: 238–44.
———. 1993 [1983]. *99 Untuk Tuhanku*. Yogyakarta: Bentang.
———. 1980. "Seni Da'wah Sangat Mungkin, Cuma Soalnya . . ." *Panji Masyarakat* 21.289: 42.
Nakamura, Mitsuo. 1980. "The Reformist Ideology of Muhammadiyah." In *Indonesia: The Making of a Culture*, edited by James J. Fox, 273–86. Canberra: ANU Research School of Pacific Studies.
Naniel K. 1988. "Teater Kubur Ternyata Mampu Mengumpulkan Banyak Penonton." *Suara Pembaruan*, n.d.
Noer, Deliar C. 1973. *The Modernist Muslim Movement in Indonesia 1900–1942*. Singapore: Oxford University Press.
Oei Eng Goan. 1994. "'Marsinah': A Play Depicting Anguish of Female Workers." *Jakarta Post*, 21 September.
Oemar, Priyantoro. 1996. "Teater Indonesia dalam Kebingungan Seorang Kaspar." *Republika*, 12 October.
Ortner, Sherry B. 1995. "Resistance and the Problem of Ethnographic Refusal." *Comparative Studies in Society and History* 37.1: 173-193.
Otong, Boedi S. 1995. "Teater Kata Kita." *Buletin Dewan Kesenian Surabaya* 2.16: 20–21.
———. 1994. Personal Interview, 7 July.
Otong, Margesti S. 1996. "Kondisi Teater Buruh." *Media Kerja Budaya*, 3: 26.
———. 1994. Personal Interview, Jakarta, 31 July.
———. 1993. "Dari Catatan Harian Seorang Pembimbing." Typescript.
Pagelaran Drama Kolosal Lautan Jilbab. 1991. Performance Program. Surabaya: Organizing Committee.
Pané, Armin. 1933a. "Kesoesatraan baroe: sifatnja." *Poedjangga Baroe* 1.1: 9–15.
———. 1933b. "Kesoesastraan Baroe: Jang Koeno dan Jang Baroe." *Poedjangga Baroe*, 1.2: 37–43.

Pelras, Christian. 1996. *The Bugis*. Oxford: Blackwell.
Pemberton, John. 1994. *On the Subject of "Java."* Ithaca: Cornell University Press.
Pijar. 1995. "Teater Buruh Pentas di Komnas Ham." 21 September.
Pijar-KDP. 1995. "Oposisi Telah Bangkit." 001 edisi November.
Pracoyo. 1996. "Ketika Kaleng Menjadi Saksi Demokrasi." *Forum Keadilan*, IV.21 (29 January): 66.
Pracoyo, Haryanto, Hanibal, and Irawati. 1995. "Politik Versus Budaya." *Forum Keadilan*, IV.4 (8 June): 25.
Pracoyo and Riza. 1995. "Diskriminasi bagi Koma." *Forum Keadilan*, 18 December: 27.
Price, Jason. 1997. "Middletown Comes to Malang." *Inside Indonesia* 50 (April–June): 15–17.
Purnasatmoko, Setiaji. 1994. "Mentok." *Prospek*, 19 February.
Purnawady, Eddy. 1996. "Kaspar Memukau Publik Surabaya!" *Pikiran Rakyat*, 9 July: 18.
Pusat Data & Analisa Tempo. http://www.pdat.co.id/hg/apasiapa/html/J/ads, 20030620-41,J.html accessed 24 February 2008.
Putera, Indera et al. 1995. "Hanya Membangunkan Orang-Orang" (and attached articles). *Panji Masyarakat*, 829 (1–10 June): 10–19.
Quinn, George. 1983. "The Case of the Invisible Literature: Power, Scholarship, and Contemporary Javanese Writing." *Indonesia* 35: 1–36.
Rachmat, Denny. 1991. "Dunia Tanpa Makna: Si Cilik Mencari Arti." *Bandung Pos*, 22 February.
Rahardjo, Toto et al. 1994. "Pak Kanjeng Tidak Pangling." Press release 31 January.
Rahman, Fazlur. 1966. *Islam*. Chicago: University of Chicago Press.
Rakit. 1991. July. Yogyakarta: Kelomopok Teater Rakyat Indonesia.
Ramage, Douglas. 1995. *Politics in Indonesia: Democracy, Islam and the Ideology of Tolerance*. London: Routledge.
———. 1994. "Pancasila Discourse in Indonesia's Late New Order." In *Democracy in Indonesia 1950s and 1990s*, edited by David Bourchier and John Legge, 156–67. Clayton, Victoria: Monash Centre of Southeast Asian Studies.
Rendra, W. S. 1983. *Mempertimbangkan Tradisi*. Jakarta: Gramedia.
———. 1981. *The Mastodon and the Condors*. Calcutta: Writers Workshop.
———. 1979. *The Struggle of the Naga Tribe*. New York: St. Martin's Press.
———. 1975. "'Goro-Goro Rendra.'" *Tempo*, 30 August: 50–52.
Rizal, Ray. 1994. "Marsinah . . ." (full title obscured). *Mutiara*, 27 September–3 October.
Robison, Richard. 1996. "Megawati's Downfall Is Indonesia's Loss." *The Asian Wall Street Journal Weekly*, 8 July: 11.

———. 1992. "Industrialization and the Economic and Political Development of Capital: The Case of Indonesia. In *Southeast Asian Capitalists*, edited by Ruth McVey, 65–88. Ithaca: Cornell University Southeast Asia Program.

———. 1986. *Indonesia: The Rise of Capital*. Sydney: Allen and Unwin.

Robison, Richard, and Vedi R. Hadiz. 2004. *Reorganising Power in Indonesia: The Politics of Oligarchy in An Age of Markets*. London: Routledge Curzon.

Röling, Niels G., and Elske van de Fliert. 1998. "Introducing Integrated Pest Management in Rice in Indonesia: A Pioneering Attempt to Facilitate Large-scale Change." In *Facilitating Sustainable Agriculture: Participatory Learning and Adaptive Management in Times of Environmental Uncertainty*, edited by N. G. Röling and MAE Wagemakers, 153–71. Cambridge: Cambridge University Press.

Sabur Rachman. 2004. *Teater Payung Hitam: Perspektif Teater Modern Indonesia*. Bandung: Kelir.

Sabur, Syah. 1994. "Ratna Sarumpaet: Apa 'Arwah' Mau Dicekal Juga?" *Suara Pembaruan*, 19 September.

———. 1990. "Para Pekerja Pabrik Mementaskan Teater Berdasarkan Pengalaman Hidup." *Suara Pembaruan*, 12 September.

Sahid, Nur. 1989. "Kontekstualitas Mitologi Dajjal." *Kedualatan Rakyat*, 16 April.

Saini K. M. 1999. "Masalah Gaya Dalam Teater Indonesia." In *Teater Indonesia: Konsep, Sejarah, Problema*, edited by Tommy F. Auwy, 275–83. Jakarta: Dewan Kesenian Jakarta.

———. Nd. "Indonesian Theatre—Historical Background and Current Trends" posted at http://www.mindspring.com/~accra/indoXchange/rendraRef.html

Sarumpaet, Ratna. 2000. "Marsinah Menggugat." In *Silenced Voices*, edited by Frank Stewart and John McGlynn, 155–66. Special Issue of *Manoa* 12.1.

———. 1994a. *Nyanyian Marsinah: Dari Bawah Tanah*. Jakarta: Typescript.

———. 1994b. Personal Interview (with Dindon), Jakarta, 3 August.

Scarry, Elaine. 1985. *The Body in Pain: The Making and Unmaking of the World*. New York: Oxford University Press.

Schiller, Jim, Anton Lucas, and Priyambudi Sulistyanto. 2008. "Learning from the East Java Mudflow: Disaster Politics in Indonesia." *Indonesia* 85 (April): 51–77.

Schimmel, Annemarie. 1982. *As Through a Veil: Mystical Poetry in Islam*. New York: Columbia University Press.

Schwarz, Adam. 2000. *A Nation in Waiting: Indonesia's Search for Stability*. 2nd Edition. Boulder, Colorado: Westview Press.

———. 1994. *A Nation in Waiting*. Boulder, Colorado: Westview Press.

Sears, Laurie J. 1996. *Shadows of Empire*. Durham, Norh Carolina: Duke Universiy Press.
Sen, Krishna. 1994. *Indonesian Cinema: Framing the New Order*. London: Zed Books Ltd.
Sen, Krishna, and David Hill. 2000. *Media, Culture and Politics in Indonesia*. Melbourne: Oxford University Press.
Seymour, Susan. 2006. "Resistance." *Anthropological Theory* 6.3: 303–21.
Shiraishi, Takashi. 1990. *An Age in Motion*. Ithaca, N.Y.: Cornell University Press.
Sihombing, Wahyu, Slamet Sukirnanto, and Ikranegara, eds. *Pertemuan Teater 80*. Jakarta: Dewan Kesenian Jakarta.
Simon H. T. 1991. Personal Interview. Yogyakarta. 17 August.
Sinar Harapan. 2002. "Penayangan 'Alia Luka Serambi Mekah' di TVRI Ditunda." 14 December.
Sirait, Arist Merdeka. 1995. "Akankah Nasib Buruh Terpuruk?" Program for *Pentas Kontekstual Senandung terpuruk Dari Balik Tembok Pabrik*. Jakarta: Padepokan Teater Buruh Indonesia: 3–4.
———. 1994. Personal Interview. Jakarta. 2 August.
Sjafari, Irvan and Yanto, Noor. 1997. "Jika Sarumpaet keserempet/Saya Perlu Jawaban." *Sinar* 20 Desember: 16.
Sjahrir, Sutan. 1938. "Kesoesastraan dan Rakjat." *Poedjangga Baroe* Vol. Peringatan Lima Tahun *Poedjangga Baroe* 1933–38: 17–30.
Sofian, Iskandar, Muhammd Rusli Malik, Avhos Pasajo, and Kaharuddin Anyad. 1989. "Seni Membungkus Dakwah," *Panji Masyarakat*, 622 (1–10 September).
Studio Audiovisual Puskat. 1984. "Motivating the Village." Videotape.
Suara Pembaruan/Naniel K. 1989. "Pembawa Paham New Wave." *Suara Pembaruan*, 12 July.
Sudradjat, Djadjat. 1995. "Kaum Estetikus tak Usah Marah." *Media Indonesia Minngu*, 3 September.
———. 1991. "Dunia Tanpa Makna, Prototipe Manusia Primitif." *Media Indonesia*, 11 August.
Suharto. 1976. "Sambutan Presiden Republik Indonesia Pada Acara Kunjungan ke Taman Ismail Marzuki, Jakarta Pada Tanggal 25 Juni 1976." *Budaya Jaya*, 9.98 (July 1976): 385–88.
Sularto, Agus. 1994. "'Kami Berangkat dari Kemiskinan yang Sesungguhnya.'" *Media Indonesia*, 20 February.
Sullivan, John. 1991. *Inventing and Imagining Community: Two Modern Indonesian Ideologies*. Clayton, Victoria: Monash University Centre of Southeast Asian Studies, Working Paper 69.

Sullivan, Norma. 1990. "Gender and Politics in Indonesia." In *Why Gender Matters in Southeast Asian Politics*, edited by Maila Stivens, 61–86. Monash Papers on Southeast Asia No. 23. Clayton, Victoria: Monash University Centre of Southeast Asian Studies.

Sumardjo, Jakob. 1992. *Perkembangan Teater Modern dan Sastra Drama*. Bandung: Citra Aditya Bakti.

Suriaji, Yos Rizal. 1995. "Inilah 'Kesaksian' Teater ABU!" *Republika*, 4 June.

———. 1994. "Protes Eksistensialis Kaum Rombengan." *Republika*, 16 February: 5.

Suryakusuma, Julia. 1996. "The State and Sexuality in New Order Indonesia." In *Fantasizing the Feminine*, edited by Laurie J. Sears, 92–119. Durham, N.C.: Duke University Press.

Sutherland, Heather. 1979. *The Making of a Bureaucratic Elite: The Colonial Transformation of the Javanese Priyayi*. Kuala Lumpur: Heinemann.

Sutrisno and Wijiono. 1994. Personal Interview, Jakarta, 31 July.

Syaid, Kardy. 1989. "Pementasan Sirkus Anjing Teater Kubur." *Suara Karya Minggu* Minggu Kelima Desember.

Tammaka, Mh. Zaelani. 1997. "Dongeng Batu-batu Tentang Kesia-siaan Hidup." N.p., N.d.

Teater ABU. 1993a. *Nyanyian Pabrik*. Video recording of performance at Sanggar Satu Merah Panggung, Jakarta, 19 January.

———. 1993b. *Nyanyian Pabrik*. Theater Program. Jakarta, 6 February.

Teater Buruh Indonesia. 1993. *Bercanda dalam Duka*. Typescript.

Tejo, H. Sujiwo. 1994a. "Membahas Buruh Dengan Bahasa 'Wek-Wek'." *Kompas*, n.d. (probably between February 7–13).

———. 1994b. "Dindon dan Teater Kuburan." *Kompas*, 17 February.

———. 1994c. "Aktor dalam Ziarah Televisi dan Sinepleks." *Kompas*, 18 February.

———. 1994d. "Belum Ada Mutiara dalam teater Buruh." *Kompas*, 12 March.

———. 1993a. "Dengan Lauk Janji-Janji." *Kompas*, 11 February.

———. 1993b. "Bercanda Dalam Duka." *Kompas*, 6 September.

Tejo, H. Sujiwo, and H. Witdarmono. 1995. "Teater Buruh: Sebuah Kesenian untuk Meringankan Beban." *Kompas*, 15 October.

Tempo. 1981. "Larangan Lagi di Yogya." 12 December, 25.

———. 1980. "Diskusi, Bukan Interogasi." 16 February, 32.

———. 1978. "Setelah kejadian Rendra, bagaimana?" 20 Mei, 52–57.

———. 1975. "Mengapa Rendra? Mengapa bukan Rendra?" 23 August: 47–51.

———. 1973. "Rendra membuka dada." 8 December.

Thamrin, Husni. 1996. "Menyoal Pencekalan Teater Buruh." *Media Kerja Budaya*, 3 (February): 25–28.

Tickell, Paul. 1987. "The Writing of Indonesian Literary History." *Review of Indonesian and Malaysian Affairs* 21.1: 29–43.

Tjitrosoewarno, Soeharmono. 1993. "Studiklub Teater Bandung (STB) dan Saya." In *Teater Untuk Dilakoni: Kumpulan Tulisan Tentang Teater*, edited by Sugiyati S. A., Mohamad Sunjaya, and Suyatna Anirun, 88–89.

Triyanto, Gatot et al. 1991. "Seragam Harus, Jilbab Boleh." *Tempo*, 19 January: 76–77.

Triyanto, Gatot, Kelik Nugroho, and R. Fadjri. 1991. "Kembalinya Anak Berkerudung." *Tempo*, 2 March: 100.

Tsuchiya, Kenji. 1987. *Democracy and Leadership: The Rise of the Taman Siswa Movement in Indonesia*. Honolulu: University of Hawai'i Press.

Turner, Victor. 1982. *From Ritual to Theatre: The Human Seriousness of Play*. New York: Performing Arts Journal Publications.

Van Erven, Eugène. 1992. *The Playful Revolution: Theatre and Liberation in Asia*. Bloomington: Indiana University Press.

———. 1989. *Stages of People's Power: The Philippines Educational Theatre Association*. Verhandelingen No. 43. The Hague: Centre for the Study of Education in Developing Countries (CESO).

Vatikiotis, Michael R. J. 1993. *Indonesian Politics under Suharto*. London: Routledge.

Waskito, Agung. 1988. Letter dated 5 December.

———. 1989. Letter dated 23 June.

———. 1990. *Dajjal*. Revised typescript version of 1989 script.

Weintraub, Andrew N. 2001. "Contesting Culture: Sundanese *Wayang Golek Purwa* Competitions in New Order Indonesia." *Asian Theatre Journal* 18.1 (Spring): 87–104.

Wibowo, Fred. (n.d.) "Komunikasi Horizontal: Sebuah Pendekatan Dalam Rangka Mengembangkan Prakarsa dan Swadaya Petani." Typescript.

———. 1991a. *Ombak-Ombak*. Typescript.

———. 1991b. *Tiga Buah Buku Teater Rakyat*. Ms. 3 vol.

———. 1986. *Tumbal*. "Yogyakarta." typescript.

Widodo, Amrih. 1995. "Stages of the State: Arts of the People and Rites of Hegemonization." *Review of Indonesian and Malaysian Affairs* 29.1–2 (Winter/Summer): 1–35.

Widyawan, Rosa. 1994. "Klangenan Kaum Buruh." *Wawasan* 14 February.

Wijaya, Putu. 1997. *Ngeh: Kumpulan Esai*. Jakarta: Pustaka Firdaus.

———. 1991. "Lakon Diskusi Suami dn Istri." *Tempo*, 21 September: 110.

Williams, Michael. 1990. *Communism, Religion, and Revolt in Banten in the Early Twentieth Century*. Athens, Ohio: Ohio University Research in International Studies, Southeast Asia Series no. 86.

Williams, Raymond. 1989. *The politics of Modernism*. London: Verso.

———. 1977. *Marxism and Literature*. London: Oxford University Press.

Winet, Evan Darwin. 2005. "The Critical Absence of Indonesia in W.S. Rendra's Village." In *Staging Nationalism: Essays on Theatre and National Identity*, edited by Kiki Gounaridou, 141–66. McFarland and Company, Inc.: Jefferson, North Carolina.

———. 2001. "Facing Indonesia: Character, Actor, and Nation in Jakarta's Modern Theatre." PhD diss., Stanford University.

Wiyanto, Hendro. 1987. "Teater Kubur: Teater Tanpa Penonton." Gadis n.d.: 58–59.

Wolf, Diane. 1996. "Javanese Factory Daughters." In *Fantasizing the Feminine in Indonesia*, edited by Laurie J. Sears. Durham: Duke University Press: 140–62.

Wright, Astri. 1994. *Soul, Spirit, and Mountain*. Kuala Lumpur: Oxford University Press.

Yampolsky, Philip. 1995. "Forces for Change in the Regional Performing Arts of Indonesia." *Bijdragen tot de Taal-, Land- en Volkenkunde* 151.4: 700–25.

YLBHI (Yayasan Lembaga Bantuan Hukum Indonesia). 1996. *Tahun Kekerasan: Potret Pelanggaran HAM di Indonesia*. Jakarta: Yayasan Lembaga Bantuan Hukum Indonesia.

———. 1994. *Demokrasi: Antara Represi dan Resistensi*. Jakarta: Yayasan Lembaga Bantuan Hukum Indonesia.

———. 1990. *Laporan Keadaan Hak Asasi Manusia di Indonesia*. Jakarta: Yayasan Lembaga Bantuan Hukum Indonesia.

Yayasan Perempuan Mardika. 1993? *Strive for Workers' Theatre*. Jakarta: Yayasan Perempuan Mardika, N.d.

Yoga, Busyra Q. 1994. "Saya dan Sebagian Perjalanan Teater Sae." Unpublished Manuscript.

Yohanes, Benny. 1996. "Ketika Bahasa Menjadi Bunyi dan Bunyi Menjadi Orgi." *Pikiran Rakyat*, 3 December: 10.

Zal. 1996. "Teater Musik Kaleng Kelompok Payung Hitam: 'Indonesia dan Demokrasi Kaleng'." *Republika*, 9 January.

Zurbuchen, Mary. 1989. "The Cockroach Opera: Image of Culture and National Development in Indonesia." *Tenggara* 23: 123–50.

Performances seen in person or in recorded form

Agung Waskito and Sanggar Shalahudin. 1989. "Dajjal." 3–5 August, Gelanggang Mahasiswa UGM, Yogyakarta.

Agung Waskito, Teater Jiwa, and Teater Aisyiah. 1990. "Keluarga Sakinah." 16–19 December, Sporthall Kridosono, Yogyakarta.

Budi S. Otong and Teater Sae. 1991. "Pertumbuhan di Atas Meja Makan." 12–15 September, Teater Tertutup, Taman ismail Marzuki, Jakarta.

Budi S. Otong and Teater Sae. 1992. "Biograpfi Yanti Setelah 12 Menit." 3–6 December Tetater Tertutup, Taman Ismail Marzuki, Jakarta.

Dindon and Teater Kubur. 2000. "Trilogi Besi." May, Pusat Kebudayaan Jepang.

Emha Ainun Nadjib dan Komunitas Pak Kanjeng. 1993. "Pak Kanjeng." 23–24 November, Taman Budaya Surakarta.

Margesti S. Otong and teater ABU. "Nyanyian Pabrik." 19 January, Teater Satu Merah Panggung, Kampung Melayu, Jakarta.

Margesti S. Otong and Teater ABU. 1994. "Mentok." 6 February, Gelanggang Remaja Bulungan, Jakarta.

Margesti S. Otong and Teater ABU. 1997. "Mesin Baru." Rehearsal, 17 August 1997, Depok, Jakarta.

N. Riantiarno and Teater Koma. 1990. "Suksesi." 28 September-8 October Graha Bakti Budaya, Taman Ismail Marzuki, Jakarta.

Rahman Sabur and Teater Payung Hitam. 1995. "Kaspar". August 14, Teater Arena Taman Budaya Solo, Solo, Central Java.

Rachman Sabur and Teater Payung Hitam. "Teater Musik Kaleng." 6–7 Januari 1996, Teater Tertutup, Taman Ismail Marzuki, Jakarta.

Rahman Sabur and Teater Payung Hitam. 1997. "Merah Bolong Putih Doblong Hitam." August 2, Teater Arena Taman Budaya Solo, Central Java.

Ratna Sarumpaet and Satu Merah Panggung. 1994. "Marsinah: Nyanyian dari Bawah Tanah." Rehearsal 3 August 1994, Sanggar Satu Merah panggung, Kmpung Melayu, Jakarta.

Ratna Sarumpaet and Satu Merah Panggung. 1999. "Marsinah Menggugat." Later version, 31 August 1999, Graha Bakti Budaya, Taman Ismail Marzuki, Jakarta.

Popular Periodicals Cited

Berita Buana
Bernas
Bisnis Indonesia
DeTik
Editor
Fajar
Forum Keadilan
Harian Terbit
Harian Umum Karya Darma
The Jakarta Post
Jawa Pos
Jayakarta

Kedaulatan Rakyat
Kompas
Kompas Online
Masa Kini
Media Indonesia
Media Indonesia Minggu
Memorandum
Merdeka
Nova
Panji Masyarakat
Pedoman Rakyat
Pos Kota
Republika
Republika Online
Sinar
Sinar Pagi
Suara Indonesia
Suara Merdeka
Suara Pembaruan
Surabaya Minggu
Surabaya Pos
Surabaya Post
Surya
Swadesi
Target
Tempo
Tempo Interactive
Tiras
Wawasan
Yogya Post

Index

"A Short Organum for the Theater," 62, 337
AA II UU, 168
Abad Berlari, 344
Abu Zar al-Ghifari, 126
Aceh, 313, 358–59
adiluhung, 169, 317
Aduh!, 195
Ahmed, Leila, 106
Aisyiyah, 122, 341
Aji, Arwinto Syamsunu, 168
Ajidarma, Seno Gumira, 312, 314
Ajoeb, Joebaar, 31
Akademi Sinematografi Bandung, 194
Akhudiat, 348
Al-Hallaj, 102, 340
Alia, Luka Serambi Mekah, 313, 331, 358–59
Amaral, Clementino dos Reis, 299
Anderson, Benedict, 3, 148
Anirun, Suyatna, 31, 192
Anwar, Chairil, 29
Appiah, Kwame Anthony, 40
Arabia, 99, 105
Arahmaiani, 196, 321
Archipelagic Writers' Conference, 295
Arena Teater, 14–15, 39, 56–74, 76–95, 321–22, 324, 327, 337–38
Arge, Rachman, 354
Aristophanes, 37, 79, 289
Aristotelian theater, 61, 79, 240
Art Summit, 349
asas tunggal, 46, 100, 101, 112, 317
Asia Theater Forum Partnership, 60
Asian Wall Street Journal, 160
Aspinall, Edward, 45, 190
ASTI Bandung (STSI), 190, 193, 194–95, 331–32

ATNI, 332
ATOR, 60
Attar, Farid Uddin, 102
Aum, 195
Australian Freedom from Hunger Campaign, 75
avant-garde, 2, 4, 5, 6, 7, 14, 15–16, 17, 19, 20, 29, 33, 40, 43–45 52, 132–33, 144–45, 148, 166–67, 172, 175, 180, 186–87, 189, 200, 219–20, 230, 231, 310, 311
Azwar A. N., 354

Bachri, Sutardji Chalzoum, 354
Bag Big Bug, 260, 262–63, 268, 317
Bahasa Indonesia, 16, 23, 140, 189, 200, 202, 208, 209, 217, 219
Balai Budaya 135
Bali, 325
Bandarlampung 288, 299–300, 308
Bandung, 10, 16, 18, 31, 133, 172, 188, 191–94, 195, 196, 199, 200, 208, 231, 250, 288, 293, 307, 313, 328, 331, 346, 348, 349, 354
Bandung Post, 144
Bani Khidlir, 342
Bank Duta, 113
Banurusman, 252
banyolan, 70, 83, 87–88, 317
Bapindo, 208
BAPPENAS, 77
Basic Christian Community, 61
Bawantara, Agung, 176
Bebek-Bebek, 195
Beckett, Samuel, 199
bedug, 124, 317, 342
Ben Go Tun, 195
Benda, Julien, 155

Bengel Teater Rendra, 18, 19, 43, 58, 330
Bennett, Susan, 12
Bentang, 44, 334, 350
Bercanda Dalam Duka, 233–34, 243, 251, 253, 286, 317, 350
Bespoke Overcoat, The, 192
Bila Malam Bertambah Malam, 195
Bila Saatnya Tiba, 268
Biografi Yanti Setelah, 12; *Menit*, 144, 145, 146, 159–66, 179, 317, 344–45
Biran, Misbach Yusa, 192
Boal, Augusto, 61–62, 67, 79, 81, 95
Board of Film Censors (BSF), 48
Bogor, 226, 293, 336
Bom Waktu, 332
Bond, Christopher, 142
Bourdieu, Pierre, 11, 24
Brecht, Bertolt, 34, 57, 60, 61–62, 67–71, 95, 193, 194, 337–38
Brenkman, John, 222
Brenner, Suzanne, 106, 339
Broadway, 279, 281
Broer, Tony, 203–8, 212, 331–32, 349
BUBUTAN (Budaya Buruh Tangerang or Tangerang Workers' Culture), 259–61, 264, 268, 270–71, 330, 352
Büchner, Georg, 142
Budianta, Eka, 259
Budiman, Arief, 292, 295
Budyanto, Novi, 322, 356
Bulungan Youth Arena, 137, 230, 236–38
Bung Besar, 192
Buried Child, 142, 144

Caligula, 149, 151, 153–54, 192, 345
calung, 226, 350
Camus, Albert, 149, 192, 199, 345
censorship (banning, bans), 1, 2, 7, 8, 17, 22, 45–52, 53, 128, 149–50, 152, 153, 154, 156, 187, 188–89, 201, 202, 204, 205, 209–10, 221–22, 244, 245, 249, 250, 252, 254–56, 257, 264, 267, 271, 273–309, 310, 319, 320, 321, 322, 323–24, 334–35, 355, 358–59
Central Java, 2, 14, 18, 49, 56, 63, 74, 75, 81, 88, 93, 96, 112, 119, 128, 314, 318, 319, 321–22, 325, 330, 356
Chekhov, Anton, 192
Cimanggis, 240, 350
cinema, 46, 47, 48–49, 131, 146, 162, 289, 331, 341
Cirebon, 192, 332
Cisalak, 226, 254, 293
Citayam, 172
colonialism, 149–50, 155, 284, 315, 323, 333

commercialization, 26, 30, 43–44, 131–32, 142, 147–48, 175, 244, 334. 335–36, 338
Conroy, Rebecca 358
conscientization, 12, 15, 60–61, 74, 86, 89
consumerism, 41, 104, 163, 177, 178, 179, 182, 183, 184, 185, 198, 323
Council of Indonesian Ulama (MUI/ Majelis Ulama Indonesia), 128

Dag Dig Dug, 195
dagelan, 93, 112, 318
dagelan mataram, 119, 318
Dahana Radhar Panca, 135
Dajjal, 97, 118, 119–22, 129, 318, 341
dakwah, 115, 318
Damar Wulan, 28
Danarto, 168, 169, 172
dangdut, 50, 84, 88, 125, 226, 231, 318, 338
Darmawan, Whani, 124
Darul Islam, 100
Darusman, Marzuki, 299
Das Badener Lehrstück vom Einverständnis, 338
Das Verhör des Lukullus 337
demang 63, 318
Depok 240, 350
Depot Kreasi Seni Bandung 196, 208, 321
Der Hauptmann von Köpenick 194
Der Kaukasische Kreidekreis 337
desa binaan 76, 318, 338
DeTik, 180, 278, 345
development (pembangunan), 15, 32–33, 35–36, 37, 38, 41, 45, 53, 56–95, 102, 118–19, 120, 128, 132, 140, 160, 164, 176, 186, 224, 245–46, 248, 273, 283, 322, 324, 327, 333, 338, 344, 346, 355
Dewan Kesenian Jakarta (DKJ/Jakarta Arts Council), 135, 168, 169, 193, 291, 303, 329, 331, 332, 344
Dewanto, Nirwan, 42–43, 145, 174, 334, 345
Di Mana Aku Berpijak 240, 349
Die Ausnahme und Die Regel, 337
Die Maßnahme, 337–38
Dilarang untuk Melarang, 134, 343
Dim, Harry, 196–98, 321
Dimyati, Ipit S., 347
Dinaldo, 153
Dindon W. S., 133, 141, 167–86, 199, 242–43, 323, 324, 329, 346–47
Diponegoro, Muhammad, 114, 115
Directorate of the Arts, 188
Diyanto, 196, 321
Djayakusuma, D., 195, 236
Djody, Setiawawn, 125, 342–43
Doblo, Deden, 208

DOM, 358–59
Domba, Zainal Abidin 133, 144, 151, 156, 157–59, 161, 329, 343
doxa, 4, 24, 30, 38, 42
DPR (Dewan Perwakilan Rakyat or National Legislature), 285, 301
Dutch East Indies, 26–30, 113, 149, 194, 319
Dwi, Bambang, 137

Eagleton, Terry, 10
East Java, 93, 96, 101, 102, 109, 114, 124, 221, 243, 245, 252, 282, 285, 287, 291, 302–3, 320, 321, 325, 328, 355
Editor, 232, 278, 296, 345
Effendi, Djohan, 55
Effendy, Herman, 196
Egon, 354
El-Sadawi, Nawal, 314
El Teatro Campesino, 227
electronic media, 148
Eliot, T. S., 199
Emha (Ibrahim Ismail Hamid), 31

Fajar, 340
Fals, Iwan, 125
Family Planning, 93
FAO (Food and Agriculture Organization of the United Nations), 77
faranji, 120
Faruk H. T., 356
foreign funding agencies, 74, 94, 95
Formless Organizations (OTB/Organisasi Tanpa Bentuk), 262
Foucault, Michel, 40, 42
Freire, Paulo, 57, 59–60, 61, 63, 72, 95, 124
French Cultural Center, 307–8
Friedrich, Georg, 195

Gajah Mada University, 37, 64, 109, 110, 119, 294, 320, 323, 327, 339
Galaxy Theater, 225–26, 254, 256, 293
gamelan, 108, 192, 323
Gantra, Maman 232
gedongan, 54, 318
Gelanggang, 29
gender relations (gender roles) 105–8, 114, 151, 161, 163, 178, 181–82, 183, 185, 229, 237, 245–46, 280, 313, 321, 324
Genesis II, 192–93
German Expressionism, 136
Geusun Ulun, 193
Gilbert, Helen, 13
Gillitt, Cobina, 19
Glass Menagerie, The, 192
Goethe Foundation, 195, 199

Golkar, 125, 128, 283, 296, 358
Gontor, 102, 327, 342
grass roots theater, 6, 7, 8, 13, 14–15, 19, 20, 39, 52, 56–95, 99, 123–24, 130, 311, 314, 338
Grotowski, Jerzy, 345
Guided Democracy, 114
Gumeulis, Linda, 235–36, 237–38, 250, 257, 352
Gunawan, Indro, 76–77, 81, 93, 94, 321, 337, 338
Guruh, 44, 50–51

Habibie, B. J., 54, 97, 116, 126, 128
habitus, 24
Hadaning, Diah, 259
Hadith, 99
Hafiz, 102
Hall, Stuart, 11, 24
halus, 29, 174, 281, 289, 302, 318, 358
Hamid, Syarwan, 305, 358
Hamka, 114, 115
Hamlet, 192
Hamlet Menjelang Pemilu, 346
Hamzah, Amir, 160
Hamzah, Sheila, 177, 180
Handke, Peter, 188, 199, 200, 201, 319, 348
Happening Channel, oo 142
Harmoko, 283, 290, 301, 355
Hartono, General R., 128, 358
Harvey, David, 53
Hasan, Fuad, 300
Haté, Simon, 60, 74–76, 78
Hatley, Barbara, 18, 39, 128, 237, 314, 338, 339–40, 346, 359
Hatta, Mohammad, 149, 152, 155–56, 157, 346
Hendardi, 299, 305–6
Hendropriyono, 303
Herfanda, Ahmadun Y., 121, 259
Heryanto, Ariel, 42–43, 291, 297, 334, 355
hikayat, 31
Hinduism, 155
Hitam Menunggu Putih, 228, 349
Hofmann, Rüdi, 59, 61, 91
Hollywood, 281
Honna, Jun, 359
Horison, 136
Hübner, Zygmunt, 47
Human Rights Watch/Asia, 351, 356
hybridity (hybridization), 13, 15, 19, 23, 26, 29, 31

IAIN Sunan Kalijaga, 294
ICMI (Ikatan Cendekiawan Muslim Indonesia), 54, 97, 101, 126, 128, 129

identity, 18, 40, 85, 106, 111, 131, 140, 147, 160, 163, 164, 175, 179, 189, 198, 206, 317; gender, 108, 114, 151, 161, 178; individual, 138, 146–47, 152, 154–57, 160, 161–63, 165; and language, 199–207, 219–20, 319; national, 4, 16, 149, 214, 215–16, 315
Idrus, Taslim, 144, 161
Igor, 260–64, 317, 318
ijtihad, 100, 318
IKIP Jakarta, 135, 172
Ikranegara, 34, 137–38, 291, 297, 354
Impian Diantara Cerobong Asap, 260–62, 270, 318
indah, 333
Indonesia Bagian Dari Desa Saya, 339
Indonesian Military Academy, 126
Inspector General, 354
installation of ideas, 147, 149
Institute Kesenian Tangerang (Tangerang Arts Institute), 259
integrated pest mangement, 77–78, 93
inter-class alliances, 57, 71–73, 338
Ionesco, Eugene, 136, 142, 192, 194
Irama, Rhoma, 50, 125, 338
Islamic aesthetics, 96, 121–22, 130
Islamic consumerism, 125
Islamic culture, 54–55, 99, 116–17, 126, 130; and commercial culture, 122–23, 124, 125, 131, 320, 323, 338, 341, 342
Islamic modernism, 99–100, 102, 103, 107–8, 111, 112, 114, 129, 340
Islamic neo-modernism, 100–1, 103, 112, 129
Islamic theater (*see also* Muslim theater), 6, 7, 8, 9, 13, 19, 20, 39, 96–130, 131–32, 311, 319, 323, 340–42
Islamic traditionalism, 32, 99–100, 102, 107, 108, 112, 114–15, 129, 340
Ismail, Usmar, 30
Istiyanto, Agus, 74, 76
ITB, 172, 193
ITRJ (Institut Teater Rakyat Yogyakarta), 93, 337

Jabbar, Hamid, 137
Jabo, Sawung, 125
jahiliya, 105, 106, 107, 119, 318
jaipongan, 231, 232, 318
Jakarta, 1, 2, 14, 15–16, 17, 18, 20, 33, 37, 39, 44, 56, 125, 132, 133, 134, 135, 136, 137, 167, 172, 178, 184, 186, 191, 193, 220, 222, 224–25, 229, 230, 244, 254, 257, 264, 279, 282, 285–86, 287, 288, 293, 300, 303–4, 306, 307, 311, 312, 313, 323–24, 330, 332, 336, 341, 343, 344, 346, 349, 354, 356, 357
Jakarta Academy, 38
Jakarta Artists' Solidarity, 294–95
Jakarta Arts Center (*see also* Taman Ismail Marzuki), 14, 45
Jakarta-Jakarta, 296
Jakarta Post, The, 144, 265, 296, 345
Jakarta Youth Theater Festival (Festival Teater Remaja Jakarta), 135, 136, 168, 169, 172, 173, 236–37, 328
Jamaah Shalahuddin, 109, 339–40
Jameson, Frederic, 10, 161, 166
Jamila dan Sang Presiden 331
Japan, 59, 331–32, 349
jaringan, 5, 6, 40, 186–87, 220, 222, 318
Jassin, H. B., 137–38
Jatinegara Timur, 167
Javanese, 2, 18, 41, 49, 54, 58, 63, 69, 70, 83, 85, 86, 87, 96, 108, 109, 112, 119, 153, 221, 237, 243, 244, 265, 280, 288, 307, 314, 315, 317, 319, 320, 321, 322, 323, 325, 329, 333, 355, 357
Javanese Performances on an Indonesian Stage, 340
Jawa Pos 340
Jayakarta, 173
JEJAK, 312
Jember, 288
Jenar, Syech Siti, 340
Jenderal Anjing, 354
jilbab, 96, 97, 103–8, 110, 111, 115, 116, 318, 339
Joni, Asril, 133, 135, 343
Jonson, Ben, 194

kampung, 54, 58, 131–32, 135, 152–53, 167, 168, 172, 173, 174, 175, 180, 185, 312, 319, 346
Kampung Kober, 167–69, 174, 311–12
Kampung Melayu, 164
Kamto, Joko, 74, 76, 322, 356
Kanjeng Ratu Kidul (Kanjeng Roro Kidul), 83–87
Kantata Taqwa, 125
Kapai-Kapai, 110, 135, 168, 169, 171, 231, 321
Kaplun, Mario, 337
Kartarejasa, Butet, 322, 356
Kartasasmita, Ginandjar, 54
Karya, Teguh 34, 168–69, 282, 328, 332
kasar, 289, 319
Kaspar, 188–89, 194, 199–207, 209, 211, 215, 319, 331, 348–49
Kaspar Hauser, 199, 200
Kayam Omar, 331
kecapi, 110, 319

Kedaulatan Rakyat, 340, 341
Kedung Ombo, 93, 126, 128
kekeluargaan, 163, 280, 319
Kelompok Pinggiran 93, 337
Kelompok Teater Rakyat Indonesia (KTRI), 75–76, 336
Keluarga Sakinah, 97, 118, 122, 129, 319, 342
Ken Arok, 193
Kershaw, Baz, 7
Kesaksian, 257
kesatria (satria), 155, 157, 319, 323
keterbukaan (*see* openness), 42, 55, 188–89, 273, 274, 279, 300, 319–20
ketoprak, 18, 58, 63, 70, 93, 320
Kidd, Ross, 67, 73, 81
Kirjomulyo, 192
Kisah Perjuangan Suku Naga, 37, 70
Kompak, 330
Kompas, 144, 180, 243, 251, 253, 296, 298, 345, 354
Komunitas Kecil Pak Kanjeng, 1, 273, 277, 290, 293, 319, 336
kongko, 137, 138, 344
konglomerat, 76, 320
Kontras, 312
Kopkamtib, 37
Kruger, Loren, 3
Kucak Kacik (Darim Mencari Darim), 168, 195
Kussudiardjo, Bagong, 38
Kusuma, Mulyana W., 297
kyai, 99, 320

La Trahison des Clercs, 155
Laskar Panggung, 194
Lauckner, Rolf, 136, 142
Lauk-Lauk Janji, 227, 250, 349
Lautan Jilbab (play), 96–97, 101, 107–13, 115–18, 119, 121, 122–30, 131, 132, 317, 320, 323, 340–42; cycle of poems, 102–5, 108, 121, 122, 130, 131, 339
LBH (Lembaga Bantuan Hukum or Legal Aid Institute), 256, 257, 258, 293, 297, 299, 305–6
Lehrstücke, 62, 337
Lekra, 31–32, 320
lenong, 320
Les Chaises, 142
Lewoleba, 62
liberation theology, 59
Liburan Seniman, 30
Liga Teater Bandung, 194–95
Lim, Jim, 31, 192, 348
limits of language, 139, 140, 143, 147–48, 150, 154, 157–59, 163, 189–90, 197, 202, 203–5, 209, 215–17, 219, 322

longser, 192, 193
Luthfianti, Adinda 265
Lysistrata, 37
ludruk, 58, 320

Ma'af, Ma'af, Ma'af, 354
macapat, 265
MacBeth, 354
Macherey, Pierre, 10
Madiun, 96–97, 109, 113, 115, 122, 126–28, 340, 342
Madura, 285
madzhab, 99, 321
Mahabharata, 324, 341
Majalaya, 250
Majid, Nurcholish, 55
Makassar, 18, 313, 314, 354
mailaikat, 117, 321
Malang, 109, 288
Malari riots, 37, 59, 354
Malay cultural ideologies, 333
Malna, Afrizal, 45, 136–67, 172, 197, 322, 323, 328–29, 344, 345–46
Mangkudilaga, Benyamin, 298
Manifes Kebudayaan (Cultural Manifesto), 32, 22–23
Mankowitz, Wolf, 192
Marcuse, Herbert, 243
Margesti, Titi (Margesti S. Otong), 144, 146, 150, 151, 157–59, 161, 186, 230–33, 235–38, 242–43, 244, 250, 252, 257–58, 264–68, 270–71, 313–14, 328, 344
Marsinah, 17, 186, 221, 222, 244, 245, 246, 248, 249, 252, 256, 258, 270, 285, 286, 287, 288, 295, 312, 321, 350–51, 356
Marsinah: Bersatulah Buruh Indonesia, 252, 253
Marsinah Menggugat 17, 277, 288, 294, 299, 306–9, 312, 321, 331, 355–56
Marxism, 10
Marxism and Literature, 334
Masa Kini, 328
Massardi, Noorca, 137
mass activities permit system, 47, 49
mass media (*See also* print media, television, film, radio), 45, 144, 146–48, 150, 163, 166, 179, 184, 201, 219, 223, 234, 260
Masyumi, 52, 100
Mastodon dan Burung Kondor 35–37
Matra, 332
May declaration, (1995) 254, 285, 292–93, 304
Medan incident, (1994) 252
Media Indonesia, 144, 180, 242, 256

Media Kerja Budaya, 264, 334
Mega-Mega, 135
Memet, Yogie S., 305
Menak Jinggo, 28
Mengapa Kau Culik Anak Kami?, 312, 314
Mentok (see also *Bebek-Bebek*), 236–38, 243, 252, 253
Merah Bolong Putih Doblong Hitam, 208–19, 321, 349
Mernissi, Fatima, 105–6
Mesin Baru, 265–68, 321
Messiah II, 192–93
Meta-Ekologi, 136, 195
Metateater: Dunia Tanpa Makna, 195–99, 200, 205, 321, 348
Migrasi dari Ruang Tamu, 167, 345
Minikata, 195
Ministry of Education and Culture, 188
modernism, 28, 29, 40, 43, 44, 137, 189, 190, 214, 344, 345
Moelyono, 243, 257
Moerdani, Benny, 54, 276
Moerdiono 282, 291, 300–1, 303, 356
Mohamad, Goenawan, 34, 36–37, 289–90, 292, 295, 335
Monitor, 113
Mrozek, Slawomir, 136
Muhammadiyah, 122, 319, 341
Muid, P. H., 31
Murtopo, Ali, 37
Murwaty, Sri, 225
Muslim Theater, 15

Nahdlatul Ulama (NU), 32, 305–6
Nadjib, Emha Ainun, 6, 9, 15, 39, 58, 60, 96–98, 101–5, 107–13, 115–18, 121, 122–30, 131–32, 208, 273, 282–83, 290–93, 297, 302–4, 318, 319, 320, 322, 323, 327–28, 336, 339–42, 356
Nashar, 135
Nasution, Adnan Buyung, 297
national art theater (modern theater), 4, 5, 9, 12, 14, 17, 18, 22–23, 25, 26, 27–45, 47–52, 57, 125, 132, 166, 169, 172, 187, 189–90, 191, 193, 195, 214, 215, 218–20, 239–42, 249, 273–309, 310, 311, 313–15, 323, 335, 345
national arts ideologies, 6, 9, 12, 14, 18, 25, 38–39, 41, 98, 102, 114–15, 135–36, 168–69, 172, 173, 174, 190, 218–19, 232, 239–40, 247, 270, 277, 289, 295, 308, 311, 335, 350, 352
National Cultural Congress, 42
national culture, 2, 4, 5, 14, 25, 27–45, 133, 142, 160, 188, 190, 214, 268, 301, 322, 333, 345

National Human Rights Commission, 258, 278, 291, 294, 297–98, 299, 309
national modern theater festival, 188, 349
national personality, 41, 43
nationalism, 3, 25, 132, 149–50, 155, 160, 217, 218
nativism, 41
Navis, A. A., 295
neo-feudal aesthetics, 38–39, 41, 174, 277, 281, 288, 289, 295, 308, 357
New Order, 1, 2, 3, 4, 5, 6, 8, 12, 16, 17, 18, 19, 20, 21, 22–23, 25, 32, 34–55, 56, 58, 59, 74, 91, 94, 96, 100–1, 102, 104, 107, 119, 120–21, 126, 128, 129–30, 132, 140, 142, 144, 146, 147, 148, 149, 152, 156, 159, 163–64, 174, 183, 184, 185, 186, 187, 189, 190, 192, 193, 198, 200–3, 204, 206, 209, 210, 215, 217, 218, 220, 222, 223–25, 237, 239–40, 244, 245–49, 252, 254, 257, 269, 272, 273–89, 293, 295, 296–97, 302, 304, 306, 308, 309, 310–14, 317–18, 319, 321, 330, 334, 335, 338, 354, 358
New Tradition (neo-traditionalism), 18, 33–34, 125, 188
NGO/LSM (non-government organizations), 4, 13, 15, 17, 40, 56, 59, 73–78, 81–83, 91–92, 93–94, 95, 101, 102, 123–44, 137–38, 145, 167, 186, 220, 221, 222, 223, 224–36, 238–39, 244, 245, 249, 250, 252–53, 254–58, 259, 261, 269, 270–71, 276, 278, 285, 311, 312, 313, 314, 320, 330, 349
Nipah, 285
noblesse oblige, 3, 26, 311
Noer, Arifin C, 19, 34, 110, 132–33, 135, 136, 168, 169, 171, 172, 173, 195, 231, 237, 256, 308, 321, 328, 335
Noer, Jajang C , 237, 308
Noor, Maman, 196, 321
North Suamtra, 314, 329, 330, 351
Nyanyian Marsinah: Dari Bawah Tanah (*Marsinah: Nyanyian Dari Bawh Tanah*), 221, 222, 223, 244–49, 253, 263–64, 271, 306, 321, 331, 350
Nyanyian Pabrik, 231–33, 235, 237, 241, 242–43, 250, 264, 267, 321

Oedipus at Colonus, 37
Ombak-Ombak, 81–92, 321
openness (see *keterbukaan*), 1, 42, 55, 95, 150, 189, 225, 273–82, 285, 289, 296, 297, 300, 301, 319
Opera Julini, 332
Opera Kecoa, 1, 282, 301, 322, 332, 357

orientalism, 120
Orkes Madun, 195
Otong, Boedi S., 133–67, 171, 186, 328, 329, 344, 345, 346

Padang, 18, 306
Padepokan Teater Rendra, 172, 265, 294, 334
Padmodarmaya, Pramana, 50
Pak Kanjeng, 50, 277, 282–85, 290–92, 296, 302–4, 320, 322, 336, 356
pakem, 300, 357
Pakpahan, Mochtar, 351
Pancasila, 32, 33, 45, 100, 112, 280, 285, 290, 317, 322; and aesthetics, 277, 301, 303, 304–5
Pané, Armin, 29
Pané, Sanusi, 27–28, 149, 154, 155, 323
Panji Koming, 193
Pantai Baron, 73
Pantai Sundak, 81, 83, 90, 91
Parahyangan University, 256, 293
Paranggi, Umbu Landu, 327
Parangtritis, 62, 81, 321
Parung Panjang, 313
pasemon, 335
Pasuruan, 285
PDI, 208–9, 215, 264, 306, 355
Pedoman Rakyat, 340
pendopo 83
Pengalaman, 225–26, 349
Penggali Intan, 192
Peranakan, 322
Perempuan-Perempuan Pemimpi, 79
Permadi, 137
Pertumbuhan Di Atas Meja Makan, 144, 145, 148–59, 161, 163, 164, 166, 179, 322, 323
pesantren, 27, 102, 322, 327, 342
pesantren seni, 109
pesta rakyat, 80–82, 322, 337
Petruk Dadi Ratu, 289
Pheline, Jean, 307
Philippines Educational Theater Association (PETA), 60, 62, 67, 74
Pikiran Rakyat, 144, 188, 197, 348
Pinter, Harold, 136
Pirandello, Luigi, 354
PKI (Indonesian Communist Party), 31, 32, 91, 317–18, 320, 333–34, 358
PNI (Indonesian Nationalist Party), 32, 52
Polemik Kebudayaan (Cultural Polemic), 27, 322
Polish Laboratory Theater, 345
popular culture (mass culture), 44, 125, 149, 150, 167, 180, 232, 319

popular theater, 4, 18, 169, 192, 227, 237, 240, 319, 320–21, 338
Porong Sidoardjo, 287
postcolonial practice, 15, 23, 40, 71, 215
postcolonial theory, 13–14
postmodernism, 39–45, 142–44, 146–47, 149, 152, 154, 159–60, 165–66, 317, 333, 334
Prabowo, Jujuk, 124
Prabowo, Wowok Hesti, 259–61, 264, 268, 270, 313, 330, 352–53
preman, 185
print media, 14, 19, 33, 43, 46, 47, 48, 131, 144, 146, 147, 148, 149, 153, 173, 174, 180, 182, 183, 186, 188, 201, 202, 226, 238, 239–44, 253, 256, 257, 270, 278–79, 294, 296–300, 309, 311, 312, 313, 319, 320, 335, 341, 347, 354, 356, 357
priyayi, 133, 284, 323, 333
pro-democracy movement, 22, 40, 44, 57, 258, 264, 271–72, 274–76, 278–79, 287, 310–11, 319
Prospek, 144, 238
PRRI, 100
PTUN, 293
Pujangga Baru, 322
Puntila, 193, 194
Purnasatmoko, Setiaji, 238
PUSKAT (Studio Audio Visual PUSKAT), 57, 58, 59, 74, 76, 79, 91, 93–94, 327, 337
Qori 119, 323
Qur'an, 99, 104, 105, 113, 119

radio, 146, 182, 183, 312, 347
Radio Mara, 196
Rahardjo, Dawam, 55
Rahardjo, Sapto, 110, 113, 119, 124, 129
Rahardjo, Toto, 356
rakyat, 321
Ramayana, 341
RCTI, 175
Reform era, 167, 311, 312, 313, 315
Relief Air Mata, 314–15
Rembulan Terbakar, 265, 267
Rendra, W. S., 19, 34–38, 43, 50, 58, 125, 168, 172, 195, 265, 278, 282, 289, 292, 294, 296, 297, 301, 304, 330, 335, 354, 356, 357
Republika, 180
resistance, 2, 5, 8–9, 11, 14, 18, 20, 39, 52, 107, 204, 208, 215, 222, 243, 247, 264–68, 269
Revolutionary Realism (Socialist Realism), 31

Index 387

Rhinoceros, 192, 194
Riantiarno, N., 1, 6, 34, 44, 237, 279, 284, 289, 296, 305, 322, 324, 332, 334, 358
Riantiarno, Ratna, 237, 332
Riffandi, Nandi, 192
Rilesta, Dingu, 261, 268, 330
Ritonga, M. H., 300
Roesli, Harry, 196–98, 207, 208
Rollies, Gito, 122, 125
Romeo and Juliet, 331
Rubaiyat, 331
Rukmini, 297, 357
Rumemper, Hare 153
Rumi, 102

Sabtu Kelabu (Dark Saturday), 208–9, 306
Sabur, Rachman, 190–91, 193–220, 321, 331
Sabur, Syah, 240
Sadikin, Ali, 37
Sahetapy, Ray, 44, 45, 265, 294
Sahid, Nur, 121
Sahilatua, Franky, 149, 150, 158
Said, Salim, 291
Saini K. M., 192, 193, 195, 348, 354
sampakan, 70, 234, 323
samroh, 124, 323, 342
Sandhyakala Ning Majapahit 27–28, 149, 151, 153, 154, 155, 323
Sandiwara Dol, 175
Sanggar Merah Putih, 18
Sanggar Pabrik, 17, 258, 264, 267, 271, 273, 277, 285, 287–88, 294, 297–99, 304–5, 306, 308, 324, 357
Sanggar Shalahuddin, 39, 109, 119, 126, 129, 318, 320, 323
Sanggar Tetater Buruh Wanita, 349
Sani, Asrul, 354–55
Sanjaya, Tisna, 200–1
santri (students at a traditional Islamic boarding school), 342, 351
Sardjono, Agus S., 348
Sardono, 136, 137–38, 195, 328
Sari'ah, Bi, 150, 153
Sarumpaet, Ratna, 1, 6, 17, 186, 208, 221, 222, 223, 231, 244–49, 253, 254, 258, 263–64, 270–71, 273, 287, 288, 294–96, 299, 306–9, 312, 313, 321, 323, 330–31, 350, 355–56, 358–59
Sarwono (Sarwono Kusumaatmadja), 300
Satu Merah Panggung, 1, 6, 208, 221, 222, 273, 277, 288, 321, 323
satuan-satuan kecil, 42
SBSI, 235, 250, 258, 287, 306, 351
Scarry, Elaine, 209–10
Schiller, Friedrich, 34

Schrei aus der Straße, 142
SDSB, 113
Section 510 Joint Field Instructions, 298–99, 305–6, 308
Sediawati, Edi, 295, 308
Sekolah Lapangan Penendalian Hama Terpadu (Integrated Pest Management Field School), 78
Seks, Sastra, Kita, 335
self-actualization, 147, 230, 231, 238, 242–43
Semar Gugat 50, 305
Semarang 288
Sen, Krishna 48
Senandung Terpuruk Dari Balik Tembok Pabrik 221, 254–56, 285–87, 294, 297–98, 323, 357
Senayan Stadium, 125
Sesa'at Rasa, 265–66, 268
Shafi'ite School of jurisprudence, 99, 100
Shakespeare, William, 331
Shepard, Sam, 142, 144
Siagian, Bachtiar, 31
Sidang Puisi 261, 268
Silenced Voices, 355
Simanjuntak, Lena, 314
Sinar Pagi, 168
Sirait, Arist Merdeka, 225–29, 236, 239, 249–50, 251, 252, 254, 256, 270, 286, 313, 329 -30
Sirkus Anjing, 169–73, 175–80, 183, 323, 329
Sjahrir, Sutan, 29–30
social alliances (see also inter-class alliances), 2, 4, 6, 12, 17, 52, 59, 71, 73, 92, 94–95, 222, 253–64, 269, 272, 278, 286, 298, 310–12, 313
social networks (see also *jaringan*), 5, 12, 271
Soe Hok Gie, 160
Soeratin, Aat, 196
Solo (Surakarta), 18, 93, 194, 209, 212, 282, 288, 293, 307, 337, 346, 349, 356
Sontani, Utuy Tatang, 31
Sophocles, 37
Sopyan, Yayan, 176
Srimulat, 44
Stadion Wilis, 97
Sternagel, Peter, 199
structure of feeling, 41
STSI Surakarta, 194, 331
student activism, 35, 45, 52, 53, 187, 190–91, 207, 276, 278
Studiklub Teater Bandung (STB), 18, 31, 190, 192, 193, 194, 195, 348
Suara Pembaruan, 144, 240
Sudarman, Susilo, 305
Sudarno, Haris, 303

Sudharmono, 54
Sudirman, Basofi, 303, 355, 357
Sudomo, 290, 301, 303, 304
Sudradjat, Djadjat, 256–57
Sudrajat, Edi, 305, 358
Sufi poetry, 102–3, 124, 129
Sufism, 99, 102–3, 107, 111, 124
Suharto, 1, 2, 4, 5, 6, 17, 18, 19, 20, 21, 25, 32–33, 37, 48, 53, 56, 97, 101, 131, 150, 153, 154, 167, 185, 190–91, 272, 273, 274–78, 280–85, 290, 295, 296, 301, 305, 306, 307, 311, 312, 313, 314, 317, 319, 334, 352, 355, 358; and the military, 54, 55, 126, 276
Suharyono, R. Bagus, 221–22, 254, 257, 293, 298, 304, 358
Sukarno, 32, 45, 51, 52, 114, 149, 152, 154, 155, 190, 292, 317–18, 319, 320, 346
Sukarnoputri, Megawati, 209, 264, 306, 355
Suksesi, 1, 17, 273, 277, 279–82, 283, 289, 296, 300–1, 324, 356, 357
Sulawesi (*see also*, Makassar, Ujung Pandang), 129
Sultan of Yogyakarta, 85
Sumardjo, Trisno, 33
Sumardjo, Jakob, 193
Sumatra, 288
Sumitro, 37
Sundanese (West Javanese), 133, 153, 192, 193, 215–17
Surabaya, 109, 116, 118, 122–23, 124, 125, 126, 128, 243, 245, 282, 288, 290, 294, 303, 304, 306, 307, 314, 317, 320, 322, 330, 336, 340, 341, 342, 348, 349, 357
Surabaya Arts Council (Dewan Kesenian Surabaya), 291, 303
Surat Cinta Bagi Marsinah Di Sorga, 258, 287–88, 297, 305, 324, 357
Surowo, 93–94
Sutomo, 27
Sutrisno, 232
Sutrisno, Try, 358
Suzanna, 227, 250
Sweeney Todd, 142
Sylado, Remy, 192, 225, 227, 230, 249, 256

Tabir, 294
Tablig Akbar, 125
TABUR, 17, 259, 260–64, 267, 268, 270–71, 317, 318, 352
Taman Ismail Marzuki (TIM), 33, 37, 38, 49, 50, 135, 172, 180, 207, 221, 227, 230, 236, 240, 254–55, 258, 285–86, 293, 294, 312, 323, 324, 336, 341
Tamara, Nasir, 137

Tanen Pakem, 63, 72, 73, 90, 337
Tangerang, 226, 257, 259, 261, 313, 330
Tanjung, Feisal, 302–3, 358
Tasikmalaya, 288, 307
Team, 10, 54
Teater ABU, 17, 223, 229–33, 234–38, 239, 241, 242–44, 248, 250, 252, 253, 257, 264–68, 270–71, 313, 317, 321, 328, 350; Teater ABU Tangerang, 257–58, 259, 264
Teater Adinda, 329
Teater Alam, 354
Teater Bumi, 18
Teater Buruh Indonesia (TBI), 17, 221–22, 223, 225–34, 236. 238, 239, 240, 241, 242, 248, 249–50, 251, 252, 253, 254–57, 258, 259, 264, 267, 268–69, 270–71, 273, 277, 285–87, 293 -4, 297–98, 304–5, 306, 313, 317, 323, 330, 336, 350–51, 357
Teater Dalam Gang Tuti Indra Malaon, 334
Teater Detik, 259
Teater Dinasti, 18, 58, 74, 102, 110, 131, 328, 336–37
Teater Gajah Mada, 354
Teater Gandrik, 18
Teater Garasi, 315
Teater Gedag-Gedig, 18
Teater Hitam Konstruksi Keterasingan, 136–38, 169
Teater Jagat, 18
Teater Jiwa, 319, 379
Teater Kecil, 18, 133, 135, 172, 328, 329
Teater Kita Makassar, 314
Teater Koma, 1, 6, 17, 44, 50, 273, 277, 279–82, 289, 300–2, 305, 322, 324, 332, 334, 354, 358
Teater Kubur, 6, 9, 16, 20, 45, 131–33, 148, 167–86, 189, 198–99, 202, 242, 311–12, 323, 324, 329, 346–47
Teater Mandiri, 18, 196
teater mbeling, 192–93
Teater Musik Kaleng, 207–8, 209, 324
Teater Muslim, 57, 114
Teater Oncor (Studio Oncor), 44, 256, 265, 268, 293, 294, 334
teater paripurna, 196
Teater Payung Hitam 6, 9, 16–17, 20, 186–87, 188–91, 193, 195–220, 311, 312, 313, 314–15, 319, 321, 324, 331, 347–49, 358–59
Teater Pengantar Ekstase Kematian Orang-Orang, 139–42, 169
Teater Perintis, 192
Teater Populer, 282, 332

Index 389

teater rakyat (*see also* grass roots theater), 39, 56, 76, 93, 110, 338
Teater re-Publik, 193
teater rakyat (people's theater; *see also* grass-roots theater), 5
Teater Sae, 6, 9, 15–16, 20, 43, 131–67, 168, 169–72, 173, 179–80, 186, 189, 197–99, 202, 203, 230, 311, 317, 322, 323, 328, 329, 343–46
Teater Saja, 18
Teater Utan Kayu, 334
Tegal, 288
Tejo, H. Sujiwo, 253–54
television, 23, 43, 46, 49, 79, 98, 117, 131, 146, 147, 149, 162, 175, 176, 182, 183, 331, 341, 352, 359
Tempo, 33–34, 36–37, 144, 148, 180, 278, 292, 296, 297, 312, 335, 345, 347
Theater of the Oppressed, 61
Tiang Setengah Tiang, 313
Tiga Buah Buku Teater Rakyat, 79, 91, 94
tirakatan, 35, 324
Toer, Pramoedya Ananta, 314
Tombol, 13 (*Topeng Monyet Bola Plastik*), 172, 174, 175, 176, 180–85, 324, 329
Tompkins, Joanne, 13
topeng, 324
tradition, 9–10, 13, 19, 25, 27–33, 34, 38, 40, 41, 42, 43, 51, 58, 67, 98, 99, 102, 103, 106, 113, 115, 119, 121, 137, 163, 167, 214, 215, 217, 220, 262, 278, 315, 317, 322, 333, 336
traditional culture, 12, 19, 23–26, 28, 33, 41, 58, 77, 98, 108, 110, 114, 124, 129, 155, 160, 217, 226, 345
traditional theater, 4, 18, 23, 24, 27–28, 31, 33, 38, 57, 58, 63, 70, 88, 90, 93, 98, 121, 186, 189, 192, 193, 237, 240, 241, 273, 281, 300, 320–21, 324, 336, 341,
Tranggono, Indra, 356
Trilogi Besi, 175, 176–85
Tuhan dan Kami, 195
Tumbal, 64–73, 83, 84, 87, 92, 324
Turner, Victor, 5–6
TVRI, 46, 359

Udin, 299
Ujung Pandang (see also Makassar), 109, 113, 115, 126, 340, 341, 342
ulama, 102–3, 104, 115, 128, 324
Umang-Umang, 135, 136
umat, 105, 324
U.N. Universal declaration of Human Rights, 291
Uncle Vanya, 192
UNESCO, 160

Unggaran, 75
universal human values, 40, 146, 190, 239, 241, 249
Universal Humanism (liberal humanism), 29–32, 33–34, 38, 41, 51, 56
urban alienation, 131–32, 136–37, 138, 139–42, 145, 163, 164, 165, 177, 179, 219, 323, 324
Usman, Utoyo, 305

Vagina Monologues, The, 314
Van Erven, Eugène, 62, 74, 91
Volpone (*Karto Loewak*), 194

WACC (World Association for Christian Communications), 92
Wahabi movement, 99
Wahid, Abdurrahman, 55, 305–6
Warisman, Neno, 122
Waskito, Agung, 110, 112–13, 118, 119–22, 124, 126, 129, 318, 319, 320, 323
wayang golek, 324–25
wayang kulit (shadow puppet theater), 27, 31, 58, 70, 237, 281, 284, 289, 325, 341, 357
wayang wong, 121, 325, 341
West Java (Sunda), 328, 331, 332
West Papua, 76
West Sumatra, 295, 343
Western mass culture, 13
Whalers of the South Seas, 332
Wibowo, Fred, 59–61, 62–74, 78–95, 321, 322, 324, 327, 337
Widodo, Dibyo, 308–9
Wijaya, Putu, 19, 33, 34, 145, 195, 196, 212, 294, 335, 349
Wijoyanto, Bambang, 299
Williams, Raymond, 11, 24–25, 334, 344
Williams, Tennessee, 192
Winardi, Eko, 76
Winarto, Yasso, 327
Winet, Evan, 19, 26
Wiyanto, 168
Woman at Point Zero, 314
women's movement, 40
women's theater, 331
workers' theater, 6, 7, 8, 17, 19, 20, 39, 40, 44, 56–57, 93, 186–87, 220, 221–23, 225–72, 278, 285–88, 293, 309, 311, 312, 313, 349
World Bank, 126
Woyzeck, 142

Yasanti (Yayasan Annisa Swasti), 75, 224, 225, 337, 349

Yayasan Perempuan Mardika (YPM), 224, 229–33, 235–36, 250, 252, 257, 264
Yayasan Sisbikum, 224, 225, 226, 229, 230, 313, 320
Yeats, William Butler, 199
Yoga, Busyra, 133–35, 343
Yogyakarta (Yogya, Jogja), 1, 10, 14–15, 18, 20, 37, 39, 44, 46, 49, 56, 57–58, 60, 64, 74, 75, 76, 85, 96, 98, 102, 109–10, 112, 115, 124, 125, 126, 128, 131–32, 224–25, 282, 288, 294, 315, 318, 323, 328, 340, 341, 342, 346, 354

Yohanes, Benny, 193, 348
youth counter culture, 58
YPKS (Yayasan Pimpinan Kesejahteraan Sosial), 93
Yusuf, Busro, 150, 152–53
Yusuf, Daud, 38, 296

Zainuddin MZ, 125
Zaman, 332
zikir, 104, 124, 325
Zuckmayer, Carl, 194

www.ingramcontent.com/pod-product-compliance
Lightning Source LLC
Chambersburg PA
CBHW031229290426
44109CB00012B/218